THE Horizon BOOK OF THE
RENAISSANCE

THE

The
cHorizon
Book of

RENAISSANCE

by.

J. H. PLUMB

and the Editors of
HORIZON MAGAZINE

With biographical essays by
MORRIS BISHOP
GARRETT MATTINGLY
KENNETH CLARK
RALPH ROEDER
J. BRONOWSKI
IRIS ORIGO
H. R. TREVOR-ROPER
DENIS MACK SMITH
MARIA BELLONCI

COLLINS, *St. James's Place, London*

cHORIZON

PUBLISHER
James Parton

EDITOR
Joseph J. Thorndike, Jr.

MANAGING EDITOR
William Harlan Hale

Staff for this Book

EDITOR
Richard M. Ketchum

EDITORIAL ASSISTANTS
Martha House
Norman Kotker
Katharine H. McCagg
Mary Sherman Parsons

EUROPEAN BUREAU
Gertrudis Feliu, *Chief*
Timothy Green
Ann Natanson

COPY EDITOR
Margaret Robinson
Assistant: Sally Dreyfus Carr

ART DIRECTOR
Irwin Glusker

DESIGNER
Joel Szasz

HORIZON Magazine is published by
American Heritage Publishing Co., Inc.,
551 Fifth Avenue, New York 17, N.Y.

Above, an angel by the Florentine Filippino Lippi.
Title page: a detail from Cossa's Triumph of Venus.

CONTENTS

INTRODUCTION

Art reflects society—its aspirations, confusions and inheritance. But the future is there as well as the past and the great ages of man only have meaning so long as they create modes of expression and behaviour which will hold unborn generations in unconscious subjection. And this was peculiarly true of the Renaissance in Italy which started themes capable of infinite variation, so that Shakespeare and Poussin, and even Isaac Newton and Edward Gibbon, were carried along by its impetus into new worlds of creative achievement. Iconoclastic scholars have belittled the originality of the Renaissance; attempts have been made to isolate it; to demonstrate its overwhelming debt to former ages; to confine it to the realm of art. Not even the most prejudiced mediaevalist, however, can deny the astonishing vigour and originality of fifteenth-century Italy in painting, in sculpture, and in architecture. True, it adds depth to our understanding to realise the power of Gothic influence in the tragic nudes of Michelangelo and to appreciate the ironic handling of his inheritance by Uccello. Yet, as these splendid pages show, artists from the days of Masaccio to the death of Tintoretto not only equalled the triumphs of Greece and Rome, to which they were so deeply indebted, but excelled them. By their exploration of perspective, of landscape, of the nude, and of the human face, they opened up fresh dimensions in art. Although there were aspects of Renaissance painting that are as private and as esoteric as anything that modern art can produce, yet mostly it possessed a universality of appeal that shows little sign of diminishing, even as the last relics of the social structure which gave rise to it vanish from the Western world. Both capitalist and communist can gaze at Leonardo's self-portrait and be moved by the dignity of man and feel pity for his lonely fate. Perhaps the most profound themes of Renaissance painting and sculpture are concerned with the destiny of men, caught in the inexorable process of Time. And the originality of its greatest artists lies not in the virtuosity of their technical experiments, or the boldness with which they explored landscape and the naked body, but in their concentration on the uniqueness of the human temperament and the significance of individual experience. This became the preoccupation of Renaissance society; of its poets, philosophers and educators as well as its artists.

Renaissance art possessed, however, mundane roots: and the dung that fertilised them was golden. Without patrons, without the careless extravagance of popes and princes, cardinals and merchants, it could never have flourished. Italy in the fifteenth century was once more really rich; not as affluent as in the days of Imperial Rome but wealthy enough to support an extravagant and self-indulgent merchant aristocracy. The devastations of the barbarian invasions, the onslaught of Vikings, Magyars, Slavs and Moslems had destroyed the fabric of European society and impoverished its peoples. For centuries rich men had been few, money hard to come by, and what profits there were from agrarian toil and feeble commerce were needed for castles and cathedrals and the courts of kings. There were always pockets of luxury and sophistication, which provoked occasional originality in art and in thought; at times an eagerness for knowledge, and even a love for the classics, so that much of the Renaissance seems foreshadowed in earlier centuries. Foreshadowed, yes, but never achieved. Before Dante and Petrarch, and even after them, the iron dogmas of theology limited speculation, inhibited change, and gave preference to argument over observation.

In spite of setbacks, however, Italian cities, particularly Venice, Genoa, Florence, Milan, Naples and Palermo grew in population and in wealth: their merchant communities, vigorous, competitive, questing, increased steadily until their numbers, strength and riches began to bring into being a new form of society, that involved a fusion of aristocratic and bourgeois principles which found its expression in Italy of the Renaissance.

This fusion took place slowly, for the inertia of mediaeval society was very strong. Religion was neither overturned nor undermined. The Madonnas, Pietàs, Crucifixions, and the innumerable saints of Renaissance art speak eloquently of the traditional faith of Machiavelli's princes or of the Borgia's cardinals: plenty of painters of pagan nudes remained ardent Christians, Michelangelo did, so also Botticelli. Nor was the aristocratic structure of society submerged by the growth of the merchant class: indeed the Renaissance witnessed as much, if not more, penetration of the ideas and manners of the nobility into the ethos of the bourgeoisie as the other way about. In the fifteenth-century Italian world of violence, in which soldiers of fortune secured a dukedom for their prowess, noble birth was never necessary but always desirable, and feudal genealogies were manufactured with alacrity. Yet the prosperous and sophisticated merchants of Florence and Venice helped to promote civility and to widen the horizons of aristocratic life. A knowledge of the ancient classics, an appreciation of art, of literature, of music and of conversation became the hallmark of a gentleman, whether he was a soldier, statesman, priest or merchant. As wealth spread and the rich multiplied, their sophisticated demands created new tastes and encouraged new techniques. The permanent theatres for the performance of operas and plays became a necessity for any city with pretensions to civilised living. The rapid exploitation of the invention of moveable type in 1451 made libraries possible for men of modest means and so revolutionized education. Culture was constantly extended, thereby creating opportunities for advancement for those without the privilege of birth or the security of wealth. The gradations in society increased as well as thickened: individual enterprise, creative imagination and weight of temperament became of great potential value in a world in which the lines of class structure grew blurred. Pietro Aretino, the scourge of princes and the first man to live in splendour by his pen alone, is as much a part of Renaissance Italy as Petrarch, Michelangelo, Machiavelli, or Pius II, whose lives are discussed in this book.

As the old certainties slowly dissolved or grew more limited in application, curiosity took their place; of course, previous ages had contained men of ample curiosity, but society had not encouraged its practice nor inflamed its appetite. It had had to find its satisfaction in argument based on the dogmatic certainties of revealed religion. During the Renaissance it became easier for a few men to look at the world about them with the desire to understand it on its own terms, not God's. In the drawings of Leonardo that explore the formation of rocks or the turbulence of water, one can see this habit of truth being formed; so, too, in the historical and political writings of Machiavelli or Guicciardini there is a quest for truth, no matter where it may lead. Nor did Renaissance society discourage these tentative steps towards an open mind to man and his nature: other forces—particularly the great discoveries of continents beyond Europe—nourished and strengthened an attitude which was often during the Renaissance intermittent and unrealised. Such stirrings might have withered had not the circumstances of society been appropriate for their growth. And they would have lost all significance had not Italian society of the Renaissance been the prototype of those great empires that were to grow in Western Europe as the trade of the Atlantic flourished. Humanism took root elsewhere and its greatest triumphs were not to be Italian: but open minds, the use of trial to discover error, and the acquisition of knowledge for its own sake were vital for the growth of the commercial, and increasingly secular, societies of Western Europe. Italy of the Renaissance began hesitantly to experiment with what they so greatly developed. Attitudes of mind are difficult to pin-point in an historical context, but it is obvious that neither Machiavelli nor Leonardo could have pursued their own genius in the Middle Ages as they did in the Renaissance. And this Renaissance in Italy is as important for understanding the intellectual attitudes of Western Europe as for its art.

As will be seen from the pages that follow, Italian society, which gave rise to this stupendous achievement, was complex, exciting, dramatic, a world of violence that threw up geniuses with the ease of a juggler. An age of genius and one of extraordinary *panache*, it has never in all its variety ceased to entrance generations of men and women.

J. H. Plumb

RENAISSANCE ITALY, revering the landmarks of ancient and medieval glory, built splendid cathedrals and palaces to reflect its own proud age. Centered in Florence, the tide of the Renaissance stretched north to the rich Lombard plain and as far south as Naples; but beyond Naples, at the foot of the peninsula, medieval civilization still retained its hold. In the mountainous reaches of the Papal States, warrior families blazoned their shields with feudal symbols; but like Italy's other ruling houses, whose emblems are shown within their domains, they welcomed the rebirth of culture. The boundaries shown on the map are those of 1492, when the Renaissance was at its height. They are only approximate, however; throughout the era they shifted rapidly, like the fortunes of Italy's princes.

Trieste

VENICE

Ravenna

ROMAGNA
Cesena
Rimini
MALATESTA
San Marino
Pesaro
Fano
Sinigaglia
Burgo
San Sepolcro
Urbino
MONTEFELTRO
Ancona
Anghiari
THE
MARCHES
Perugia
Assisi
Lake
Trasimeno
Siena
STATES OF
THE CHURCH
Orvieto
Lake
Bolsena
Viterbo
TIBER RIVER
Aquila
ADRIATIC SEA
Foggia
Tivoli
KINGDOM OF
NAPLES
Rome
COLONNA
THE PAPACY
Ostia
Benevento
ARAGON
Naples
ISCHIA
TYRRHENIAN SEA

THE DAWN OF THE
RENAISSANCE

The face of medieval Europe was scarred with the ruins of its past. In Rome itself, the Colosseum housed the barbarous Frangipani and their armed retainers, greedy, lawless, destructive; the Forum provided a quarry for churches and rough pasture for the cattle market, and beneath the broken columns of the temple of Castor and Pollux the bullocks awaited their slaughter. The Campagna was littered with the crumbling ruins of its aqueducts; the pavements of those splendid Roman roads were narrowed by the returning wilderness. Elsewhere scraps of walls, the ruins of arena, temple, and triumphal arch, sometimes embedded in the hovels and houses of a town struggling to regain its life or lost forever in the countryside, constantly reminded the man of the Middle Ages of the fleeting life of man, of the unknowable nature of Providence. For him the past was dead, and its relics but morals in stone, a terrible warning of the wickedness which God had punished.

The wealth that was wrung from the soil and the tenuous trade of those dark centuries was poured into the splendid barbaric churches, noble if grotesque, that soared to heaven in violation of all the harmonies of ancient art. Or it served a grimmer purpose, and from it grew the towering fortresses, the embattled towers, the walled cities that were a necessity in a society in which the clang of armor was as common as the church bell.

Yet relics there were, and the miracle is that so much survived the ravages of violence. The barbarian hordes had swept away the thin veneer of Roman culture in Northwestern Europe and broken the powerful web of trade, law, and government that had bound the Mediterranean world in unity. This breach, on which time had worked, was widened by the surge of Islam which swept across and absorbed not only Northern Africa, the islands of Sicily and Sardinia, but also the huge peninsula of Spain, and poured over the Pyrenees only to be checked on the plains of France. Under the hammer blows of Vikings, warrior colonists and traders by the sword, Europe and its culture had nearly bled to death. Violence,

insecurity, and poverty reduced trade and city life to pitiful dimensions. Yet even in the worst of times, groups of peasants spread like a virus through the wastes and forests, colonizing those vast tracts of Europe which the Romans had dominated but never peopled.

Their lives were controlled by a warrior caste which attempted to give them protection, but battened on their labor; or by priests and monks who controlled the ritual of their existence and taught them that life was as fleeting as the crops they harvested. Men of this Western world lived simple, isolated, primitive lives in which pestilence, famine, and war marked the passage of the years.

Yet the past was never quite destroyed, the structure of society never utterly broken. Trade with the great civilizations of Islam and Byzantium transfused a little wealth into the shattered society of the West. More than wealth—ideas, too, could leap across the frontiers of hate and heresy to stimulate the cunning of men. So Byzantium lured men, warriors

as well as traders, and so did the challenge of the Moslem world, which called the knights to battle and sanctified the blood-crazed warriors of Europe, offering them riches in life or glory in death.

This curious society of peasant and priest and warrior, which drew its strength from individual men rather than from nations or countries, was held together by the Catholic Church and by feudal law. The secular ideal, often expressed but rarely achieved, was of an ordered, graded society, unchanging and unchangeable, compounded of obligations and rights fixed by law, both written and customary. At all times the majority of men, including the most bloodstained baron, accepted unquestioningly the superior merits of the religious life; the liturgical worship of God and the contemplation of the spirit, by which man subordinated his nature and exorcised his desires, became a social ideal. And like all ideals dreamed of by many, it was attained by few. The institutions for its fulfillment were everywhere created, but frequently

they served mere mundane ends. For the sake of power and wealth, men forgot their obligations, and found it sufficient to expiate their sins in age or defeat. Even for those who genuinely sought the ideal in the most ascetic monastery, the instincts of men broke through and compelled them to draw, to paint, and to sing for the glory of God.

In the darkest decades, there was a force at work—trade—which was inimical to this world of warriors, priests, and peasants. Trade drew Moslem, Jew, and Christian together; trade fattened towns, sometimes bred them. In so primitive a world, the personalities of kings and popes could lead either to strong government or to social anarchy; peace and good harvests could lift prosperity with outstanding rapidity; war and disease and famine could hold in check all progress, all growth, for a generation. At times it seemed as if the forces of expansion would lift Europe to a higher level of civility than it had known since the decay of Rome; at others that it would vanish and leave nothing but barbarism. In the eleventh century, towns and trade and craftsmanship grew rapidly. An intense interest in ancient learning, particularly in Aristotle, followed; the surging success of the Crusades promised new power and new prosperity. But the prospect faded and disaster followed. The Western Christians savaged the Byzantine Empire; the Moslem world revived under the powerful leadership of the Ottoman Turks; the scourge of the bubonic plague emptied the towns and reduced Europe's population by at least a third. A new death rather than a rebirth seemed Europe's prospect. Indeed, the dance of death became a threnody of life, haunting the imagination of men. Yet in the middle of the fourteenth century there were forces working like yeast in the economy and in the spirit of Italy. During the Renaissance these were to ferment and turn life into a new form, not only in Italy itself but throughout the Western world.

Throughout the Middle Ages, Italy never belonged wholly to Europe. The Romans had thoroughly colonized the land,

13

Simone Martini's well-known painting of Guidoriccio da Fogliano occupies a prominent position in the Palazzo Pubblico of Siena, commemorating the condottiere's great victory over the rebellious nobles of Montemassi and Sassoforte in 1328. He is seen riding in a fanciful landscape, dressed in colorful robes embroidered with the diamond and foliage (fogliana) pattern of his coat of arms. At the far right is a military camp, and in the background are two crenelated castles, the one at right with a newly developed defense mechanism for hurling stones. Fogliano lived in Siena and died there in 1352.

creating an urban life which neither Goth nor Lombard nor Saracen ever totally destroyed. Feudalism was planted in Italy but never rooted deeply there. Gothic art achieved one or two outstanding successes, but never dominated the Italian imagination. Italy remained a prey of, not a breeding ground for, warriors. During the waves of invasion there were times when it seemed that Italian society might be destroyed or transmogrified. The hemorrhage of war weakened Italy's strength, emptied her towns, diminished her trade, and enfeebled all institutions save the Church of Rome, whose universality endowed it with some of the authority, if little of the strength, of the Caesars. But always there was trade, there was an urban life. When Belisarius landed in the sixth century at Naples with his Byzantine troops, intent on recapturing Italy for the Eastern Empire, his leading ally was a Syrian businessman, Antiochus. Aistolf's laws for the Lombards, about 750, legislate for merchants. A pair of Venetian traders, in 828, stole the relics of Saint Mark from Alexandria.

By 836 there was at least one merchant, Semplicianus, rich enough to endow a monastery at Milan. Indeed, during these barbarous centuries, Venice was laying the foundations of its future greatness by exploiting the natural advantages that Italy possessed as the link between the primitive world of the North and the sophisticated East. The most valuable traffic was probably in men, women, and children, who were shipped to Alexandria where there was a ready slave market. Paid in coin, the Venetians then bought luxuries—the silks which the concubines of Charlemagne's court found so ravishing, the great silver dishes which might find their way into the ship-graves of chieftains by the northern seas, the papyrus that the papal Curia needed for its administration. As well as slaves, the Venetians traded the salt from their lagoon for the products of the Lombard plain. Nor was Venice the only mercantile community among Italian cities. Ships from Pisa, Genoa, and Amalfi ventured to the eastern Mediterranean, carrying pilgrims to the Holy Land, trading

with the Greeks or the Moslems or the Jews, creating a spider's web of commerce. Yet progress was neither steady nor constant. Pirates infested the inland seas, war was endemic, and risks, like profits, were huge. Nor must the amount of trade be exaggerated; often it consisted of nothing more than a pedlar plodding dusty roads by the side of the Rhone, carrying his pack laden with eastern marvels to the rural fairs of Champagne.

Trade, however, was not the only catalyst at work in Italy and medieval Europe. The world of armed knights was not cheap; the courts of kings have never tolerated poverty; and though princes of the Church might preach self-denial, they rarely practiced it. As war became more highly technical, it became more costly; as kingdoms grew in strength, their administration needed larger funds; as the network of churches and monasteries honeycombed Europe, so the wealth and expenses of the Church became more vast. The result was that the merchants quickly found themselves in fresh and

lush pastures. They became financiers. As with trade, so with finance, the seeding ground for the rest of Europe was Italy. The great banking street of London was, and still is, called Lombard Street after the Italian moneylenders who settled there in the thirteenth century. Of course, this high finance of popes, emperors, and kings could be as dangerous as trade. The Venetians rarely made any loans to a prince: the risk was too great and default too common. Yet in the handling of taxes, in the loans for war, in the purchased rights of justice, there were men who amassed fortunes. And by the High Middle Ages the structure of international finance, based on Italy, was as advanced as that of the ancient world. This helped to make Italian life more complex and more secular.

The burgeoning both of trade and of finance rested primarily on the growth of Europe's population. The great empty lands of Gaul, Britain, and Germany absorbed generation upon generation of men; in the struggle to conquer the forests, the marshes, and the wastes, few could be spared

15

from the toil of the land save for prayer or for war. Although Italy was ravaged often, its thickly spread peasant population possessed remarkable powers of recuperation from famine, pestilence, and war, and this numerous people nourished crafts and industries. Wealth and commerce aided their growth, and the old walled Roman cities gave them protection. Cities, not states or kings or princes, dominated the land. The sole exception was the Pope, whose superiority in the hierarchy of universal power even emperors had, after bitter conflicts, reluctantly admitted. The popes intended both to protect the Patrimony of St. Peter and to prevent any secular ruler from achieving the hegemony of Italy. To achieve this aim they were rarely reluctant to call to their aid the warriors of France—an ominous precedent for the future. To check the Pope's territorial ambitions, some cities were not averse to asking on occasion for military help from the Emperor, to whom they owed a certain allegiance. It is true that the powers and rights of the Holy Roman Empire were more often ig-

nored. Theoretically, the emperors claimed universal secular authority as the popes claimed universal spiritual power, but in practice the emperors' strength was based on the lands that they possessed in Germany, their estates in Italy, and a vast, ill-defined collection of rents, dues, and legal powers over the cities and states of Italy, the Netherlands, and parts of Burgundy. And any threat to the riches of Italy brought the imperial armies across the Alps. Invasion and war, sometimes desperate and tragic and bloody, threaded the history of Italy for a millennium, making her poets and philosophers dream of freedom, of unity, of peace. No great power ever succeeded for long, and the absence of a powerful state-system, the lack of any corpus of national law or secular jurisdiction, bred an openness to political experiment that was in itself a powerful stimulus to the new age which dawned in Italy toward the end of the fourteenth century, an age which was dominated by the city-state that was born in the violence and anarchy of medieval Italy.

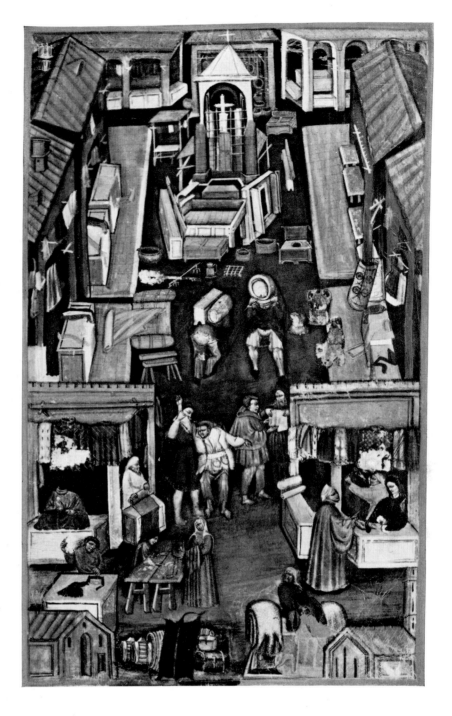

Trade, high finance, a large and partially urbanized population, quickening industry, the absence of a deeply rooted all-powerful political structure—all of these were seminal. There were, however, other forces—equally important, if less measurable—that were needed to change the whole life of Italy at the Renaissance as certainly and as dramatically as the Industrial Revolution changed the face of Britain in the late eighteenth century. Ideas, like heresy, traveled in the Middle Ages along the lines of trade. From Byzantium, from Islam, from the prosperous and flourishing lands of France, Burgundy, and the Flemish towns came ideas in art, in technology, in science, and in philosophy. And even in the most barbarous times, cultivated Italians never forgot the great traditions of their imperial past nor their splendid achievements in literature. Throughout the Middle Ages the classics had been copied, studied frequently for their moral virtues, occasionally enjoyed for themselves. Monks appreciated Horace as well as Seneca, and even Ovid was not unknown to the cloister. There were high points of excitement and discovery. The recovery of many of Aristotle's works in the twelfth and early thirteenth centuries, from Arabic sources, created an intellectual ferment in scholastic circles. As secular life grew in complexity and stability and urbanity, the laws of Justinian became the object of devoted research, and long before the Renaissance, Roman ideas of law, of order, and of government had permeated Italian city life. This complex society, never far from barbarism yet close to civility, threw up men of great intellectual stature and brilliant literary gifts. Long before the Renaissance dawned, Saint Thomas Aquinas had provided a philosophic argument for dogma that was to serve men for century after century. Dante, the Florentine, produced the first great poem in Italian—a poem that is medieval in spirit but modern in technique—and Petrarch, who followed, showed that Dante's achievement was not likely to remain unique. These were but the brightest stars in a luminous firmament.

Europe of the Middle Ages was not a closed world. The Crusades had ripped open the Near East and given the hordes of warriors a taste of sophisticated, cultured society which previously had only been the experience of merchants and pilgrims. And Italy was the door through which the Crusaders passed. There had been more distant seekings, too. Marco Polo had reached Peking; links, unfortunately to prove as fragile as gossamer, had been made with the long-lost Nestorian Christians of India and China. At one time it seemed as if the Great Khan himself might turn Christian and link Europe with the eastern seas. The glimpse of the wider world proved brief—the Khan remained a Buddhist, the Chinese threw off Mongol control, and Ottomans swept the Christian powers out of Asia Minor, seized the Balkans, and threatened Italy itself. Yet this ebb and flow of European power interlocked the Christian and Moslem worlds. Methods and materials passed from one to the other. At the splendid court in Sicily of Frederick II, it was an Arab who taught geography

and presented the Emperor with a silver sphere on which the map of the world was drawn. Indeed, at that court the Renaissance itself seemed at hand. Frederick, ruthless, amoral, violent, a realist in politics as in philosophy, might have been an uncle of Cesare Borgia. Although he was the Holy Roman Emperor, possessing vast lands and vaster rights beyond the Alps, the core of Frederick's strength and power lay in his kingdom of Sicily, which contained most of southern Italy as well as the island itself. Here he introduced laws based on Justinian's code, fostered city life, and favored the bourgeoisie. He patronized the arts; encouraged literature, poetry, science; kept an astrologer; dabbled in alchemy; brought together a menagerie of rare animals and an exotic collection of mistresses. He lived flamboyantly and realistically and delighted in the creative activities of man. But he was a portent, not a man of his time. Legends festooned his name, and they called him *stupor mundi* as much from awe as from flattery. The delight of his court in literature and in philosophic in-

The miniature on the facing page shows the monarchs of France (left) and England (right) setting out on the Third Crusade in 1189. Forty years later Emperor Frederick II succeeded where they had failed and liberated Jerusalem. Frederick, whose portrait (left) appears in a treatise he once wrote on falconry, had many interests, and his court was the great intellectual center of the time. One of his residences was the stronghold of Castel del Monte (below), on which work began in 1240.

quiry, the efficiency of his administration, the energy of his diplomacy, and above all the openness of his mind to all ideas, whether Moslem or Christian or pagan, struck a rare chord in thirteenth-century Europe. Yet about him and his courtiers there is still an air of barbarism, a lack of sophistication, even of experience, that makes his world, in truth if not in appearance, closer to that of Charlemagne or Otto I than that of Lorenzo de' Medici or Lodovico Sforza.

By the time of Lorenzo and Lodovico, Italy had changed fundamentally and dramatically, and this change is rightly called the Renaissance. In Rome broad streets had been driven through the chaotic slums that crouched amid the rubbish of antiquity. A new city had arisen about the Vatican, and the plans for the huge Basilica of St. Peter were slowly taking shape. The palaces of the cardinals proclaimed the tastes, the interests, the sophistications of this new age. As in Rome, so in Florence. The great towers in which families had sought refuge during the furious vendettas of the Middle Ages had

been razed. In their place stood the opulent homes of patrician families—Strozzi, Medici, Rucellai, and the rest. These great houses were designed according to the austere classical harmonies that the great architect of the Renaissance—Brunelleschi—had made fashionable. Out in the Tuscan countryside the first villas of modern times rivaled those of Augustan Rome. The style as well as the decoration of these buildings was in sharp and vivid contrast to the Gothic which so many men and women of the Renaissance thoughtlessly despised, not realizing the extent of their debt to their recent past. But such unawareness was scarcely surprising, for their age was astonishingly fresh, and the achievements of the fifteenth century as remarkable as they were original. Historians, concerned with origins and remote influences, stress how deeply interlocked this age of the Renaissance was with the medieval world: how much it owed to Flanders, to Paris, to Byzantium. True as this may be, it also distorts reality by the nature of its emphasis. It would be folly to underestimate the creative

strength and originality of fifteenth-century Italy. This stretched far beyond architecture, dramatic though the structural changes of the Italian cities were. In sculpture and in painting the change was, perhaps, more profound. In both these arts there had been precursors—Giotto, the great Florentine painter, Duccio, the Sienese, and Andrea Pisano, the sculptor—and the break with the past was neither so sharp nor so vivid as in building. The achievement, however, was far greater. For the next four centuries the themes, the traditions, the techniques, and the preoccupations of the artists of fifteenth-century Italy were to dominate Western Europe. The roll call of their names—Fra Angelico, Bellini, Botticelli, Donatello, Ghiberti, Leonardo, Lippi, Mantegna, Michelangelo, Pollaiuolo, Signorelli, and Verrocchio, a list that could be doubled with scarcely any loss of quality—speaks for itself: such a constellation of artistic genius, spread over a mere century and a half, would alone make this age of the Renaissance one of the great epochs of human achievement.

Yet art was only one aspect of the brilliance of Renaissance Italy, which created an image of man, a vision of human excellence, that *still* lies at the heart of the Western tradition. Rarely achieved, it has nevertheless haunted men like a mirage. The Italians, particularly the Florentines, revered antiquity—its wisdom, its grace, its philosophy, and its literature. Sensitive and deep-thinking men had done so, of course, ever since the Roman world had crumbled into decay; in monastic schools and universities Plato, as well as Aristotle, had been studied intensively. Yet such knowledge had been largely part of the private world of scholars. At the time of the Renaissance these humanistic studies spread through the upper and middle ranks of society and became a formidable part of the education of those who were to wield power and authority. The timely invention of the printing press not only multiplied the works of antiquity so that they were readily available to hundreds of thousands of men and women, but also helped to create a public for their study. What had been

private became public, and a study of the classical heritage became a necessity for a gentleman; indeed, his familiarity with the classics was the hallmark of civility. A man might still be a warrior, a priest, a merchant, with a professional outlook and professional mores, yet if he wished to be regarded as the complete man, *l'uomo universale,* more was expected of him. He needed to be well-bred, and the breeding of a gentleman was defined by Italians of the Renaissance. They insisted on a refinement of taste, an ease of manner, combined with a capacity for manly pursuits, a knowledge of the classics, an acquaintance with history and philosophy, an appreciation of music, painting, architecture, and sculpture, a connoisseurship of the rare and the beautiful whether they might be books, jewels, coins, or scraps of antiquity. All of these interests were to be lightly borne, without pedantry or excessive professionalism. This was the image that Castiglione created in his famous book, *The Courtier*—an image which was drawn from the knowledge he acquired of men such as

Lorenzo de' Medici and Federigo da Montefeltro.

To acquire, let alone indulge, such sophisticated tastes required money, for education in so many disciplines and interests, even if superficial, took time, and no one could patronize the arts without wealth. As patronage grew competitive, the arts themselves became more costly. Renaissance society was designed for rich men, rich cities, rich popes. To maintain so vast an expenditure required an active and most profitable commerce; to indulge it a prodigious concentration of costly talent was necessary. And the Italian cities possessed both. Venice, Florence, Milan, and Rome were full of exceedingly rich men, and money, which was the base of all Renaissance achievement, nurtured genius. The transmutation of gold into works of art was the result of a complex social process, the marriage between aristocratic extravagance and bourgeois ambition. The aristocrats of medieval Europe did not vanish overnight; they still lived on, maintaining their sense of caste, providing a snobbish goal toward which the

rich merchant could direct his social ambition. The patricians of Florence, Milan, or Venice might be merchants, but they wished to live like nobles. In Italy of the Renaissance, therefore, aristocratic and bourgeois attitudes fused to create a pattern of life, a tradition of social expression that was to be adopted by societies of the West as the wealth of the New World and of the Indies poured into their cities. Commercial capitalism, struggling in the framework of feudalism, learned, through Italy, not only how to express itself in art and learning, but also how to make an art of life itself.

It is a sobering thought that the great Italian achievements in almost every sphere of intellectual and artistic activity took place in a world of violence and war. Cities were torn by feud and vendetta: Milan warred against Venice, Florence against Pisa, Rome against Florence, Naples against Milan. Alliances were forged only to be broken, the countryside was constantly scarred by pillage, rapine, and battle, and in this maelstrom the old bonds of society were broken and new

ones forged. After a brief period of peace, in the second half of the fifteenth century, the confusion and carnage grew worse through the great French invasions of Charles VIII, Louis XII, and Francis I, a time of agony that did not end till the dreadful sack of Rome in 1527 by the Holy Roman Emperor, Charles V. Yet this violence worked like yeast in the thought of men, and profoundly influenced the way they were to regard problems of power and government for hundreds of years. They ceased to look for answers to the fate of man in the dogmas of the Church. They searched the histories of antiquity for precedents that might guide them to the truth, but they also sought to explain, as Machiavelli did, the world in which they lived by what they knew to be the nature of man. Indeed, it was during the Renaissance in Italy that many men came to feel that truth was elusive, a mood afterward strengthened by the discovery of the world beyond Europe. The old dogmatic certainties did not vanish at once, and the habit of trying to nail truth down by argu-

Marco Polo's departure from Venice in 1271 is the subject of the fourteenth-century manuscript on the facing page. The quaint view of the city includes such details as the bronze horses which may still be seen today over the portico of St. Mark's Cathedral. In the foreground, islands populated by strange beasts represent the many foreign lands visited by the traveler in his twenty-four year voyage in the East. At right is an illumination done by Simone Martini for a manuscript—A Commentary of Servius upon Virgil—once owned by his friend Petrarch. The Latin poet, who was honored during the Renaissance as if he were a saint, is seated in the Muses' sacred grove with his commentator and characters from his poems.

ment from fundamental principles was not lightly cast aside. Some of the most original minds, however, particularly Machiavelli and Leonardo da Vinci, sought truth not in argument but in observation. Machiavelli brooded on men and events, on the effects of political action and on the consequence of chance; Leonardo grew preoccupied with the flow of water, the flight of birds, the formation of rocks. The growth of ideas and the development of mental attitudes are difficult to pinpoint in the course of history, but this, at least, can be said: the men of the Renaissance, by the range of their inquiries, by the freshness of their skepticism, and by the sharpness of their observation, gave impetus to, and helped to acquire intellectual acceptance for, the search for truth on earth instead of in heaven.

Artistic expression, intellectual inquiry, social attainments —the Renaissance enriched all these things in an original and creative way. Its influence spread throughout Europe and continued for centuries. It was the work of hundreds of gifted men and a score of remarkable cities—Vicenza, Rimini, Ferrara, Urbino, Mantua, Parma, and the rest all made their contributions. They had their artists, philosophers, poets, and craftsmen of genius and distinction, yet the full force of the Renaissance flowed most strongly in four cities—Florence, Milan, Rome, and Venice. Florence, a very small city by modern standards, cradled the Renaissance and produced an astonishing array of genius which Rome and Milan, both far richer than Florence, patronized. The full tide of the Renaissance reached Venice late, but it lingered there longer, creating an island of delight in a world made brutal by the new clash of religious ideologies as the Reformation broke Europe asunder. Neither Reformation nor Counter Reformation, nor the economic decline of Italy, brought on by the discovery of the New World, could check the spread of the Renaissance. Its ideas and its achievements ran like an ineradicable dye through the fabric of Europe, and its monuments have become a part of the world's heritage.

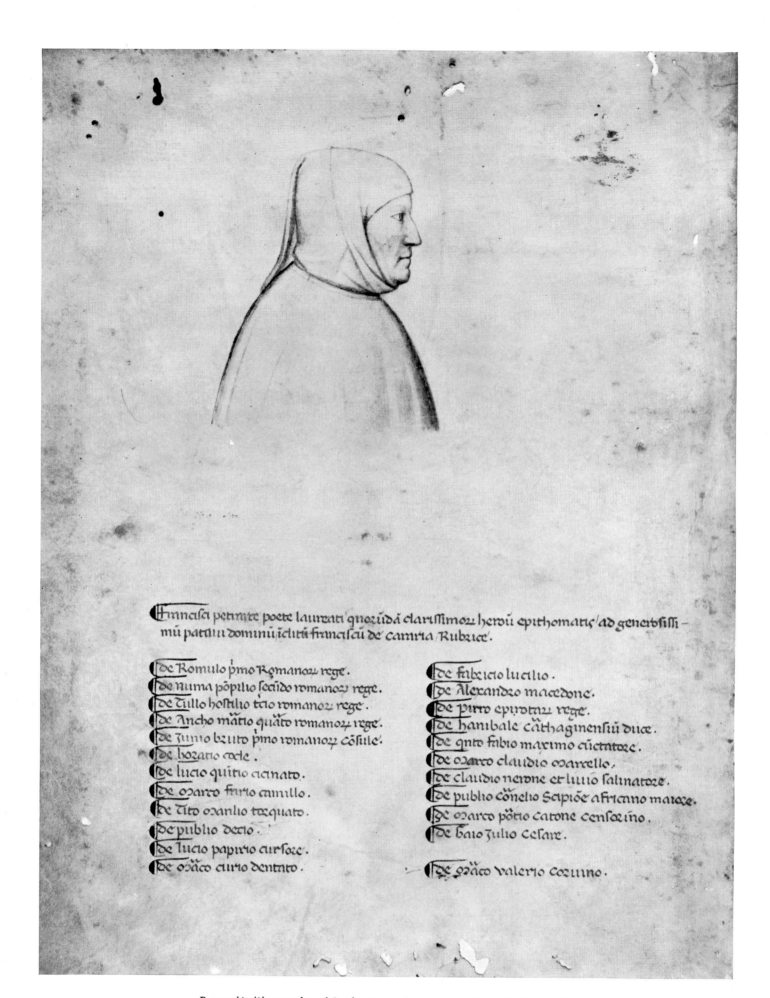

Petrarch's likeness, by a friend, appears in a manuscript of his last work.

Petrarch

by MORRIS BISHOP

"I was born to this world," says Petrarch, "in the Via dell' Orto of the city of Arezzo, just at dawn on Monday, July 20, in the thirteen hundred and fourth year of this latest age which takes its name from Jesus Christ, fountain and author of all my hope." The house of his birth still stands at the town's top, across from the cathedral. Houses occupied by great ghosts live long.

He was christened Francesco Petracco, a slightly inelegant name which he Latinized to Petrarca, which we have Anglicized to Petrarch.

He was an Aretine only by circumstance. His father, Ser Petracco, was an office-holding notary, or attorney, in Florence, living on the edge of poverty. He belonged to the bourgeois party of the Whites; and in the revolution of 1302 he was banished, together with Dante and many others, and took refuge in Arezzo, some sixty miles away. But as Arezzo gave a chill welcome to plotting Florentine exiles, Ser Petracco had soon to seek his fortune afar. His wife, Eletta, and baby were permitted to return to the family house in Incisa, on Florentine territory.

According to a dear family story, Francesco, seven months old, was transported to Incisa in a sort of sling depending from a stout stick borne over a mounted servant's shoulder. In fording the flooded Arno, the horse slipped and fell; the servant nearly lost his life in saving that of the child. This is the kind of incident that has made Fortune a deity.

In Incisa was born, in 1307, Francesco's brother Gherardo, the product of a furtive visit of Ser Petracco. In 1310 or 1311 the family was reunited for a year in Pisa, and there, or possibly in Genoa, Ser Petracco was visited by his old friend and fellow exile Dante. By this time Ser Petracco found a post in the papal court, which had removed from Rome to Avignon. There, in 1312, his wife and sons joined the exile.

Avignon was a town of some five thousand inhabitants. The arrival of the papal court affected it as would the establishment of the United Nations in a rural American county seat. Cardinals' trains were billeted in citizens' homes, petitioners and office seekers camped in the streets, on the walls, in cemeteries. Signora Petracco and the boys found lodgings in the town of Carpentras, fifteen miles away, and there they spent four happy years. Writing, years later, to Guido Sette, a schoolmate and a lifelong friend, Petrarch remembered in Carpentras only joy, security, peace at home, liberty in public, and country silence round about. He recalled tenderly how the boys watched out the night in talk on the eternal subjects. He remembered also that while his companions were studying their Latin for grammatical and rhetorical lessons, "I was noting down the substance of thought—the pettiness of this life, its brevity, haste, tumbling course, its hidden cheats, time's irrecoverability, the flower of life soon wasted, the fugitive beauty of a blooming face, the flight of youth, the trickeries of age, the wrinkles, illnesses, sadness, and pain, and the implacable cruelty of indomitable death." Already he was oppressed by the sense of time and its hurry toward the end.

One day his father came to Carpentras with Guido Sette's uncle. Despite Signora Petracco's fears, they visited the famous Fontaine de Vaucluse, fourteen miles away. Francesco was enchanted with the lovely rocky gorge and with the fountain itself, a mysterious swirling pool, where long-hidden underground waters furiously emerge under limestone cliffs. This, he said, was the place he would most wish to live, rather than in any great city.

Francesco, Gherardo, and Guido Sette were sent to the University of Montpellier and then to Bologna, to study law. Seven wasted years, Francesco called them, but although he detested the law—the art of selling justice—he had time to read widely in the classics, to perfect his Latin style, and to correct his Italian not far from the Tuscan fount. He loved fat Bologna, *pinguis Bononia,* its songs and dances; he loved also to escape on feast days for long country walks, returning after dark to climb the crumbling walls.

The parents died, and Francesco and Gherardo returned, in 1326, to Avignon. Francesco always maintained that his guardians robbed him of his small property, an act which reinforced his dislike of the law. He refused to practice—"I couldn't face making a merchandise of my mind," he said—but he must have had some employment at the papal court, for he and his brother led the life of elegant young men about town.

Francesco was tall and active, with a clear complexion, between light and dark, keen, lively eyes, and reddish-brown hair, which turned prematurely gray, to his great grief. He was vain of his good looks. He later recalled to Gherardo how the pair of them would work all night on their coiffures, sometimes burning their brows with curling irons, how they would dispose every fold of their gowns, terrified lest wind should discompose them and horses splash them with mud; and he recalled his very long, very tight boots, which would have crippled him if he had not revolted in time. He remembered their stylish talk, with dislocated words and dropped syllables, and their popularity, their swarms of visitors, and the vain, lewd songs they sang. He wrote poetry in the current mode, which he was later careful to destroy, and he had more than his share of amorous success with the light women who followed the papal court.

On April 6, 1327, when he was not yet twenty-three, he attended the early morning office at the church of St. Clare. There and then for the first time he saw Laura, and there and then the god Amor's arrow pierced his heart and made a wound never to be staunched.

To rid himself of Laura's obsessing image, he says, he traveled far. But again he says that the real reason was a great inclination and longing to see new sights. He got as far as Paris, Flanders, Germany, Rome; he would have liked to push on to the farthest Indies, to Taprobane. Even in old age he loved to travel on a map, with the aid of books and imagination. He has been called the first tourist, journeying for pleasure alone; and indeed it is hard to think of a predecessor, for even Herodotus wandered with a book in view.

For pleasure alone he climbed Mont Ventoux, which rises to more than six thousand feet, beyond Vaucluse. It was no great feat, of course; but he was the first recorded Alpinist of modern times, the first to climb a mountain merely for the delight of looking from its top. (Or almost the first; for in a high pasture he met an old shepherd, who said that fifty years before he had attained the summit, and had got nothing from it save toil and repentance and torn clothing.) Petrarch was dazed and stirred by the view of the Alps, the mountains around Lyons, the Rhone, the Bay of Marseilles. He took Augustine's *Confessions* from his pocket and reflected that his climb was merely an allegory of aspiration toward a better life.

To qualify for the right to receive income from church benefices he took the tonsure, which committed him to nothing much (though ruining his stylish coiffure). Aided, no doubt, by wealthy patrons, he bought a small house in the picturesque gorge of Vaucluse, thus linking forever the names of Petrarch, Laura, and Vaucluse. His retreat was only twenty miles from the hateful city of Avignon, the Western Babylon, with its traffic noise, its scavenging pigs and dogs, and its filthy dust blown by the mistral. When he went to town he tried to make himself insensible, but he had much business in Avignon, for he was already well known as a poet and scholar, and of course Laura was there.

If he did not exactly discover the love of wild nature, he established it as a literary convention for all later times. His beautiful descriptions of country sights and sounds, of the little Sorgue, with its crystal waters and the emerald luster of its bed, moved and still move the poetic imagination of the Western world. But his solitude was laborious. "I rise at midnight, leave the house at dawn; and in the fields I study, think, write, and read. I fight off sleep as long as I can, and keep dainties from the body, pleasures from the soul, sloth from my behavior. All day I wander on bare mountains, dewy valleys, and in mossy caves, alone with my thoughts." He lived simply. A servant once asked him, "What do you eat?" "Polenta, toasted turnips, greens, vegetables, sometimes delicious cows' milk." "No meat?" "I'm not a wolf that feeds on flesh."

He worked fruitfully, producing, in Italian, poems of love's longing and despair, which were passed from literary hand to hand, with copies taken on the way. They were diffused throughout Italy, sung to the lute in such gatherings of gentlefolk as Boccaccio describes. In Latin he wrote giant compendiums of ancient learning, an epic poem which was to rival Virgil's, and endless enchanting letters. His retreat was not a rejection of the world; it was a roundabout means of attaining worldly fame.

This he gained. For him Rome revived its ancient custom of crowning a poet with symbolic laurel. On April 8, 1341, on the holy ground of Rome's Capitol, he became the first laureate of modern times. His celebrity spread far: an old blind poet from near Genoa had himself led, and often carried, by his son to Naples, in order to hear and feel the presence of his idol. Missing Petrarch there, the pilgrims pursued him to Parma, and for three days

blessed God for their companionship with poetic divinity.

The attainment of one's ambition is always disillusioning, or so we are told. Petrarch's sense of human vanity and void increased; he went through a period of crisis. His dear brother Gherardo, shocked by the death of the woman he loved, entered a Carthusian monastery, to spend a six-year novitiate in virtual silence. Was not this, indeed, the better way? In his self-questioning mood Petrarch wrote a beautiful series of penitential psalms, and also his extraordinary *Secretum*. This, his secret book, never revealed during his life, is a dialogue with Saint Augustine. The saint, with robust assurance, explores Petrarch's character and faults and brings to light his subconscious motives. He berates Petrarch for his sensuality, his overweening love of fame, his really ridiculous sighing for unattainable Laura, and his *accidia*, or fits of unreasoning gloom. "Give yourself back to yourself!" says the saint. The little book, stemming from Augustine's own *Confessions*, is the first example of introspective self-analysis of modern times.

His sensuality bore its fruit. He had a son, Giovanni, born in 1337, and a daughter, Francesca, born in 1343. Whether there was one mother or two we do not know. Petrarch did his best for his children. He had them legitimized, gave the son the best education obtainable, and procured for him an ecclesiastical living; but the boy was a sad scapegrace, at least in the father's eyes. He died at the age of twenty-four, in the Plague of 1361. The girl, on the other hand, was the consolation of Petrarch's later years.

From 1343 onward Petrarch spent more and more of his time in Italy, partly because he obtained comfortable canonicates there, partly because Vaucluse had nearly served its purpose, and partly because he enjoyed implication in great affairs. In Parma, during the Great Plague of 1348, he learned that his Laura had died on the sixth of April, twenty-one years to the hour from the moment he had first seen her in the church of St. Clare. (The coincidence is astounding; whether too astounding for belief depends on one's capacity for belief.) He lived for a time in Padua; he visited Florence and was triumphally received. The city restored his family property to him; but as he did not immediately make his residence there, it took the property back again. He returned for two years to Vaucluse. After his departure, his house was robbed of everything except his books; he never saw it again. He settled in Milan, city of the Visconti tyrants, hateful to all Florentines. For this he was much blamed even by his best friends; and indeed it does seem a surrender to an ambition he affected to despise. He served the Visconti as envoy to Venice and to the Emperor Charles IV, and he made an official trip to Paris to felicitate the bloodthirsty King John the Good of France on his release from an English prison.

In Milan, in 1359, he received a visit from Boccaccio, nine years his junior. The two became fast friends; their precious correspondence is a literary treasure. (Petrarch left Boccaccio, in his will, money to buy a warm dressing gown for "winter study and lucubrations by night.")

Restless, he left Milan in 1361 for varying stays in Pavia, Padua, and Venice. The city of Venice gave him a palazzo on the Riva degli Schiavoni, whence he could watch the ships setting forth for the Black Sea and Egypt and the Holy Land. In return, he offered his books to the city, expecting them to be the nucleus of the first public library since ancient times. (But after his death they were not delivered; at least twenty-six of them arrived, after centuries of adventure, in Paris.)

Venice did not satisfy him; nothing satisfied him. Four young Aristotelians visited him, and made clear that they thought him an old fogy. He was shocked by a cleric à la mode, who praised only Averroes, and called Paul and Augustine and the rest a lot of gabblers. He was inspired to write the treatise *On His Own Ignorance and That of Many Others.*

He was old and tired and conscious of being out of date. He removed to Padua and bought a country house at Arquà in the hills to the southward. It still stands, in its olive groves and vineyards, flower-framed, bird-beloved, as in his day. His daughter Francesca joined him. She had married well; her son Francesco was the image of his grandfather. The child's death at the age of two nearly broke the old man's heart. "I never loved anything on earth as I loved him," he grieved, but he came to love no less his winsome granddaughter Eletta, named for his mother.

Illnesses gathered: fevers, fainting spells, foot trouble, and the itch. He was so thin that he was afraid of vanishing. Boccaccio urged him to take things easy, to stop writing. "No," he said; "nothing weighs less than a pen, and nothing gives more pleasure; it is useful not only to the writer but to others far away, perhaps even to those who will be born a thousand years from now."

In the morning of July 19, 1374, he was found dead at his writing desk, the pen dropped from his hand on his *Life of Julius Caesar.* (But some distrust this story, too exquisitely apt.) He lacked a day of reaching seventy years, the Psalmist's span.

"What am I?" he had asked himself, a few years before. "A scholar? No, hardly that; a lover of woodlands, a solitary, in the habit of uttering disjointed words in the shadow of beech trees, and used to scribbling presumptuously under an immature laurel tree; fervent in toil, but not happy with the results; a lover of letters, but not fully versed in them; an adherent of no sect, but very eager for truth; and because that is hard to find, and because I am a clumsy searcher, often, out of self-distrust, I flee error and fall into doubt, which I hold in lieu of truth. Thus I have finally joined that humble band that knows nothing, holds nothing as certain, doubts everything —outside of the things that it is sacrilege to doubt."

Petrarch is important to us in three ways—as a poet, as a humanist scholar, and as a living human being.

The irruption of Laura—or love's reality—into Petrarch's life turned him from a rhymester in the prevailing mode into a great poet.

Who was Laura, his muse? Some have doubted if she ever existed. They point to the Provençal convention that a poet must sigh forever for an unattainable lady, to Petrarch's presumed desire to outdo Dante's mystical love for Beatrice in his *Vita Nuova,* to the discord between Petrarch's proclaimed devotion for Laura and his simultaneous gross amours, and to the convenient triple meanings of the word *Laura: il lauro,* or the poetic laurel; *l'aura,* the zephyr; *l'auro,* gold. Laura, they say, is merely an allegory, a useful fiction.

No, Laura was a real woman. Many efforts have been made to track her down. The identification with Laure de Sade, née Laure de Noves, is very old, and while it presents difficulties, it is not at all unlikely. An identification is not, perhaps, very important, but readers always want to know how much is true in any fiction, as writers are usually reluctant to tell.

His *Rime in Vita e Morte di Madonna Laura*, 366 poems (the leap-year number), give us plenty of specific facts. Laura was young, golden-haired, noble, rich; she came from the hill country near Vaucluse, and she was married and settled in Avignon. She was one of a group of young matrons who went bathing and boating together. Many of the poems take their rise from an incident—the poet's attempt to purloin a glove; an eye affliction of Laura's; a new dress, purple with pink spots, blue-bordered, reminding the poet of phoenix feathers.

We have other evidence of her reality. In Petrarch's *Secretum*, his private, undivulged self-examination, Saint Augustine sneers that Laura's body, worn out by illness and frequent childbirths, has lost its old beauty. Petrarch admits the fact, but protests that she cleansed his youthful soul of all filth and taught him to look upwards. "Nonsense!" says Augustine, a hardheaded confessor. "She has ruined your life! She turned you from the love of the Creator to the love of the creature!" Augustine makes his charge admit that Laura's youthful beauty, and her significant name, allured the poet, and that he had besieged her with his sensual desires. "But she never yielded!" protests Petrarch. "I could never love anything else! My soul is so used to adoring her, my eyes so used to gazing on her, that all that is not she looks dark and ugly!"

What exactly did he want? He is always pleading in his poems for "pity," for "yielding," for the gift of mercy forever sought by the Provençal poets. One may amuse oneself by imagining that one day she might have decided to "yield." How he would have fled! She would have ruined his whole book.

Long, hopeless fidelity is the poet's best theme. But it has to be sincere, it has to be true. Then it has to be converted into beautiful poetic form. Every reader of Petrarch's poems must feel their truth and must recognize their beauty.

His commonest device was to take an incident of the endless courtship and develop it in sonnet form into a "conceit," or a fancy, or a coherent rounded thought. Some of the conceits are very thin-spun, elaborate, on the edge of absurdity. The form was enthusiastically adopted by the poets of Italy, France, and England, and the Petrarchan sonnet gained a universal vogue which eventually brought upon it nearly universal scorn. (But the "conceit" has returned to poetry today.) The fading of the Petrarchan tradition has left in many minds an aversion from Petrarch, wholly undeserved, for much of his poetry is simple, straightforward, expressing a deep emotion in everyday words which magically turn to lovely harmonies.

Instead of describing unknown, unread poems, let us take an example.

T. S. Eliot said that, knowing no Italian, he picked up a copy of Dante and stumbled through a few lines, and knew that this was great poetry. We may attempt the same test with a sonnet of Petrarch's, to see, in reading it aloud, how some of the sound and sense come through. (The reader is warned to notice the triple pun in the first line, and advised that *crine* means *hair*, and that *leggiadrette* is a diminutive of *charming*.)

> L'aura che 'l verde lauro e l'aureo crine
> soavemente sospirando move,
> fa con sue viste leggiadrette e nove
> l'anime da' lor corpi pellegrine.
>   Candida rosa nata in dure spine,
> quando fia chi sua pari al mondo trove?
> Gloria di nostra etate! O vivo Giove,
> manda, prego, il mio in prima che 'l suo fine;
>   sì ch'io non veggia il gran pubblico danno
> e 'l mondo remaner senza 'l suo sole,
> né li occhi miei, che luce altra non hanno,
>   né l'alma, che pensar d'altro non vole,
> né l'orecchie, ch'udir altro non sanno
> senza l'oneste sue dolci parole.

What does it mean? Why this:

> The gentle airs, breathing a little sigh,
> lift the green laurel and her golden hair;
> and Laura's face, so delicately fair,
> sets free the vagrant soul from body's tie.
>   She is the candid rose, thorn-compassed, shy,
> and yet our age's glory and despair.
> O living Jove, grant me this single prayer,
> grant only that before her death I die.
>   So I'll not see the sun go out, to bring
> the world's disaster, and to leave behind
> my eyes, no other light discovering,
>   my soul, to one unending thought confined,
> my ears, that never hear another thing
> but the sweet language of her virtuous mind.

Laura died; and Petrarch commemorated her in his *Triumphs*, mostly a very exhausting parade before her of ancient heroes and heroines, in *terza rima*. But there are few sweeter poetic passages than his description of Laura's death:

Non come fiamma che per forza è spenta,
ma che per sé medesma si consume,
se n'andò in pace l'anima contenta,
a guisa d'un soave e chiaro lume
cui nutrimento a poco a poco manca,
tenendo al fine il suo caro costume.
Pallida no, ma più che neve bianca
che senza venti in un bel colle fiocchi,
parea posar come persona stanca.
Quasi un dolce dormir ne' suo' belli occhi,
sendo lo spirto già da lei diviso,
era quel che morir chiaman gli sciocchi:
morte bella parea nel suo bel viso.

Not like a suddenly extinguished light
her spirit left its earthly tenement.
She dwindled like a flamelet, pure and bright,
that lessens in a gradual descent,
keeping its character while waning low,
spending itself, until its source is spent.
Not livid-pale, but whiter than the snow
the hills in windless weather occupying,
only a mortal languor did she show.
She closed her eyes; and in sweet slumber lying,
her spirit tiptoed from its lodging-place.
It's folly to shrink in fear, if this is dying;
for death looked lovely in her lovely face.

This is not, in fact, true; for Laura died of the plague. And anyway, Petrarch was far away. But what of it?

Petrarch was the first modern scholar, the first modern literary man (for Dante we must call medieval). He loved to write, rising often at midnight to get to his desk. A friend tried to force a vacation on him and locked up his books and papers; Petrarch fell into feverish headaches, and the friend, alarmed, gave him back the key.

He wrote, as he read, with passion. He said: "I write to please myself; and while I write I converse eagerly with our elders, in the one way I can. And I gladly forget those among whom I was forced by evil fate to live; I employ all my power of mind to escape them and seek out the ancients. As the very sight of my contemporaries offends me, the remembrance, the splendid deeds, even the bright names of men of old allure me and fill me with inestimable joy; so that many would be shocked to learn how much more I find my delight among the dead than with the living."

His reading was a communion with ancient spirits, alive in books. He wrote them personal letters; he called Cicero his father, Virgil his brother. A great volume of Cicero, disturbed on his shelves, fell and wounded his ankle, making him wonder what he had done to make Cicero angry. He called books "welcome, assiduous companions, always ready to appear in public or go back in their box at your order, always disposed to speak or be silent, to stay at home or make a visit to the woods, to travel or abide in the country, to gossip, joke, encourage you, comfort you, advise you, reprove you, and take care of you, to teach you the world's secrets, the records of great deeds, the rules of life and the scorn of death, moderation in good fortune, fortitude in ill, calmness and constancy in behavior. These are learned, gay, useful, and ready-spoken companions, who will never bring you tedium, expense, lamentation, jealous murmurs, or deception." What a fine quotation for a library, or a publisher!

He served well his ancient friends. He discovered several lost works of Cicero and gave them to his world. With Boccaccio, he engaged an Eastern scholar to translate Homer into Latin. He loved to examine and caress Greek books, though unable to understand them, and he tried in vain to learn the language.

"I have got rid of most of my passions," he wrote a friend, "but I have one insatiable thirst—book-buying." Yet in the end his library numbered only two hundred volumes, partly, to be sure, because he was always giving books away.

We call him the chief reviver of ancient learning. His example stimulated others to collect the classics and to copy them or have them copied. He aroused also a vogue for the critical study of ancient texts, which abounded with copyists' errors. He said that if Cicero or Livy should read current examples of their writing, they would disavow them as the work of barbarians. He developed principles of stylistic analysis, rejecting, on the basis of style alone, works ascribed to Cicero and Virgil. He found a treatise of Saint Ambrose so un-Ambrosian that he took it from the saint and gave it to Palladius.

His own formal Latin style was, and is, recognized as a modern model. It is thoroughly Ciceronian—exact, subtle, sensitive. When a Pope wanted to make him apostolic secretary he escaped the unwanted task by submitting an essay couched in such high style that the Pope rejected it as unpapal. In his letters he employed a lower, familiar manner, easy and flowing, and individual. "The style is the man," he said, long before Buffon. "We all have naturally, as in our person and movements, so in our voice and speech, something singular and our own." He advised a friend not to cling slavishly to the ancients, but to graft the new on the old, for the first inventors were men, too. "Don't believe the common statement that there's nothing new under the sun, and nothing new can be said. True, Solomon and Terence said that; but since their time how much is new!"

His critical sense was keen. He called a treasured document of Julius Caesar a fake; he read an absurd, ill-written life of Saint Simplicianus and said outright that he did not believe a word of it. He opposed supernatural explanations, preferring to rest on plain reason. He was anti-Aristotle, he said, whenever Aristotle was anti-common-sense. He rejected astrology (which was formally taught in Italian universities) because it denied human liberty. "Can celestial bodies deviate from their courses, break all their laws, run in irregular orbits, to give warnings to men? Ridiculous!" He was skeptical even of miracles, since so often lies, follies, and frauds hide under the veil of religion and sanctity.

Essentially, he taught the blending of faith and love with exact, rational, critical method, as he blended in himself the poet and the scholar. One must approach knowledge with emotional desire; one must examine it with cool distrust. "Theology is a poem, with God for subject," he said. But theology is also a rational science, susceptible to reason.

This attitude, this union of love and reason, is humanism. Properly we call Petrarch the first humanist.

With all his modernism, he retained much of the medieval. The word "medieval" would have surprised him; he thought medieval times were modern times, and he thought they were very bad times. He took for granted their social, political, and religious structure, the antithesis of human and divine, the contempt of this world, which is a mere proving ground for the next. But he had no interest in scholastic philosophy or in medieval literature in general. He pinned his faith to Plato, not to Aristotle, the supreme medieval master. While, of course, he knew his immediate poetic predecessors in France and Italy, he never mentions most of the great medieval classics, barely even Dante. He did not own a copy of the *Divine Comedy* until, late in life, he received one as a present from Boccaccio.

He loathed the world that he saw, with a good deal of justification, for it was filled with wars, plagues, tyranny, cruelty, ignorance, and political and religious cynicism. He turned backward, to the Roman classics, to the Bible and the early Fathers, to escape the present; he dimly realized that his backward-turning was at the same time a forward-turning.

His times recognized him as an intellectual leader. His fame was great, first as a poet, then as a moral philosopher. He was the counselor of princes and of the Emperor, the public critic of popes. He brought to his age a new concept, or an old, forgotten concept, of the possibilities of man's existence on earth.

Petrarch was the first man since Saint Augustine, a thousand years before, to give himself to us entire. His *Letter to Posterity* is the first modern autobiography. (With a few exceptions, the Middle Ages barely conceived of the literature of private recollection.) His intense self-consciousness prompted him to self-analysis, and since he was a literary man, his self-analysis took shape in self-expression. His enormous collection of letters makes an endless *journal intime*—and the first.

He was a great introspective. Introspection was hardly a new discovery. Every religious practiced it, especially the mystics. However, they were concerned only with the soul's welfare, with sin and salvation, whereas Petrarch, like any modern, was seeking first of all self-knowledge. "What use is it to know things if you don't know yourself?" inquired his mentor, Saint Augustine, in the *Secretum*. Most of Petrarch's work is an effort to know himself and to display himself completely, with his shortcomings and faults, and also his virtues. He never tired of exploring his inner world. We may know him as we know no other man since antiquity, until we come to Montaigne.

We know, as we might have suspected, that his self-consciousness proceeded from a profound youthful self-distrust, *diffidentia.* To gain confidence and self-mastery, he surrendered to passion and ambition. But passion and ambition led him far from self-mastery; it was necessary to subdue them. Finally, recovering his liberty, he learned to scorn the world, and thus to gain possession of himself and to find at last peace and happiness. His was a lifelong process of self-culture, prompted by and ending in egotism.

His introspection did not prevent him from looking on the external world with delighted, observant eyes. His appreciation of scenic beauty and of country charm has no parallel in medieval literature. His realization of the beauty of mountains was not to reappear in recorded words until the end of the seventeenth century. (He describes, for instance, the blue waters of Como, with the snowy peaks of the Alps overhanging the lake, with forests hiding their heads in clouds, with the dark roaring of torrents pouring out of the heights, and everywhere the murmuring of brooks and the twitter of birds.) He loved flowers and country labors, and when asked his profession liked to reply, "gardener." On the other hand, he did not notice medieval architecture. He mentions only twice, I think, a church's beauty (the golden glitter of St. Mark's in Venice, and the rising Cathedral of Cologne, *pulcherrimum templum.*) The superb Palace of the Popes in Avignon was to him only a gloomy Tartarus. Nor had he much taste for art, though he had Simone Martini paint a small, portable portrait of Laura to sigh over, and though he knew Giotto personally and left in his will one of Giotto's paintings to a friend. ("The ignorant do not understand the beauty of this panel, but the masters of art are stunned by it.") Music, however, he loved; a good concert made him cease to envy the gods their privilege of listening to the music of the spheres.

His sense of beauty awakens occasionally corresponding chords within us. Frequently in his poems, often in his prose, a phrase or set of phrases will leap out as a personal communication over all the years that separate us.

One stormy night in Venice he sat writing late, in his study overlooking the Riva degli Schiavoni. He heard a great shouting below and ran to look down from his highest window. *Deus bone, quod spectaculum!* A number of ships were casting off from the marble quay below. "Their masts considerably overtopped the two corner towers of my palazzo. And at this moment, with all the stars hidden by clouds, as my walls and roofs were shaken by the wind, as the sea roared hellishly below, the ships cast loose from the quay and set forth on their journey. One, perhaps, was bound for the river Don, with passengers for the Ganges, the Caucasus, the Indies, and the Eastern Ocean. My heart bled for these unhappy men. And when I could no longer follow the ships with my eyes, moved and stirred I picked up my pen again, exclaiming: 'Oh, how dear to men is life, and how little account they take of it!'"

Again, he writes: "I had got thus far, and was thinking of what to say next, and as my habit is, I was pricking the paper idly with my pen. And I thought how, between one dip of the pen and the next, time goes on, and I hurry, drive myself, and speed toward death. We are always dying. I while I write, you while you read, and others while they listen or stop their ears, they are all dying."

These are expressions of a modern sensibility, with its awareness of the mystery and marvel of common experience. Petrarch helped to form and define the modern sensibility, which is, indeed, an eternal sensibility. Petrarch is frequently termed the first modern man. I would go farther; I would call him one of the eternal men. As he turned back to find his companions in the great past, we too may turn back, to find in Petrarch a companion and a friend.

PRECURSORS

"Giotto alone," Vasari proclaimed, "in a rude and inept age, when all good methods of art had long been lost, dead and buried in the ruins of war, set art upon the path that may be called the true one." For a century after Giotto's death, painters imitated his naturalism and his revolutionary use of space and light, proudly signing themselves "disciple of Giotto, the good master." One contemporary, the sculptor Andrea Pisano, also had managed to free his style from the Byzantine rigidity which dominated Italian art. Approaching medieval themes with a new realism, he and Giotto collaborated on bas-reliefs for the newly built campanile at Florence. The panels on this page show Icarus flying, Adam and Eve laboring, and, at bottom, a woman at her loom. Above her, a horse and rider, infused with a vitality new to art, symbolize man's unbounded energy, which was soon to abandon medieval ideals and inaugurate a proud new era.

Although taught by Byzantine artists, Cimabue advanced toward realism. This is a detail from his Crucifix *in Arezzo.*

Petrarch compared Simone Martini to Praxiteles and Phidias, the greatest artists of antiquity. In one of the two sonnets composed to thank the artist for a small portrait of Laura, the poet said, "Surely my friend Simone was once in Paradise, whence came this gentle lady!" Two centuries later, Vasari disagreed with Petrarch's judgment. "The sonnets," Vasari wrote, "have given more luster to the poor life of Maestro Simone than it has received or ever will receive from all his works, which are rapidly perishing, while the works of Petrarch shall survive to all eternity." Despite Vasari's gloomy prediction, many of Simone's paintings have endured. The artist traveled from his native Siena to serve as court painter to the King of Naples. Pisa and Orvieto commissioned work from him, and he was called to Avignon, to the exiled papal court, where he frescoed the walls of the Pope's palace and earned Petrarch's admiration. Everywhere he went, Simone left paintings of unequaled poetic beauty. Two of the panels at right, showing Saints Ambrose and Augustine on either side of the Archangel Michael, are from his hand, but the figure of the Archangel, holding sword and judgment scales, has been attributed to one of Simone's followers.

When a papal emissary asked Giotto for a sample of his work, the painter drew a perfect circle with one stroke of his brush and told him to send it back to Rome. All Italy sought out this artist, who became so famous that, according to one legend, even Dante came to watch him paint. For Florence, Giotto designed the cathedral's campanile, the most beautiful Gothic tower in Italy. In Assisi he decorated the Basilica of St. Francis, and at Padua, in a chapel built to atone for the sins of a man so avaricious that Dante had assigned him to the seventh circle of hell, he painted his masterpieces—scenes from the life of Christ. Above, in the Pietà, weeping angels hover over the entombment. Opposite is the kiss of Judas.

THE
PRINCE
AND THE
STATE

"Horror waits on princes," wrote Webster, the Elizabethan dramatist for whom the bloodstained annals of Italy had a compulsive fascination. Certainly, the way to power was strewn with corpses; men murdered their wives, wives poisoned their husbands, brother slaughtered brother, family raged against family, city sacked city. In 1402 the chief members of the ruling house of Lodi were burned alive on the public square; at Bologna in 1445 the people, enraged by the slaughter of their favorite family, the Bentivoglio, hunted down their enemies and nailed their steaming hearts to the doors of the Bentivoglio's palace, as a token of their love.

Yet Bologna was a tranquil city compared to many, and even bloodless when matched with Foligno; there a noble—Pietro Rasiglia—cuckolded by his prince, took his vengeance. He flung his faithless wife from the turrets of his castle and killed two brothers of the prince. Retribution rapidly followed. The whole Rasiglia clan, men, women, and children, were butchered and chopped up; their joints, hung like meat,

were paraded through the streets. Of course, the ghoulish chroniclers liked to heighten the horror, and their macabre imaginations rioted in sadistic fantasy. Yet all allowance made, politics became a murderous game in which death in bed came only to the skillful or the lucky. The savagery used by men in pursuit of power was due to the nature of society and the prizes which it offered.

The city-states of Italy had won their independence by playing off the two greatest powers of medieval Europe—the Papacy and the Empire. In theory, the Pope ruled men's souls, the Emperor their bodies; the facts accorded ill with theory. The Church had acquired property which no emperor or king could match; its real estate, its pecuniary rights—first fruits, Peter's pence, and the like—made it formidably rich, rich enough to challenge the Empire and to claim the supremacy of the spiritual over the temporal power. Yet bishops were princes as well as bishops; abbots and their monasteries owed feudal obligations on their lands. The great baronage of the

Members of the Guelph party cut their fruit in one direction, Ghibellines in another; Guelphs wore red roses, Ghibellines wore white; Guelphs built rectangular-shaped battlements, those of the Ghibellines were swallow-tailed. But as power shifted bewilderingly from side to side, party symbols became hopelessly confused, until the Guelph shield (left) was almost identical to that of the later Ghibellines. Party strife expanded into a rivalry between cities, and such market towns as Orvieto (right), perched on its impregnable rock, became a stronghold of the Guelphs and a frequent refuge for medieval popes against attacks from such Ghibelline centers as Siena and Perugia.

Empire bred too many sons to view the Church's dependence on Rome with equanimity. Who should or should not select or confirm the bishops in their rights became a vital matter for emperors. And although the great struggle between the Empire and the Papacy expressed itself in the language of theology, its roots were mundane enough—land, money, power. Behind the Papacy stood the great estate of the clergy, formidable in numbers, in learning, and in authority; the Emperor had his own resources. His major strength was drawn from his lands and rights in Germany, Austria, and the Netherlands, but he was also King of Lombardy and, as such, possessed important and valuable lands in Northern Italy; yet his presence was rare in these territories, and his enemies flourished at his expense. The chief of these was the Papacy, rendered strong and inflexible by the great reforming popes of the twelfth and thirteenth centuries.

The Papacy, conscious of its God-given role in the *respublica Christiana,* had not been reluctant to encourage the revolt of the Italian communes, any more than it had hesitated to call to its aid the ferocious Norman barons, to help it in its conflict with the emperors. This great struggle unleashed on town and village and countryside the fratricidal war between the Pope's party, the *parte Guelfa,* and the Emperor's, the *parte Ghibellina,* which continued long after the defeat of the Hohenstaufen emperors had destroyed the hopes of the Ghibellines. It left behind two poles of feeling about which passion and anger and rivalry could crystallize—often to the point of absurdity, as when the Ghibellines of Milan tore down the Christ from the high altar in the Cathedral of Cremona because His face was turned to His shoulder in the manner of a Guelph. Yet the great conflict between Pope and Emperor left behind more than a tradition of internecine war. It unleashed chaos; an anarchy of power in which the strong devoured the weak, in which trivial wars, scarcely more significant than riots, alternated with struggles that involved the lives of thousands. From 1350 to 1450 Italy scarcely

knew a month, let alone a year, of peace. Yet during this time the great states—Florence, Milan, Naples, Venice—emerged as the arbiters of Italy's destiny. None powerful enough to overthrow the others, they lived in an uneasy equilibrium of power that lasted for nearly fifty years until, in 1494, welcomed by Milan, the French king invaded Italy to assert his dynastic claims. Wars more terrible and more violent than Italy had ever known ravaged the land and turned Lombardy into a cockpit in the struggle between the Hapsburg emperors and the French kings, a struggle that lasted until the sack of Rome in 1527, when Charles V brutally reasserted the Imperial power and tied the destiny of Italy to the house of Hapsburg.

In war or in peace, in freedom or in subjection, the towns grew, and in growing changed the nature of their government, sliding from hopeful democracy into greedy oligarchy. They varied greatly in size and power—a few like Florence, nearly a hundred thousand strong, a hive of trade and manu-

facture, and many like Orvieto of about twenty thousand, busy market towns of farmers, shopkeepers, and artisans. Yet, great or small, they had each undergone a novel political experience—the flowering of a qualified democracy in the midst of feudalism. Within these cities the *popolo*—not the people but the members of craft guilds—had acquired power and taken over or devised their own institutions of government. Usually they possessed no written authority or fundamental constitution; they exercised power, solved their problems, *ad hoc*. They represented not only the wealth and the enterprise of the city, but also that oligarchy of families which could hold and maintain authority. Force, and the consent of their immediate supporters, was the basis of their government. There was rarely unity in any commune—the nobility both of the surrounding countryside, known as the *contado*, which acknowledged the authority of the city, or of the city itself, had long been divided by feuds and rivalries before the division between Guelph and Ghibelline gave their

hatreds a sharper edge. And although the artisans and merchants dominated the life of the city, they frequently needed the skill and the training of the nobility both in diplomacy and in war. Furthermore, the unformalized nature of these city constitutions enabled men seeking power to manipulate the quasi-democratic methods of government, as the Medici were to do with supreme skill in Florence. And the relics of the nobility, or in the large towns the great merchant oligarchs, had little difficulty in acquiring the leadership and the control of seemingly "popular" movements. Hence there was a pronounced tendency for all communes to drift, either secretly or openly, to the despotism of a family or a clique. This was the ground swell that was to lift the Renaissance prince to power.

Chance, however, in the shape of the great bubonic plague that ravished Italy in the middle of the fourteenth century, also took a hand. Men and women died like flies, and death ate up the cities more rapidly than the countryside. Chronicler

after chronicler tells of the empty streets, the pillaged houses, the yawning pits in the graveyards, and the resulting poverty from the decay of trade. In this blighted world it was naturally easier for tyranny to flourish.

Yet plague or no plague, tyranny probably would have thrived. From the earliest days of these communes, force and expediency had governed all. Their urbanism had been as militant and as aggressive as any nationalism. They had seized villages and lesser towns by force; and war had been the lifeblood of their growth. A small town such as Orvieto, perched on its impregnable fortress of rock, quickly absorbed great tracts of countryside, stretching south to the Lake of Bolsena, westward to the coast, eastward to the Tiber, and north almost to Lake Trasimeno—almost, because greater cities than Orvieto were expanding too. Siena and Perugia wanted the territory that Orvieto coveted. Neither was without enemies on its own northern borders. Florence hated Siena and attacked or courted Perugia according to her need.

So war was endemic, and the citizens were constantly marching out to do battle with their neighbors.

The further dimension of diplomacy, with the vast paraphernalia of chicanery and pressure and secrecy, found its breeding ground in the rivalries and conflicts of these city-states, for what was true of Orvieto, Siena, Perugia, and Florence was equally true of the cities of the Lombard plain or the Patrimony of St. Peter. Only in the south, in the kingdoms of Naples and of Sicily, was the conflict of cities held in check by the rule of hereditary monarchy. The Papacy, which might have given coherence to the Patrimony of St. Peter, had been transferred to Avignon in 1309, where it remained until 1378. From then until 1417 the Great Schism provided yet additional causes for division and strife not only in the Papal States, but also throughout Italy. And it was not until 1421 that Martin V re-established the Papacy firmly and securely at Rome. The Emperor, after the defeat of the last of the Hohenstaufen, lacked the power to influence, let alone control, Lombardy's political development. Hence the appetites of the city-states for their neighbors' lands went unchecked, and war was constant. And not only war—so was treason, murder, and plot, for this reason. Some states lacked constitutions, they were without the constitutional formalization of social, economic, and political power that was sanctioned by tradition or by law. Power was captured by groups, by inter-related families, sometimes depending on oligarchic, sometimes on popular, support, and occasionally on the help of other city-states and, in time, on foreign invasion. Exiles from all states abounded, to become the instruments of aggression: murder, trickery, and civil war were accepted elements of political activity. Gradually, as war diminished the localization of power, the great city-states emerged. Florence battered down Pisa and Pistoia; Venice absorbed Padua and Verona; Milan ate up Pavia and Lodi; by skillful alliances a few smaller states—Ferrara, Mantua, and others—survived to act as pawns in the checkerboard of power. Such states

An old legend tells of a condottiere who won so many victories that his town could think of no way to reward him adequately. So to solve this dilemma, it was said, they killed him and worshiped him as a patron saint. Most real adventurers fared better. At left, in a detail from Piero di Cosimo's Passage of the Red Sea *in the Sistine Chapel, is a portrait of the condottiere Roberto Malatesta. Niccolò Piccinino is portrayed above on a medal by Pisanello. He received his name as a result of his small stature, and on one occasion he escaped from a battlefield carried in a sack.*

were too large and too rich to rely on the citizen army, which had been sufficient in the earlier days when the enemy was but a day's march away. Also, war was becoming too technical for simple peasants and workers. The cities had the need for, and the money to hire, the professional soldiers—the condottieri —who roamed Italy in order to ravage a living from its people. As the wily Venetians realized, the condottieri prevented armed power from being placed in the hands of a citizen or his faction; and so it became a fixed principle of Venetian administration that no Venetian born could command its army. At first the condottieri were foreign—Sir John Hawkwood, an Englishman, had a famous band of ravishers, the White Company. Soon the tyrants of petty states put themselves and their citizens out for hire. Some, like the Montefeltro of Urbino, kept their states, their heads, and their reputations; others, like Francesco Sforza, won a duchy; most died violently, executed, murdered, killed in battle. They lived for hire, but they could not be trusted, since bought troops

meant treacherous troops. Always the danger loomed of a condottiere turning against the state that employed him. This the Venetians and the Florentines realized clearly enough, and they saw to it that the camps of their condottieri were riddled with spies. The use of hired professional armies reduced violence even though it increased treachery, for no captain wished to waste his greatest asset—his fighting men. As a result, battles were rare, sieges infinitely prolonged. And increasingly, to the alarms and rumors of war and conspiracy were added the deliberate exaggeration and the hidden subterfuges of diplomacy.

Diplomacy as we know it arose in Italy of the Renaissance. It grew strong in the fifteenth century through the equilibrium of power created by the three great northern states of Italy—Milan, Venice, and Florence. It appealed to the leaders of these mercantile societies. They enjoyed and believed in the efficacy of hard bargaining, nor were they unaware of the merits of partnership for the destruction of

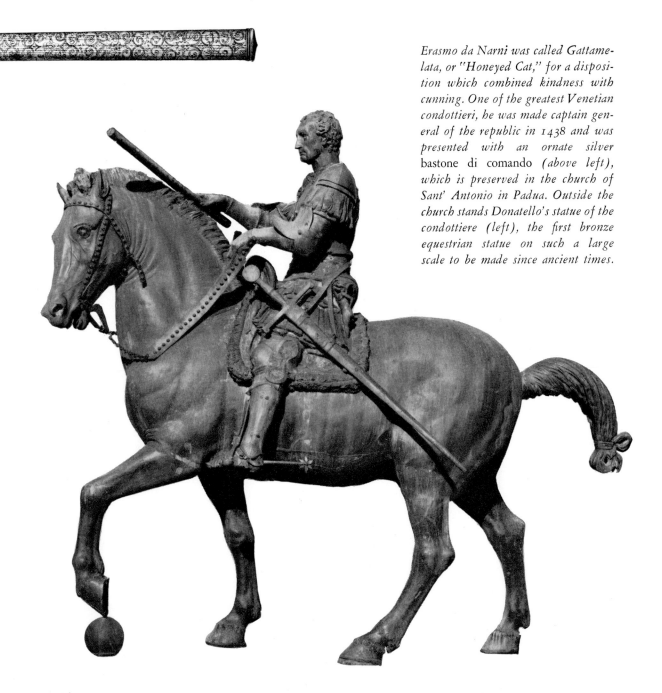

*Erasmo da Narni was called Gattame-
lata, or "Honeyed Cat," for a disposition which combined kindness with
cunning. One of the greatest Venetian
condottieri, he was made captain general of the republic in 1438 and was
presented with an ornate silver
bastone di comando (above left),
which is preserved in the church of
Sant' Antonio in Padua. Outside the
church stands Donatello's statue of the
condottiere (left), the first bronze
equestrian statue on such a large
scale to be made since ancient times.*

rivals (and partners need supervision as well as persuasion).
The collection of intelligence, the assessment of personalities
and contingencies, was early the stock in trade of bankers.
The application of these commercial techniques to the service
of the state was effortlessly made. Every Venetian abroad was
expected to spy for his country. Nor was intelligence required
solely for the purpose of foreign affairs; internally it was of
equal if not greater importance. The fear of tyrants intensified their suspicion as well as their cruelty; thus their citizens
and followers were encouraged to spy and to betray. Such
behavior was not peculiar to despotisms: in Venice men were
encouraged to report anonymously their suspicions of their
neighbors. These calumnies were meticulously sifted, at times
with the help of the rack and the boot, by the republic's in-
quisitors. Elsewhere fear took on more fantastic shapes, and
friends, relations, and children of tyrants lived on a volcano
of violence that could erupt on the slightest suspicion. Naturally, such insecurity bred a desire to survive that overrode

all claims to loyalty or affection, and frequently poison or the
dagger momentarily cleared a state of its bloodstained ruler.
Yet such actions and attitudes were an accepted part of the
political and military life.

The frequency of assassination, the perennial plots, the
constant vicissitudes, encouraged superstition and a romantic
view of Fate. Men felt themselves to be the prey of strange
destinies and turned to astrologers and magicians to strength-
en their hope, to check despair, and to help them meet the
uncertain future with confidence. The stars were studied as
intensely as diplomatic dispatches, as a guide to action; and
superstitious dread threaded the daily course of men's lives.
Even the popes felt more secure in their faith when the
heavens were propitious. Julius II fixed the date of his coronation on the advice of his astrologers, and Paul III arranged
his consistories at the dictates of the stars.

The ever-present sense of death and danger heightened
instinct as well as superstition. The possession of power,

In 1500 the Venetian ambassador told how "every night they find in Rome four or five murdered men . . ." Indeed, bravoes such as the one about to strike in Titian's painting below were employed by nearly every court for purposes of protection or revenge. Another assassination attempt is seen in a detail of a painting by the Master of the Legend of San Bernardino (left). On the facing page, the merits of peace and warfare are weighed in a miniature painted on the wooden cover of a Sienese tax register. Well-dressed citizens on the left receive funds, under the caption, "Peace enriches the citizens." On the right, armed mercenaries receive their pay beneath a legend which advises: "War enriches the foreigners."

naked and absolute, removed the barriers for its gratification, no matter how quaint the desire might be. At the courts of the despots sexual license was as common as treachery. And in the rampages of the flesh, as in the pursuit of power, the popes were second to none. The princes and the republics of the Renaissance lived in a dangerous, excitable, and exciting world of power. Morality was not involved, only success. But, of course, only a few princes, nobles, and merchants were concerned in any state. The mass of the people eschewed office, and the disasters of government troubled them only in military defeat.

Yet it would be wrong to consider the tyrants of Italy as concerned only with the pursuit of power by the most cruel methods. Many were intelligent, some sensitive; all desired fame. Since fame involved outward expression—buildings, statuary, art, pageants, tourneys, and even public benefactions—patronage, in its widest aspects, was an illustration of power, or rather of social and political grandeur. Splendor

added stature to the Doge as well as the Pope, and the Visconti with their Cathedral of Milan and their Certosa at Pavia glorified their state as well as their dynasty. Display became a part of the art of government, and the wealth of Italy permitted an extravagance that would not have been unbecoming to an ancient Roman emperor. Pageantry was also a part of the aristocratic tradition, but the riches of the Medici, the Sforza, the Gonzaga, or the Este, and the skill of their painters and sculptors, raised this art to an intenser level. The tourneys which celebrated the wedding of Beatrice d'Este and Lodovico Sforza were prolonged, extravagant, drenched in mythology, a vast spectacle that took months to prepare and days to enact. And for this Leonardo da Vinci directed his genius to the design of the costumes. The power of princes and the glory of cities could be expressed less ephemerally. All raised monuments to their greatness in buildings, in painting, and in sculpture. Leonardo da Vinci sought the patronage of Cesare Borgia as well as Lodovico

Sforza; Raphael began his career in the most bloodstained and power-ravaged city of Italy—Perugia. The patronage of tyrants took delight in all that gratified the mind as well as the senses of men. Exquisite and extravagant food, fabulous and sumptuous clothing, delicate and intricate jewelry, masterpieces of craftsmanship in silver and gold, lightened the strain and soothed the anxieties of princes. So did the memorials of antiquity, the broken torsos, the green, encrusted bronzes, the coins and medallions, which the earth yielded. Books were novel not only in their contents but also in their new printed form, and it was not long before they became as worthy of collection as the illustrated manuscripts of the recent past. The animate world also distracted the mind and ennobled the possessor. Strange animals or misshapen men were collected like curios. Popes and kings, cardinals and princes, outbid each other to persuade the great in art, letters, and science to join their entourage; rarely has so great a premium been placed on men of creative ability. These

strange courts of princes—so close to violence, yet so alive to beauty, so transient in power, yet so permanent in expression —need a closer focus, both the best and the worst.

At Mantua, high above the Piazza Sordello, swings an iron cage; throughout the fourteenth and fifteenth century it was usually occupied by a dead or dying man. The grim, embattled palaces of the Bonacolsi and the Gonzaga provided a fitting background to the sagas of their princes. The lords of Mantua had their quota of fratricide, of treasonable sons and murderous uncles, of wives caught in adultery and killed for their crime. Its citizens, as well as its princes, had their times of horror, their years of tribulation. Like all city-states it was born in feudal anarchy and nurtured by interurban strife. Gifted with a superb natural strength (on three sides the Mincio swells out into large, wide lakes that proved difficult to probe), Mantua quickly dominated the surrounding countryside and held it against the most formidable assaults of its combined enemies. Still, it is doubtful whether it could

have survived but for the aid of Venice. It was too strong and too remote for Venice to absorb, yet its powerful princes were an excellent buffer against their common enemy, Milan. So the Venetians hired the Gonzaga as condottieri and, to pay them, ceded Lombard towns that were too weak to maintain their independence and too poor for Venice to covet. The Gonzaga were too clever to allow a tradition of dependence on Venice to develop, and from time to time they sold their skill to the rulers of Milan. The balance of power kept Mantua independent, and the needs of Venice or Milan made it rich. Violent though its history was, it enjoyed more peace and greater security than was the common lot of Italian cities. The unruly, battle-scarred Gonzaga were never mere condottieri; they governed as strongly as they fought. Under Lodovico Gonzaga, in spite of plague and pestilence and flood, trade in wool and silks flourished, and the population grew to forty thousand or more. Money from war and trade was spent not only to delight the eye, but also to train the

mind. Opportunities for pageantry proved frequent enough. Pius II called a council there in 1459 to declare a Crusade against the Turks. In 1474 the King of Denmark paid a state visit and found a royal welcome. Powerful neighbors—the Sforza from Milan, the Este from Ferrara—expected and received extravagant hospitality. The births and marriages and deaths of Gonzaga princes were celebrated with appropriate solemnity and expense. So were their triumphs: few public occasions matched the reception of Francesco Gonzaga, the first cardinal of his house, a prince of the Church at seventeen and a symbol of his family's greatness.

As became Renaissance princes, the Gonzaga sought a permanent expression for their wealth and power and destiny. Lodovico (1414–1478) was, perhaps, the most gifted of his family and possessed abundantly those wide-ranging tastes and abilities that were so much admired in his day. He embodied the skill and decision of a man of action with the sensitivity of a scholar. He proved himself ruthless in war,

In 1445 Sigismondo Malatesta asked his friend Leon Battista Alberti to redesign the church of San Francesco in Rimini. A miniature (opposite, at upper left) from the Hesperides, a poem by Sigismondo's court poet, Basinio Basinii, shows the reconstruction taking place. Below it is the finished building as it looks today. Known as the Tempio Malatestiano, this is one of the finest examples of early Renaissance classical style. Inside are monuments in honor of Sigismondo, along with reliefs such as the example at left by Agostino di Duccio, which shows the zodiacal sign of Cancer protecting the town of Rimini. In the background are the mountains of San Marino. The young girl at right, painted by Pisanello, is thought to be Sigismondo's first wife, Ginevra d'Este, who died in 1440 at the age of twenty-two, quite possibly murdered by Sigismondo.

adept in diplomacy, yet more generous toward his treacherous brother Carlo than was usual in a despot, a sign of that human warmth which infused his private life and his artistic sensibilities. By 1460 he had persuaded Andrea Mantegna to make Mantua his permanent home and to become his court painter. The result was a splendid series of frescoes that still adorn the Camera degli Sposi in the Castello of Mantua; other frescoes have been destroyed, and pictures that were painted for Lodovico dispersed, but what remains is one of the great achievements of the Renaissance. As with painting, so with architecture: for Lodovico's taste was sure. He employed Alberti—a man of universal genius and a leading Florentine figure in the Classical revival—to design his churches, and urged Mantuans to give generously so that plans for Sant' Andrea could become a reality, which, as Lodovico said, "from its vast size and noble simplicity should be superior to any building of the kind in the leading cities of Italy, and worthy to stand beside the magnificence of Rome herself."

Huge buildings, sumptuous palaces, brilliant paintings—these were the common extension of a prince's greatness. Lodovico, however, was a man of wider and deeper sympathies. He encouraged philosophers and poets to stay at his court. Pico della Mirandola, Platina, Poliziano, Ognibene, Guarino da Verona, and Filelfo all, at one time or another, brought distinction to the Mantuan court. Lodovico himself took a delight in books; he collected not only manuscripts of the classics, but also of Dante, Petrarch, and Boccaccio, and employed the most gifted craftsmen to illustrate their books.

The width of Lodovico's interests was due partly to his native genius and partly also to his education, for it was in the education of princes that Mantua made one of its most remarkable contributions to the Renaissance. Lodovico's father had established the great humanist Vittorino da Feltre at Mantua. Vittorino's ideas were to influence European education profoundly for centuries. He believed that education should concern itself with the body as well as the mind, with

the senses as well as the spirit. Wrestling, fencing, swimming, and riding alternated with hours devoted to Virgil, Homer, Cicero, and Demosthenes. Luxury was eschewed, and Vittorino educated the poor with the rich. Nor was he prejudiced about the sexes; the Gonzaga princesses enjoyed the same extensive education as the princes. Above all, he encouraged the belief that individual greatness was part of the nature of man, and a desirable part, one that was in no way in opposition to the obligations which men had to their fellow men. To Vittorino the virtues were innate; they were human. Although a devout Christian and insistent on regular religious practices, he nevertheless cherished an optimistic view of man's capacities. Certainly in Lodovico, as in the great Federigo da Montefeltro, Vittorino found an apt pupil, and the traditions which he helped to create kept the Gonzaga from gross excesses and saved Mantua from the terrible sufferings which were so frequently the lot of other Italian cities. And Lodovico was as lucky in his children and his grand-

children as Mantua was in its dynasty. His son Federigo proved himself as skillful a condottiere, as wily a diplomat, and as sensitive a patron as his father, but it was his grandson Francesco and his wife, Isabella d'Este, who lifted the court of Mantua to its highest fame.

There were few among the lesser cities which enjoyed such serenity as Mantua or were led by so able a man. Ferrara under the Este, Bologna under the Bentivoglio, and Urbino under the Montefeltro were perhaps its nearest rivals, but the common lot of cities was more grievous, their tyrants more terrible. Orvieto, in little more than fifty years, was sacked and ravaged eight times, and sacked and ravaged with a brutality that was exceptional even for those murderous times. Yet even in an age which had grown immune to violence, the thought of Perugia and its tyrants made men quail.

The cities of the papal states experienced the most unfortunate fate of all the Italian communes. The absence of the popes at Avignon had given an opportunity for princely

Lodovico Gonzaga and Federigo da Montefeltro were the best-known pupils of Vittorino da Feltre's famed school, La Giocosa. In Mantegna's fresco, at the left, Lodovico is shown seated beside his wife, surrounded by his large family and courtiers. Below, in a miniature from a book by the scholar Landino, Duke Federigo appears in an unusual portrait. After losing an eye in a jousting tournament, he later insisted on being portrayed from the left.

anarchy to flourish; the Great Schism had encouraged law-lessness and rapine; and the return of the popes to Rome merely led to punitive wars. Both by geographical position and by reason of its size, Perugia was regarded as one of the most important cities of the Patrimony. By the middle of the fifteenth century its history was steeped in bloodshed that none other could equal. Chroniclers delighted in exaggeration and enjoyed recounting bloodcurdling deeds, yet after making every allowance, the Perugian story is horrifying in its utter cruelty and in its wanton disregard of human suffering. The great families, who with their armed ruffians raged and stormed and slaughtered in its streets and churches, failed to exterminate each other; some always seemed to escape, to live to plot revenge. Naturally, the cities that feared Perugia were ready to succor them and to provide them with arms and money for their campaigns of revenge. And the oppression which Perugians suffered too often lured them into thinking that any change of master might be for the better.

Here are but a few examples of Perugia's tribulations, of the curse of blood that seemed to its great chronicler Matarazzo to be the city's fate.

In 1488 the Baglioni and their enemies the Oddi fought a pitched battle in the Piazza, and the governors of the city were helpless to stop it. In 1491 the Baglioni strung up before the Palazzo dei Priori 130 men, supporters of the Oddi, who had found their way into the city. Shortly after this the Baglioni were only saved by the bravery and skill of Simonetto, a boy of eighteen, who held a narrow street with a few followers until they were nearly hacked to pieces. Then came the great betrayal in which four of the leading Baglioni were slaughtered in their beds—including Simonetto. Between 1520 and 1535 practically all who were left of the Baglioni were either publicly executed or murdered by each other. Nor were these fratricidal vendettas the only horror that the Perugians had to suffer. War was waged in their *contado* with a ferocity unusual for the fifteenth century, for

the Baglioni, as condottieri, did not believe in half measures. And to give an additional taste of horror, the plague found in Perugia a happy playground—between 1424 and 1486 there were eight severe epidemics.

Violence and sickness, suffering and death, made the Perugians susceptible to the more evangelistic expressions of religious fervor. The slaughters by, or of, the Baglioni were usually followed by days of solemn ritual and purification. On one occasion the cathedral was washed with wine and reconsecrated; on another over thirty altars were erected in the Piazza, and Mass was continuously solemnized. It is not, therefore, surprising that the vivid preaching of Fra Bernardino of Siena found a fruitful soil in Perugia. The people of the city responded eagerly to his denunciations of the vanity of all earthly life. He condemned the crimes of its citizens, called them to repentance, reconciled enemies, and made a large bonfire of worldly delights in a great act of public repentance. The results of Bernardino proved as fleet-

ing as were the reconciliations of the Baglioni and the Oddi later in the century, yet this thread of religious revivalism, of sensational open-air preaching, of the sudden need for public repentance, was not an unusual theme in city life of fifteenth-century Italy—it was a common response to the insecurities created by war and pestilence and crime.

Although the constant strife proved inimical to trade, although the population declined, these things failed to kill the vigorous artistic life of Perugia. In the midst of the turmoils, paintings of exceptional beauty were produced: Perugino and Raphael shared the city with the Baglioni and the Oddi. Perugino's frescoes of quiet, ecstatic saints, and Bonfigli's charming, tender, personal vision of the merciful Madonna, provided the background for fratricidal slaughter in a piazza reeking with blood and festooned with the grotesque shapes of slaughtered youths and men. At no other place were the dark and the light of Renaissance life brought to a stranger contrast.

After the massacre of the Baglioni family of Perugia in 1500, the mother of one of the murdered men commissioned Raphael to paint his famed Deposition in memory of her son. The artist's sketch for the painting that now hangs in the Borghese Gallery is seen at left. Above is a griffin, the emblem of Perugia, suckling the two great condottieri who were born there: Braccio da Montone, who at one time ravaged his own birthplace, and Niccolò Piccinino, who succeeded Braccio as leader of one of the two largest mercenary bands in Italy. Sano di Pietro painted the scene at right, which shows Saint Bernardino of Siena preaching in his crusade against factionalism and strife.

Sensitive, thoughtful men realized that this was a world like to none other. They searched the histories of antiquity —Livy, Suetonius, Plutarch—looking for the keys that would unlock for them the problems of princes and of cities. What made men succeed? Or fail? Why did some cities grow great and rich only to dissipate it all in war and rebellion? Why did free citizens become the prey of professional thugs? What were the causes of tyranny? Was tyranny bad? Did cities have a natural life like men—youth, maturity, age? And were learning, art, and the practice of humanism bound up with the nature of institutions? Did philosophers make the best citizens? They ransacked antiquity, read again and again Plato and Aristotle and, above all, Cicero, who seemed to demonstrate more clearly than any other the virtues of a philosopher at large in civic life. What they did not turn to was theology, to Saint Thomas Aquinas, to Saint Ambrose, or to Saint Jerome. The theological way of thinking about men and events was as alien to them as a salon painting to

Picasso. The key to their problems they knew to be rooted in the lives and actions of men, not in universal mysteries or the attributes of God. Consequently, there is an astonishing freshness about the historians and the political philosophers of the Renaissance, and, as with the painters and sculptors, the greatest by far were the Florentines, and the greatest of the Florentines was Niccolò Machiavelli, whose speculations about the nature of men's political actions are as remote from the thinkers of the Middle Ages as Leonardo da Vinci's drawings are from the illuminations of missals. Yet Machiavelli is no isolated phenomenon—from Salutati to Guicciardini, men were following the same quest. What general rules can be derived from political experience? As history enshrines political experience, thinkers grew profoundly interested in the past. In the Middle Ages political philosophers were theologians, in the Renaissance they were historians. This change had been brought about by the conflict of cities, the problems of despotism, and the crisis of liberty.

Niccolò Machiavelli wears a slightly furtive expression in this portrait by Santi di Tito.

Machiavelli

by GARRETT MATTINGLY

For most of us, Renaissance statecraft is typified by a single man, Niccolò Machiavelli—or rather, by a single name, a reputation, an epithet. After all, not many people have any clear recollection of the life and character of the man Machiavelli (not many, even, of the relatively few who have ever bothered to read anything about him). But everyone knows what the name stands for: all the complicated deviltry, hypocrisy, intrigue, secret murders, and public treacheries which for four hundred years the Western world has held typical of the Italian Renaissance. Seventy-five years ago a learned Frenchman identified the whole high Renaissance—the last decades of the fifteenth century and the first ones of the sixteenth—as the Age of Machiavelli. Certainly he realized the incongruity of labeling that bustling time after the drab little servant of a third-rate state, a man whose name even those princes and prelates to whom he had bowed probably never knew or, unless they were Florentines themselves, promptly forgot. But Maulde la Clavière was writing about Renaissance politics, and the name imposed itself. It came as naturally as saying the Age of Augustus, or of Louis le Grand, or of Napoleon, and it carried, like those labels, its own connotations, its own peculiar and, in this case, definitely sinister aura.

In a way it was appropriate that Niccolò Machiavelli should have become the interpreter of Renaissance politics to subsequent ages. He was a Florentine of the Florentines, and the citizens of his city were the quintessence of the new spirit that was then stirring in Italy. Not at first, of course: in the years after the great Guelph victory, after the popes had broken the power of the Empire in Italy forever, Florence was only one of the vigorous, turbulent city republics with which northern and central Italy swarmed. Some of these paid a token allegiance to the Papacy, although the popes knew how little that really meant, and some professed a loyalty to the Holy Roman Emperor, since no Emperor could endanger their liberties any more, but in fact they had all torn clean away from the hierarchical system in which the rest of Christendom was enmeshed, and were engaged in an external struggle against all their neighbors and an internal one of faction against faction, in which the only reality was the naked fact of power.

At first most of these new states were republics. Then, as the bigger fish devoured the smaller, not only were there fewer independent cities, but fewer of the survivors were republics. Presently came the anxious moment when on the Italian mainland only one republic was left, or only one that mattered. By force or guile the great Duke of Milan, Giangaleazzo Visconti, was building himself a kingdom. All Lombardy yielded to him from Piedmont to the Adriatic, and then Genoa and Pisa, Perugia and Siena, and finally proud Bologna. Guarded by its lagoons, the Republic of St. Mark turned its aristocratic back on Italy. Only Florence still held out.

Florence had had as checkered a political history as any of her neighbors. In the century since she had exiled her greatest poet, the bitter factional strife which Dante lamented so pathetically and joined in so energetically had never ceased and only occasionally diminished. In the moment of crisis there was, of course, a clique to say that it would be madness for Florence to pit her unaided strength against the wave of the future, that it would be better for Florentines to live as the subjects of a tyrant than to die as his victims. But the Florentines chose to resist. Apparently they preferred the uneasy vigilance which is the price of freedom to the smug lethargy of the Milanese, and were willing to risk death as free men rather than embrace life as slaves. They did not have to make so hard a choice. As he advanced against Florence, the plague struck down the tyrant, and his jerry-built kingdom fell into ruins. By resisting, the Florentines saved not just their own liberty but the liberties of Italy.

In a series of masterly studies Hans Baron has recently shown how the outcome of this crisis altered the whole tone of Florentine and so of Italian thought. Florence became the center from which spread a new humanism, a new appreciation of political liberty and civic virtue, a new attitude toward the place of man in society. It was this attitude which insured the independence of the major Italian states, and consequently that vigor and diversity of Italian artistic and cultural development which characterized the Renaissance. Now that the point has been made, it seems strange that we did not see it before, but even without Baron's fresh insight, Florentine civic humanism has long been recognized as characteristic of one aspect of the Italian Renaissance. Although he was himself no humanist, if we make that term include a polished mastery of Greek and Latin letters, Niccolò Machiavelli was soaked in the spirit of Florentine humanism.

He was soaked, too, in the Florentine obsession with politics. He came of a family which had played a great role in the political life of his city for more than two centuries. Ancestors of his had been honored, time and again, with the republic's highest offices, and if his father was too stiff-necked a republican to hold a place in a government which was becoming a more and more transparent mask for the boss rule of the Medici, we may be sure that papa Bernardo saw to it that son Niccolò was thoroughly imbued not only with the history of ancient republican Rome, but also with the great traditions of his own city. When he was forty-four, Niccolò wrote that politics was the passion of his life, that he could think and talk of nothing else, and we may guess that this began to be true when he was still young.

For fourteen years he had a chance to indulge his bent in action. When the French invaded Italy in 1494, the Florentines, who had begun to be restive under the scarcely disguised rule of Lorenzo the Magnificent and had become more so under Lorenzo's incompetent son, rose up to reclaim their ancient liberties and drove the Medici out of Florence. Niccolò was then twenty-five. We do not know whether he held any kind of post in the first years of the re-established republic, but when the revolutionary fanatics who were swayed by Savonarola's eloquence gave place to a solider, less hysterical government in 1498, Niccolò Machiavelli, just turned twenty-nine, was appointed second chancellor of the republic. Shortly afterward he was given the additional charge of secretary to the influential committee known as the *Dieci di Balìa,* the Ten of Liberty and Peace as they were sometimes grandiloquently called, or, more realistically, the Ten of War.

War was the chief preoccupation of the restored republic. Foreign armies were tramping back and forth across Italy. Spaniards slowly tightened their grip on Naples; Frenchmen periodically invaded the kingdom and were periodically chased out of Milan; Switzers and Germans were in the field, fighting sometimes for foreign paymasters, sometimes for their own hands; around Rome, first the bastard son of the Borgia Pope and then that warlike old man who succeeded to the Papacy as Julius II were trying to unify the anarchic Papal States; and once all the warring powers put aside their quarrels in order to combine against the one powerful, independent Italian state, the Venetian republic. In the midst of these big wars Florence was busy with an interminable little war, trying to reconquer Pisa, which, in the confusion of the first French invasion, had slipped from under the Florentine yoke. Since his nominal chief, the first chancellor, was more interested in Greek poetry than Italian politics, Machiavelli took a large part in these affairs. He was deep in the business of war and the diplomatic bickerings and hagglings which were the normal Renaissance accompaniments of war. Most of the correspondence of the republic passed through his hands. He wrote memoranda to inform and advise his masters on a variety of subjects, and the Signory sent him on numerous diplomatic missions in Italy, Germany, and France.

Early in his diplomatic career his path crossed that of the man who for most of us typifies the prince of the Age of Machiavelli, the typical prince of the Italian Renaissance—largely because he is the leading figure, the ostensible hero, of Machiavelli's famous little book. Actually, Cesare Borgia was not much more typical of the princes of Italy in his time than Caligula was a typical Roman emperor, or than Al Capone was a typical tax dodger of the Age of Herbert Hoover, but there is no denying that for a few years Cesare cut a wide swath and attracted a lot of attention, even eclipsing his notorious father.

Throughout his papacy, the whole family of Rodrigo Borgia, who ascended the papal throne as Alexander VI, was surrounded by a buzz of scandal. Gossiping about popes has always been a favorite Italian pastime, but probably no pope has ever afforded so much occasion for juicy gossip. Other popes had kept mistresses in the Vatican, and simony and immorality were no more rife in Rome under the Borgia Pope than they had been under his predecessors and would be under his successors. But there was a sort of childlike shamelessness about Alexander VI which invited comment. Other popes had auctioned off high ecclesiastical offices, doubled-crossed their associates and allies, and used their exalted position for the advancement of their families and for base personal ends, but usually they had pretended that they were doing something else. Rodrigo Borgia had either an honest scorn for hypocrisy or a naïve ignorance of the force of public opinion. Other popes had thrown wild parties at the Vatican, but no other pope had made the parties so flamboyant or so public. And no other pope had had a portrait of his official mistress, robed as the Virgin Mary, painted over the door of his bedchamber or, at the same time, given his official mistress so many transient but reasonably well publicized rivals. Temperate, even ascetic in most respects (in spite, or perhaps because of his gross body, he drank little wine and ate sparingly of coarse food), Rodrigo Borgia was a great lover of women, and this alone was the source of innumerable stories which grew more outrageous with each retelling.

But neither his private conduct nor his carelessness of concealment can account for all the stories about the Borgia Pope. The trouble was that although far from a saint, he was a first-rate administrator, with enormous energy and a driving will. He tried to police not only the streets of Rome, but even the Roman *campagna*, he tried to control the disorderly Roman nobility, he tried to make sure that the papal treasury received its proper cut of all the sums which the swollen papal bureaucracy and their hangers-on extorted from suitors at his court. He tried, and in part he succeeded, and this made him very unpopular with the Romans. Besides, he tried to assert the rights of the Papacy and his jurisdiction over the Papal States wherever it was challenged, whether by the Duke of Milan or the republics of Venice or Florence, by the King of Naples or the anarchic Neapolitan barons, or by the petty tyrants of Umbria and the Romagna. This made him unpopular with the ruling classes throughout Italy. Worst of all, he was a foreigner, a Spaniard, and Italians have always resented a non-Italian pope. Hence another whole cluster of stories, different and more sinister.

Two of Rodrigo Borgia's children, his eldest son, the Duke of Gandia, and his daughter Lucrezia, were less than ideal targets for malicious gossip. Gandia, although he inherited to some extent his father's disposition to run after women, was otherwise a conventional and colorless type. Lucrezia, although she had a checkered and somewhat smirched history of successive marriages before she was out of her teens —a foundation on which Roman scandalmongers readily erected a towering superstructure—was really a bland, vapid creature with nothing remarkable about her except a cowlike disposition and long blonde hair. But the Pope's younger son Cesare was something else again. Even as a mere stripling, just turned seventeen and newly made a cardinal, he was already a spectacular figure, taller by a head than most tall men, with massive shoulders, a wasp waist, classically regular features, a leonine mane, and blazing blue eyes. It was said that he could leap into the saddle without touching pommel or stirrups, bend a silver *scudo* double between his fingers, or straighten the iron of a horseshoe with a twist of his wrist. And he was a show-off. He dressed himself and his household with insolent magnificence, and he used to organize *corridas* in the Piazza Navona so that the Romans could watch him behead a bull with a single stroke of a broadsword. Before long he was trailing a legend gaudier and more lurid than that attached to his father.

It was said that he was his father's rival for his sister's incestuous bed. (Almost certainly false.) It was said that after the horrible sack of Capua he seized forty beautiful highborn maidens and added them to his personal harem. (Highly unlikely. Cesare does not seem to have shared his father's excessive appetite. The maidens were probably commandeered by Cesare's captains, though perhaps in his name.) It was said that he seduced that gallant youth Astorre Manfredi, and when he tired of him had him murdered. (Possible, but the motive for the murder was more probably purely political.) It was said that he had murdered his brother, the Duke of Gandia. (Probable. At least his father seems to have believed it.) And that he had his brother-in-law, Lucrezia's second husband, murdered. (Pretty certainly true.) But it was a dull week when one, at least, of the embassies in Rome did not chalk up another murder to Cesare's credit, sometimes by poison, sometimes by the hands of hired assassins, sometimes by his own dagger. Probably he really was responsible for a fair share of those bodies hauled out of the Tiber. Freed by his brother's death from his cardinalate, Cesare became Duke de Valentinois (Valentino, the Italians called him) and Gonfaloniere of the Church, cousin and ally of the King of France, and commander in chief of the papal army. As he marched through the anarchic Papal States, seizing one town after another, by bribery or trickery or the sheer terror of his name, his legend hung over him like a thundercloud.

When Machiavelli first encountered the Duke, the spell of the legend must have been already at work on him, and it must have been heightened by the manner in which Valentino received him and his chief, at night, by the light of a single flickering candle which showed only dimly the tall figure clad in black from head to foot without jewel or ornament, the still white features as regular as a Greek statue and as immobile. Perhaps the cold beauty of those marble features was already beginning to be marred by the pustules which led Valentino later on usually to wear a mask. Perhaps the

eyes, lost in shadow, already held that glare which another ambassador noted in them shortly afterward, the look of a savage beast at bay. And perhaps a shrewder observer might have reflected that there was the smell of comedy about these negotiations, the Duke endlessly repeating the same banalities about his eternal friendship for Florence and how wise the republic would be to employ the services of so good a friend, while his captains warned the Florentine envoys that the Duke's patience was growing short, that France would support him against Florence and the Venetians would not stir, that the army was poised to spring and could be at the city's gates before the news of its coming. It was really one of the cruder forms of blackmail, but something about the Duke's personality put the act over, and the Florentine envoys carried away the image of a great prince, subtle, inscrutable, dangerous.

Not long afterward Machiavelli had an opportunity to observe Cesare Borgia in action at the time of his greatest triumph. Cesare was not much of a general: he never learned the rudiments of tactics or strategy, logistics or supply. He was not even a good combat leader, and though he has been praised as a disciplinarian, the only available instance seems to be that once he quelled an incipient riot among some of his brawling soldiers by the terror of his presence. Similarly, if he ever gave any proof of ability as a statesman or ruler, no evidence survives. But he was a ruthless gangster and an expert confidence man, and the revolt of some of the smaller gangsters, his captains, gave him an opportunity to display his talents. Machiavelli watched, fascinated, while Cesare, all mildness and good will, lured his mutinous subordinates into a peace conference, lulled their fears, invited them to a banquet to celebrate their renewed friendship, and when they arrived unarmed and unescorted at a rendezvous where Cesare had hidden his bodyguards, had them seized and murdered. Machiavelli was delighted at the virtuosity of the performance and set it all down in detail for the edification of his countrymen and of posterity.

Machiavelli had a third opportunity to observe the Duke. He arrived in Rome on the business of the republic some months after the death of Alexander VI and just at the moment when Cesare, with incredible stupidity, had helped swing the election of his most implacable enemy. It was plain to see that Cesare was finished. Everything really had depended on his father's being Pope, and as soon as his father died, his allies deserted him, his people rose against him, and his army fell apart as his captains scrambled for the service of some luckier master. Machiavelli assessed the emptiness of the man at a glance, avoided him when he could, wrote of him and no doubt looked at him with cold contempt. But later Machiavelli seems to have preferred to forget the cringing, whimpering, blustering, dithering creature his hero had become. The picture is spread out in detail in his dispatches, but Machiavelli never openly alluded to this aspect of Cesare again.

One thing Machiavelli admired about Cesare was that he raised his soldiers in his own domain instead of hiring foreign mercenaries. It was not, in fact, a great departure. The Romagna was the great source of mercenary troops, and for years its petty despots had enrolled their subjects and farmed them out to fight other people's wars. But Cesare's action was like a project very close to Machiavelli's heart, one which after years of urging he finally got the Florentine government to adopt. They not only adopted it, they put him in charge of it, so that for the last six years of the republic, he had added to his other duties most of those of minister of defense. Instead of the cut-rate mercenaries who had prolonged the Pisan war for twelve years (being a republic in which the taxpayers held the purse strings, Florence hired only the cheapest mercenaries), Machiavelli persuaded the government to raise a militia in its own territory. Since the militia were not Florentine citizens, but conscripts from the wretched peasants of the *contado*, a folk without political rights or any material stake in the success of their bourgeois masters, the scheme had an obvious weakness, but it did not work badly at first. In 1509 Pisa fell, and Machiavelli's militia could claim a share in the long-delayed triumph. Three years later the militia failed a harder test. When the veteran Spanish infantry moved in to attack Prato, the militia ran like rabbits, and the Medici epigoni came back behind a column of Spanish pikes to rule once more in Florence. Machiavelli's active career in politics was over. But not his interest in politics. The next year he wrote that he could think about, talk about, nothing else, and from then on until he died in 1527, only a few weeks after the Florentines had again expelled the Medici, most of the writings with which he sought to allay the boredom of his exclusion from office were concerned, one way and another, with statecraft. He also wrote some verses—pretty wretched verses—and a not unamusing version of an old, smutty joke, and comedies, one of which is a masterpiece. But mostly he wrote about politics. Had he been asked to name his political writings in an ascending order of importance, surely the top three would have been his *History of Florence,* his *Art of War,* and his *Discourses on the First Ten Books of Livy.* Into these writings, and particularly into the last, Machiavelli had poured, or so he thought, all his practical experience of government and diplomacy and all his wide reading of ancient and modern history. However surprised some of the successful statesmen of his day might have been to find the little Florentine secretary the political spokesman of their age, Machiavelli himself would not have been too surprised. He would have regarded the reputation accrued as a poor compensation for the fame as a statesman which fate had denied him, but he had often said that he was the first modern man to look at politics with a clear and open eye, and he would certainly have taken the recognition of posterity as no more than due to the merit of his books.

Only, of course, the recognition of posterity has nothing to do with the books Machiavelli would have named. When people speak of the Age of Machiavelli, they are not thinking of any of them, but of one little pamphlet apparently dashed off at white heat in 1513 just after the fall of the Florentine republic. It is called *The Prince* and it bears only an ambiguous, tangential relationship to Machiavelli's big, serious works or, some people think, to the actual history of the time and place over which its fame casts such a lurid and sinister light. The discrepancy between the impression of Renaissance Italy to be gathered from *The Prince* and that given by the rest of Machiavelli's writings, to say nothing of the writings of his contemporaries, who often turn out to be more reliable about matters of fact, is sufficient to raise some doubts about the appropriateness of letting *The Prince* describe the political atmosphere of its time.

Perhaps our doubts about letting Machiavelli speak for the age which bears his name ought not to be increased by our knowledge of his private life. But among his contemporaries, surely Niccolò Machiavelli was one of the least Machiavellian. It is true that he often professed a preference for drastic methods and for sweeping all-or-nothing solutions, along with a contempt for delay and improvisation and compromise, a set of attitudes usually more characteristic of academic theorists than of practical men of affairs. But though this quirk of temperament sometimes misled him into a temporary enthusiasm for a mountebank like Cesare Borgia, it does not seem otherwise to have affected his own behavior. If the discipline of the Florentine militia had been harsher, they might not have run so soon at Prato. Machiavelli not seldom praised the efficacy of hypocrisy and smooth deceit, but in his dealings both with his own government and with foreign potentates, he was usually inept at concealing his feelings, likely to show his hand, and, in negotiation, blunt to the point of tactlessness. He often spoke of the value of clear-eyed, dispassionate observation and seems rather to have prided himself on the possession of this faculty, but, in fact, his views were usually clouded by wish and prejudice, he was easily deceived, and he was not, in the things that really mattered, those affecting the daily course of politics, a very acute, discriminating, or even very accurate observer. This judgment, suggested by comparing his dispatches with those of his contemporaries, is reinforced by the fact that his employers, the Florentine Signory, never gave him the chief responsibility for any important mission.

Niccolò not only lacked the virtues he praised, he possessed others even more incompatible with our picture of Old Nick. He was as anticlerical as most literate adult male Italians of the last six centuries have always been, and, in spite of his pious mother's teaching, no more zealously practicing a Catholic than one would expect. But as he had been baptized, confirmed, and married, so he died in the arms of the Church, having seen to it that his children followed the same conventional course. Nor—and this is farther from the popular picture of his age—is there any evidence that he indulged in any fantastic crimes or vices. He was probably no more faithful to his wife than most middle-class husbands in any age or clime, but he seems to have been a kind, affectionate, considerate husband and father, as he was a warm and true friend, a man of his word in money matters, and an admired and respected citizen.

A digression may be called for here about the handful of pornographic letters which shocked the Victorian sensibilities of J. A. Symonds. The fifteenth-century humanists had made fantastic obscenities a normal epistolary ornament. Certainly no Anglo-Saxon in the last two centuries would have written down such anecdotes about himself as Machiavelli wrote to his friends, though they are not much different from what one may hear in any locker room or thoroughly masculine bar. But they are responses, all of them, to anecdotes which his friends wrote him, and they differ from them not in essential subject matter but in elaboration and intensification. They are clearly meant to top his friends' stories, and do top them so successfully that one is led to wonder whether literary artifice and imagination have not been called in to supply the defects of experience. Machiavelli, himself, would have been the first to resent the implication that he was a saint. But there is not the slightest evidence that he was anything but the most conventional, commonplace, and prudent kind of sinner.

One inappropriate virtue is particularly surprising. It even surprised Machiavelli himself. The man who wrote that men are moved so predominantly by self-interest that princes need take account of no other motives, that "a man will resent the loss of his patrimony more than the murder of his father," was himself the devoted, unselfish servant of his ungrateful state. He lived in an age when the use of public office for private gain was perfectly customary. He had during most of his fourteen years as a servant of the Florentine republic unrivaled opportunities to enrich himself at the expense of the condottieri and other contractors with whom as secretary to the Ten of War he had to deal. Yet he quitted the Florentine service as poor as the day he had entered it. His whole public career was a testimony to the inaccuracy of his own cynical maxims. It is hard to reconcile it with the trend of his major serious books. It is impossible to square it with the lurid picture which we have drawn from his one famous little book, *The Prince*.

Drawn, in part, quite unjustifiably. Most people, whether they have read *The Prince* or not, retain the conviction that somewhere, they cannot say quite where, Machiavelli commends the famous (quite mythical) poison of the Borgia and justifies the pagan debauchery which, ever since the Reformation, Protestant countries have associated with the Italian Renaissance.

Most of these false imputations are quite old and go back to a book called *Anti-Machiavel* which a Huguenot pamphleteer wrote against Catherine de' Medici and her Italian entourage just after the Massacre of St. Bartholomew's. But even after these old vulgar errors have been cleared out of the way, *The Prince* remains a shocking book, shocking both for what it says and for the deliberately provocative way it says it, and for the discord between a part of its contents and the life and other writings of its author.

As for its contents: *The Prince* lays it down as a major premise that men in general are selfish, treacherous, cowardly, greedy, and, above all, gullible and stupid. It therefore advises a prince, and particularly a new prince who hopes to destroy the liberties of those he rules, to employ hypocrisy, cruelty, and deceit, to make himself feared even at the risk of making himself hated, to divide the people and destroy their natural leaders, and to keep faith with no one, since no one will keep faith with him. It views the world of politics as a jungle in which moral laws and standards of ethical conduct are merely snares for fools, a jungle in which there is no reality but power, and power is the reward of ruthlessness, ferocity, and cunning. In such a jungle, not the actual Cesare Borgia, but the picture of himself which Cesare succeeded in conveying at the height of his fame, a savage beast—half lion and half fox—would be the natural king. To a society which regarded the relations between its parts as ruled by justice and equity and sanctified by religion, all this was more shocking than we can quite imagine.

It was shocking, too, to find a man of staunch republican principles and flawless republican antecedents, a man who had served the Florentine republic with selfless devotion and suffered for that devotion more than most, turning, within months of his country's fall, to writing a handbook for tyrants, a book meant to teach the Medici, the enemies of his country's liberties, how to hold his fellow countrymen in thrall, and writing it all for the mean object of helping himself to wriggle back into some minor government post. If Machiavelli behaved so, he earned, for the only time in his life, the epithet Machiavellian. That his behavior seems to have been a momentary aberration, that when it was over Machiavelli returned to the defense of republican principles and the society of republican friends, makes his defection not less shocking but only more puzzling.

From the first there were at least two explanations of the puzzle. One was that Machiavelli had been inspired by the Evil One to write a plausible book of advice for princes, meant to damn the souls and ruin the fortunes of princes who followed it, and to destroy the prosperity of their subjects. This was the official view, shared by the cardinals and popes who placed and kept *The Prince* on the Index and by the Protestant pamphleteers who pointed to it as the manual of the Jesuits and the political inspiration of the Counter Reformation. Meanwhile a second view was expressed openly by some of Machiavelli's fellow countrymen (those in exile) and hinted at by some who remained in Italy, where the banned book continued clandestinely to circulate. This was that *The Prince,* under the guise of giving advice to princes, was meant to warn all free men of the dangers of tyranny. One wonders whether the originators of this explanation of the puzzle may not have been the ardent Florentine republicans who always remained Machiavelli's friends. From this second view sprang the judgment, popular in the eighteenth century, that *The Prince* was, in fact, a satire on absolute monarchy, and that all its epigrams were deliberately double-edged. The nineteenth century offered other solutions to the puzzle. The one which gained ascendancy as the cause of national self-determination triumphed in Western Europe was that, ardent republican though he was, Machiavelli made up his mind that only a strong prince could liberate Italy from the barbarians, and so chose to sacrifice the freedom of his city to the unity of Italy. Just before World War I, this solution began to be questioned by those who said that Machiavelli was not a chauvinistic patriot but a detached, dispassionate political scientist who described political behavior as it actually was. After about 1920 this view took a powerful lead over all its competitors, and among orthodox Machiavelli scholars it still dominates the field.

Obviously none of these answers is entirely satisfactory. It is possible that Machiavelli was mean enough to sell his birthright of republican ideals for the chance of some third-rate civil service post under a petty tyrant; but that he was at the same time stupid enough to believe that a book like *The Prince* was the best way into Medici favor, and to let advice which, if it was seriously meant, should have been highly secret escape into general circulation, seems much less credible. Both the notion that *The Prince* was inspired by the devil and the counternotion that it was the subtle weapon of republican idealism seem equally oversimplified. And, of course, the proposal that *The Prince* was conceived as a satire is the kind of anachronism which only the eighteenth century could have perpetrated. Machiavelli knew perfectly well that satires were compositions in verse after the manner of Horace and Juvenal, such as his friend Luigi Alamanni wrote. He would have failed completely to understand the proposition that *The Prince* was a satire. As for the theory that Machiavelli was willing to accept a tyrant prince in order to effect the unification of Italy, there is not the faintest indication anywhere in his writings that he would have grasped the idea if anybody had put it to him. There is nothing about unifying Italy anywhere in *The Prince,* only about driving out the barbarians, a commonplace of Italian rhetoric from Petrarch to Paul IV. But Machiavelli the Italian patriot is a little easier to swallow than Machiavelli the dispassionate scientist, unless someone can explain how the scientific temper can accord with facts and generalizations equally distorted by emotion and prejudice.

It is probably hopeless to try to explain the whole puzzle of *The Prince.* How do you reconstruct the motives at a particular moment of a man more than four hundred years in his grave who has left only the scantiest and most ambiguous clues to what they might be? How do you tell, in the case of a man like Machiavelli, how much of the demonstrable distortion in *The Prince* was due to faulty observation (he was a passionate man), and how much to the deliberate irony which he certainly sometimes practiced? How do you probe the bitterness and agony of spirit which must certainly have been his on the collapse of all his hopes, and decide which wild statements come from anger, which from despair, and which from a calculated will to undermine his enemies by indirection?

Probably, like most insoluble problems about men of genius, this one has taken up more time and energy than it deserves. The real importance of Machiavelli, his claim to give his name to a whole period of history, lies elsewhere, not in the points in which *The Prince* differs from his other writings, but in those in which it agrees. Here the transformation of his legendary figure from a diabolist or a rebel, a spirit who says "No," to a major culture hero, offers the clue. What had happened, in almost three centuries between the time when Machiavelli was either praised as a daring rebel or denounced as an emissary of Satan and the time when he began to be acclaimed as a prophet, was that all Europe had become what Italy in Machiavelli's lifetime already was, a congeries of autonomous, purely temporal sovereign states, without any common end to bind them into a single society or any interest higher than their own egotistical drives for survival and expansion.

To pretend that the relations between such states were governed by Christian ethics seemed to Machiavelli a contemptible hypocrisy. Many Italians since Dante had lamented that the nearer one came to Rome the wider the gap between Christian teaching and Christian practice, and charged that the Papacy had corrupted the morals of Italy. Indeed, the major assumption of the stern reformers of what we call the Counter Reformation was not much different. But Machiavelli went further. He compared his own embittered picture of the degeneracy of his countrymen with Livy's of the virtues of republican Rome, and without asking how much exaggeration there might be in either, he leaped to one of his drastic all-or-nothing conclusions. Christianity, whatever its value as a guide in private life, was not a viable fountain for the good society. So for the religion of Christ he proposed to substitute the religion of patriotism. In politics the Christian ethic was worse than valueless, it was positively harmful. It might serve to keep the masses more law-abiding in their private lives, but when it came to public actions the only test of good or bad was what best served the safety and aggrandizement of the state. Since every state was an autonomous entity, recognizing no superior and no interest higher than its own, no rules of ethics whatever applied to relations between states. The only test was success. This was Machiavelli's consistent position. It appears in his earliest state papers and is as firmly held in his writings in praise of republics as it is in *The Prince.* In 1513 it was a desperate paradox. By 1813 it was an axiom of statecraft. By 1914 it was the tritest of platitudes. Machiavelli did not invent it. It was apparent in the behavior of the Italian states of his time and more or less openly acknowledged in the memoranda of statesmen and diplomats. But Niccolò Machiavelli first gave the fresh attitude of his age toward statecraft a permanent literary form, and the progress of history compelled general recognition of his insight. For that reason, perhaps he does deserve to be accepted as the voice of the Renaissance State. Perhaps his age should be called "The Age of Machiavelli."

Machiavelli's Statecraft

Machiavelli's fame rests on a code of conduct designed to teach ambitious princes the devious art of governing men. An age dominated by rulers and upstarts as fierce as the seasoned condottiere shown above in Leonardo da Vinci's drawing had made the art of war the paramount concern of a prince's life, and Machiavelli introduced an analysis of tactics and weapons, fortifications, and military history into most of his writings. But the astute prince never relied solely on arms; and Italy's despots acknowledged Machiavelli's bold advice on how to run a state, heeding such precepts as those which appear on the following two pages in a selection of quotations from *The Prince* and from the *Discourses on Livy*. Only when diplomacy or guile failed to control the tumultuous course of events did princes have recourse to warfare, now made more terrible by new advances in military technology.

Everybody knows how laudable it is in a prince to keep his faith and to be an honest man and not a trickster. Nevertheless, the experience of our times shows that the princes who have done great things are the ones who have taken little account of their promises and who have known how to addle the brains of men with craft. In the end they have conquered those who put their reliance on good faith.

You must realize then that there are two ways to fight. In one kind the laws are used, in the other, force. The first is suitable to man, the second to animals. But because the first often falls short, one has to turn to the second. Hence a prince must know perfectly how to act like a beast and like a man. . . .

Since then, it is necessary for a prince to understand how to make good use of the conduct of the animals, he should select among them the fox and the lion, because the lion cannot protect himself from traps, and the fox cannot protect himself from the wolves. So the prince needs to be a fox that he may know how to deal with traps, and a lion that he may frighten the wolves. Those who act like the lion alone do not understand their business. A prudent ruler, therefore, cannot and should not observe faith when such observance is to his disadvantage and the causes that made him give his promise have vanished. If men were all good, this advice would not be good, but since men are wicked and do not keep their promises to you, you likewise do not have to keep yours to them. Lawful reasons to excuse his failure to keep them will never be lacking to a prince. . . . the prince who has best known how to act as a fox has come out best. But one who has this capacity must understand how to keep it covered and be a skillful pretender and dissembler. Men are so simple and so subject to present needs that he who deceives in this way will always find those who will let themselves be deceived. *The Prince,* Ch. 18

. . . a prince need not pay much attention to conspiracies when the people are well-disposed to him. But when they are unfriendly and hate him, he must fear everything and everybody. *The Prince,* Ch. 19

Contempt is [the prince's] portion if he is held to be variable, volatile, effeminate, cowardly, or irresolute. From these a prince should guard himself as from a rock in the sea. He should strive in all his actions to give evident signs of greatness, spirit, gravity, and fortitude. Also in the private affairs of his subjects he should make it understood that his opinion is irrevocable. In short he should keep up such a reputation that nobody thinks of trying to deceive him. *The Prince,* Ch. 19

A prince, then, must have no other object and no other thought than war and its methods and conduct and must not take anything else as his specialty, for this is the only branch of knowledge that is required of him who governs; and it is of such value that it not merely keeps in power those who are born princes, but causes men to rise from humble positions to that rank. . . . it may be seen that princes have often lost their rank when they have thought more on luxuries than on arms. The first cause that makes you lose your position is neglect of the art of war; and the cause that makes you acquire it is skill in that art. *The Prince,* Ch. 14

Is it better to be loved than to be feared, or the reverse? I answer that a prince should wish for both. But because it is difficult to reconcile them, I hold that it is much more secure to be feared than to be loved, if one of them must be given up. The reason for my answer is that one must say of men generally that they are ungrateful, mutable, pretenders and dissemblers, prone to avoid danger, thirsty for gain. So long as you benefit them, they are all yours . . . But when need comes upon you, they turn around. So if a prince has relied wholly on their words, and is lacking in other preparations, he falls. Men hesitate less to injure a man who makes himself loved than to injure one who makes himself feared, for their love . . . is broken on every occasion for the sake of selfish profit; but their fear is secured by a dread of punishment which never fails you. *The Prince,* Ch. 17

Nevertheless, the prince should make himself feared in such a way that if he does not win love, he escapes hatred. This is possible, for to be feared and not to be hated can easily co-exist. In fact it is always possible, if the ruler abstains from the property of his citizens and subjects, and from their women. And if, as sometimes happens, he finds that he must inflict the penalty of death, he should do it when he has proper justification and evident reason. But above all he must refrain from taking property, for men forget the death of a father more quickly than the loss of their patrimony. *The Prince,* Ch. 17

. . . as every history shows with many examples, it is necessary for anybody who organizes a republic and establishes laws in it to assume that all men are wicked and that they are always going to make use of the malice of their spirits whenever they have a good opportunity to do so. If their malice remains concealed for a time, there is a hidden cause for it. *Discourses,* I, Ch. 3

. . . anyone who seizes control of a state ought to consider carefully all the injuries he must do, and do them all at one stroke, so that he will not have to undertake new ones every day, but may be able, since he does not repeat them, to give men a feeling of security and gain them to his side by benefiting them. . . . Injuries should all be done together in order that men may taste their bitterness but a short time, and be but a little disturbed. Benefits ought to be conferred a little at a time, that their flavor may be tasted better. *The Prince,* Ch. 8

A prince should also show himself a lover of excellence by giving preferment to gifted men and honoring those who excel in some art. Besides he should encourage his citizens . . . in trade and agriculture and every other occupation of man. A citizen should not hesitate to increase his property for fear it will be taken away from him or to open a new business for fear of taxes. On the contrary the prince should offer rewards to those who undertake to do these things and to anybody who thinks of improving in any way his city or his dominion. Besides this, at suitable times of the year he should engage the attention of the people with festivals and shows. And because every city is divided into guilds or wards, he should take account of these bodies, meet with them sometimes, and give in person an example of humanity and generosity. *The Prince,* Ch. 21

THE ART OF WAR in Italy was transformed by the French invasion of 1494. Before then, condottieri were reluctant to hurt enemies who could pay them ransom; military etiquette frowned on the use of artillery and forbade campaigning at night, and hopefully prescribed a level field as the most comfortable place for an encounter. Machiavelli scorned the Italian system. "Mercenary and auxiliary troops are useless and dangerous," he wrote. "He who bases his government on hireling soldiers will never be solid or secure, because they are disunited, ambitious, without discipline, unfaithful, vigorous among friends, vile among enemies; they have no fear of God or faith with men." In 1495, when the Italians finally ventured to join battle with the French invaders at Fornovo, their mercenary force failed to defeat a highly trained regular army only one-third its size. The battle, shown in the con-

temporary woodcut above, raged fiercely for an hour, until the mercenaries turned aside to pillage the French camp. The Italians suffered most of the casualties and allowed the enemy to escape; but because they had captured French booty, they claimed a victory. In the years that followed, when the peninsula became the battle-ground of rival European powers, Italian troops were forced to imitate the ferocity of foreign armies. Assessing Fornovo, Machiavelli's friend the historian Guicciardini declared: "Before the year 1494, wars were protracted, battles bloodless . . . and although artillery was already in use, it was managed with such want of skill that it caused little hurt . . . But the French infused so much liveliness into our wars, that up to the year 1521 [when newly designed fortifications proved effective], whenever the open country was lost the state was lost with it."

Cheratelli di polnare

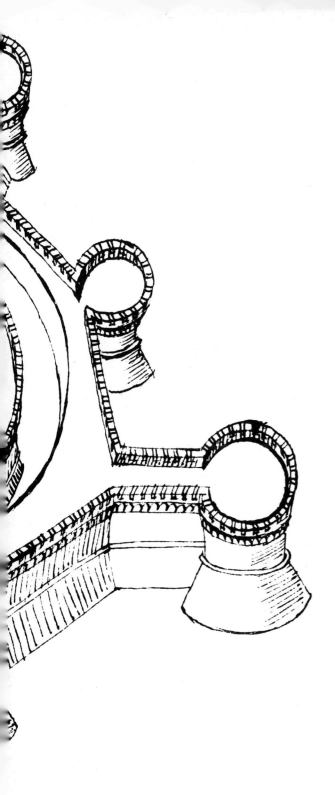

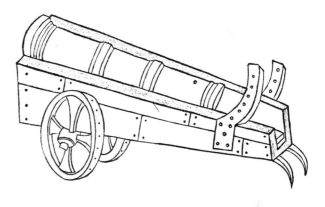

Until 1494, when the invading French army demolished Italian forts with iron cannon balls, the peninsula's artillerymen had relied on bombards of stone; easily shattered on impact, however, they were hardly more effective than a medieval catapult. The foreigners' revolutionary use of iron forced Italian military architects—among them Leonardo da Vinci and the Sienese painter Francesco di Giorgio—to design fortifications which could withstand the fiercest assault. At first, round towers, like those in the fortress (left center) designed by Francesco di Giorgio, were considered strongest, but they were soon replaced by triangular bastions, where covering fire could provide full protection to all the defenders. Although he played a major role in developing the science of fortification, Francesco studied problems of attack as well. His technique for mining, seen beneath the picture of his fort, was probably used for the first time at Naples in 1495. As fortresses became stronger, scaling ladders and wheeled assault platforms (top and bottom, far left) became less useful; and battering rams, such as the one shown at left, with its aptly designed head, were soon completely ineffective, for cannon became the chief engine of siege. On its primitive carriage, the one above was relatively inefficient as a battlefield weapon, but once it was set in place against a city, it was a match for the strongest fort.

"A great and monstrous Arabian engine for storming cities, filled with men, bridges, ladders and various instruments of war" (left) appeared in a treatise on warfare published in Verona in 1483. It shot immense arrows from its mouth, and used an enormous scaling ladder to claw abreast enemy fortifications. The same book displayed a revolving gun with eight barrels, which is shown at right. Although it could imperil friend and foe alike if a spark accidentally ignited all the barrels at once, it was actually seen in battle. So, for that matter, was a less fanciful version of the Arabian engine. Inventing such fantastic weapons as these failed to overtax the ingenuity of Renaissance men. Leonardo da Vinci, who planned the bombard shown below with projectiles which explode in mid-flight, was one of the most industrious of military engineers. His notebooks are filled with designs for immense crossbows and mechanisms for raining shot, with scythed chariots and armored cars, rock-throwing machines and assault bridges. Few were built, for new techniques of war forced inventors to concentrate instead on improvements in artillery. Machiavelli regretted the trend, and nostalgically praised the projectiles used by the ancients, which "although not so noisy as cannon, yet were equally effective in the killing of men." But for once the Florentine was proven wrong. Within his own lifetime, artillerymen and their new weapons came to dominate the battlefields of Italy and all Europe.

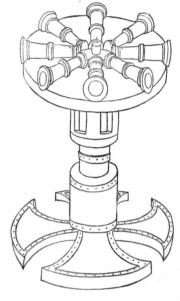

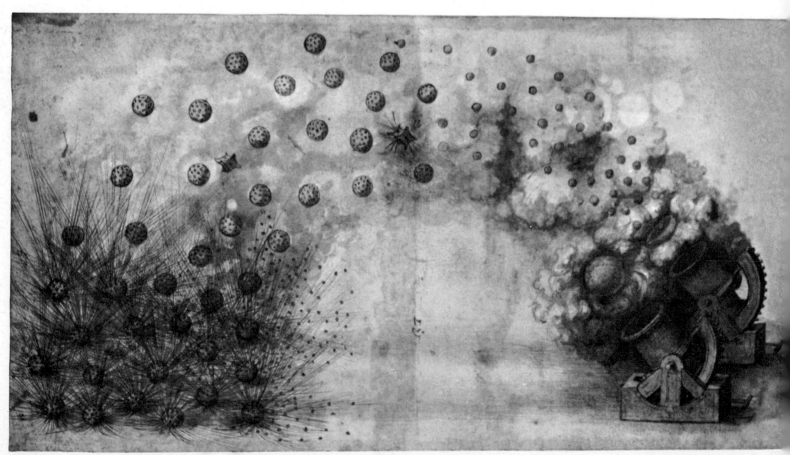

A CONTENTIOUS PENINSULA

The "canker'd hate" of Montagues for Capulets had its origins in an actual feud between the houses of Montecchi and Cappelletti in Verona, but Shakespeare might have found prototypes for his play in any other city of Renaissance Italy. Time and again, the Guelph-Ghibelline conflict was echoed in vendettas between Orsini and Colonna in Rome, Pazzi and Medici in Florence, Baglioni and Oddi in Perugia, with the blood feuds such, as Mercutio put it, that "Thou wilt quarrel with a man for cracking nuts, having no other reason but because thou hast hazel eyes." The fifteenth-century manuscript above, with a bellicose Mars presiding over a scene of battle, was symbolic of the continuous strife. Factionalism existed on every level of society, as family fights developed into wars between rulers, cities, guilds, or towns. With Italy a hotbed of warring factions, it became an easy prey for the increasingly powerful and grasping monarchs of Northern Europe.

CAESAR Borgia de Francia Dei Gratia Dux Romandiole valentie Princeps Hadrie et venafri Dnus Plumbini &c &c Ac sancte Romane Ecclesie Confaloncrius et Capitaneus Generalis Omnibus et singulis ad quorum notitiam presentes pervenerint esse volumus Manifestum Q. Nos omnibus melioribus modo via iure causa & forma quibus melius & efficatius de iure possumus & debemus Facimus Constituimus & sollemniter Deputamus per pntes nros veros Certos Legitimos et indubitatos Procuratores Actores & Factores &c [illegible manuscript Latin text continues]

MACHIAVELLI'S HERO

Cesare Borgia, archetype of *The Prince,* was theatrically handsome, eloquent, and skillful enough to kill a bull with one stroke of a sword. His spectacular achievements impressed Machiavelli and all Italy, but what fascinated men then and since were his private dealings, cloaked in secrecy and surrounded with ugly rumors. A brother who was unfortunate enough to outrank him was stabbed and thrown into the Tiber; a brother-in-law, so rash as to wed his sister Lucrezia, was strangled in the Vatican. Cesare was suspected of both crimes, but his bereaved father, Pope Alexander VI, looked the other way. This son's talents were too valuable to waste. The Pope gave him command of the Church's armies, and with treachery, bribery, military force, and a persuasive reputation for ruthlessness, Cesare conquered Romagna, humbled Florence, and terrified Italy. In his wake, murdered princes left no avenging heirs; rebels who trusted his offers of amnesty were trapped and led to the gallows. But once his control of the land was secure, Cesare's rule was just, if stern. He might have unified Italy had he not been seriously ill on the day his father died. Unable to seize enough money to buy the papal tiara for a member of the Borgia party, Cesare for once was outmaneuvered. He had foreseen every contingency, he told Machiavelli later, except his own illness, and that one mistake ended his career. With his reputation for invincibility shattered, Cesare was exiled to Spain and killed in a minor skirmish at the age of thirty-one.

Three of Cesare Borgia's many victims are shown at far left. Astorre Manfredi (top), the youthful ruler of Faenza, resisted Borgia's assault on his city for six months, but finally yielded on the promise of leniency only to die in the papal dungeons. Caterina Sforza (center), the virago of Forlì, personally led her armies against Cesare and escaped with her life through the intervention of the King of France. Below, in Turkish costume, is the Duke of Gandia, favorite son of Pope Alexander VI. After his mysterious death, Cesare inherited their father's affections. At the bottom is Cesare's sword, etched with illustrations of Julius Caesar's conquests and the incongruous motto, Fides prevalet armis: faith prevails over arms. Another Borgia weapon, fully as dangerous, was the document shown at left, which offers peace to a band of rebel condottieri. When they swallowed his bait, Cesare had them executed.

·CAES·BORGIA·VALENTINVS

Colleoni and the bearded King of Denmark appear (left) in one of Romanino's frescoes commemorating the royal visit to Bergamo.

On May 24, 1458, a fleet of gondolas swept out on the blue lagoons of Venice to welcome Bartolommeo Colleoni, the captain general of the Venetian armies, with lavish ceremony. Later, his name was inscribed in the ancient Golden Book, along with those of the nobility. It was a striking contrast to the day, a few years earlier, when Colleoni, under sentence of death for treason, had barely escaped arrest by the agents of the Council of Ten. But Colleoni, like all condottieri, was accustomed to abrupt changes of fortune. If a Renaissance general was successful, he risked the jealousy of his employer; if he failed, he was dismissed or sometimes even executed. There was a degree of honor among condottieri, but few illusions of chivalry survived in this milieu; war was a profession chosen for pay, not patriotism, and loyalties usually belonged to the highest bidder.

Fighting for or against his Venetian homeland, Colleoni was as ambitious as all condottieri, as treacherous as most. He had worked his way up through the ranks, receiving his first command under a professional soldier in the pay of the aging Queen of Naples. Before long he was faced with challenges more unpredictable than the whims of royalty. Venice captured his family and held them as hostages, paid his salary with castles and then stole them back; rival condottieri vowed to drink his blood if they caught him. If he was not the greatest soldier of his time, he succeeded in bringing off some rather notable victories (he is credited by some with being the first general to use artillery successfully), and as a result he managed to achieve the goals coveted above all others by condottieri —respect, and a small state to govern in his old age. As lord of Bergamo, the unschooled Colleoni assumed the role of a model prince, welcomed royalty to his castle, patronized philosophers and artists, and even wrote a book on the art of war. Ambitious to the end, he left his fortune to Venice with a proviso that the republic commission a statue in his memory and place it conspicuously in the great square of St. Mark's. More than any deed of valor or military skill, it is this monument, still standing in the Campo Santi Giovanni e Paolo, which has made Colleoni the personification of the warlike spirit of the Renaissance.

The noble equestrian statue of Colleoni (opposite), modeled by Andrea Verrocchio, was included in his bequest to Venice.

THE CONDOTTIERE

This panel from Uccello's stylized Rout of San Romano, *memorializing Florence's victory over Siena in 1432, hung in Lorenzo de' Medici's bedroom. The knight falling from his white horse is Bernardino della Carde, the Sienese leader.*

A TRIBUTE TO HEROISM

To a public weary of the endless round of petty warfare, the condottieri were generally objects of contempt or fear. But there were able, honorable men among them, men such as Giovanni delle Bande Nere, about whom Aretino wrote this moving tribute after his death from a wound: "He valued brave men more than he did riches and indeed only desired the latter to keep the valiant, who served him, from going hungry. There was nothing about his men's lodgings or their conduct in action that he did not know about, for in battle he fought side by side with privates in the ranks and in peacetime he made no distinction between himself and others. Indeed, the very clothes he wore proved he was himself a fighting man. They were worn and shabby and they had armor stains upon the legs, and arms, and chest. . . . But what more than anything else won the hearts of his followers was that he said 'Follow me!' instead of 'Go ahead of me!' in time of peril. . . . He sought only honor and not his own interest, and . . . sold all his possessions . . . to pay the army's overdue salaries. He was always the first to bestride his steed, and always the last one to dismount." No soldier could ask more of his commander.

The Gonzaga receive the keys to Mantua after downing the Bonacolsi, in a detail from Domenico Morone's painting (above).

THE
PRINCES
OF
MANTUA

In January of 1462, Lodovico Gonzaga, Marquis of
Mantua, presided over one of his greatest triumphs
—the welcoming home of his second son, Francesco,
who had just been made a cardinal. It was not a
chance appointment; Lodovico had quarreled with his
own brother over the succession and purposely placed
Francesco in the Church to avoid any such rivalry between his sons. It was a policy continued by later
Gonzaga princes. Having wrested control over Mantua from the ruling house of Bonacolsi in 1328, the
Gonzaga had maintained and strengthened it by election, legitimization (upon payment of a substantial
fee to the Emperor), and wise rule. Lodovico, a
skilled condottiere, as were most of his family, kept
the city peaceful and free from the encroachments of
Milan by taking service with the Milanese. But it
was in internal rule that he excelled; he carefully nurtured Mantua's prime industry, the cloth trade; he
built hospitals to combat the frequent epidemics of
plague, and bridges to span the marshes surrounding
the city; he reformed laws and ruled justly (a rare
quality in those days); he patronized humanists and
authorized one of the earliest printing presses in
Mantua; and he invited Alberti, Mantegna, and other
artists to adorn both the city and his court. With only
meager funds, Lodovico managed to contract several
brilliant marriages for his family and died in 1478
with the knowledge that his dynasty was loved and
secure. Gonzaga relatives were married into most of
the ruling houses of Italy, and Lodovico's grandson
Francesco was engaged to a princess of Ferrara, Isabella d'Este, who was, in time, to bring Mantua to the
zenith of its fame, influence, and prosperity.

*Cardinal Francesco Gonzaga's triumphant return from
Rome (right) was painted by Mantegna in a famous fresco in the Camera degli Sposi in Mantua. He is greeted by
his father (left) and nephews (front). The elder nephew,
also named Francesco, who later became marquis and
married Isabella d'Este, appears again kneeling at the
Virgin's feet in Mantegna's Madonna of Victory (left).
It was painted to commemorate his victory over the
French King, Charles VIII, at Fornovo in 1495—a ques-
tionable triumph, since Charles escaped with most of his
outnumbered army and sustained many fewer casualties.*

DESPOTISM
IN RIMINI

If the Gonzaga princes were loved and respected, others were not, and off to the southeast of Mantua ruled the most hated and feared tyrants in all Italy. In 1216 the first members of the powerful house of Malatesta (Evil-heads) had been granted citizenship in Rimini, and by the end of the century the family was in complete control of the town. Their history was filled with bloody tales of tragedy and brutality, such as Giovanni Malatesta's murder of Francesca da Rimini and her lover, Paolo, but the crimes of Sigismondo Pandolfo Malatesta outdid those of all his predecessors. He became lord in 1432 at the age of fifteen, already accomplished in the warlike arts and known for his headstrong bravery. For the duration of his long reign his people saw no respite from war, pillage, and hardship. An active condottiere, Sigismondo was continually fighting for one state or another, earning the enmity of nearly all who employed him by his treachery, while rumors and stories of his personal crimes sealed his evil reputation. Pope Pius II, with whom he feuded over land holdings, said, "Of all men who have ever lived or ever will live [Sigismondo] was the worst scoundrel, the disgrace of Italy and the infamy of our times." He was said to have murdered his first two wives, attempted sodomy with his son, committed incest with his daughter, and been guilty of rape, adultery, and murder on many occasions.

In surprising contrast to such acts were his extraordinary brilliance and his profound

Hanged and decaying corpses such as those painted by Pisanello (left) were a common sight in Italy.

In one of the frescoes remaining in the Tempio Malatestiano, Sigismondo may still be seen (below), his pose one of sham piety. Piero della Francesca executed the painting and showed the Rimini tyrant kneeling before his patron saint. Now badly damaged, the fresco was once brilliantly colored in jade green, coral, and azure blue. Sigismondo employed the famed medalist Matteo de' Pasti, who in 1446 cast a medal of Isotta degli Atti, his patron's mistress (left); reverse (right) shows the Malatesta symbol, an elephant.

knowledge of and respect for ancient philosophy. His closest friends were humanists and artists, upon whom he lavished patronage, and his proudest deed was the exhumation of the ashes of Gemistus Pletho, the apostle of Renaissance paganism. They were brought to Rimini and entombed with all the pomp and devotion that might have been accorded a Christian saint.

The chief monument to Sigismondo's fame, and one of the major works to show the classical revival in architecture, was the church of San Francesco in Rimini, which was transformed into a Roman temple by Leon Battista Alberti, the leading architect of the time and a close friend of Sigismondo's. Called the Tempio Malatestiano, it was so filled with pagan reliefs and decorations that Pius II said "it seemed less a Christian sanctuary than a temple of heathen devil-worshipers." Within the classical façade were housed all the Malatesta tombs (Sigismondo's carved with horns and a scornful epitaph) and the famed chapel "sacred to the divine Isotta," Sigismondo's mistress. For his heresies and other crimes, Pius II excommunicated Sigismondo and said, "No mortal heretofore has descended into Hell with the ceremony of canonization. Sigismondo shall be the first deemed worthy of such honor." A few years later a council of cardinals sentenced him to burn as a heretic, and when they could not capture him, consigned his effigy to the flames. Sigismondo only laughed. But it was the Church that defeated him in the end. He was brought to his knees in 1463, was forced to surrender most of his realm, and died in 1468, unloved and unregretted.

In the court scene at right, one of Carpaccio's eight canvases on the legend of Saint Ursula, two typical ambassadors make their departure while a third has a final word with a scribe. The document above directed the Venetian ambassador in Rome to complain about Cesare Borgia's kidnaping of the wife of a Venetian condottiere.

DIPLOMACY

As the risks and expenses of mercenary warfare mounted, the Italian states were forced to seek new avenues of advancing or safeguarding their interest. Most of them had merchants and traders traveling abroad, whose experience in bargaining suggested a means of obtaining information about enemy plans or resolving problems of state. Frequently business or banking interests paved the way for an exchange of envoys, and by 1500 resident embassies were established in most European capitals. The earliest ambassadors, equipped with little training and less money, were expected to gather and report information, entertain lavishly, make diplomatic contacts, and uphold the prestige of their states. They engaged in endless wrangles over precedence and were highly suspect (in Venice, the penalty for discussing politics with a foreigner was banishment), but in spite of such difficulties, diplomats were remarkably successful, and none more so than the Venetians, who set the pattern for diplomacy as we know it today. In her proud isolation, and with a relatively stable and legitimate government, Venice preserved her diplomatic records systematically, thus lending continuity to her policies. A Venetian humanist envoy, Ermolao Barbaro, first laid down the rules governing the duties of a resident ambassador; and Venice initiated the first triumph of the new diplomacy—the League of Lodi in 1454. This twenty-five-year nonaggression and defense pact between all the major states of Italy was grudgingly adhered to at first, and later blatantly ignored; but it was the foundation upon which Renaissance diplomacy grew.

A victorious Neapolitan fleet, flying the banners of Aragon, tows the defeated French galleys into Naples (above) after the battle of Ischia in 1464. This was the last futile Angevin effort to regain the throne they had lost in 1442. Castel Nuovo, the home of the kings of Naples, is at left center. Below, a contemporary manuscript depicts the grand entry of Charles VIII into Naples. The young King is shown at right, in full regalia, riding under a canopy borne by eight traitorous Neapolitan noblemen. It was a short-lived triumph, however; not long afterward Charles was scurrying north, having received word that the contentious states of Italy were rallying their forces against him.

THE
CONQUEST
OF
NAPLES

Under a golden canopy, the short, ugly King of France, Charles VIII, marched unopposed into Naples in 1495, to receive the acclamation of Italy's great southern kingdom. In 1442 the ambitious Alfonso of Aragon had wrested its crown from the French house of Anjou, but his hold was a precarious one. Partly out of fear, partly from greed, Naples' neighbors seized every opportunity to advance the claims of Alfonso's rivals, and Naples became the objective of nearly every move on the diplomatic chessboard. To protect her banking interests beyond the Alps, Florence supported the French claim. Milan, fearful of French power, allied with Alfonso, then switched sides. Venice favored anyone who threatened Milan, and Pope Calixtus III, hoping to put a Borgia nephew on the Neapolitan throne, claimed the kingdom as a lapsed papal fief. Instead of a balance of power, there was a vacuum, and Charles VIII's easy—if short-lived—conquest caused other European powers to turn their eyes southward.

THE ARTS

In 1546 a young, successful painter, Giorgio Vasari, was at a small supper party in Cardinal Farnese's palace in Rome. The conversation turned to the extraordinary flowering of Italian art in the previous century and to the exceptional artists who had revolutionized painting and sculpture since the far-off days of Giotto and Pisano. Yet Vasari's presence was even more remarkable still, for even a hundred years earlier it would have been unthinkable for a young painter to have been a frequent guest at a cardinal's table. The social position of the artist had changed as much as art itself. To the men at that supper party, the age of heroes was passing; only the formidable genius of old Michelangelo could challenge, Vasari thought, the giants of the past. Encouraged and helped by the others, Vasari determined to collect all that men knew about these remarkable artists of True recent past; to immortalize, above all, the painters of Florence, which, for Vasari, was the cradle of the arts. Florence had nurtured what Rome had used. There had been a time when Milan, with Leonardo

da Vinci at the court of Lodovico Sforza, had seemed about to be the leading city of the Renaissance. The great invasions cut that short. And it was Venice, secure and rich, that became the heir of Florence and the rival of Rome. Yet it was these four cities—Florence, Milan, Rome, and Venice—in which the practice and patronage of art had become a civic virtue; it was these cities that witnessed the triumphs of painting and sculpture and the emergence of the artist from the confines of a craft to the lonely pursuit of his genius.

In the early fifteenth century the artists had been as certain as Vasari that they were heralding a new age; behind them stretched dark and barren times. They acknowledged the genius of Giotto and Cimabue, but few others. Their admiration was kept for antiquity, which they yearned to equal, if not surpass, but certainly the modern age began with them: painting with Masaccio, sculpture with Ghiberti, architecture with Brunelleschi. And, indeed, this was not idle boasting. Donatello's statues possess exceptional originality. In paint-

Masaccio, as critic Bernard Berenson has observed, was "Giotto reborn." Like Giotto, he gave each figure its proper weight, and made saints and madonnas as strong as Tuscan peasants. His masterpiece, The Tribute Money, *painted when he was about twenty-six, set a standard for painters of the following generations, who made pilgrimages to the church of the Carmine at Florence to study it. The figure of Christ, sending Saint Peter to find tribute money in the mouth of a fish, dominates the fresco. At the extreme right, Peter, outside the gates of the city, hands his coin to the Roman tax collector.*

ing the break is, perhaps, less vivid than in Donatello's free-standing statues, but it is remarkable enough. In architecture success came more slowly. In literature and in music men were equally confident of their own originality and in the superiority of their age: between their own time and antiquity stretched the "barbarous Middle Ages." Seen against the broad sweep of modern history, their claims seem wholly justified. The language of Renaissance art is the language of the modern world—at least until recent times—whereas the art of the Middle Ages possesses some of the same difficulties as the art of Islam or India or China. Its beauty can be recognized, its contents discerned, but its impact on the feelings is never, or rarely, immediate.

And yet, as soon as one considers individual works of Renaissance art or considers the purpose for which they were painted or modeled or built, one is immediately aware how entangled the artists of fifteenth-century Italy were in the traditions not only of Gothic art but also of Byzantium. They were also deeply indebted to the imaginative originality and technical skill of the great Flemish and Burgundian school of painting and illumination. These strands of tradition and of foreign influence give an added richness of texture to the achievement of the Renaissance painters; but when all debts and obligations are acknowledged, what a fabulous achievement in painting and sculpture remains! Great artists are as common as peaks in the Himalayas, leading one to believe that the ability to draw or to carve is no rarer in human beings than mathematical skill and only requires the appropriate social circumstances to call it forth in abundance.

And certainly the social circumstances were exceptionally favorable for artists and craftsmen. Firstly there was a strong, deep-rooted tradition, which went back to the earliest days of Christian Europe, that men whom God had prospered should give thanks for their good fortune by embellishing the churches and monasteries in which He was worshiped. Building for God and the adornment of God's buildings were a

part of the Christian life—sanctioned by time and anchored in belief. After all, it was the most vivid, the most dramatic way of reaching the illiterate. Therefore, it was inevitable that as the men of affairs flourished in Venice, in Florence, in Milan, or in Naples, they should wish their wealth to be reflected in their parish churches, in the monasteries and nunneries which they founded or patronized, and in the cathedrals of their cities. And in this exercise of artistic benevolence in the service of God, they had a supreme mentor in the Pope. At Avignon, and afterward at Rome, the popes had fostered a visual splendor that was the envy of the kings of Europe as well as the princes of Italy. The sense of merit in the visual expression of piety was universally held even by such naturally puritanical characters as Bernardino of Siena or Savonarola. Although they called for the burning of vanities, that did not include pictures of sacred subjects. To all men, even the most ascetic, these were a part of religion as old as the Church itself.

Furthermore, it had long been the custom of princes to adorn their palaces; to encourage the skilled crafts of metalwork and jewelry; to take delight in tapestries and frescoes that told them a well-loved story such as the Virgin and the Unicorn or reminded them of the pursuits—hunting or the art of love—in which they took delight. It satisfied their senses, as well as enhanced their pride, to read their prayers from costly books, illuminated with exquisite skill. By 1400, however, there were hundreds of merchants in Italy, and in Burgundy, who could afford the artistic elegance that had once been the prerogative of the country's aristocracy. And these merchants were city-born; often their families had risen to greatness with their towns, and their civic pride was as strong as chivalry, stronger perhaps than a knight's loyalty to his prince. And they wished their city to mirror their own greatness, to reflect in its buildings and their adornment the wealth in which they took such sturdy delight. The competitive state system of Renaissance Italy was not merely con-

cerned with power; it flourished equally strongly in the arts. It added to the stature of kings to have a world-renowned artist attached to their courts; and the republics—particularly Florence and Venice—were as jealous of their geniuses as any king.

Into the pursuit of art, therefore, both money and social energy were poured, and the effect was as dramatic as the investment of capital during the nineteenth century in technology and invention—and in many ways similar in its results. Naturally, the need for artists drew some men into a career which they might otherwise have ignored. Any poor peasant boy who showed some natural skill was likely to find a sponsor among the neighboring gentry or local merchants, as did Mantegna, who had herded sheep in the fields near Padua until discovered by Squarcione. Of course, the greatest source was the families of craftsmen—the jewelers, goldsmiths, metalworkers, and decorative painters—in which there was a tradition of design and the opportunity for early

apprenticeship. Yet probably only the religious life had before drawn its practitioners from such a wide social background or caught in its orbit such a rich variety of human temperament. And this in itself had a fertilizing effect on artistic expression.

To the competition for artists was added the competition by artists. In early centuries, the craftsman could spend a lifetime beautifying one cathedral or monastery, adding, perhaps, a personal variation to the traditional themes and colors in which he worked, but unconcerned with public reputation or rivalry with his fellow artists. By 1450 personal vendettas and public rivalry between artists had become a commonplace of Florentine and Venetian life, and again to the advantage of art, for they led men to attempt to exploit their techniques to the fullest, to give their imagination free rein, to emphasize the singularity of their personal vision. It needs the skilled eye of a connoisseur to distinguish between one Burgundian master of illumination and another; a child can tell

The first large bronze free-standing nude done since antiquity, Donatello's David *(opposite) states a Renaissance theme which Michelangelo employed a generation later, after years of anatomical study by Florentine artists. Scientific advances in perspective kept pace with research in anatomy. The painting of the ideal city (below) probably owes its complex perspective scheme to Brunelleschi and his followers, its round temple and broad piazza to the architect Alberti's theories of city planning. Draftsmen's tools were sometimes as carefully wrought as their scientific studies. The beautiful set of instruments at right— compass, dividers, and damascened ink box—was made in the sixteenth century.*

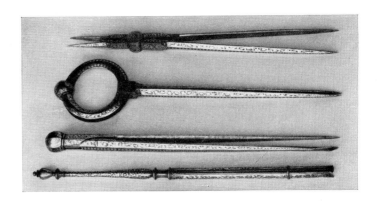

the difference between a Botticelli and a Uccello. Of course, this does not mean that attribution is easy or absolute. A successful painter of the Renaissance was the head of a workshop —often, as with the Bellini or Tintoretto, a large-scale family affair in which brothers, sons, and even daughters joined. And, furthermore, apprentices abounded, and so did journeymen who were skilled in hands or costumes or backgrounds or *putti*. And, as ever, the works of the second rate emulated slavishly the genius of a few.

The circumstances of the Renaissance encouraged the cultivation of individual style. And the rewards of the successful creation of a deeply personal idiom were so large that artists took risks which craftsmen in earlier days would never have dared take. Some men followed their daemons wherever they might lead, and painters committed themselves to their artistic vision with the fervor of a saint following his calling. The stories that Vasari tells may or may not be true, but they reveal what Italian society expected of the lives of its artists—

Andrea del Castagno killing Domenico out of envy; Piero di Cosimo boiling the eggs that he lived on, fifty at a time, with his varnishes to save time; Paolo Uccello loving perspective so much more than his wife. What is common to all is the acceptance of dedication and the acceptance of self. This swarming crowd of painters, sculptors, goldsmiths, decorators, jewelers, contained men of widely differing gifts and most varied temperaments: men of profound curiosity such as Leonardo, of soaring imagination such as Michelangelo, of highly intellectual powers such as Piero della Francesca, of exquisite sensitivity such as Giorgione, and of supreme technical accomplishment such as Raphael.

The three great arts—painting, sculpture, architecture— changed most profoundly between 1400 and 1500. Indications that change might come had not been infrequent in the fourteenth century. Painting in the thirteenth century had been largely dominated by Greek (that is, Byzantine) influence—indeed, many of the artists were themselves Greek;

The perspective scheme of Piero della Francesca's Brera Madonna (opposite) focuses upon an egg which hangs above the Virgin's head. Fra Angelico's naturalism was less scientific; above, a detail from the life of Saint Nicholas shows two workmen unloading a shipment of wheat.

the olive-skinned, slant-eyed, ikonlike madonnas of Cimabue and Duccio di Buoninsegna are refined expressions, with a hint of personal involvement, of established traditions. In comparison, Giotto towers like a giant, even if by fifteenth-century standards he is naïve and primitive. His figures have, to use Berenson's excellent phrase, "tactile values"; you feel that you could touch them, walk round them, and that they could walk round you. He used with great economy light, shade, color, and strongly featured men and women to give this sense of solid form and three-dimensional space. Yet for a hundred years there was little or no advance from his innovating skill, only imitation. Florentine art was, apart from Orcagna, less imaginative, less technically dexterous than the achievement of the great painters and illuminators of Burgundy, Flanders, and Avignon, whose skills were steadily to seep through the Alps to enrich Italy. Certainly Florence lacked the achievement of Siena, where strong Byzantine and weaker Gothic influences blended to create a

school of painters—Lorenzetti, Martini, Duccio—of great charm and some originality, particularly in landscape.

Then, suddenly, as Italian art seemed to be drifting gently and skillfully into its own version of the Gothic, the promise of Giotto was fulfilled in one of the greatest of all Florentine painters—Masaccio. His frescoes in the Brancacci Chapel of the Carmine were revered by generations of artists, who subjected them to the closest study. His great abilities were not, however, like Giotto's, exercised in isolation. From 1400 onward two artists of outstanding ability—one a sculptor, Donatello, and the other an architect, Brunelleschi—also helped to create a totally new attitude to art. Both were entranced by perspective, by human nature, and by reality as they saw it—not through symbol or myth but directly and clear-sightedly. Donatello's *David* was a piece of amazing originality; the beauty of a boy's naked body displayed frankly for the first time since antiquity. It marks as emphatically as Watt's invention of a modern steam engine the

birth of a new age. Brunelleschi contributed as much, perhaps, by his ardent proselytism of the rules of perspective as by the soaring dome that he built for Florence's cathedral. And in addition to these three great Florentines there were others—Ghiberti, Uccello, Luca della Robbia, Fra Angelico—painters and sculptors of exceptional talent, perhaps even touched with genius, who were deeply moved by the new technical triumphs which the study of perspective had brought; indeed, Uccello painted with scarcely any other object in view than to demonstrate his skill in handling perspective in the most unlikely circumstances. Naturally, those men who in more recent times would have turned to the career of a scientist or a mathematician were deeply stirred by the complex harmonies that could be achieved by following the strict rules of perspective. The greatest of these was undoubtedly Piero della Francesca of Borgo San Sepolcro, an artist of genius who in the end preferred his mathematics to his art and painted nothing for the last fourteen years of his life. He

combined an exceptional control of linear relationships with a sense of life that was both grave and serene. A preoccupation with, as it were, the density of things, combined with a tragic view of life, became the dominant theme in Florentine art. A further preoccupation was a sense of movement which infuses the reliefs, the statues, the pictures of this extraordinary city, and was to culminate in the writhing nudes of Michelangelo, locked forever in their struggle with Fate. Power of intellect, gravity of feeling, a sense of Time, these qualities artists were able to express visually.

Both Donatello and Brunelleschi, who were devoted friends, were concerned with other intellectual preoccupations apart from perspective. They searched deliberately and consciously for the antique. They went off together to Rome. Brunelleschi measured and drew ruin after ruin; Donatello studied the few Roman and fewer Greek bronzes and statues that men were beginning to collect at this time. And both men felt that they were the heirs of Rome, that between them

and the fifth century there was a great gulf of barbarism.

And yet the art of the early fifteenth century was deeply entangled in its past. The scenes which painters were called upon to paint were the traditional scenes of Christian mythology—Nativities, Circumcisions, Crucifixions—the miracles of saints, the Stations of the Cross—and they were expected to execute them in traditional places, on the walls of churches and monasteries and on panels for altars. And skill in the control of perspective, or even a delight in the antique as absolute as Mantegna's, did not abolish the old symbols or the traditional iconography: four or five jagged rocks, realistically drawn, still represented mountains, as they had done for centuries in Byzantine art. The egg, hanging in the apse in Piero della Francesca's great picture of the Madonna and Child with saints, in the Brera, Milan, represents the four elements of the universe—a purely medieval symbol—as well as being a perfect conic section and the central point of a complex composition, requiring superlative skill in perspec-

tive. And although Uccello might gently mock the traditions of chivalry in his *Saint George and the Dragon,* nevertheless they absorbed his imagination; and Gozzoli's *Journey of the Magi* is as Gothic in feeling and intention as a fifteenth-century tapestry from Burgundy. Indeed, the new art of Donatello and Masaccio had no easy victory except in technique, for the Gothic feeling from the North seeped like an estuarine tide through the brushes and canvases of Italian artists of the fifteenth century: they were no more conscious of it than children playing with new toys in the sunshine, yet it caught them inexorably.

The other great triumphs of Renaissance art—the painting of landscape, the exploration of space and light through color, the full acceptance of the nude, and the development of the portrait—came only slowly.

And again they were partly due to foreign influence. Landscape in early Renaissance art was mainly the landscape of symbol, such as the paradisal gardens derived probably from

Leonardo da Vinci kept a room full of botanical specimens; Uccello collected sheaves of perspective drawings of the mazzocchio, which was the turban-shaped headgear worn in Florence. Leonardo's drawings of the star-of-Bethlehem plant (right) and Uccello's Saint George and the Dragon *(left) both transform the artist's scientific studies into masterpieces of grace. Although his battle is in a medieval setting,* Saint George *is fully a Renaissance creation, with sculptured armor, charging horse, and a lance tilted so as to add depth to the painting. Dated about 1455, Uccello's picture is an early example of a painting on canvas instead of wood.*

Persia—containing sometimes delicately observed flowers and plants and animals, but painted for their value as symbols, not to stir feeling, not to evoke mood deliberately, except in a formalized and quasi-theological sense—or the terrible mountains, rocks, and forests which were the age-old symbols of hell and horror. But as individuality began to creep out from traditional expression, and as the control of technique became more certain, painters and illustrators could not resist the challenge of the outward-seeing eye. In the *Très Riches Heures* of the Duc de Berry, ordinary life is revealed—peasants cut the crops, the children swim, the sheep feed on the mountain side. About the time that these were being painted by the Limbourg brothers, a Flemish artist, Jan van Eyck, began to give small background landscapes to his great altarpieces, which influenced Italian art as profoundly as his discovery of oil painting. Both his feeling for landscape and his knowledge of oils were taken back to Italy, where Antonello da Messina was one of the first to employ the new technique. The exploration of color, of light and shade, of the intimate relation of man and nature, became dominant themes in Venetian art. Actually, Florentine artists had not been entirely indifferent to landscape; its study was partially involved in their preoccupation with perspective. Also, feeling inspired by natural objects was an integral part of their Neoplatonism. Brunelleschi made an optical device for viewing the city, and Alberti told how nature stirred him to tears and to joy. The intellectual problem of drawing figures against a distant background was bound to preoccupy Piero della Francesca, and he solved it about 1465, when he painted his great Urbino diptych. And realistic landscapes, particularly of the Val d'Arno, were painted shortly afterwards by Pollaiuolo. But neither painter responded with such a deep sense of personal discovery as did Giovanni Bellini, although the stimulus for his preoccupation may have come as much from della Francesca as from van Eyck. Bellini loved light, loved the first clear

light of morning that touches the mountaintops and leaves the plain in shadow, and the golden light of the last hours of day, the time that Leonardo was to love so deeply, a time that gives depth to shadow and softness and glow to color. Even the full light of midday in all its hardness and brilliance did not repel Bellini. He could drink in its heat and intensity, as his Saint Francis does with his outstretched arms, raised as much to the sun as to God. Although his delight in light and its effects on color passed into the Venetian tradition, his almost Brueghel-like concern with the detail of landscape did not.

Landscape was used by Giorgione, by Titian, by Tintoretto, to interpret mood, to reflect the emotion felt by the painter and to stimulate it in the beholder. In Giorgione and in the early works of Titian, landscape painting reached hallucinatory heights of feeling, reflecting mystery, horror, fear, tenderness, security, bliss, and love. As with perspective, so with landscape, a new world of artistic expression had been created.

The Venetians, of course, were not the only artists in the early sixteenth century to take delight in the painting of landscape. True, Michelangelo largely ignored it, and Botticelli used it merely as decoration or to emphasize his flowing, vibrant movement, but the Umbrian painters—Perugino and Pinturicchio—drew much from the tradition of Piero della Francesca; a tradition that was absorbed with masterful ease by Raphael. And, naturally, Leonardo da Vinci's sense of beauty as well as his avid curiosity were stirred by nature. The geological structure of mountains as well as their evocation of emotion caught his imagination, as did the turbulence of water as well as the mechanics of its flow; as did the flight of birds or the botany of flowers as well as their beauty; and, as in so many other aspects of Renaissance art, the scientific spirit and the delight in the eye were combined in one aesthetic pleasure, for in Leonardo the creative imagination was as multidimensional as geometry.

Throughout the Renaissance, artists were working for a

With the introduction of oil painting, at the time of Antonello da Messina, Italian art was revolutionized. The Sicilian artist copied the new technique from Flemish painters, whose characteristic style he imitated, too. Saint Jerome in His Study *(opposite) devotes meticulous attention to detail, with each shelf in the room displaying a miniature still life, and the whole set in a frame of Gothic architecture. Another revolution in Italian art, initiated by Giorgione, brought increased importance to landscape painting. Giorgione's* Castelfranco Madonna *utilizes an idyllic landscape on either side of the figure of Mary (right) to soften its symmetrical composition.*

small public. They were well known in their cities, they were familiar to popes and princes. The atmosphere in which they worked was intimate. Also, their art served a civic as well as a religious purpose. The Venetians realized early that narrative paintings about their heroic moments could have a public function, could impress both citizen and stranger with the republic's greatness. For the same reason, artists were paid to paint the vast pageants that gave drama and color and pomp to the Venetian year. In such pictures Venetians as well as Venice appeared, citizens as recognizable as the Piazzetta itself. The princes, too, helped to domesticate art. Their profiles had long adorned medals—indeed the only claim to fame of some of them is that Pisanello made a cast of their features. They hungered, as princes will, for eternity, and they needed not only to patronize painting or to construct huge palaces, but also to see themselves immortalized by one in order to adorn the other. They appeared, as the Medici did, in the retinue of kings making their offerings to the in-fant Christ, or in symbolic pageant, as Federigo da Montefeltro and his wife, Battista, did in the Urbino diptych. And, of course, the preoccupation with the nature of man must of itself lead to the attempt to interpret character through portraiture; and for this the treatment of the face in profile was insufficient. Although there were brilliant portraits elsewhere—Pollaiuolo's *Portrait of a Man,* Botticelli's *Giovanni di Pierfrancesco de' Medici,* and many others—Venice was the true home of the portrait. A great series of doges, unhappily destroyed by fire in 1577, was painted by Bellini for the Doge's Palace. And the portrait rapidly became fashionable. Procurators and merchants quickly followed in the steps of the doges, and the walls of private palaces were adorned with the portraits of their owners, many of them masterpieces of human interpretation by Titian.

Through perspective, through the introduction of oils, through the exploitation of landscape and the human body, Renaissance Italy created the traditions of Western art, in

which it was to remain embedded for centuries. Sculpture and architecture had flourished in like manner. Donatello's *David* remained an isolated phenomenon only for a generation. Verrocchio, Leonardo, and, above all, Michelangelo created statues of a beauty that equaled the best that the ancient world had to offer; and Michelangelo infused his statues with an emotional force that none have equaled since. The tragic nature of man—his immense loneliness and his inevitable end—gripped him like a vise. His tension and suffering, generalized for mankind, passed into stone or paint. Social circumstance and technical change allowed such supreme artists to flourish. And the distance traveled in a little over a hundred years—from Lorenzo Monaco, Gentile da Fabriano, or Lorenzetti to Leonardo, Michelangelo, or Raphael—is stupendous. Such a leap was only possible because art had become the expression of complex social forces.

By the High Renaissance, art had come to pervade all aspects of life. From the arrangement of sweetmeats to the con-

struction of fortifications—all were matters of moment upon which an artist's opinion might be needed or offered. And most of the great artists, too, regarded themselves as Jacks-of-all-trades. Leonardo did not think it beneath his dignity to design the costumes for the masques which his patrons loved or to fix the heating for a duchess' bath. And most of the great figures of the Renaissance displayed exceptional versatility. Michelangelo felt himself to be a man wholly dedicated to sculpture, yet after his reluctance had been overcome, he could paint the frescoes of the Sistine Chapel. And, of course, he could, and did, turn to architecture with equal facility and, when the mood was upon him, express his deepest feelings in poetry. The versatility of a Leonardo or a Michelangelo was far from being unusual. Princes and patrons wished their lives to be embellished richly, ostentatiously, beautifully, and they were willing to pour out their ducats and florins on all the arts and crafts that adorn the life of man. They pursued physical beauty like a drug. Their

In modeling the figure of Hercules (opposite), Pollaiuolo distributed muscular stresses as though he were solving a problem in physics, for unless artists studied science they remained mere artisans, linked with masons and bricklayers like the sculptor shown below. The distinction between art and artisanship remained vague in the Renaissance. The craftsman in the plate at left, painting portraits of a betrothed couple, might work in other arts, too. The highly developed craft of majolica (bust at right) was an inexpensive substitute for the fine arts.

heightened sensibilities, due to the sudden turns of chance which threaded their days with light and shadow, lusted for color, richness, wanton display. This aristocratic spirit at large in a world of bourgeois delights had no use for pewter dishes, sober costume, modest feasting, or chaste jewelry. It reveled in gold, in silver, in bronze, in gaudy dishes of majolica, and in silks, in satins, and in damasks, in cunningly wrought pearls, in sapphires, in rubies, and in emeralds. And the pageantry, the masquerades, the feasts, the dancing, and the music provided the background to this peacock world. This pride, this ostentation could find expression in the intellectual world as well as in the senses, and collections of antique bronzes, marble statues, splendidly illuminated manuscripts, beautifully bound books from the new presses, ancient rings and seals, became a prince as much as his palace or his pictures. The mania for collecting, as a reflection of social grandeur, emerges during the Renaissance. This delight in the eye, this desire to impress, created a constant demand for

the services of the great masters, even for the most trivial and most ephemeral commissions—the molding of pastry, the decoration of a table, the casting of a candlestick, the cutting of an intaglio, the design of a dagger—almost all of which have disappeared into limbo. The works of a few craftsmen of genius—the terracottas of della Robbia, the metalwork of Cellini, the bronzes of Riccio—survive. Those of nameless craftsmen who achieved high excellence are more plentiful. Their ornate *cassoni*, their haunting bronzes, their brightly patterned majolicas, and, above all, their exquisite jewelry, scattered about the museums of America and Western Europe, give a glimpse of the sumptuous world for which they worked.

This was the way, they thought, the great Romans had lived. They loved to act the parts of classical mythology, to be Jupiter or Hebe or Apollo or Diana for a day. And although, of course, they never gave up their Christian roots, they were drawn increasingly closer to the pretense of a

101

In collaboration with his pupil Titian, Giovanni Bellini painted The Feast of the Gods *(facing page), an involved allegory based on a tale taken from Ovid. The metamorphosis of Daphne was another of Ovid's stories; Pollaiuolo shows the nymph (left) fleeing from Apollo's advances. Sprouting branches in place of arms, Daphne turns into a laurel tree to elude the god's pursuit. Pollaiuolo's mythological paintings were an early result of the revival of interest in the classics. By the time of Titian, the ideals of humanism had come to dominate all painting. Titian decorated one room at the court of Alfonso d'Este at Ferrara with three pictures tracing a favorite humanist theme, the evolution of love, and placed* The Feast of the Gods *on the fourth wall. One scholar has conjectured that the amorous couple sitting behind a bowl of fruit at the right center of Bellini's painting represents Lucrezia Borgia and her third husband, Alfonso d'Este.*

pagan world. It gave them what all aristocracies need, a sense of separateness, as certainly and as completely as chivalry and feudalism had given a sense of caste to the warrior knights of the Middle Ages. Classical mythology, Neoplatonism, the mysteries of the pagan world, became chic. The education of a gentleman took on the strong classical bias which it was not to lose until modern times. The popular philosophers—Ficino, Pico della Mirandola, the friends of painters as well as their patrons—encouraged the revival of these ancient allegories. But they were not to be shared with the vulgar. Taste, sensibility, were to be linked with esoteric, almost private, knowledge. Poets, philosophers, painters, should speak in the language of riddles, of mysteries, which the *cognoscenti* alone could read. Such an attitude bred a sense of singularity, of exclusiveness, which courts and courtiers found as seductive as sin. Even Leonardo jotted down in commonplace books the trivial riddles of the Sforza, and Pico boasted in a philosophical essay, "If I am not mistaken

it will be intelligible only to a few, for it is filled with many mysteries from the secret philosophies of the ancients." The esoteric, the mysterious, developed a fashionable cachet, and its cult opened the floodgates not only to much of the nonsense of late Neoplatonism, but also to astrology, to the language of emblems, and to the absurdities of late medieval bestiaries, and in the revival of learning was intermingled a great deal of hocus-pocus. Much, however, of this is germane to the image that Renaissance man created of himself and will be dealt with later, but this delight in an exclusive world of myth and mystery also influenced artistic expression profoundly. A naked Mars and Venus, tired but happy from their wanton sport, might shock the uninitiated, but the cultivated knew better. Mars, of course, was War, and Venus Love, so Love could conquer War and bring forth Peace. And if by chance Venus was wearing a bit of the armor, that merely illustrated that Love itself involved Strife. Such were simple allegories which even the fringe of the elite could

read, but the theology as well as the mythology of poetic virtue grew ever more complex in its expression. Bellini's *Feast of the Gods* is the subject of a monograph, and all the iconographic scholarship of the Western world has failed to probe the hidden meanings of Giorgione's *Tempest.* For those artists who felt keenly the mystery of things, the way of allegory often proved enriching. It enabled them to explore feeling, to describe atmosphere, to hint at hidden presences, and to still in one luminous moment the fever and the fret of life and give its transience significance. So the *Virgin of the Rocks,* or even the *Mona Lisa,* possesses a sense of depth, of the abiding value of individual life, of eternal knowledge, that is both nostalgic and humane.

Giorgione responded to this sense of awareness as well as to Leonardo's mastery of light and shade. In Giorgione's paintings, and in many of Titian's, the value of earthly life is increased and given a significance that is as remote from the Middle Ages as it is from China.

A great artist like Giorgione could give universality to a private and exclusive myth, indeed deepen his genius by indulging in it, but many lesser artists could not. In their hands the mysteries became hollow, the allegories obvious and banal. Also, this cult of a private language of art marks the drift of the tide. The great masterpieces of the Renaissance had been, and many of them even in the first quarter of the sixteenth century still were, great public performances, even if they were created for popes or princes. But increasingly the direction of art was toward private enjoyment, and its style both more aristocratic and more exclusive. This was bound to be, as the heroic age of the city-state waned; as power and wealth and the sense of opportunity passed to the sea-borne nations of the West. Yet the achievement was so fabulously great that the traditions created in four or five generations proved far too strong for the creative imagination to wither quickly, and for the next four hundred years the arts of Italy continued to entrance the mind of Europe.

The Young Michelangelo

by KENNETH CLARK

Michelangelo belongs to that small company of poets, artists, and musicians whose greatness has never been seriously questioned; but he differs from his companions—Dante, Shakespeare, Goethe, Titian, Mozart—in one important way. All of them have maintained this hold on our admiration by appealing to a wide range of human experience, so that each generation may extract from their works what suits it best. But Michelangelo has made his own terms with posterity, just as he did with his employers. He is the most concentrated and undeviating of great artists. We come to him for one particular revelation, communicated by one particular means. And the revelation is so important to us, and the mastery of means so absolute, that having once experienced it we, like his contemporaries, can never get it out of our systems. It makes everything else seem small and tame and worldly.

When we speak of an artist's greatness, as opposed to his talent or even his genius, we are usually referring to an aspect of his personality, and this is particularly true of Michelangelo. We know about him from many contemporary records, including the two *Lives* of Condivi and Vasari, men who knew him well, and every one of these records gives us the impression of an awe-inspiring character. Leaving aside the great religious teachers, I cannot think of any other man in history who has commanded such respect.

Our visual image of Michelangelo is of an old man, his face deeply marked by spiritual struggles. But there is a quantity of evidence that as a young man his force of character was equally apparent. The following episode recorded by Condivi will serve as an example. In 1506 Michelangelo had left Rome in a huff because he had been debarred from immediate access to Pope Julius II. Seven months later Michelangelo was brought into the papal presence. Julius asked him why he had walked out. Michelangelo answered, "Not from ill will, but from disdain" (*ma per isdegno*). A bishop who was present nervously intervened, "Pay no attention, Your Holiness; he speaks out of ignorance. Artists are all like that." But before the wretched bishop could finish his apology he was hustled out of the room with blows; and Michelangelo resumed his former relationship with the Pope. Julius was then the most formidable figure in Christendom; Michelangelo was thirty-two.

Michelangelo in later years, by one of his followers.

Michelangelo used this transcendent force of character, which was like the spiritual power of a medieval saint, to transform the physical perfection of antiquity. He appeared at the moment when Greco-Roman sculpture was a new and compelling discovery, accepted by artists and patrons alike as an ultimate model. But in fact the bland materialism of antique art could not alone have expressed the crisis of the human spirit which took place during the years between Luther and Galileo. Michelangelo, by changing and twisting the forms of antique sculpture, created an instrument through which the spiritual turmoil of the sixteenth century could be made visible.

He was born in Florentine territory on March 6, 1475, and was one of the very few artists to come of aristocratic stock, although by his time the family fortunes had declined. His father, who claimed descent from the counts of Canossa, strongly objected to his son becoming an artist, which at that date meant an artisan; and when Michelangelo was one of the most famous men in Italy, his father still regarded the whole affair with bewildered incredulity. He was, as Condivi says, "somewhat old-fashioned"; but Michelangelo treated him with patience and respect, asked for his prayers and sent him money, and often said that his sole aim in life had been to help the family regain its former status.

From the very first no one had any doubt that he was supremely gifted in the arts of design. After a short apprenticeship with Ghirlandaio, the most successful Florentine painter of the period, he is said by his biographers to have joined the privileged youths who were drawing antiques in the Medici gardens of the Via Larga, under the direction of the sculptor Bertoldo, and where he attracted the attention of Lorenzo the Magnificent. I see no adequate reason for disbelieving this tradition, and Michelangelo's earliest carvings seem to confirm it, for they consist largely of imitations of the antique, of a kind which he would have learned only in this particular school. Bertoldo's own masterpiece was a bronze relief of a battle, done in imitation of an antique sarcophagus in Pisa; and Michelangelo's earliest carving is also an imitation of a battle sarcophagus, although the nominal subject is the *Rape of Dejanira*. Although it was surely begun in the Medicean academy (and was perhaps left unfinished on Lo-

renzo's death in 1492) it looks out of this enchanted garden, both backwards and forwards: back to the charged and passionate Last Judgments of the Pisani and forward to the achievements of Michelangelo's maturity. There is no more striking example of Proust's saying, *"Les grands artistes n'ont jamais fait qu'une seule oeuvre."* Michelangelo's first great carving foreshadows not only the classical style of his Florentine period, but the anticlassical expressiveness of his later works. In many respects it is closer to the *Last Judgment* of the Sistine than to the cartoon of the *Battle of Cascina*. And the affinity with the Dantesque spirit of Giovanni Pisano is also very revealing, for Michelangelo's heroic seriousness was, perhaps unconsciously, a reaction away from the daintiness of the *quattrocento,* back to the passion and gravity of the first founders of Tuscan art. His earliest drawings were copies of Giotto, and the poems of Dante were his continual inspiration.

But the Dejanira relief is exceptional. During his years in the garden of the Via Larga, and for some time afterward, Michelangelo's whole conscious effort was directed toward the imitation of the classical style, and he succeeded so well that one of his works, a sleeping cupid, was actually sold as an antique, having been buried in a vineyard by a Roman dealer. When the fraud was discovered, Michelangelo, unlike modern imitators of antiquity, derived nothing but credit for his skill, and the cupid was afterwards purchased by that most pedantic of collectors, Isabella d'Este. It has now disappeared, and the *Bacchus*, which survives from about the same epoch, suggests that the loss is not a serious one. For the *Bacchus* is an all too successful imitation of Hellenistic sculpture at its least attractive. The swaying, dreamy movement of the body and a certain Dionysiac beauty in the head do not compensate for the lack of tension in the modeling, and one is left wondering how Michelangelo, even in a technical exercise, has contrived to suppress his energy of hand.

The *Bacchus* was executed in Rome, soon after Michelangelo's arrival there in 1496. After the death of Lorenzo de' Medici in 1492 he had remained two years in Florence, and it was at this time that he is supposed to have begun a scientific study of anatomy, under the protection of the Prior of Santo Spirito. These were the years when Savonarola was the virtual ruler of Florence, and although Michelangelo was never a direct follower, he read Savonarola's books throughout his life, and told Condivi that he could still hear the *frate*'s voice ringing in his ears. So two essential ingredients of Michelangelo's art, a passion for anatomy and a consciousness of sin, were, so to say, poured into his mind at the same moment. But he was not happy in the Florence of Piero de' Medici; and in October, 1494, there occurred the first of those panic flights which were to be repeated three times in the course of his life. Psychologists have occupied themselves with the question why this man of immense moral courage, who was utterly indifferent to physical hardship, should have suffered from these recurrences of irrational fear; and perhaps it is true that continuous inner tension led to an occasional snapping of the spirit, which expressed itself in a sudden need to escape. Or perhaps in each case there really was some ground for running away, and Michelangelo, who recognized his own genius, felt that he must preserve his life at any cost. In 1494 he fled to Bologna, where, as usual, his gifts were immediately recognized and he was commissioned to work on the chief sculptural project of the town, the ark of Saint Dominic; but fifteenth-century Bologna offered no scope to a youth of Michelangelo's genius, and as soon as possible he returned to Florence, and thence to Rome.

He arrived in Rome in the summer of 1496, having a letter of introduction from Lorenzo di Pierfrancesco de' Medici, the pupil of Marsilio Ficino and friend of Botticelli; and a week after his arrival he wrote back to Lorenzo, "There are many beautiful things here." Medieval Rome, the city of vineyards and cow pastures, with its stranded basilicas and aggressive watch towers, was just beginning to give up its buried treasure; and Michelangelo's chief patron at this epoch, Jacopo Galli, had already a considerable collection of antiquities, amongst which Michelangelo's *Bacchus* was given a place of honor. However, the outstanding work during this first visit to Rome was of an entirely different character, the *Pietà* in St. Peter's. It was commissioned by a French cardinal, Jean Bilheres, and this may account for the fact that Michelangelo accepted a Gothic motif in which the full-grown Christ lies on Our Lady's knees. This was originally a wood-carving motif,

and the difficulty of adapting it to the crystalline character of marble has led Michelangelo to a marvelous feat of technical skill. This is the first work in which he shows that consummate mastery of his craft which his contemporaries, both artists and patrons, valued so highly. It has also involved a new stretch of the imagination, for he has achieved what theorists tell us is impossible, a perfect fusion of Gothic and Classic art. The motif and sentiment are northern, the physical beauty of the nude Christ is Greek; and Michelangelo has given the Virgin's head, so painfully distorted in Gothic Pietàs, a union of physical and spiritual beauty which is entirely his own. Ever since the *Pietà* was put in place, people have asked how the mother of a grown man, in the depths of grief, could appear so young and beautiful; and Michelangelo's reply is recorded in both Vasari and Condivi. It expresses in vivid, colloquial form the doctrines of Neoplatonism, which he had absorbed from the Medicean philosophers of his boyhood: that physical perfection is the mirror and emblem of a pure and noble spirit. This is the belief that had led his friend Lorenzo di Pierfrancesco to commission Botticelli's *Venus*; and we know, from Michelangelo's sonnets, that it justified to his mind his passionate admiration of the naked beauty of young men. Our scientific modern way of thinking, with its reliance on experience and psychology, may reject Neoplatonism as a compound of myth and self-deception. But there is no question of the sincerity with which Michelangelo believed (in Spenser's words) that "soule is form, and doth the bodie make."

In 1501 Michelangelo returned to Florence. These were the years in which the Florentine republic was able to assert some of the heroic virtues which had made it great a century before, and Michelangelo must have found the atmosphere of his native city a sharp contrast to the Medicean *douceur de vivre* of his youth, or the parasitic, antiquarian Rome of his more recent experience. It was an atmosphere which suited him perfectly, and he was immediately called upon by the city magistrates to carry out commissions which should express the pride, vigor, and austere idealism of their regime; and the results were the *David* and the cartoon of the *Battle of Cascina*.

The *David* was carved out of a gigantic block of marble from which, seventy years earlier, the sculptor Agostino di Duccio had begun to carve the figure of a prophet. Agostino had completed little more than a knot of drapery, and when at last the derelict block was given to Michelangelo, his first symbolic act was to cut this drapery away. In his austere and uncompromising nudity the *David* states for the first time the essence of Michelangelo's ideal. As a piece of modeling the torso is equal to the finest work of antiquity, both in science and plastic vitality. Cut out the head and the hands, and you have one of the most perfect classical works of the Renaissance. Put them back and you put back the rough Tuscan accent, which was part of his birthright. It is possible to feel that there is a certain lack of harmony between the two elements: the *David* is in many respects an imperfect work. The marble block was too thin, and apart from this material shortcoming, Michelangelo has made a mistake common at the time; he has taken a motif from a relief as the basis for a figure in the round. But if the whole is unsatisfactory, the *David*, taken part by part, is a work of overwhelming power and magnificence, and it is Michelangelo's first great assertion of that quality which is so often in our minds when we think of him—the heroic. I suppose that the heroic in life or art is based on the consciousness that life is a struggle; and that in this struggle it is courage, strength of will, and determination which are decisive, not intelligence nor sensibility. The heroic involves a contempt of convenience and a sacrifice of all those pleasures which contribute to what we call a civilized life. It is the enemy of happiness. But we recognize that it is man's supreme achievement. For the heroic is not merely a struggle with material obstacles; it is a struggle with Fate. Insofar as it magnifies the individual in his conflict with the blind forces of destiny it is the highest expression of a humanist ideal, and was recognized as such in antiquity. But the heroic stands on the borders of humanism, and looks beyond it. For to struggle with Fate man must become more than man; he must aspire to be a god. Now apotheosis announced the end of humanist art. If there is a single point at which the art of classical antiquity turns toward the Middle Ages, it is when the emperor is accepted as a god. The first great medieval work of art is the statue of Constantine at Barletta: and like the *David* it is of heroic size. So on the perfectly antique body of the *David* is set a

head which looks, with proud and conscious heroism, away from the happy, concrete world of the *quattrocento*. Like other great revolutions in history, we may wish that it had never happened, but once it has taken place we must accept it with all its potency for good or evil.

The mere size of the *David* (the statue stands over sixteen feet high), which is embarrassing to us, impressed Michelangelo's contemporaries. As a technical achievement alone it was a source of civic pride, like a space rocket. Significantly, the committee of artists who considered its site took it away from the cathedral and placed it in front of the Palazzo della Signoria, the center of democratic government. A few months later Michelangelo began, in this building, the other great composition of these heroic Florentine years, the *Battle of Cascina*. It was executed in rivalry with Leonardo da Vinci, but unlike his *Battle of Anghiari*, it was never carried out as a painting, and the cartoon on which it was drawn proved so irresistible to artists that it was soon cut up and lost. Vasari called it "the school of all the world," and Benvenuto Cellini was certainly voicing the professional verdict when he said that Michelangelo never did better. What gave it this immense authority? We can see from copies and from Michelangelo's original studies that it consisted of a number of naked men grouped in such a way as to show off the human body in action. Each body was not only an admirable human specimen modeled with scientific knowledge, but was in a pose selected for its completeness and nobility. Such poses were the legacy of antique art, surviving almost like symbols, through four hundred years of attrition; and in fact some of Michelangelo's drawings for the *Battle* are not done from nature, but from wax models he had made of antiques. So the *Battle of Cascina* was the foundation of the academic ideal, that strange, compelling approach to form which dominated art education until the present century; and the fact that Michelangelo himself transcended this ideal has always been a source of confusion to his more academic admirers.

For Michelangelo's vision of antique art was not bounded by the firm and finished outlines of the Cascina drawings. Throughout his life he had two ideals of antiquity which were in a sense complementary to each other. One of these was the ideal of perfection, the belief that what gave antique art its durability was the unflinching firmness with which every detail was realized. This had inspired the *Bacchus* and the *David*, and was to be realized, in later life, in those curious labors of love, the drawings executed for his friend Tommaso de' Cavalieri. For these the source of his inspiration was chiefly cameos and gems. But parallel with this admiration for its completeness, Michelangelo was fascinated by the fragmentary character of ancient sculpture; and the appeal of these weather-worn survivors of a mightier age was all the stronger because they gave a free play to the imagination. This attitude to ruins and fragments became common in what we call the Romantic Movement. Michelangelo was not the first man to feel it—Mantegna had already made evocative use of ruins—but he was the first to let it influence his style. Like the half lines in Virgil, the rough and unfinished state of Michelangelo's sculpture has evoked a whole literature of explanation, and no doubt the cause lies deep in his temperament. But I am certain that he was encouraged in this means of expression by the suggestive decay of antique sculpture. A proof of this dates from the very period of the *Battle* cartoon, the unfinished figure of Saint Matthew, commissioned by the Duomo in 1503 and executed a year or two later. It is imitated from a battered Roman figure, the so-called *Pasquino*, which had already inspired Donatello; and I doubt if this rather grotesque work would have had so compelling an appeal to the imaginations of two great artists had it been better preserved. In decay only the large lines of movement were perceptible, and gave the effect of a giant struggling out of the mists of antiquity.

This sense of titanic struggle was an aspect of Michelangelo's character which had appeared already in the Dejanira relief, and came more and more to dominate his art; and the crumbling magnificence of antique sculpture showed him that he could express it by leaving a great deal to the spectator's imagination. This also involved two other advantages which, although not consonant with the artistic principles of Michelangelo's time, appeal most strongly to our own: it allowed him to preserve the character of his material with the vivid mark of his own hand upon it; and it allowed him to dispense with those parts of a figure which did not fit into the main rhythm of his design, just as time has lopped off such excrescences as the arms of the *Torso Belvedere*.

This titanic struggle of form to emerge from matter reaches its climax in the marble figures destined for the tomb of Julius II. Michelangelo had been summoned to Rome in March, 1505, and commanded to design and execute the greatest tomb in Christendom. His new master was a formidable man of action, with a powerful mind and boundless ambition. He was also as proud and wilful as Michelangelo himself. Gorki once said of Tolstoy, "His relations with God are very uneasy: like two old bears in a den"; and such were Michelangelo's relations with God's vicar on earth. Yet it was one of those momentous conjunctions for which posterity must be grateful, for without Julius II, Michelangelo might never have had the opportunity of developing the full power of his imagination.

In the summer he went to Carrara to superintend the quarrying of blocks of marble big enough for the tomb, and for eight months he remained inaccessible in that awe-inspiring landscape, surrounded by stone. These long sojourns in Carrara, repeated several times in his life, were to Michelangelo like religious retreats, and were the prelude to spells of his greatest activity. He returned to Rome in the winter of 1505–1506, ready to concentrate all his force on executing his grandiose ideas. Then there occurred the first catastrophe in what, since Condivi, all writers on Michelangelo have called the tragedy of the tomb. Pope Julius refused to see him. It was Michelangelo's first experience of court intrigue and of the readiness with which princes allow themselves to be swayed by rival coteries. Later in life he accepted such intrigues with a firm and melancholy stoicism. But to the young man of thirty-one, his mind charged with colossal images, his spirit burning like a fire, this treachery was intolerable; and in April, 1506, he left Rome without a word and returned to Florence. For seven months the Pope tried to lure him back to Rome, but Michelangelo was suspicious and the Florentine government protected him. Finally, when the Pope conquered Bologna in November, Michelangelo felt bound to go there and ask for forgiveness, and there follows the scene I have already described. I should add that although Condivi says that he had this account from Michelangelo's own lips, contemporary documents suggest that the artist was considerably more penitent. Al-

A QUARREL WITH THE POPE

A letter from Michelangelo to the papal architect Giuliano da Sangallo, sent from Florence in 1506.

I learn from a letter sent by you that the Pope was angry at my departure, that he is willing to place the money at my disposal and to carry out what was agreed upon between us; also, that I am to come back and fear nothing.

As far as my departure is concerned, the truth is that on Holy Saturday I heard the Pope, speaking at table with a jeweler and the Master of the Ceremonies, say that he did not want to spend another baiocco on stones whether small or large, which surprised me very much. However, before I set out, I asked him for some of the money required for the continuance of my work. His Holiness replied that I was to come back again on Monday, and I went on Monday, and on Tuesday, and on Wednesday, and on Thursday,—as His Holiness saw. At last, on the Friday morning, I was turned out, that is to say, I was driven away; and the person who turned me away said he knew who I was, but that such were his orders. Thereupon, having heard those words on Saturday and seeing them afterward put into execution, I lost all hope. But this alone was not the whole reason of my departure. There was also another cause but I do not wish to write about it; enough that it made me think that, if I were to remain in Rome, my own tomb would be prepared before that of the Pope. This is the reason for my sudden departure.

Now you write to me on behalf of the Pope, and in similar manner you will read this letter to the Pope. Give His Holiness to understand that I am more eager to proceed with the work than ever I was before, and that if he really wishes to have this tomb erected it would be well for him not to vex me as to where the work is to be done, provided that within the agreed period of five years it be erected in St. Peter's, on the site he shall choose, and it be a beautiful work, as I have promised: for I am persuaded that it be a work without an equal in all the world if it be carried out.

If His Holiness now wishes to proceed, let him deposit the said money here in Florence . . .

most as a penance, he was commissioned to make a gigantic bronze statue of the Pope to go over the door of San Petronio in Bologna. It cost him one of the most miserable and unproductive years of his life; and shortly after it had been put in place, was broken up and melted down for the bronze.

At the beginning of March, 1508, he left Bologna for Florence, intending to settle down in his native town and complete the commissions that he had left unfinished there. He thought that he was "free of Rome"; but within two months his terrible old master had forced him to return there. What was worse, Julius did not allow him to finish the tomb, but gave him a new and in many ways unsuitable commission, to paint the ceiling of the papal chapel in the Vatican, known as the Sistine. Michelangelo's early biographers believed that the proposal was put forward by his enemy, Bramante, in order to discredit him; and it is true that Michelangelo accepted the commission under protest, complaining that painting was not his art. Documents show, however, that the proposal had been discussed two years earlier; and there is no doubt that Michelangelo had practiced painting. The *Holy Family* in the Uffizi, known as the Doni *tondo*, dates from 1504; and as an apprentice to Ghirlandaio he seems to have had a hand in the frescoes of Santa Maria Novella.

It was not as a technical, but as an intellectual feat that the Sistine ceiling involved such a vast extension of his faculties. Hitherto his sculptures had been concerned with single figures or traditional themes, and in the *Battle of Cascina,* the subject had been only a pretext for a pictorial exercise. Now he had to illustrate the first phase of human destiny, and what theologians called the world *ante legem.* He was no longer concerned with problems of form alone, but with problems of philosophy.

In the chief history paintings of the Renaissance, the artist was usually given a "program" by his patron or some attendant poet or philosopher. But Michelangelo, in a well-known letter, explains that he was told to work out his subject for himself. Even he could not conceive the whole theme in a single flash of inspiration. Both in subject and style it developed prodigiously as the work continued. Yet at some early point, Michelangelo recognized that the story of the Creation could be transformed from a fanciful narrative into a profound philosophy. He did so by compelling us to read his "histories" in a reverse order. Over our head, as we enter the chapel, is the *Drunkenness of Noah;* at the far end, over the altar, is the *Creation.* Thus the ceiling illustrates the Neoplatonic doctrine, so dear to Michelangelo, and so often expressed in his sonnets, that life must be a progression from the servitude of the body to the liberation of the soul. It begins with the inert figure of Noah, where the body has taken complete possession, and ends with the figure of the Almighty dividing light from darkness, in which the body has been completely transformed into a symbol of the spirit, and even the head, with its too evident human associations, has become indistinct.

The same evolution, both of spirit and style, can be seen in the so-called athletes, those deeply personal creations which come first to most people's minds at the mention of Michelangelo. They are not, as used to be supposed, mere decoration, but symbolize the thoughts of the prophets and seers in the spandrels and are a link between them and the histories. But because this subject is limited to the representation of a single naked youth, we are made more conscious of changes in style. At first they are classical in the narrow sense. They are symmetrical, bound by a firm outline, forming a closed rhythm, and several are actually derived from antique gems. The athletes on the middle of the ceiling, beside the Creation of Eve, are already less symmetrical and the unity of planes has been abandoned. In the last pair of athletes, those beside the Creation of Light, a balanced and reciprocal movement is entirely abandoned, and Michelangelo has created a continuous movement which twists round the central scene.

In the use of this twisting rhythm he is realizing an experience which he had stored away in his mind almost five years earlier, the impact of the famous antique group known as the *Laocoön.* It had been discovered in January, 1506, and Michelangelo had been one of the first to identify and admire it. No doubt he recognized immediately that it confirmed his own feelings about the potential expressiveness of the nude. But like most great poets and artists, he had a long period of gestation, and it was not till about 1510 that a reminiscence of the *Laocoön* is perceptible in his work. Then, finally, in the corner spandrels depicting the *Crucifixion of Hamar* and the *Brazen Serpent,* this new system of form, in which tormented rhythms and violent foreshortening are used to express mental and physical agony, is pushed to a limit never surpassed. By 1511 Michelangelo had anticipated almost every extremity of style which would engage the ingenuity of mannerist and baroque artists in the next hundred years.

Two years before the ceiling was completed it had begun to make itself felt by premonitory rumblings, like those which anticipate the theme in the last movement of Beethoven's Ninth Symphony. Raphael himself had been smuggled in by Bramante, and had immediately added a Michelangelesque figure to the already complete design of his fresco of the *School of Athens.*

When, on October 31, 1512, the frescoes were officially unveiled, artists and connoisseurs were prepared for something which should change the course of painting; and that, in fact, is what it did; and not only painting, but the whole mode of feeling. The freshness and wonder of the early Renaissance, the delight in living things unburdened with a conscience, birds, children, flowers—all this was crushed by the oppressive awareness of human destiny. And instead of a natural ease of arrangement in which flower was set beside flower and face beside face, there came into being the new unity of struggle, the unity of Hercules grappling with the lion.

On October 31, 1512, when the ceiling was finally unveiled, Michelangelo was thirty-seven. He lived to be eighty-nine. In this half century he executed some of his greatest works—the marble prisoners, the Medici tombs, the *Last Judgment,* the marvelous and tragic Pietàs of his old age. The mood becomes graver; the confidence in physical beauty diminishes, and is at last rejected with a kind of horror. But fundamentally there is an unvarying aim; to use the human body as an instrument with which to reveal the ascent of the human soul. The body must perish: and Michelangelo became increasingly preoccupied with death; the soul must be judged; and he became more and more burdened by the consciousness of sin. But in his imagination body and soul remain indivisible, fatally united in their struggle; and out of this involvement he creates movements, gestures, limbs, proportions which allow us poor worldlings, with our sordid material interests, to become, through the contemplation of form, momentarily capable of spiritual life.

Two Sonnets by
MICHELANGELO

Although Michelangelo wrote his impassioned sonnets on art and love and his controversial verses against papal corruption only for circulation among his friends, after the artist's death his great-nephew published them in an expurgated version which smoothed out rough versification and censored any ideas which might be objectionable to the Church. In this translation by the nineteenth-century Renaissance scholar John Addington Symonds, the sonnets are restored to their original form.

ON THE PAINTING OF THE SISTINE CHAPEL

to Giovanni da Pistoia

I've grown a goiter by dwelling in this den—
     As cats from stagnant streams in Lombardy,
     Or in what other land they hap to be—
     Which drives the belly close beneath the chin:
My beard turns up to heaven; my nape falls in,
     Fixed on my spine: my breast-bone visibly
     Grows like a harp: a rich embroidery
     Bedews my face from brush-drops thick and thin.
My loins into my paunch like levers grind:
     My buttock like a crupper bears my weight;
     My feet unguided wander to and fro;
In front my skin grows loose and long; behind,
     By bending it becomes more taut and strait;
     Crosswise I strain me like a Syrian bow:
     Whence false and quaint, I know,
     Must be the fruit of squinting brain and eye;
     For ill can aim the gun that bends awry.
     Come then, Giovanni, try
     To succor my dead pictures and my fame,
     Since foul I fare and painting is my shame.

THE ARTIST AND HIS WORK

How can that be, lady, which all men learn
     By long experience? Shapes that seem alive,
     Wrought in hard mountain marble, will survive
     Their maker, whom the years to dust return!
Thus to effect cause yields. Art hath her turn,
     And triumphs over Nature. I, who strive
     With Sculpture, know this well; her wonders live
     In spite of time and death, those tyrants stern.
So I can give long life to both of us
     In either way, by color or by stone,
     Making the semblance of thy face and mine.
Centuries hence when both are buried, thus
     Thy beauty and my sadness shall be shown,
     And men shall say, "For her 'twas wise to pine."

A RENAISSANCE IN ART

Grieving over the disappearance of arts which had once flourished in antiquity, the architect Leon Battista Alberti came to Florence, and to his delight encountered there a new generation of artists with a "talent for every noble thing." They even surpassed the ancients, he decided, for with no models to imitate or teachers to follow, they had discovered "arts and sciences unheard of and never seen." Alberti caught their spirit; he codified new rules of perspective and determined harmonious proportions for his architecture by measuring musical intervals. Other Florentine artists invented ideal proportions for the human form, dissected corpses to learn anatomy, composed pictures upon mathematical formulas. The Venetian school soon rivaled Florence, and its richly painted nudes and sensitive landscapes established an enduring tradition in European art. But Florence produced Michelangelo, the supreme artist of the Renaissance. He found landscape painting trivial and portraiture almost as unsatisfactory; his great obsession was the human figure, which he employed as the expression of man in torment, struggling heroically, as in the red chalk drawings of Hercules reproduced above, against the forces of destiny.

Within the "Zone of Heaven," the central section of the Sistine Chapel ceiling, Michelangelo painted a series of heroic nude athletes, whose beauty and energetic movement reflect the artist's physical and spiritual ideals. The figure on the facing page, who borders the panel where God divides the light from the darkness, and the one in the drawing at right, a chalk study for another of the youths, reveal Michelangelo's careful study of Roman sculpture. The clay model of a reclining river god (below), designed for one of the Medici tombs in the New Sacristy of San Lorenzo at Florence, bears the influence of classical Greece and is similar to figures on the Parthenon. Although Michelangelo's inspiration was classical (his system of proportion probably was derived from Polyclitus), his unique treatment of the male nude, with its flowing movement, tensed muscles, and massive torso, was a major departure from the blander forms of antiquity.

THE
PATRONAGE
OF
POPES

Banging against the scaffolding, clattering tools, groaning over the discomfort of working on his back, Michelangelo loudly interrupted the celebration of Mass while he painted the ceiling of the Sistine Chapel. Pope Julius II, raging at his slowness, threatened to throw him off the scaffolding unless he speeded up the work, but Michelangelo ignored him. The Pope finally clambered up to his perch and whacked him with his cane, but it still took four years for the artist to complete the enormous frescoes.

Other papal taskmasters were less excitable than Julius, but fully as difficult. The thrifty Giulio de' Medici, later Clement VII, refused to use Carrara marble on the façade of his family's church in Florence, so Michelangelo had to waste a year organizing new quarries in Florentine territory, where the revenues would revert to the Medici treasury. At Clement's orders, Michelangelo ignored his commitments to the heirs of Julius II, who were badgering him to finish Julius' tomb, and devoted his efforts instead to projects glorifying the Medici family. When Clement asked for a colossus over three times the height of the gigantic *David*, Michelangelo finally rebelled, and pointedly proposed putting bells in its head to peal for mercy for parishioners of the Medici church.

THE GREAT SCULPTOR

If his marble developed a flaw or was so hard that the chisel struck sparks, Michelangelo had to abandon a statue, no matter how far he had progressed with it; and when the Arno dried up, no shipments of marble reached his studio in Florence at all. Incompetent assistants who mutilated toes, overpolished, or knocked noses out of joint exasperated him constantly; but the chief obstacle to Michelangelo's progress was his own rigid standard of criticism. If he were compelled to satisfy himself, he told Vasari, he would show little or nothing. Once a work had been seen in public he never tried to correct it, but began another version resolved not to make the same mistakes again. Patrons were understandably impatient; one Roman, who had waited seven years for a figure of the risen Christ, panicked when Michelangelo offered to take back the second version of his statue and start all over again. "It shows the loftiness of your mind," the patron wrote diplomatically, "that you wish to replace a work which could not be better by one that is better," but he refused to allow a replacement, and for once Michelangelo was forced to be satisfied.

Michelangelo was working on the Rondanini Pietà *(right) during the week in which he died. The* Captive *at left, planned for the colossal tomb of* Julius II, *is also unfinished. It was Julius who commissioned Michelangelo to paint the Sistine Chapel ceiling (overleaf). The artist's original plan called only for figures of the twelve Apostles, but he later substituted the great series of Old Testament scenes—the stages of Creation, man's temptation and Fall, the Deluge, and other Biblical events—on the huge ceiling.*

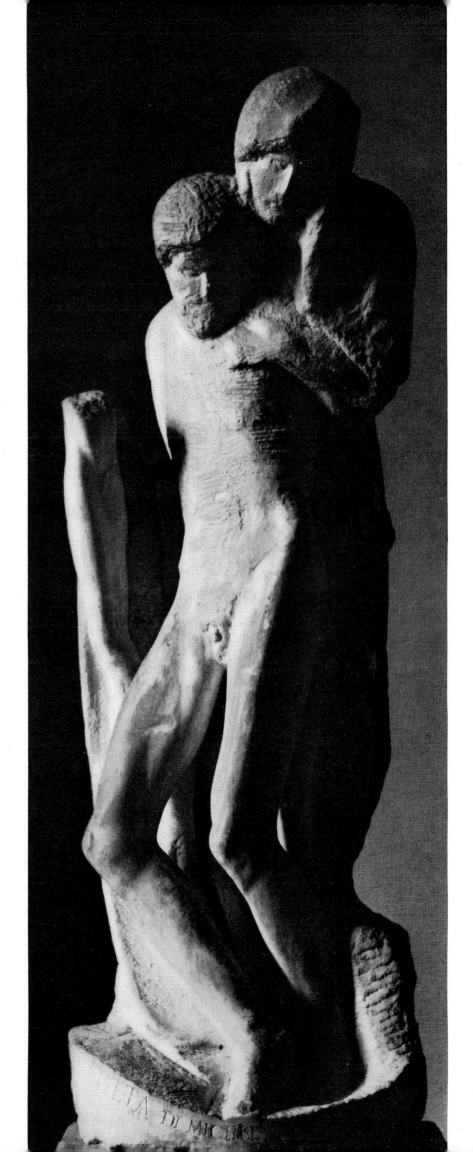

Fascinated by the scientific study of art, Renaissance painters filled their sketchbooks with measured drawings of the human figure, like the full face above by Leonardo, and the tilted one, at far right, by Piero della Francesca. Uccello preferred to draw detailed perspective studies of complex forms; typical are the skeletal chalice above, and the swirling rosette of ribbons, which is a mosaic in the Cathedral of St. Mark at Venice. The greatest mathematician of all was Piero, whose mysterious Flagellation of Christ (right), perhaps painted for the court of Urbino, was carefully constructed on a geometric framework. The basic unit of measure, one-tenth the width of the canvas, is a horizontal black bar above the hat of the bearded figure in the foreground. Mathematical ratios relate this unit to ceiling panels and pavement squares, to columns, figures, and the radius of the circle in which Christ is bound.

PERSPECTIVE

Painting had been largely a craftsman's trade until Brunelleschi and others began demonstrating their new theories of linear perspective with the aid of mathematical principles. The rules of mathematics helped raise painting to the realm of the liberal arts, and painters, alert to social as well as aesthetic advantages, were quick to grasp them. Soon artists were studying optics, writing textbooks on geometry, laboring over complex formulas to perfect tiny details of compositions. Hats, mountains, even people began to assume geometric forms; and tiled pavements and rows of columns, receding with mathematical regularity into the distance, were used to increase a painting's depth. To echo the fashionable humanist theory that harmonious numbers unify the universe, pictures were constructed on a mathematical framework in which a numerical ratio related every object to the total composition. But painters rarely used a perspective as strict in its limitations as the one Brunelleschi had developed, which depended on a single point of view. Most artists varied their techniques. They retained the old craftsmen's rules—warm colors jump forward; cool ones, like blue and green, recede—to supplement linear perspective; and adapted Brunelleschi's theses to focus compositions from several points of view, to keep perspective from tilting awry as the observer shifted his position.

THE PORTRAIT

The laws of antiquity, one Renaissance scholar stated, had forbidden artists to paint the portrait of anyone who was not a prince or a wise or virtuous man; but now, he complained, any low or infamous man could have his picture painted. The art of portraiture had been developed to glorify the great, and Pisanello's first portrait medal, a Byzantine emperor, continued an imperial Roman tradition which the Renaissance copied from ancient coins that had lately been unearthed. But soon petty princes, humanists, and even merchants began to commission their portraits on medals to send to friends as mementos. Florentine painters filled church frescoes with pictures of recognizable individuals, and sculptors modeled their work—statues of saints and of Plato himself—on the features of specific men. Scandalized preachers complained that these portraits served vanity, not religion, and painters soon realized that they distracted observers from the fresco itself.

The use of idealized images returned to fashion, and the taste for easel portraits spread as fresco portraiture waned. The sharply limned likenesses of the fifteenth century gave way to dramatic character studies, representing both the sitter's image and his inner nobility, propaganda portraits designed to satisfy the Renaissance thirst for individual glory.

Future generations, a court poet predicted, would praise the union of art and nature in Leonardo da Vinci's portrait (above) of Cecilia Gallerani, Lodovico Sforza's beautiful mistress. Leonardo had striven to reproduce far more than Cecilia's appearance: "Paint the face," he once recommended, "in such a way that it will be easy to understand what is going on in the mind." Earlier painters, like Pisanello, had ignored psychology, recording only the sitter's features. His medal of Leonello d'Este (right) posed the Marquis of Ferrara in a realistic but uncharitable profile, for in low relief a profile could be more precise than a full-face view. Botticelli balanced his own psychological insights with detailed description of the sitter; his glowing portrait (opposite) of Giovanni di Pierfrancesco de' Medici, who posed holding a medieval religious image, is idealized but highly suggestive of the young man's characteristics.

THE NUDE

"Begin with the bones," the scholar Alberti advised in the first scientific treatise ever written on painting. "Then add the muscles, and then cover the body with flesh in such a way as to leave the position of the muscles visible." Anatomy lessons were part of an artist's training, and the results were soon as explicit as Alberti's instructions had been. Painters labored patiently over muscular nudes rippling with anatomical detail, and were so fascinated by scientific study of the human body that Signorelli, it was said, even dissected the corpse of his own son. But artists eventually outgrew the need to display a pedant's knowledge of anatomy. Instead, they idealized the male body, like Michelangelo, or like the Venetians, turned to the female form for the more subtle and difficult transitions of its soft contours. Florence preferred demure female nudes, and Botticelli's Venus seems almost virginal; but in Venice sensuality was more assertive. There, painters endowed their compositions with mature, unblushing nudes, on the humanist theory that the naked body was a symbol of innocence, and its beauty a reflection of intellectual or spiritual splendor. Renaissance artists saw no conflict between flesh and spirit, and their uninhibited love for the body recreated a concept of the nude which was as voluptuous and idealized as that of the classical artists whom they longed to equal.

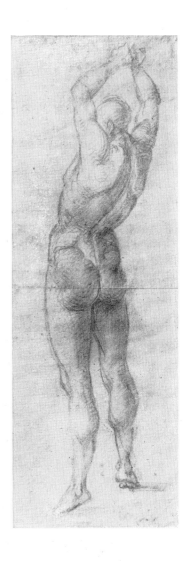

Titian was eighty when he painted the sensuous nudes of Diana and Actaeon. The goddess of chastity and her attendant nymphs are conceived with a ripe freedom which had been developed by Italian artists after more than a century of careful anatomical studies, such as Signorelli's fine drawing (right) of a muscular torso.

As ambitious princes cleared the highways of robbers and cultivated model farms according to agricultural precepts recommended by Virgil, the Italian countryside emerged as a new Arcadia. Fashionable poets, mooning over rural scenery, scribbled eclogues celebrating the joys of country life; painters followed their lead, cradling Holy Families and pensive saints in a hospitable landscape of gentle meadows and hills. Far behind was the stony wilderness of earlier paintings where hermits wandered through deserts to prove their saintliness, where jagged rocks, borrowed from Byzantine art, reflected nature's hostility to man. Now another tradition predominated. Man was completely at home in nature. Fantastic rocks, once merely emblems of mountains, were painted as realistic studies of natural formations. Portraits showed, beyond the sitter's shoulder, lovingly detailed views of the countryside; even in altar pieces and other religious paintings it was the custom to use the local landscape as the background for a Biblical event. Finally the landscape became important enough to dominate a picture. Florentine landscape painters were factual observers. The Venetian school began with a realism as exact but under Giorgione's lead soon transformed it, modeling precise details of the countryside into luminous idyls. The Venetian ideal—tranquil, poetic, and unified by light—eventually became traditional in European art.

Meticulous concern for the description of nature is evident in Giovanni Bellini's masterpiece, Saint Francis in Ecstasy *(right). But there were alternate ways of treating landscape. Giorgione idealized his pastoral scene (top left, a detail from* The Adoration of the Shepherds). *The painter of the* Thebaid *(center) used bleak conventional rock forms symbolically, to show the desert's hostility. Lazzaro Bastiani placed Saint Jerome (below) in a landscape of sheer fantasy, beside a rocky but optimistic highway to heaven.*

LANDSCAPE

FLORENCE
CRADLE OF HUMANISM

"In a few hours they were burnt, their legs and arms gradually dropping off; part of their bodies remaining hanging to the chains, a quantity of stones were thrown to make them fall, as there was a fear of the people getting hold of them; and then the hangman and those whose business it was, hacked down the post and burnt it on the ground, bringing a lot of brushwood, and stirring the fire up over the dead bodies, so that the very least piece was consumed. Then they fetched carts, and accompanied by the mace-bearers, carried the last bit of dust to the Arno, by the Ponte Vecchio, in order that no remains should be found," wrote Landucci in his diary after watching the execution of Savonarola and his disciples. So ended the strange, doom-haunted Dominican monk from Ferrara, whose bitter tirades against luxury, greed, extortion, and tyranny had torn Florentine society apart.

The Piazza in which Savonarola met his end was adorned with some of the most profoundly moving works of Renais-

sance art. He had given the apocalyptic sermons for which he was condemned under the vaulting dome of the cathedral, itself a triumph of the new architecture. Among his audience had sat the flower of Italian humanism—Pico della Mirandola, Poliziano, and Marsilio Ficino, the president of the Platonic Academy—and he told them roughly that an old woman knew more of faith than their Plato. Even Lorenzo de' Medici, the greatest of all Florentine patrons, had sought his friendship, only to be spurned. Savonarola rejected the Renaissance. He would have none of it, ignoring the fact that for a hundred years Florence had led Italy in painting, in sculpture, in philosophy, in sophistication. Of all Italian cities, Florence had been the cradle of the Renaissance, but curiously, except in its very earliest days, the spirit of Savonarola had always been abroad. Florence was a city of violent contrasts, a city of the light and the dark.

Physically Florence deceives: the golden Tuscan land-

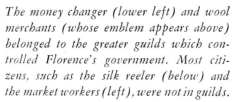

The money changer (lower left) and wool merchants (whose emblem appears above) belonged to the greater guilds which controlled Florence's government. Most citizens, such as the silk reeler (below) and the market workers (left), were not in guilds.

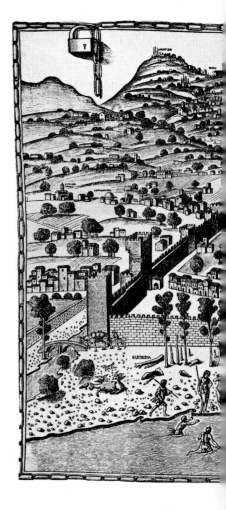

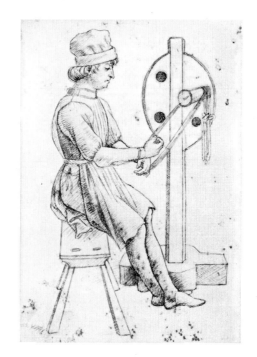

scape, so rich, so fertile, so gentle in climate, bespeaks a pastoral, idyllic, Virgilian life in which the rhythms of living achieve a harmony with nature. Here, if anywhere, is a countryside made for a Giorgione or a Titian, yet Florence produced neither, nor indeed any painter who sought to immortalize the poetry of nature. The facts of Florentine life were brutal, not gentle. Rich and beautiful its situation might be; economically and strategically its position was always desperate. To the west, controlling its only outlet to the sea, lay Pisa, prosperous and powerful, linked by its commerce with the four corners of the Mediterranean world. Athwart the route to Pisa, Florence had an unbeatable enemy in Lucca. To the north, the peril was worse—Milan, ravenous for land and rich in men and money. To the south, almost on Florence's doorstep, Siena controlled the road to Rome, and the Sienese were as fiercely proud and warlike as the Florentines. To the east were the wolves, the ravagers, the petty tyrants of

the Papal Patrimony who lived by war and violence; for these despots the rich lands of Tuscany were sweet to plunder. To survive, therefore, let alone expand, Florence required from its citizens both courage and resourcefulness, a willingness to practice the arts of diplomacy as well as war. Both needed money, and, in the last analysis, wealth and wealth alone enabled Florence to survive and to triumph over the disadvantages of its geographical situation. The realities of Florentine life were the sword and the florin. The use of both was improved by skill in reading human nature, and it is not surprising that a preoccupation with man and his destiny lies at the heart of the Florentine Renaissance.

Despite all its perils, Florence triumphed. The prime source of its strength and wealth lay in its *arti*—the guilds which drew together its merchants and skilled craftsmen. One of the earliest to be organized was the *arte di Calimala,* and throughout the golden age of Florence it held its dominating

Brunelleschi's dome dominates Florence in a woodcut done about 1486. Feudal towers dot the city, but new mansions such as the Pitti palace, in the center of the walled section at far right, across the Arno from the cathedral, relieve the medieval appearance.

position. It was a company of merchants who traded with England, Flanders, and France, bringing undressed cloths to Florence, where they were reworked into fine materials and dyed in the splendid, vivid colors that the Renaissance painters have made so memorable—the blues and crimsons and reds in which they dressed their saints and madonnas. They exported the finished goods throughout Europe, and the stamp of the guild became a guarantee of worth and workmanship. The guild was meticulously ruled and its members subjected to a close discipline not only in their public, but also in their moral life. The *Calimala* became a model for the other great guilds that began to dominate Florentine economic and political life in the late twelfth and early thirteenth centuries. Including the *Calimala* there were seven of them—the wool merchants, the silk weavers, the bankers, the notaries, the druggists (Dante was a member of this guild, which also dealt in spices and precious stones), and

the furriers. These seven included all the great merchants of Florence, who formed the heart of its economic life. But Florence was a large town, and it served a populous hinterland, and its shopkeepers were numerous enough, and powerful enough, to form their own guilds, which were known as the lesser arts—the innkeepers, shoemakers, carpenters, blacksmiths, grocers, bakers, and the like—fourteen in all. Each guild had its officers of state—its consuls, its notaries, and its banner-bearer (*gonfaloniere*) who carried the heraldic symbols in the great processions which were held on the day of their patron saint. Each guild, too, had its church which it patronized and in which were held its special masses, for these merchants were as deeply steeped in religion as in trade. (At the head of each page of one of their surviving account books is the sign of the cross, made to make forgery hell-worthy.) The Florentine guilds were small worlds unto themselves, closely regulated, self-conscious, jealous of their

Thirty thousand neighboring farms, one
Florentine citizen boasted, annually yield
"bread and meat, wine and oil, vegetables
and cheese, hay and wood to the value of
nine hundred thousand ducats in cash."
Even in time of want, Florence tried to
feed the poor. The miniature opposite
shows refugees from a famine in Siena receiving supplies outside the walls of Florence. Behind them is the octagonal Baptistery, with façade patterned of black and
white marble. Even in the midst of plenty,
famine could strike Florence, too. At left,
an angel hovering over the grain market
trumpets a call for rejoicing at abundance,
with a reminder that scarcity may follow
it. Both miniatures illustrate a fourteenth-
century trader's record of prices and profits.

rights and customs, and fully aware of their power.

Naturally, relations between the greater and lesser guilds
were often uneasy. The lesser guilds felt their numbers gave
them a right to power; the greater knew that, in the last resort, it was their money which sustained the government of
Florence both in peace and in war. Yet there were never more
than three or four thousand men in these twenty-one guilds,
and Florence embraced nearly a hundred thousand souls. The
bulk of the population was proletarian—workers for a day
wage: spinning, dyeing, weaving, carding, or hauling the
great bales of wool and cloth and silk—the citizens who, in
the very beginning, had fought for the liberties within the
city and for its rich territories without, the people into whose
hearts Savonarola's words burned like fire. They were organized into four districts, each with four quarters led by a gon-
falon—the Unicorn, the Viper, the Lion—under which each
citizen was enrolled to fight, if need be, for his city's liberty.

From these quarters were drawn the governors of the city
who made up the Signory which ruled Florence, made peace
or war, and levied the taxes. Naturally, the Signory was attended with immense ceremonial and its chief officers, the
priors, lived in grandeur, but their tenure was as brief as a
butterfly's, for they ruled for two months only. To control
this complex governmental machine, men fought in the
streets, assassinated, exiled, pillaged, and destroyed each
other generation after generation, so that one Florentine
gloomily remarked that there were enough citizens in exile
to populate another city. The main strife revolved about who
should or who should not be prior-worthy—whether, in fact,
power should be widely distributed or kept close—and
whether the major arts or the minor arts should dominate
the institutions of government. There was factional strife not
only within the ranks of the guilds but among the restless
proletariat, often made politically conscious by the hunger

of their bellies, for Florence suffered the sharp economic storms of an uncontrolled capitalism. So over the centuries power in Florence swayed like sea-weed in a tide, drifting into the hands of oligarchs only to be snatched out, but never for long, by a great upsurging wave of popular feeling.

During most of the Renaissance, political power in Florence was in the hands of a group of very rich merchants, led by the Medici family. This closely knit oligarchy controlled all the elections to office with the sureness of a Tammany machine. Better still for them, they handled the city's taxes. And, of course, they were the inheritors of the vast wealth which the far-flung trade of Florence had drawn from the four quarters of Europe.

Suspicious, guarded, rich, the oligarchs clung tenaciously to their power, willing to serve the Medici only as long as the Medici served them. Their greed and envy occasionally drew them close to conspiracy, and the plot of the Pazzi family to kill the Medici in the Duomo toppled some of them into disastrous treason. Politically and financially these men had little foresight: they exploited their power to siphon the city's riches into their own pockets. Yet they had one saving grace: they had been born into a tradition of civic patronage. Their fathers, and their fathers before them, had endowed monasteries, beautified churches, and established charities. A sense of sin still clung to usury and to the banker's trade, and they had felt a need to return a tithe of their profits. Naturally, they were stirred by particular acts of God's goodness to them, and then their piety turned more quickly into patronage. Yet about 1400 this tradition began to change, both in its nature and its expression.

This change was wrought by a desperate war, working on the literary and artistic movements which had already seeded themselves in Florence, and the result was a remarkable leap forward in painting, in sculpture, in architecture, in phil-

Reliefs on the façade of Giotto's campanile reflect Florence's devotion to humanist studies. The medallion at left represents logic, with portraits of Plato and Aristotle. The one below it shows a grammar lesson.

osophy, and in the countless arts and crafts that adorn the life of man. The change was as dramatic as water turning into ice.

After its failure by 1343 to secure dominion of Tuscany by force of arms, Florence had resolved to ally, whenever possible, with neighboring city-states, to protect rather than absorb. As Coluccio Salutati, the chancellor of Florence and one of its first great humanists, wrote, the Florentines who hated tyranny at home were willing to defend the liberties of others. The feeling was strong in the city's governing circles that Florentines were the true heirs of republican Rome: Salutati, Bruni, and Poggio studied Cicero in their leisure from running Florence's diplomacy and collecting its taxes. His ideas, which lie at the heart of humanism, struck them with the force of a new discovery, and they began to weave afresh the belief that the full life, indeed, the good life, could only be lived if a man dedicated himself to civic virtues. It was about

Rome, about Cicero, about Plato, that they talked when they lingered in the sun in the Piazza or gathered together in each other's houses. Nor did they disdain to discuss their ideas with the sculptors and artists—Ghiberti, Donatello, Brunelleschi—whom they and their friends patronized. And how right they seemed in their interpretation of the past and the present, when Florence withstood alone the might of Gian Galeazzo Visconti, who, in 1402, stood poised to overwhelm the city and so bring the whole of Lombardy and Tuscany under his sway. Then, as in some Athenian tragedy, the Fates took up their shears. Gian Galeazzo, in the prime of life, with the cup of success at his lips, sickened and died. So the threat to Florence passed, but, in passing, fused a mood into an attitude to life.

The Florentines did not consider themselves saved by chance. For them it was a triumph of civic virtue, of steadfast republicans thwarting tyrants. The ancient Roman virtues of

Beauty pervaded Florentine schoolbooks as well as religious tomes. Part of an arithmetic problem in the primer at right reads: "The King of France was routed in battle, with ¼ of his soldiers killed and ⅖ wounded and 1000 were taken prisoner and 6000 escaped." And the illustration almost makes its solving palatable. The high literacy of the populace inspired such humanists as Coluccio Salutati (above) to dream of Florence as the ideal city of man. An artist portrayed Saint Augustine writing The City of God *(left), and hopefully included Florence in the background of his illustration.*

which Cicero spoke and of which old Cato was the ideal, had been, they felt, reborn in Florence, which gave the city an identity with the past. The year 1402 represented a triumph and a liberation, and this sense of freedom renewed, of the breaking of the shackles of the immediate past, invigorated not only philosophy and history but also the plastic arts. It is not surpising that Masaccio's grave saints should wear their cloaks like togas.

Interest in classics, interest in ancient art, delight in new techniques of painting, sculpture, and architecture, existed before the cataclysmic struggle with Milan, but none can doubt that it gave an immense impetus to the peculiar qualities of the Florentine Renaissance. Symbolically, at the height of the struggle the city appointed Chrysoloras, the first and most deeply influential teacher of Greek, a public lecturer. A belief in the value of classical learning as the molder of a citizen's character, a conviction that great moral value could be derived from a study of its philosophy, became as deeply embedded in the Florentine tradition as it did in nineteenth-century England. And when the Medici founded and encouraged a Platonic academy, and patronized handsomely the great philosophers—Ficino, Pico, and the rest—they were no innovators, and the purpose of their patronage was widely understood. It would strengthen an attitude to human life that was thought to be singularly Florentine. Although humanistic study had its roots in civic life, naturally it developed rapidly within the terms of its own disciplines and needs. Scholars dedicated themselves to the textual and philological problems inherent in the study of the classics—and as scholars will, became obsessed with their own techniques. Yet even if preoccupation with style, grammar, emendation, and the minutiae of criticism often took the place of creative imagination, there was nevertheless a great deal of fine poetry and fine prose, written in a Latin

Florentines delighted in the themes of antiquity. In this allegorical procession, an unknown artist conceived a throng of satyrs, tambourine a

that would have been no disgrace to the age of Augustus. And the encouragement to classical studies given by the humanistic Renaissance in Florence was in harmony with scholarly activity scattered throughout the courts and cities of Italy.

Yet the greatest gains from this self-identification with the antique were in the arts, particularly sculpture. As in ancient Athens, statues taught citizens the lessons of their public life. The mysterious David of Donatello and the vast David of Michelangelo both told the Florentines that their city had always been a giant-killer, proud of its liberty: the citizens themselves dragged Holofernes and Judith from the Medici palace and set them up in front of the Palazzo della Signoria to underline what should be the fate of tyrants. In no other place were sculptors so handsomely patronized or so deeply admired. Florence, in consequence, produced the greatest masters of the fifteenth century, whose work graced Rome, Venice, Milan, and the lesser cities of Italy. So, too, in architecture:

while Milan and Venice still lingered in the grip of the Gothic, and Rome lay in ruins, Brunelleschi began recreating the austere harmonies of the classical world and giving to the Florentines a proper setting for their intense civic consciousness. In painting there was the same sense of *gravitas,* of weight of human character, of the power of human destiny, particularly before the sophistication and self-indulgence of the High Renaissance produced in some artists a more esoteric cultivation of art. Even so, the last great artist of Florence, Michelangelo, still recalls the tradition of his city, created by Giotto and Masaccio.

The struggle with Milan did more than render humanism fashionable, or encourage a cult of the antique, or stimulate the arts, or make a study of Cicero an essential part of the education of a gentleman. It consolidated the power of the oligarchy, and peculiarly so, as the lucky death of Gian Galeazzo not only plucked them from the jaws of destruc-

…orn players, and weird beasts with serpents' heads parading past Ariadne slumbering on the isle of Naxos—all without interrupting her nap.

tion, but set them on a course of military success. Surging economic prosperity was linked with the triumph of their arms. Florence, still free, still republican, enjoyed a prosperity, a fame, a serenity unparalleled in her annals—giving further point, if point were needed, to the antique virtue of her government and its citizens. Oligarchies, however, are rarely stable for long; after the first difficulties, criticism is quickly followed by intrigue. The death in 1417 of Maso degli Albizzi, the most powerful member of the ruling oligarchy, unleashed a struggle for power in which the old class and guild antagonisms once more erupted to the surface. By dexterous exploitation of these jealousies, Giovanni de' Medici and, after his death in 1429, his son Cosimo were able to establish their family so securely in power that Cosimo's grandson Lorenzo enjoyed the power if not the title of a prince. Yet even at the height of the family's greatness, respect was always paid to the letter of the republican con-

stitution. The survival of the Medici and the ease with which they defeated the conspiracies of the Neroni and, afterward, of the Pazzi, were due to the loyal support of their fellow merchants as well as their dependents.

During this half-century of Medicean rule, Florence dominated the intellectual and artistic life of Italy: Cosimo poured out a torrent of wealth on buildings—palaces, monasteries, churches—on sculpture, and on paintings. Feeling himself to be God's debtor, he did his best to make restitution—reconstructing and embellishing his favorite monastery of San Marco, as well as his parish church of San Lorenzo. Following in his footsteps, his son Piero ordered a sumptuous tabernacle for the miraculous crucifix in San Miniato al Monte, and another for the wonder-working image at Santissima Annunziata, which bears the proud boast that the marble alone cost four thousand florins. Cosimo built his own palace modestly but strictly according to the new style; he patron-

137

ized Donatello for as long as he lived, and sculpture, as might be expected from so dedicated a Florentine, was his greatest passion after architecture. He preferred his sons to deal with mere painters and decorators, but *he* paid. And many superb frescoes of Fra Angelico, Filippo Lippi, and Benozzo Gozzoli were the fruits of Medicean gold, of their sense of the usurer's sin, of a need to return the riches that one man had acquired in beauty that all could enjoy.

Lorenzo the Magnificent, his grandson, amazed by the staggering sums that his grandfather had spent, preferred the cheaper patronage of philosophers. Nevertheless, he maintained the tradition of his ancestors, and the beauty and splendor of Florence steadily grew. The citizens were continuously regaled with pageants, tournaments, and carnivals. It proved to be a reckless world in which capital was too easily squandered on military maneuvers, diplomatic activity, and Lorenzo's anxiety to cut a figure in Italy whatever the cost.

As the fame of Florence reached new heights, so did its public debt (not that the debt worried the oligarchy overmuch, for they lent the money on excellent security and at a splendid interest). The world was a rich man's oyster: the tentacles of Florentine trade stretched from Cairo to the Cotswolds, and even the shocks and disasters in the eastern Mediterranean—the spread of the Ottoman Turks and the fall of Constantinople—seemed, for a time at least, to be turned to Florence's advantage by a benign Providence. The loss of Byzantine alum, so vital to the luxury cloth trade, was immediately countered by the discovery of huge deposits at Tolfa in the Papal States, for which, naturally, the Medici secured the concession. Wandering Greeks with manuscripts to sell and an ancient tongue to teach were welcome as a further adornment to a refined household. Secure and self-indulgent, the leaders of Florentine society tried to evade present disasters and future cataclysms, while the

*The Medici always put on an impressive
show. To house their bank in Milan, they
erected the imposing building shown below in Filarete's drawing. When Lorenzo
was born, the circular panel at right was ordered by his family, prophetically illustrat-
ing the* Triumph of Fame. *Cosimo, who
is shown at left in a detail from the Gozzoli fresco on page 156, spent money liberally for charity and public works, devoting
to them a fortune almost twice as large as
the one he left to his family at his death.
Nonetheless, a royal inheritance remained.
"He did not take his gold florins and the
rest of his money and bonds with him into
the other world," an admirer wrote, "nor
his banks and storehouses, nor his woolen
and silken cloths, nor his plate and jewelry: but he left them all to his worthy
sons and grandsons." With this immense
fortune, Cosimo's sons and grandsons continued the tradition of largesse, realizing
that charity, like art, enhanced family glory.*

Florentine government sought to survive by the use of mercenaries, diplomacy, subsidies, and bribes. The call to civic
virtue, the mobilization of the city's wealth and the city's men,
no longer appealed to a bourgeois aristocracy. Their exclusive
world possessed too much delight to be foolishly risked. In
the soft elegance of Lorenzo di Pierfrancesco de' Medici's
villa, in the golden glow of the Tuscan evening, young men
might listen to Ficino's subtle explanations of the hidden
meanings in Botticelli's *Primavera,* which adorned its walls;
for them the bales of wool, rolls of cloth, stacked hides, and
piled spices were a necessity, not a way of life, and although
they could use the dagger and the sword, they felt no com-
pulsion to sweat in arms amid the horrors of war for the
future of their city. All the authority, all the skill, of Lorenzo
were used to avoid such bleak necessities. This elegant world
was perched precariously, however, on the edge of turbulence, and it depended on the subtlety and statesmanship of

Lorenzo not only to prevent the system from collapsing in
internecine strife, of which the Pazzi conspiracy was a clear
enough warning, but also to still the dangerous antipathy of
a restless population whose fears and hopes were already
being played upon by a master demagogue, some years before Lorenzo's death.

The Florentine Renaissance has entranced generations of
men by the astonishing range of its artistic and scholarly
achievements—from the serene perfection of Leonardo to
the tragic realism of Machiavelli—and all too often the endless toil of the laboring men and women, whose grievous lives
made it possible, is forgotten. It was the tragic situation of
the common man that stirred deeply the creative imagination
not only of Michelangelo, but also of Botticelli, who reflected the bright elegance and exclusive charm of the Florentine world more faithfully than any other painter. The compulsive rantings of Savonarola haunted them both.

The last decades of the fifteenth century brought a sharp contraction of Florentine trade. Englishmen were beginning to make their own cloth, the Flemish were showing a more than Italian skill in dressing and dyeing it. In 1478 the London bank of the Medici was closed; in 1483 the Tolfa alum concession had to be abandoned; for a time the merchants of Florence even lost their traditional role as papal bankers. Trade with the eastern Mediterranean steadily wasted away. Renewed wars, with expensive alliances and even more costly condottieri, added further strain to an economy which had already accumulated far too many obligations. The Florentines had been dealing in futures for too many generations, and, skillful as their financiers were, they could not conjure increased wealth from diminishing trade. For centuries urban poverty had helped to breed epidemic diseases that raged with the ferocity of a prairie fire through the dirt-encrusted slums. Plagues, fevers, and consumption

made death a constant visitor at the houses of the poor, who, to exorcise horror, fortify their courage, and set their hopes on future blessedness, pleaded for the intercession of the Virgin and the saints. Religion—ecstatic, even apocalyptic—assuaged the wounds of their poverty and its pain. For them the elegant, exclusive domain of the scarlet-wearing burghers who exercised authority in their city was a bright, elusive world as impossible to understand as dreams in a language they could never comprehend. The sufferings of Christ and the pity of God lay closer to their knowledge, and in their lives the priest was as necessary as bread. This contradiction —poverty, suffering, and pain amid a world of profusion, extravagance, and delight—stirred the consciences of deeply sensitive men. It was this that made Pico della Mirandola seek the solace of Savonarola's mysticism, that led him, at his death, to adopt the habit of a Dominican; it was this that brought about that stranger conversion which drew Botticelli

To commemorate the Pazzi conspiracy, Lorenzo commissioned the medal below, showing his brother's assassination in the Cathedral of Florence. Giuliano's picture, seen above the choir enclosure, may have been copied from Botticelli's portrait of him which appears on the facing page. Pallas and the Centaur (right) was painted by Botticelli as a tribute to Lorenzo. The goddess of wisdom, wreathed in olive branches and taming a centaur, has been thought to symbolize the Medici talent for ruling through suasion rather than force. But Lorenzo was not always gentle; when the Pazzi conspirators were hanged, heads down, Botticelli was asked to paint a picture of them.

away from the gaieties and urbane moralities of the antique to an acceptance of Savonarola's prophecies; it was this that fused Michelangelo's tragic sense of human destiny with Savonarola's apocalyptic vision.

The story of Savonarola is a mixture of tragedy and hysteria, in which a genuine pity for man's condition became enraveled in hate and muddled by political intrigue. His denunciation of worldliness, his childish burning of vanities, his fiery condemnation of a lazy and corrupt clergy, were a part of the threnody of the life of Europe, frequently heard, frequently forgotten; but Savonarola spoke at a time when the young Piero de' Medici was displaying a singular lack of his family's genius. Behind Savonarola loomed the discontented poor, eager for a change, eager for secular as well as religious hope. Those families whom the Medici had excluded and despised knew how to manipulate this superlative demagogue, whose wild sermons could inflame a multitude. So

what started in evangelism finished in political revolution.

The little people, the *piagnoni* (snivelers) as the old oligarchs called them, became a power in the land. *Popolo e Libertà* frequently echoed in the Piazza—a cry which Pisa promptly adopted as it threw aside the Florentine yoke and claimed the protection of the French, when invasion of Italy had triggered the revolution against Piero. Savonarola combined a dependence on the French that was quite unrealistic with a hatred of the Papacy that bordered on insanity. His loud denunciations of papal sins (interlarded from time to time with staggeringly sane bits of hardheaded diplomacy) grew more shrill as the French left him in the lurch. Alexander VI—aware of, and tolerantly amused by, his own shortcomings—bore with the fulminations so long as his diplomacy required it. Time, of course, favored the Pope. The French were content to use Florence, but naturally disinclined to save it from the consequences of its own folly, or to restore its

To replace the recently exiled Medici as protectors of Florence's liberty, Savonarola proclaimed Jesus Christ as the new ruler of the city. Shouting "Viva Cristo!" excited crowds roared their approval, for the friar's impassioned sermons had transformed Florence. From his cloister in the monastery of San Marco, shown in the photograph at right, Savonarola ruled the city. His preaching was so famous that even the Sultan of Turkey read translations of his sermons. A woodcut (right) taken from his Book of Revelations, shows him exhorting his flock. Savonarola castigated the Medici, the Pope, humanists, and painters, and found time to write a tract against astrologers. An illustration from the work appears above.

Tuscan empire. And in Florence itself, the oligarchs disliked both the rantings of Savonarola and the government of the people; in the wings lurked the exiled Medici—*they* were powerful in Rome. The inevitable end came: the rack and the fagot for Savonarola; the defeat of his *piagnoni*; and in the fullness of time, the return of the Medici.

The whole Savonarola episode is a curious mixture of idealism, ineptitude, and iniquity. Certainly Savonarola wanted a Florentine government that represented more fully the whole citizenship—the poor and the dispossessed as well as the rich and the powerful. He also hated life, grew drunk on his own megalomaniac visions, preferred prophecy to policy, and welcomed the disasters he had done so much to promote. Ignorance married to prejudice, blind hatred linked with a disgust for life, proved an unsatisfactory basis for statesmanship, even when practiced by a saint.

Never again was the republic the same; the power of Flor-

ence was greatly diminished. For a decade after the burning of Savonarola in 1498 for heresy, and after the failure of her mercenaries, Florence's blood and treasure were poured out in the Pisan war. In 1509 Pisa was captured, but the expense was far beyond the weakened resources of Florence's dwindling trade. Indeed, three years later a refusal to act in concert with the Papacy was treated by Julius II as an impertinence. His professional Spanish troops scattered the Florentine militia. The papal-inspired revolution followed, and the Medici returned. They lacked the ability of their ancestors, and proved little better than pawns in the hands of the Medici Pope Leo X, and it required further rebellions and plots, another brief republic haunted by the puritanism and religiosity of Savonarola, as well as the sack of Rome by Charles V, before Florence was finally subjected to the rule of the Medici as dukes of Tuscany. In the first three decades of the sixteenth century the greatness of Florence faded. Eco-

nomically—and the splendor of the Florentine Renaissance was based on its wealth—Florence lacked a future. The heart of its trade—cloth—was lost to England and to Flanders, and banking followed trade. Florence was far more vulnerable than Venice, or even Milan, to the great decline in Mediterranean prosperity which followed the discoveries of the New World and the sea-route to the Indies.

Artists lived uneasy lives in post-Medicean Florence, for patronage grew scarce. Art and humanism no longer reflected the civic virtues—these were adequately exercised by private prayer and public repentance. During the middle decades of the sixteenth century, the cult of sensitivity, of elegance, and of learning as the peculiar attributes of a gentleman had also narrowed the social basis of art and, to some extent, limited its appeal. In the wanderings of Leonardo and of Michelangelo, in the frustrations that marred their lives and marked their art, there is a reflection of the growing impotence and decay of the society in which they were born and grew to manhood.

Yet that tradition of individual destiny, of the worth of man, which the Florentines had cultivated so carefully in their heroic days, remained strong enough not only to sustain them in spite of the tribulations of their age, but also to buoy up a number of artists of lesser genius—Bronzino, Pontormo, del Sarto, and Fra Bartolommeo. And to one art, namely history, the decay of Florence provided a greater stimulus than its climb to greatness. The cataclysms of Florentine experience opened the same creative vistas for Machiavelli and Guicciardini as neuroses in individuals were to do for Dostoevsky or Proust. Indeed, even in its last, sad days, republican Florence still produced an astonishing array of genius, and no city of so small a compass has ever, before or since, made a greater contribution to art and letters within the brief span of a hundred and fifty years.

Lorenzo de' Medici

by RALPH ROEDER

Lorenzo de' Medici was, first and last, a financier; he was much more besides—politician, statesman, patron of art and letters—but these were merely functions of the financier developed by his forefathers, which he inherited together with the fortune of his family, and in each of these roles his performance was the consummation of theirs. His biography begins before he was born, and he sits for his portrait under his family tree.

His great-grandfather, Giovanni di Bicci de' Medici, was the first millionaire of the family. Of plebeian origin, the Medici had risen by prosperous trade to the front rank of the *nobili popolani*—the merchant princes of the major guilds—but they had not abandoned the class from which they sprang, and it served them steadily in their subsequent ascent to power. The banking business which Giovanni built up with branches in sixteen European capitals entitled him to a leading position among the eighty banking firms of Florence, and would have assured him a corresponding influence in the government had he chosen to claim it, since the bankers' guild supplied the capital and the connections for the enterprises of the state; but Giovanni was prudent and avoided politics. Retiring by nature, modest and unassuming, he spent his money on the construction of churches, the encouragement of art, and works of charity (the Foundling Hospital built for him by Brunelleschi, and the church of San Lorenzo rebuilt for him by the great architect as a family temple, were his monuments), and as long as he confined his public spirit to such modest activities, he passed for a safe man and honors came to him unsought. Summoned to the Signory, he revealed a different form of public spirit, however, by supporting against powerful opposition a tax reform, which substituted for the universal poll tax and the arbitrary assessments of the past a $1\frac{1}{2}\%$ levy on capital. This innovation was a boon for the poor, who reckoned it among his major charities; and since it was enacted when an unsuccessful war was about to be resumed and the tax rate raised, it won him high favor with the little people; but it incensed the rich. "Since the burden was to be distributed by law and not by men," Machiavelli, the official biographer of the family, observed, "it weighed heavily on the powerful citizens and was received with extreme displeasure by the mighty." Their anger rose and turned to alarm when the little people proposed to make the reform retroactive to compensate the losses they had suf-

A terra-cotta bust of Lorenzo, by Andrea Verrocchio.

fered in the past; but Giovanni dissuaded them from this abuse of his bounty, and having done his duty impartially by both sides, retired to private life and the practice of his private charities. When he retired to the grave in 1429, he was widely missed and mourned by those whom he benefited.

The eldest son of this model Medici followed closely in his footsteps. Equally modest and unassuming and no less charitable, Cosimo also minded his own business carefully; but that business was constantly growing, and with it the motives to ruin it. The rich had not forgotten the tax reform imposed on them by his benevolent father, nor the fund of good will he won with his churches and his charities. For four years Cosimo was not molested, but in 1433 the blow fell. The Albizzi, a rival family which had long been conspiring with the former nobles to uproot the upstart Medici, judged the moment ripe to strike. Before a Signory predisposed in their favor and a *gonfaloniere* in their debt, they preferred charges against the opulent family as a danger to the state because of their wealth and ambition. Among other proof, they cited a new mansion which Cosimo was building on a scale and in a style unbefitting a private citizen. The evidence, based on prejudice and suspicion, prospered; Cosimo was arrested and imprisoned. The Albizzi, bent on obtaining the death penalty, summoned a popular assembly to appoint by acclamation a *balia*—a commission created in emergencies and entrusted with absolute power for a limited length of time—and the *balia*, composed of two hundred leading citizens, deliberated without reaching a decision. Many were for death, many for banishment, many more, moved by compassion or fear, were silent. For four days the prisoner refused food until a friendly jailer shared it with him; with his jailer's help he smuggled a substantial bribe to the *gonfaloniere*, and the sentence was commuted to banishment for himself and his family for ten years. A year later, a friendly Signory canceled the decree and recalled him. "Seldom," said Machiavelli, "has a citizen returning from a great victory been greeted by such a concourse of people and with such demonstrations of affection as Cosimo on his return from exile." The Albizzi, after failing to seize the government by force before his return, fled, two hundred of their partisans were banished or bled, and when Cosimo was reproached for so drastic a purge of prominent citizens, he replied that new nobles could be made with two

lengths of crimson cloth and that states were not ruled by Paternosters. "Better a city destroyed than lost," he added.

As a result of this experience, and to prevent its recurrence, Cosimo sought and secured a controlling influence in the government. The forms of the republic were respected and adapted to his purpose. Profiting by the reaction in his favor, he served a brief term as *gonfaloniere*, but soon abandoned public office in favor of a less conspicuous but far more permanent and powerful position as banker to the republic and confidential adviser to the government. His foes having fled, his friends assumed office, and he kept them there by the customary methods of the politician. One was purely Florentine—the *balia*—employed whenever a direct appeal to the people was needed to support his authority, but discarded when he was so firmly established that he could afford to restore normal elections and humor his enemies by the free play of Florentine democracy. The other was money, universally valid in all times and places. Reviving the famous tax reform of his father, which had fallen into disuse, and enforcing it in favor of his friends and against his foes, he wielded it as a defensive and offensive weapon more deadly than daggers.

Neither of these methods would have availed him long, however—and they served him for thirty years —had he not identified his interests completely with those of the state and guided and guarded them wisely and well. As banker to the commonwealth, he put the republic in his pocket by liberal loans and assumed many public expenses himself to lend it luster and prestige. He entertained distinguished visitors at his own expense and went out of his way to attract them to Florence when they were worth it. On one such occasion he traveled to Ferrara where a council of the Pope, the Primate of the Eastern Church, and one of the last Byzantine emperors was sitting, and induced them to transfer their deliberations to Florence, where he lodged them magnificently and converted the city for a season into a brilliant political, religious, cultural, and commercial convention town. The council accomplished nothing, but it left a lasting impression on Florence, where the painter Benozzo Gozzoli commemorated the sumptuous exotic costumes of the Eastern dignitaries on the walls of the Medici chapel.

In foreign affairs Cosimo took the same risks as a statesman. Like his father, he loved peace and avoided war, and with a single exception he made war to secure peace. Reversing the traditional alliance with Venice against their mutual enemy, the aggressive duchy of Milan, he supplied a soldier of fortune, Francesco Sforza, with money and means to overthrow the Visconti dynasty, and won an equally peace-loving friend in their place; and when Venice and Naples turned against him, he paralyzed their military operations by calling in his loans.

Again like his father, he was a great builder of churches and a liberal patron of art. Architects of the stature of Brunelleschi and Michelozzo, sculptors of the grace of Donatello and Luca della Robbia, painters of the demure splendor of Fra Angelico, Filippo Lippi, and Benozzo Gozzoli, worked for him building or adorning his monuments—the monastery of San Marco, the church of San Lorenzo, the Medici palace, among others—and he added to his laurels by the encouragement of learning. Learning he encouraged with the curiosity of close acquaintance, for he was uncommonly well educated. He maintained agents abroad searching for rare prizes to fill his library and found the best at home: the Bishop of Bologna, a fellow collector who borrowed from his purse to satisfy his passion for books, repaid his debt first by cataloguing his library and later, when he became Pope Nicholas V, by awarding the management of the papal finances to the Medici bank in Rome, whose books showed a fair profit in the Jubilee year of 1450.

But it was in the art of politics that Cosimo shone. Studiously effacing himself and remaining in the background of government, he was recognized, nevertheless, both at home and abroad as the real Head of State—*Capo della Repubblica*—by virtue of financial sovereignty and adroit brainwork without the support of armed force. Living simply and soberly, he reached the ripe old age of seventy-five, but as he aged he was crippled by gout, his grip on the government weakened, and his last days were darkened by fear for the future of his family. Of his two sons, one was a chronic invalid and the other died before he did; and he was heard to murmur as he was borne through the rooms of that mansion which almost cost him his life, "Too large a house for so small a family." His fears were well founded, for his grandsons were mere boys; and his party, loyal and obedient while it was curbed by opposition, became unruly and insolent as soon as resistance subsided, and outraged Florence by unbridled oppression, corruption,

and excesses which, weary, old, and infirm, he could no longer control and which threatened to wreck his lifework. It was a tribute to his own moderation and political tact that he preserved public respect to the end, and when he was laid to rest with his father in 1464, his countrymen inscribed on the tomb of the man who had given them thirty years of domestic peace and external stability the title PATER PATRIAE.

The second model Medici left a son, Piero, hampered by gout, the indolence of an invalid, a mild disposition, and perfidious advisers. Finding that his father's liberality had left his financial affairs in confusion and disorder, he consulted a trusted friend of his father's, who advised him to call in his loans, counting on a panic to wrest the state from his hands. Piero fell into the trap, many business failures followed, and he was denounced by his debtors as an ungrateful miser and accused of jeopardizing the prosperity of Florence to protect his capital; but he survived this blow as well as two attempts to overthrow him by force of arms.

His five brief years as head of state, marred by civil dissension, saw one event which was to set the reputation of his son and successor. So well had Cosimo gilded the Florentine lily that Louis XI of France conferred on Piero the right to add the French fleur-de-lis to the five red balls of the Medici coat of arms, and Piero took advantage of the favor. He married his nineteen-year-old son Lorenzo into the house of Orsini, one of the great feudal families of Rome, but as this was a departure from custom (Cosimo had made it a rule to marry the Medici at home), the match was unpopular in Florence. Malcontents complained that the ambition of the rising bourgeois was unbounded, that the city was no longer big enough for the citizen, that the Medici were satisfied with nothing less than a foreign and baronial alliance, and that they would soon be assuming the style of princes themselves. The betrothal was celebrated by a tournament, an aristocratic spectacle so foreign and unfamiliar in Florence that Machiavelli felt it necessary to explain it: ". . . a scuffle of men on horseback in which the leading young men of the city contended with the most renowned cavaliers of Italy; and among the Florentine youth the most famous was Lorenzo, who carried off the prize not by favor but by his own valor." Gorgeously accoutered in ornate armor, bearing the French fleur-de-lis on his shield and the Medici device on his banner, the powerful young athlete unhorsed all his opponents easily, and the pride which his countrymen took in his prowess reconciled them to his marriage. It was celebrated splendidly, and his father, who had once been called a miser, made ample amends with the wedding feast. As Machiavelli added slyly, "Piero decided to celebrate the nuptials of his son Lorenzo with Clarice of the house of Orsini magnificently, and they were held with the pomp of apparel and all other manner of magnificence befitting such a man." Long before he earned the title of Magnificent, Lorenzo learned its political value and developed an appetite for it.

Such was the heritage of Lorenzo de' Medici. "Two days after the death of my father," he wrote in later life, "although I, Lorenzo, was very young, being only in my twenty-first year, the principal men of the city and the state came to our house to condole on our loss and encourage me to take on myself the care of the city and the state, as my father and grandfather had done. This proposal being contrary to the instincts of my youthful age and considering that the burden and danger were great, I consented unwillingly, but I did so to protect our friends and our property, for it fares ill in Florence with anyone who possesses great wealth without any control in the government." *I, Lorenzo!* How lonely, how isolated the identification! More fortunate than his father, however, he found faithful friends who rallied to him loyally, and it was due to their devotion that he succeeded him peacefully. With the backing of a body of eminent citizens bent on banishing civil dissension from Florence, he began governing under singularly favorable conditions, and the first years were fairly easy—peaceful at home and only briefly disturbed abroad.

For nine years Lorenzo was indeed the most fortunate of his family. His father had been called the most mediocre of the Medici, because of his mild disposition; but no one could cast that slur on his son. Sheltered by his family tree and with no opposition to overcome, Lorenzo encountered only critics. Guicciardini was one of them, and he echoed many others. Lorenzo, he said, "desired glory and excellence above all other men and can be criticized for having had too much ambition even in minor things; he did not want to be equaled or imitated even in verses or games or exercises and turned angrily on anyone who did so." Unlike his father and grandfather, who were mature men when they became heads of the house, he was in the first flush of youth, and youth claimed its privileges of pleasure and the

carefree enjoyment of life. Besides his other accomplishments, he was a poet—another variation from his breed, for though his ancestors took many risks they never ventured to write verses—and he composed fluently for festive occasions. Improving on his father, he entertained Florence continually with masquerades and revels, pageants and processions, engaging the best artists to design the masks and decorate the floats, and taking part in them himself; for these he wrote his *Trionfi*, his *Canzoni a Ballo,* and best of all, his famous carnival songs. Later historians were scandalized by the obscenity of these songs and lamented that Lorenzo catered to the taste of the common people, forgetting that Lorenzo was young, virile, and lusty. The tournament was an aristocratic entertainment; these spectacles preserved his ties with the people. A more serious charge was raised by his elders, who professed to see in these lighthearted frolics a profound political design to beguile the people and divert them from public affairs, as his father had done; but this was to credit him with sagacity beyond his years and needless guile, for these were untroubled times of peace and plenty, and public affairs went well. If ever history could be happy, it was then, and wisely he made the most of life while he could sing:

> *How passing fair is youth,*
> *Forever fleeting away;*
> *Who happy would be, let him be;*
> *Of tomorrow who can say?*

It was as if an uneasy premonition of doom prompted the haunting refrain; for, in fact, the triumph of time was approaching.

In every generation plots had been laid to ruin his family; they were part of his heritage; and his turn came, long belated, in 1478, with the most formidable threat of all—the Pazzi conspiracy. The Pazzi were an old and numerous family with aristocratic pretensions superior to those of the Medici, and they had old scores to settle with Lorenzo.

Wealthy and proud, the Pazzi had been denied public office and the honors to which they were entitled, and they bore discrimination and abuse bitterly. The most sensitive of the family, Francesco, unable to suffer any longer, fled to Rome, where he fell in with a nephew of one of the most grasping and turbulent of the popes, and between them they hatched a plot for their mutual benefit. As ambitious as he was lowborn, Pope Sixtus IV was burdened with six covetous nephews, three of whom he placed profitably in the Church and a fourth in Imola, one of the poorest and smallest of the papal fiefs. When Francesco proposed to create a vacancy in Florence, Sixtus fell in with the scheme and consented to second the Pazzi in ousting the Medici. Thus encouraged, Francesco returned to Florence to enlist his family. Jacopo de' Pazzi, the head of the house, hesitated until he was convinced that the scheme had the blessing and the backing of the Pope.

The scheme was senseless on the face of it. A foreign potentate aiming to add Florence to the papal domain and impose a papal cub on a fiercely freedom-loving people, and relying on a Florentine family ambitious to fill the vacancy themselves—the plot was a patchwork of cross-purposes perfectly calculated to fail. Yet it nearly succeeded.

The Pope opened hostilities by canceling the concession of the Medici bank in Rome and transferring it to the Pazzi; then he lent a helping hand to the plot by appointing as Archbishop of Pisa a member of another family hostile to the Medici, the Salviati. Notwithstanding these unfriendly acts, Lorenzo seems to have suspected nothing, although he refused Salviati admission to his see. In April, 1478, the conspirators assembled in Florence and were hospitably entertained in Lorenzo's villa at Fiesole, where they planned to kill him during a banquet. However, his brother Giuliano was absent, and since the murder of both was essential to success, they postponed the blow until the following morning, during the celebration of High Mass in the Duomo, where both were bound to appear for the celebration of Easter Sunday. The change created an unforeseen difficulty; the hired assassin suffered an attack of conscientious scruples and shrank from committing sacrilege as well as murder in the cathedral; Francesco de' Pazzi, a priest, and an accomplice assumed his duties, but still another hitch developed. Giuliano was missing when the service began, and they were forced to fetch him to the slaughter, coaxing him out of bed, where he was nursing a bad knee. They braced him between them, embracing him fondly and feeling his body to make sure that he was unarmed, and brought the laggard limping to the altar; then, having finally united the victims, they struck. The church was crowded; the signal for attack was the solemn moment when the Cardinal who was officiating (another papal cub but not privy to the plot) raised the Host and hundreds of heads bowed devoutly. Giuliano bent obediently, the priest behind his back

struck the first blow, and Francesco finished him off with eighteen more—so furiously that he hacked himself in the leg and in the confusion was mistaken for one of the victims. Lorenzo defended himself, escaped with a gash in the neck, and ran into the sacristy, where his friends bolted the doors and waited for help. In the meanwhile Archbishop Salviati, entrusted with the most difficult part of the undertaking, entered the palace to seize the government. His confederates waited below in the chancery, where they locked themselves in by mistake, while he mounted to the upper floor to parley with the Signory, but his agitation betrayed him and aroused their suspicion, and before he could summon assistance the *gonfaloniere* hanged him, stammering, from the window. The city was now in an uproar. Francesco de' Pazzi, weak from loss of blood, took to his bed and begged his uncle to rally the people to their cause. Sallying forth with a hundred armed men, Jacopo de' Pazzi roamed the streets raising the cry of *Liberty!* without arousing a response, and running into a mob acclaiming the Balls, abandoned the attempt and fled. Lorenzo, escorted by his friends, returned home unharmed.

The mob avenged him loyally. Francesco de' Pazzi, dragged from his bed, was hanged beside the body of the Archbishop, dangling limply with a cluster of comrades overhead. A furious man-hunt followed: everyone even remotely connected with the conspiracy or suspected of sympathizing with it was brought to justice or mobbed; seventy perished in the first four days and two hundred more before the tumult subsided. Jacopo de' Pazzi, caught and killed, was not allowed to rest in his grave: a horde of scavenging boys unearthed his body, dragged it through the streets, and flung it naked into the Arno. Of his ten sons and nephews, two were beheaded; one was saved by Lorenzo, who was his brother-in-law; the survivors were sentenced to imprisonment or exile, and even the name Pazzi was wiped out by proscription.

Infuriated by the failure of the plot, the Pope demanded that Lorenzo surrender and that the Florentine government answer before an ecclesiastical court for the crime of sacrilege committed on the person of the Archbishop. Lorenzo protested that his only crime was that he had not allowed himself to be murdered; the Signory seconded him, circulated the confession of one of the conspirators exposing the complicity of the Pope, and appealed to the sovereigns of Europe for support. The sovereigns of Europe sided with the Medici; the Pope excommunicated the Florentine state; the Florentine clergy outlawed him in turn; the Pope declared war. Brandishing both his spiritual and temporal arms, he forbade the faithful to trade with the rebellious republic, broke their previous alliances, prohibited any state from forming new ones or any soldier from taking service with them, and summoned to his assistance the Sienese republic and his feudal ally the King of Naples; and their troops invaded Tuscany. The fortunes of war ran against the Florentines, and Lorenzo, unwilling to tax the loyalty of his people, volunteered to surrender himself, but the issue had long since outgrown a personal sacrifice and the Signory refused to abandon him. He insisted, however, slipped off to Pisa, and sailed for Naples to treat with King Ferrante. Ferrante was a notoriously treacherous monarch, but, impressed by Lorenzo's daring, he detained him less as a prisoner than as a guest, listened to his arguments, and consented to abandon the Pope. The Pope fumed, but an incursion of the Turks in Calabria compelled him, like Ferrante, to make peace.

The Pazzi conspiracy, formidable in its folly, failed; but it created a crisis and marked a turning point in Lorenzo's political career. To prevent its recurrence, he surrounded himself with an armed guard and adopted those precautions which his enemies denounced as a tyranny. He tightened his grip on the government, subordinated the Signory and the councils to a self-perpetuating privy council responsible to himself alone, and converted the controlling influence created by Cosimo into absolute personal rule. Before the Pazzi conspiracy, he was the most fortunate of the Medici; after it, the most masterful; and *I, Lorenzo* now assumed its full meaning for Florence. But the crisis had a further effect: it stimulated his powers as a statesman, and he devoted them diligently to preserving the balance of power and keeping the peace in Italy.

No sooner was the crisis over than his critics found fault with his conduct. The expedition to Naples was blamed as a rash, foolhardy, and unnecessary adventure. It was argued that he could have attained the same success sitting safely at home, instead of risking his life in the hands of a faithless enemy and returning to Florence as a hero. Also, instead of antagonizing the Pope and playing the injured party, if he had concealed his grievance and handled him

gently he might have averted a war that caused the greatest damage to the city, especially in trade and taxes. Also his punishment of the Pazzi was excessively cruel. By some he was considered unnaturally vindictive and heartless for imprisoning the innocent young men of the family and preventing the Pazzi girls from marrying and breeding more of their kind; although Guicciardini admitted that "the event was so bitter that it is no wonder that he was extraordinarily angered by it. And it was seen later that, softened by time, he gave permission for the maidens to marry and was willing to release the Pazzi from prison and let them go and live outside of Florentine territory. And also it was seen that he did not employ cruelty in other matters and was not a bloodthirsty person." But while suspicion lingered, and it lingered long, he intervened vigilantly in domestic affairs, preventing powerful families from intermarrying, arranging matches to suit himself, and permitting no important marriage in Florence without his intervention and consent.

No sooner was peace restored than he returned to his pleasures and won his final and most undeniable triumphs in their pursuit—the patronage of art and letters and the pursuit of women. In both he was resolved to excel. The lover of art and letters more than maintained the fame of his family—he increased it by his boundless liberality. Under his enlightened lead Florence became the mother of arts and the cultural capital of Italy, imitated but unsurpassed by rival states. He set the pace, and other princes were compelled to compete; but he was the highest bidder for the services of scholars and artists and carried off all the prizes for the glory of Florence and the greater glory of the Medici. In Pisa he founded a superfluous branch of the University of Florence for the sheer pleasure of surpassing rival schools, paying the highest salaries and sparing neither trouble nor expense to secure the most famous teachers in Italy. In Florence the Platonic Academy formed part of his household and boasted the best philosophers he could find. Sharing the craze for ancient learning which was widening the mental horizon of his age, he introduced it even into his home and made philosophy a household word, collecting intellectuals at his table to discuss it and teach Florence that no one could live without it. He could not. "When my mind is disturbed by the tumult of public affairs and my ears are stunned by the clamor of turbulent citizens," he confessed to a friend, "how could I bear such dissensions unless I found relief in learning?" Study was a refuge from politics and an escape from statecraft. Educated as a boy by humanists, he was one of them and collected them to preserve the most precious of his treasures, his peace of mind. His Poggio, his Poliziano, his Pico della Mirandola, his Marsilio Ficino, were bosom friends who formed his intellectual family. On books alone he spent more than half the annual income of the state, and for art his bounty was unbounded. Ambitious to be the most universal as well as the most glorious of the Medici, he befriended all the arts, and they flourished abundantly at his bidding. "For vernacular poetry, music, architecture, painting, sculpture, and all the fine and mechanical arts he showed the same favor, so that the city overflowed with all these graces," Guicciardini acknowledged. Artists flocked to Florence from far and near, attracted by the magnetic name of Lorenzo de' Medici. Not merely for pecuniary reward, either, for he was a connoisseur who appreciated their gifts, understood their problems, and defended them against fools. (When someone found fault with the music of Squarcialupi, he scolded the critic as sensitively as if he were the composer himself.) "If only you knew how difficult it is to attain perfection in any art!" he admonished.

When it came to his other ruling passion, Guicciardini found it difficult to forgive his fidelity to it: "He was licentious and very amorous and constant in his loves, which usually lasted several years. In the opinion of many, this so weakened his body that it caused him to die comparatively young. His last love, which endured many years, was for Bartolommea de' Nasi, wife of Donato Benci, who was by no means beautiful but with a style and grace of her own. . . . What folly that a man of such great reputation and prudence, forty years old, should be so infatuated with a woman who was not beautiful and already well along in years, that he was led to do what would be disgraceful in any boy!" Physically, also, he found fault with him: "Lorenzo was of medium height, his countenance coarse and dark in color, yet with an air of dignity; his voice and pronunciation harsh and unpleasing, because he spoke through his nose." But the fact remains that he was attractive to women; neither his nasal voice nor his coarse features nor his swarthy complexion nor the natural blemishes with which he was born were displeasing to them.

As he matured he mellowed and became as tolerant of his critics as they expected him to be. Though Guicciardini was one of them, he was the most indulgent and judicious of his judges, and his final verdict was fair. "Though the city was not free under him, it would have been impossible to find a better or more pleasing tyrant. From his natural goodness and inclination came infinite advantages, but through the necessity of tyranny some evils although they were restrained and limited as much as necessity permitted . . ."

Twelve uneventful years followed the Pazzi conspiracy, cloudless and carefree until Lorenzo succumbed to gout and to another, graver affliction. He neglected his financial affairs, which fell into confusion and disorder, and the fall was fatal. Machiavelli blamed his misfortunes on mismanagement by his banking agents abroad, stating that Lorenzo, to avoid further reverses, abandoned his mercantile enterprises and turned instead to "possessions, as a more stable and firm form of wealth." Among his possessions was the state, and his forays into the public coffers played havoc with the public finances. Insolvency became so acute that in 1490 a commission was created to reform the fiscal administration of Florence; the currency, hitherto the most stable in Europe, was depreciated to a fifth of its face value; and the government was driven to desperate measures to avoid bankruptcy. Lorenzo was just enough of a financier to save his private fortune by withdrawing it from commerce and investing in real estate, but at the cost of his good name. Financial acumen was the foundation of the Medici political fortunes, and he who lacked it was exposed to the ruin which the enemies of his house had tried in vain to bring about for three generations.

Under these gathering clouds, his last days were also darkened by a new adversary. An alien agitator raised his voice in Florence to echo the complaints of his enemies and disturb his peace of mind; the sermons of Savonarola kindled contention anew and in an unexpected quarter. From the pulpit of San Marco—a Medici foundation—a foreign reformer called Lorenzo to account for his political sins. The festivities with which Lorenzo entertained Florence were denounced as political snares: "The tyrant is wont to busy his people with spectacles and festivities, that they may think of their pastimes and not of his designs, and becoming unaccustomed to the conduct of the commonwealth, leave the reins of government in his hands." The charge, old and familiar though it was, could no longer be ignored in the gloom of changing times, and it was followed by graver ones. Summoned to preach before the Signory, Savonarola said: "Tyrants are incorrigible because they are proud, because they love flattery, because they will not restore their ill-gotten gains. They allow bad officials to have their way; they yield to adulation; they neither heed the poor nor condemn the rich; they expect peasants and paupers to work for them gratis or they tolerate officials who do so; they farm out the taxes to aggravate the people more and more . . . The people are oppressed by taxes, and when they come to pay unbearable sums, the rich cry: Give me the rest . . . When widows come weeping, they are told: Go to sleep. When the poor complain, they are told: Pay, pay." The preacher was popular, his following grew, and in the Lent of 1491 he moved into the Duomo, where, before a congregation packed to the doors, he preached inflammatory sermons which terrified his hearers, predicting a coming calamity, ordained by divine wrath, which would sweep away the princes of Italy, including the Medici and all their iniquities. Lorenzo was tolerant, but he was troubled: what the Pazzi failed to accomplish, the prophet promised to perform. He made advances to mollify him, but he was rebuffed. He sent a delegation to reason with him. They hinted at banishment. "Tell Lorenzo to do penance for his sins," Savonarola replied, "for God will punish him and his. I do not fear your banishments. Though I am a stranger here and he a citizen, and the foremost in the city, I shall remain and he will go. I shall remain," he repeated proudly, "and he will go." And he foretold the death of Lorenzo within a year.

A year later Lorenzo lay dying in his villa at Careggi. He was in great pain, suffering from an abdominal disorder aggravated by his physicians, who fed him powdered pearls, and he sent for Savonarola to relieve his soul. Savonarola came. According to a popular but probably apocryphal account of the scene, the priest's price of salvation included the restoration of all ill-gotten gains and the restitution of liberty to Florence; to the first Lorenzo agreed, but he gave up the ghost and expired unabsolved before he could consent to the second.

Machiavelli was kinder. He acquitted Lorenzo of his political sins for the sake of the statesman whom Florence had lost, and acquitted him in a bountiful obituary. "Of Fortune and of God he was supremely loved, wherefore all his enterprises ended well and those of his enemies ill . . . All the citizens mourned his death and all the princes of Italy . . . and that they had good reason to grieve the result soon showed; for Italy being deprived of his counsels, none of those who remained found any means of curbing or satisfying the ambition of Lodovico Sforza, the governor of the Duke of Milan . . . as soon as Lorenzo died, all those bad seeds began to sprout which not long after, he who could quell them being no longer alive, ruined and are still ruining Italy."

And so it proved. Lorenzo was the pivot of Italian politics, and his eldest son, Piero, was born to be unfortunate—for himself, for his family, and for Florence. Two years after the death of Lorenzo, a revolt broke out, the Medici were driven into exile, and their palace sacked by a mob of vandals. Of Lorenzo nothing was left but the memory. The financier was a failure, the politician and the statesman were ephemeral, and of all the titles to fame which he left on deposit for posterity, only the patron of culture was remembered as Lorenzo the Magnificent.

FLORENCE OF
THE MEDICI

High and daring as the hopes of the city, the great dome, designed to astonish Italy, crowned the cathedral of Florence. Like the city's vaulting ambitions, it was based on the example of the ancients, but the new age's wealth and venturesome spirit provided a foundation even more solid. Spurred by the patronage and personal example of the Medici, Florence (shown above in a detail from di Michelino's *Allegory of the Divine Comedy*) welcomed art and learning, and under their rule became the cultural capital, the Athens, of Italy. As the center of taste and creativity, the city attracted artists from the entire peninsula and from all the countries of Europe. But with the death of Lorenzo the Magnificent in 1492, the Golden Age of Florence was no more.

The Medici established the foundation of their collection with masterpieces such as Donatello's Judith and Holofernes *(below) and* The Adoration of the Magi *(left) by Fra Angelico and Fra Lippo Lippi. Each generation continued the patronage of art. The humanist manuscript below the painting is a translation of Plotinus which was commissioned by Cosimo, dedicated to Lorenzo, and illuminated for Piero. Eventually Medici treasures, such as the medieval cup set in silver and enamel, were scattered; the rebel mobs which looted the palace in 1494 set up the statue of Judith slaying Holofernes in the public square as a warning to tyrants.*

THE MEDICI
AS PATRONS
OF THE ARTS

Afraid to defy the traditions of Florence, Cosimo chose a sober façade when he built the new Medici palace, but within its walls he freely indulged his own princely tastes. Donatello's *Judith and Holofernes* stood beside a courtyard fountain, and tapestries, designed in Italy and woven in Flanders, hung on the walls. Lavish commissions filled the rooms with pictures of saints and classical heroes, for merchant princes now shared the Church's role as patrons of the arts. Supported by Cosimo, Castagno experimented with the effects of light and shade, and each week Donatello called at the Medici bank to collect a regular stipend. Under Lorenzo the family even kept a court sculptor, Bertoldo, who watched over its collection of ancient art and tutored apprentices in the Medici garden. Promising artists, Michelangelo and Botticelli among them, were welcomed into Lorenzo's circle and were generously supported, for their work, like the Medici art collection, reflected glory on the family. Inventories of the Medici palace catalogued a rich assortment of antique busts and painted shields, goblets and haloed madonnas, an elephant's tooth and a serpent's tongue, each carefully described and valued. *The Adoration of the Magi* by Fra Angelico and Fra Lippo Lippi (opposite) was rated at a hundred florins, whereas a unicorn's horn set in gold was appraised for sixty times that. Most highly prized were ancient coins and cameos, over five thousand in all, which drew scholars and artists from all Italy to study the Medici treasures.

OVERLEAF: *On the chapel walls of the Medici palace Benozzo Gozzoli painted the story of the journey of the Magi. Leading the procession on a white horse is a handsome youth thought to be Lorenzo, in the golden robes and red hose he wore at an Oriental fete given in Florence in 1459. Cosimo, soberly dressed in blue, follows him, his mule plodding along beside a Negro page. Well back in the crowd between two bearded ancients is Gozzoli's self-portrait, with his name written along the rim of his red hat. The vivid fresco was commissioned by Piero de' Medici, who is seen in profile, riding on a spirited white horse behind his son Lorenzo.*

THE DOORS

The church of St. John the Baptist was the only link connecting Florence with its mythical Roman past. Once, according to legend, it had been a temple of Mars; now it was dedicated to the city's patron saint. Despite a plague which racked the city in 1400, the cloth merchants' guild determined to fulfill an old resolve and adorn the church with another set of bronze doors. Seven Tuscan artists competed for the commission, and when the trial panels were in, the judges unanimously awarded the prize to the sculptor Lorenzo Ghiberti. Even those artists who had competed with him agreed with the choice. It was twenty years before the doors were finished, and then they won such praise that the merchants asked for another pair. It was Ghiberti's second set of doors (at right) that Michelangelo judged worthy to stand at the entrance to paradise. Their graceful figures, modeled as in a painting by the play of light and shade, recall Ghiberti's careful study of classical sculpture. Their daring use of perspective, which Ghiberti had learned from his rival, Brunelleschi, lends a realistic sense of depth to the Old Testament scenes gleaming in high relief under a coating of gold.

"I had surpassed everyone," gloated Ghiberti after his famous victory, and he felt no reservation about including his portrait (opposite) twice in the decorative borders of the doors. The sacrifice of Isaac in the panel above and the nibbling squirrel below reflect the sculptor's profound concern for "compositions rich with many figures."

THE CITY OF PAGEANTRY

At tournaments in Florence's Piazza Santa Croce (above), display was as important as military skill. Armored knights on richly caparisoned steeds were identifiable to ladies on the balconies, to red-robed merchants, and to boys squinting through knotholes in the fences, by means of names embroidered on their bridles. But the city's most dazzling spectacles were reserved for processions. The fantastic helmet at right and the shield on the facing page, which Castagno painted with the figure of David, are typical of parade trappings in the Renaissance.

The Florentine year was rich with celebrations given in honor of guilds and state visitors, feast days, military victories, and cleverly manipulated Medici marriages. But the city's traditional festival season began on May Day, when the young danced at twilight in the public squares, and the streets echoed to the boisterous songs of reveling apprentices. The two months that followed glittered with fireworks and tournaments, masques and lavish wedding feasts, reaching their midsummer climax on the day of the city's patron saint, John the Baptist.

Through the streets wound a procession of gorgeously painted chariots, masked allegorical figures, fantastic giants on stilts, beggars and nymphs and prophets on horseback, who paused in the great Piazza to present their show. Angels and devils battled before the gaping citizens while God the Father rolled by on top of a wooden tower, peering out from behind a woolen cloud to watch

the spectacle below. As the spirit of humanism gradually triumphed, more secular and sophisticated displays followed in His train. Early in the century Brunelleschi had designed an intricate heavenly sphere surrounded by hovering angels; it opened up to release the Angel Gabriel, who flew to earth over the heads of the astonished burghers. Under Lorenzo the crowds witnessed effects as spectacular, but now the city's ingenious artists preferred to celebrate the triumphs of ancient Roman generals and of the reborn pagan gods. Visitors were awed by Florence's riches and artistic vitality, and Florentine festival masters were in demand throughout Italy. So long as Florence prospered, this splendor and gaiety kept the lower classes content (a fact which critics of the Medici were quick to observe). The citizens enjoyed themselves, and instead of the slogans of factional strife, the streets rang with Lorenzo's spirited and lusty carnival songs.

Following the example of Saint Augustine, the humanists sought to reinterpret Christianity in philosophical terms. Botticelli painted the admired saint (opposite) in a typical humanist's study, with the gleaming rings of the scholar's armillary sphere outshining his faint halo. Augustine's fusion of Christian and classical studies was echoed by Pico della Mirandola, seen at left in a medal by Niccolò Fiorentino. Contemporaries found Pico even more learned than Saint Augustine had been, but some of his ideas did veer perilously close to heresy.

THE HUMANISTS

Inspired by an imaginative pedigree that hailed Julius Caesar as founder of the city, Renaissance Florence proudly resolved to equal the glories of classical Rome. Humanist scholars labored enthusiastically to recreate the exciting world of the ancients, and the grateful city rewarded them with adulation. Reverent crowds flocked to their lectures and applauded classical quotations, until one virtuoso succeeded in cramming quotes from every ancient author into one discourse. "The whole state is turned to look at me," gloated one scholar, and like actors vying for an audience, he and his fellows fiercely exploited their precarious fame. Humanists jostled bishops for precedence, sternly warned kings that only they could confer immortality. One even married into a branch of the waning royal family of Byzantium. High-minded Florentines were more dazzled by the scholarship of Byzantium than by the studied splendor of its princes, however. A Byzantine scholar, rumored to be Plato's reincarnation, had lectured to them so persuasively on Greek philosophy that when he returned home to attempt to revive paganism, he left behind a flourishing cult of Plato. Florentine humanists gathered on the slope of Fiesole overlooking the city and formed a philosophical academy in imitation of Plato's school in the olive grove of Academe. They dreamed of seeing Plato's portrait, and rejoiced when an "authentic" bust was opportunely discovered in the ruins of Athens. Lorenzo bought it and enshrined a copy for them; it was devoutly crowned with laurel; and on November 7, supposedly the day of Plato's birth and death, a lamp was lit before it. But the humanists did more than play at classicism: they translated Greek philosophy, pioneered the science of archaeology, and put the study of manuscripts on a scholarly basis. Above all, they labored to reconcile Christian philosophy with the teachings of their classical mentors, whose universe revolved around man instead of around God.

No one was a better spokesman for humanism than the scholarly prince, Pico della Mirandola. Rich, handsome, reportedly master of twenty-two languages, Pico abandoned Mirandola, his tiny feudal principality in central Italy, to rule in the world of learning. At the age of twenty-four the young prince startled the learned with a collection of nine hundred theses boldly summarizing all of human knowledge. Prefacing it with a proud humanist manifesto "On the Dignity of Man," he challenged the scholars of Europe to debate his propositions. Timid churchmen refused to dispute, scented heresy in his defense of magic, and Pico found it wise to flee Rome. Eventually he took refuge at Lorenzo's court, where he continued to study Hebrew, Arabic, and Chaldaic, the soothsayer's language. His researches led him to the Cabala, an obscure Hebrew philosophy whose intoxicating mysticism even the rabbis feared. In it, to the scandal of the Church, Pico found proof of the divinity of Christ. But no form of magic was a match for the urgent message of Savonarola, which was sweeping Florence at this time. Savonarola threatened to scourge Pico unless he became a monk, but the humanist wavered, reluctant to surrender either his mistress or his secular freedom. He caged his humanist doubts behind monastery walls, but refused to take vows. When Pico was on his deathbed, Savonarola finally convinced him, and there the prophet triumphantly robed the humanist in the habit of a monk.

SIC AVGVSTINVS SACRIS SE TRADIDIT VT NON
MVTATVM SIBI ADHVC SENSERIT ESSE LOCVM

A boyhood spent writing Greek epigrams prepared Angelo Poliziano to tutor the Medici sons. Ghirlandaio's eloquent portrait shows him with Giuliano, a prince so gentle that his brother, Leo X, refused to let him govern Florence.

THE BATTLE
OF THE BOOKS

Accusing each other of debased morals or what was even worse—a degenerate Latin style—rival humanists squabbled furiously over the relative merits of obscure Roman authors. Invective was the favorite humanist pastime, and a good pen, the scholars boasted, could stab even a king. The Medici diluted the fighting spirit of Florentine humanists with generous patronage, but they failed to tame it. In the midst of the Pazzi troubles Lorenzo had to brave another violent battle, between his obstinate wife and his dearest friend, the humanist poet Angelo Poliziano. While teaching her son the Book of Psalms, Clarice was indignantly shouted down by Poliziano, who fiercely defended the purity of his pupil's classical education. In retaliation, she banished the scholar and confiscated his manuscripts, and it required months of negotiation by the patient Lorenzo to compose their quarrel. Poliziano continued his battles, but he confined them now to the field of scholarship, leading an attack against the group of humanists who tried to enthrone Cicero as sole dictator of a correct Latin style. But his polemics have been forgotten, and Poliziano is remembered best for his flowery and tranquil nature poetry. His lyrics written to match tunes the Medici women sang, and his poems celebrating the beauty of their rivals, the Florentine favorites of Lorenzo and Giuliano de' Medici, are among the undisputed classics of Italian poetry, and have made Poliziano the major poet of the Florentine Renaissance.

Platonic philosophy sought harmony everywhere, and the translator of Plato, Marsilio Ficino (far right in Ghirlandaio's group portrait of Florentine scholars, below), was the least pugnacious of humanists. His pupil, fourth generation of Medici scholar princes, was Pope Leo X, whose portrait by Raphael (detail above) lovingly displays a reading glass and illuminated manuscript, symbols of humanist learning.

As Lorenzo de' Medici lay dying, lightning struck the great cathedral dome, symbol of Florence's pride. "Behold," shouted Savonarola, "the sword of the Lord, swift and sure over the peoples of the earth." Fulfilling the friar's prophecy, French armies swept down to scourge Italy's sins, but Florence, having exiled the Medici, was reserved for a tyrant immeasurably harsher. Roused by Savonarola's fanatical sermons, crowds of boys raced through the city attacking gamblers, pastrymongers, and richly dressed women. Repentant merchants, terrified by his rasping threats, surrendered ill-gotten gains. Painters abandoned harlots who posed for them as the Virgin Mary, and embraced religion instead. But war, economic depression, and his own fanaticism unleashed an opposition strong enough to challenge Savonarola's hold on Florence. Impoverished butchers nagged the friar for subsidies or for an end to frequent compulsory fasts. Youths, frustrated by blue laws which exiled the harlots, smeared his pulpit with ordure and poured ink into the holy water font. So fierce were the taunts of rivals that one of Savonarola's monks volunteered to walk through fire to prove the truth of the prophet's visions. He was protected, enemies claimed, by an enchanted red cloak, but when he removed it, rain delayed the trial. Cheated of the spectacle, the volatile Florentines turned on Savonarola, and eventually imprisoned him high in the tower of the Palazzo Vecchio (left). There, at the command of his torturers, he made a delirious recantation, confessing that he had deceived Florence in order to gain glory for himself.

With two followers, Savonarola was hanged and then burned on a gibbet cut to destroy its resemblance to a cross. An unknown artist recorded the scene (left) in the great square of Florence. The friar's posthumous portrait (right) is by Fra Bartolommeo, a painter who burned his nude studies and became a monk under the influence of Savonarola.

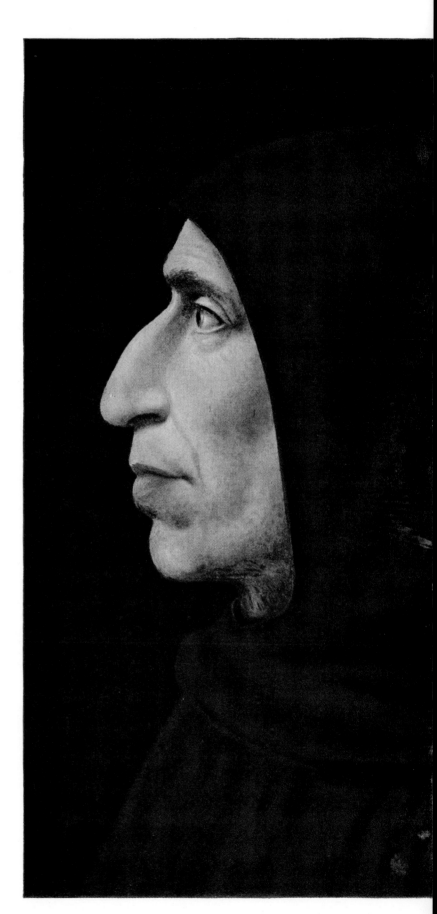

MILAN
CITY OF STRIFE

Milan seemed singularly favored by nature; to the south, over an easy pass in the Apennines, lay the great seaport of Genoa, a city of such majesty that the Venetians feared its power and envied its wealth; to the west and north swept the great arc of the Alps, as natural a frontier as a statesman could wish for; the few mountain passes that led to France or southern Germany gave Milan control of the routes from the great Genoese emporium to the markets of the North. Seen spread across an atlas of physical geography, the great, fertile valley of the Po seems one of the more natural places in Europe for the development of a strong unified state. Between the fall of the Roman Empire and the unification of Italy in the nineteenth century this was achieved only once—by Napoleon. The history of the Lombard plain is a history of invasion and war. For more than a thousand years some of Europe's bloodiest battles were fought on it. If Florence belonged to Minerva, Milan belonged to Mars.

The trouble lay partly in the fertility of the alluvial plain: the great walls of the Alps and the Apennines gave it some of the forcing quality of a hothouse. Crops grew with ease; heavy crops meant a large and prosperous population; and the whole of Lombardy was studded with thriving cities—Turin, Pavia, Lodi, Brescia, Bergamo, Vicenza, Verona, Padua, Ferrara, Bologna, Mantua, Parma, Piacenza, and Alessandria, among others. Only in times of desperation were these cities capable of acting in unity, as when the Emperor Frederick Barbarossa attempted to extend his power over them; otherwise they were content to intrigue and plot and fight among themselves. From time to time a city or a family arose like a bubble in this boiling cauldron, and like a bubble burst. Furthermore, the Holy Roman Emperor often found it advantageous to strengthen his natural aristocratic allies at the expense of the communes, for the Emperor preserved the legal right of overlordship, even if he failed often enough to exercise it in fact. What he never failed to do, once he possessed the strength, was to angle for greater power in these

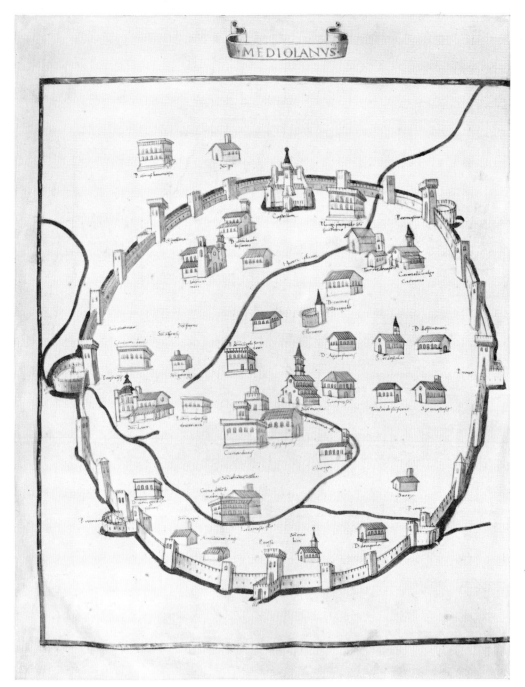

MEDIOLANVS

troubled but fish-laden waters. In this he was not alone. The princes of Savoy found morsels of the Lombard plain far sweeter than the granite wastes of the Alps which their country bestrode. Beyond Savoy were the French, whose king was willing to try to hold Savoy in check—at a price—or urge him forward if they were unpaid. And naturally the two great parties, the Guelphs and the Ghibellines, which polarized so many ancient feuds, thought that they could manipulate the great European powers to their advantage.

Milan and its satellite cities had failed to do what Florence and the Tuscan towns had succeeded in doing—they had never subjected the feudal nobility to the authority of the merchant class. In this bull ring of Europe, it is not surprising that men harassed by invasion, ruined by petty strife, and hamstrung by vendettas should dream of a "natural" state in which princes—powerful, all-wise, and intensely patriotic—should succeed generation after generation, wielding an iron authority that brought peace and fame. At times the imagina-

tion of poet and panegyrist soared in a wilder flight and saw the princes of Milan, whether Visconti or Sforza, adding to the duchy of Lombardy the kingship of all Italy. There were three dukes of Milan—Gian Galeazzo Visconti, Francesco Sforza, and Lodovico Il Moro—who, for the brief periods of their rule, removed, at least, all absurdity from this vision, although they were far too realistic ever to indulge themselves in such fantasies. Nevertheless, they did between them what no other rulers did: they created a state equal in power and wealth to Florence and to Venice. Milan, which became the epitome of the Renaissance state, is best seen reflected in the lives of its three greatest dukes.

The Visconti's emblem was a viper, and they had needed all the serpent's cunning not only to survive the vicissitudes of a fickle and bloody fortune but also to grow in riches and in authority. By the time Gian Galeazzo Visconti was born in 1351, his family had played a leading part in Lombardic affairs for over two hundred years. They had resolutely de-

Gian Galeazzo Visconti, seen at left in Pisanello's drawing, ousted his uncle as lord of Milan, then, it was rumored, tried to poison him. Bernabò's bust, above, is part of a funeral monument fortunately commissioned while he was still in power.

fended the interests of the merchants, acquired increasing judicial authority from the Holy Roman Emperor to provide a legal basis for their power, and arranged their marriages with dynastic prudence. Nevertheless, his father had been forced to fight for his inheritance, for the death of a Visconti ruler, followed as it was by the division of his lands among his heirs, always provided an opening to rebels and exiles in the discontented cities on the fringes of their lands. Galeazzo II shared the Visconti territories with his brother Bernabò, who ruled in Milan, while he remained at Pavia. Bernabò struggled to regain Bologna, Galeazzo to push westward to the Alps; in so doing they aroused a hornets' nest, and in 1373 they were nearly overwhelmed. It was a typical story of treachery, turbulence, and violence that fed the darker side of Galeazzo's nature—his suspicion, his avarice, his hate. His son Gian Galeazzo, born of his diplomatic marriage with Blanche of Savoy, was turned as quickly as possible to dynastic ends. At the age of nine he was married off to Isabelle of

Valois, a princess of France, and by the time he was fourteen she had produced him a son. Both in battle and in diplomacy he proved equally precocious; but when he inherited his father's lands in 1378, his position was far from enviable. His uncle Bernabò, with a reputation for brutality and violence even in his own age, still ruled in Milan, and he had five sons, all ambitious, all land-hungry.

Gian Galeazzo was already known for his resource and cunning, but the latter got the better of his discretion. He suddenly made a wild bid for greatness. He secretly negotiated his own betrothal (his first wife had died at twenty-three) to the heiress of Sicily—a bargain that stood if he consummated the marriage within twelve months. The news outraged the particularist sentiments of the Italian princes, and they made certain that the bride never got within five hundred miles of her groom. And while Gian Galeazzo was wrestling with his strange problem of logistics, his uncle Bernabò extorted concession after concession from him, to

According to family tradition, the marriage of Venus and Anchises inaugurated the Visconti dynasty. The nuptial ceremony, performed by Jupiter himself, is illustrated at right; in line beneath the couple are their descendants, headed by Aeneas, a collateral ancestor of the Visconti. The lady at left displays a shield and a helmet crested with the suggestive family emblem, a serpent eating a man.

make certain that the Visconti of Pavia should never be linked with the power of Sicily to the discomfiture of the Visconti of Milan. When the year had passed, Gian Galeazzo found himself without a wife and tied dynastically far tighter than he had ever been to his uncle, for the latter insisted that, having failed with the heiress of Sicily, Gian Galeazzo's bride should be his daughter Caterina, and no obstruction was placed before the immediate consummation of this marriage.

Gian Galeazzo complied, and brooded. He cultivated his garden. He devoted his considerable intelligence and remarkable concentration to the problems of government. He reduced taxation, reformed administration, weeded out corruption, and what leisure he had from the cares of government he spent on the adornment of his palace, the conversation of scholars, and consultation with astrologers. Although he enjoyed a reputation for piety, he placed his trust in the efficacy of the zodiac rather than of prayer, and when the stars were truly propitious, he set out on a pilgrimage to the Madonna

del Monte at Varese. His timidity was known, and his entourage therefore surprised no one by its size; he hesitated (it was assumed through fear) to enter Milan, so his uncle and his cousins rode out to meet him. After an affectionate greeting they were taken prisoner, and Gian Galeazzo entered Milan to cries of "Long live the Count, and down with the taxes!" Gian Galeazzo's wife seems to have taken the destruction of her father and brothers with the phlegm usual in a Renaissance princess. The boldness of his enterprise was widely admired, and even Geoffrey Chaucer in far-off London turned a few verses on the event in his *Canterbury Tales.*

This success naturally gave Gian Galeazzo confidence, and since he was highly intelligent, he learned from it. More important than the timing of the plot, in the proper conjunction of the stars, was the fact that the Milanese did not close their gates but welcomed him as a liberator—a sentiment which he quickly turned to an article of faith by distributing some of Bernabò's treasure to the great financial relief of those whom

Seated on the lap of the Virgin Mary, the infant Christ welcomes Gian Galeazzo Visconti to heaven. This miniature and the family tree on the facing page are taken from a manuscript of the Duke's funeral eulogy.

he needed as allies. For the next seventeen years he exploited the paternalism of his government so that he might realize his almost insatiable dynastic ambitions. In order to impose his iron despotism, he posed as the liberator of cities and men. His success was the result of unwearying application, aided by good fortune and blended with a nice sense of contingencies. "He was wont," wrote his chronicler, Giovio, "to give himself up to meditation during solitary walks, to hold discussions with those who were most experienced in every branch of affairs, to quote instances from the annals of the past. He found relaxation for his mind in the conversation of scholars and in constant reading." Not for him, it would seem, "the delights of hunting or hawking, nor games of dice nor the allurements of women, nor the tales of buffoons and jesters." He thought, he planned, he acted. In two swift campaigns, having made certain that treachery was rife in the cities he wished to conquer, he had absorbed all of eastern Lombardy save Mantua and Ferrara.

The Florentines, of course, were deeply disturbed to see one tyrant control all the Alpine passes on which so much of their trade depended, and they used their powers of persuasion, of which the florin proved the most efficacious, to raise a league against Gian Galeazzo. This merely succeeded in enlarging Gian Galeazzo's ambitions, for he was quick to realize that his gains could never be consolidated so long as Florence remained unsubjected. To do this he proceeded with skill and caution; each city-state had its party that hated Florence or the powers that ruled it. He fought wars when he had to, but he adroitly avoided a head-on collision with the combined powers of Florence and Venice. By 1402 he had acquired control of Pisa, Siena, Perugia, and Bologna, and it was within his power to strangle Florence politically and economically. The foundation of a great northern Italian kingdom seemed within his grasp, when he caught a fever and died.

By that time Gian Galeazzo had done more than enlarge the boundaries of his dukedom, for he had created a state as

well as a despotism. He centralized government, reformed administration, and removed inequalities and special rights and privileges. Where possible he weakened the feudal nobility and encouraged the merchant class. He tried to fulfill the ideal which his humanists at Pavia had delineated—that of a "natural prince" whose state was serenely based on justice and equality. And by these means he had created the duchy of Milan, a coherent state that was to last until Napoleon swept it away. In many ways he is the prototype of the Renaissance prince—unscrupulous in diplomacy, yet deeply concerned for the welfare of the state; passionately ambitious for his dynasty, yet aware of the needs of his country; scholarly, remote, and dedicated to the pursuit of power.

Gian Galeazzo's death broke up his empire. His captains of war thought no opportunity better for taking their pickings; the Tuscan and Umbrian cities, mindful now of the power of Florence, threw off their allegiance. The Venetians' indifference to Gian Galeazzo's success turned to alarm; his

demise brought about a fundamental change in their policy. They decided to be a Lombard power—to secure territorial control of the Alpine passes which they needed for their trade, and of sufficient territory to give them ground for maneuver against a resurgent Milan. Once again the great feudal families whose power Gian Galeazzo had attempted to reduce flourished their standards. The Colleoni, Anguisola, Cavalcabò, and Correggio demanded their pounds of flesh, and the plain of Lombardy once more reeked of blood and slaughter, pillage and rape. In the midst of this desolation the Milanese core of the Visconti state held firm. It is a measure of Gian Galeazzo's success that it did so, for in some ways his heir was a greater disaster than the conflagrations of war that consumed Lombardy. Although it is certainly untrue that he fed his hounds on human flesh, such were his tyrannies that the Milanese had no difficulty in believing the story. His assassination in church in 1412 caused no surprise. Perhaps as a tribute to his brother's memory, his successor, Fi-

Upon the completion of the Certosa of Pavia (opposite), the income from its building endowment was supposed to revert to Pavia's poor. Citizens clamored for the work to end, but it took one hundred and fifty years before the poor finally enjoyed their revenue. Scholars were rewarded more promptly. When the humanist Filelfo, whose portrait medal appears at left, found his salary in arrears, his strident complaints soon elicited cash from Francesco Sforza. The Duke was awed by scholarship, and gave liberal support to the University of Pavia, a center of Italian legal studies. The relief below shows one of the lecturers at the university.

lippo Maria, had the murderers put to death by the most refined tortures. By nature Filippo Maria was not excessively cruel, merely neurotic. He was obese to the point of ridicule, and ugly to the point of embarrassment. His portrait was never painted, his marriage never consummated, and his appearance in public rare. Nevertheless, he ruled with skill if without panache. He maintained the machinery of the state and kept his head above the turbulent waters of Italian politics. Precluded by nature from the pursuit of martial glory, he was content to employ one of the best condottieri for this duty—Francesco Sforza—at least from time to time, for Filippo could never trust anyone for long.

Sforza, the son of one of the first great Italian condottieri —Muzio Sforza—came, as most condottieri did, from the Romagna, which had little to sell but the strength of its men. Sforza proved himself a great captain. His direct manner, tough physique, and aggressive nature made him an excellent general; his attention to detail, ferocious discipline, and deep personal loyalty gave him a band of soldiers of passionate devotion and exemplary technique. His personal magnetism was such that he won the enduring friendship of the two most outstanding men of his day—the highly sophisticated and cultivated banker Cosimo de' Medici, and the equally highly cultivated condottiere Federigo da Montefeltro. In the hard, tough school of war he won himself a vast reputation and a small territory, too small either for his purse or his ambition. And the situation in Milan was as clear to him as to his friends. Cosimo de' Medici did not relish the steady advance of Venetian power across the Lombard plain (the Alpine passes were vital to Florentine trade, and the Venetians were traders first and republicans second). A powerful, friendly Milan had become a necessity to Florence, so Cosimo provided Francesco with good advice and handsome loans. Federigo, as generous a condottiere as ever lived, admired Francesco's prowess as only a professional could, but he preferred, naturally enough, that Francesco should win his kingdom in

FRAN·SFOR·VIC·
N
DX
MLI
IIII
PATER PATRIAE

Filippo Maria Visconti, whose medal by Pisanello is at left, was so timid that he had double walls to shut the sound of thunder out of his chamber. The reverse, below, shows the Duke on horseback, attended by guards. Francesco Sforza (lower left) was bolder; he rode through Milan every day on his way to hunt, and exchanged greetings with the citizens. A predecessor, Bernabò Visconti, had been so fond of hunting that he kept 5,000 hounds and tortured anyone who interfered with them. Francesco, whose interest in the sport was more temperate, paid an authority to compose a treatise on it for him. On the facing page is an illustration from it, showing courtiers hunting waterfowl.

Lombardy and not on *his* doorstep in the Romagna, where the Sforza had their patrimony.

Filippo Maria did not need to be instructed in the drift of their thoughts, for he was as subtle as his father if less ambitious. It proved toil enough for him to weld together the Visconti lands, bring the recalcitrant nobles and cities to a proper subjection, and withstand the encroachments of Venice. For these projects he needed Francesco, and to stay alive for his natural span in his castle of Milan, it was necessary to keep Sforza both expectant and dependent. So Francesco rattled his sword, and Filippo Maria dangled his daughter—not a legitimate daughter, of course, but a mistress had been more skillful than a wife, and Bianca was the result. The long wrangle ended in a betrothal; a longer engagement ended in a wedding; the wedding ended in a son and heir. Before, however, his succession had been determined, Filippo died, when Francesco was away from Visconti territory.

The Milanese erupted with republican sentiment, abolished

the dukedom, and created chaos. Neither Venice nor Florence was amused by the advent of a sister republic and gave no help as its troubles multiplied. Sforza moved cautiously until the republic crumbled, and when he finally entered Milan, the citizens went wild with delight, rushed him and his horse into the Duomo, and acclaimed him duke. For many years that was the sole right the Sforza had to their dukedom—that and the sharp edge of their swords—for the emperors refused to acknowledge them. The powers of Italy, however, lacked the prejudice of the Germans, and while Francesco consolidated his power with military precision, the Medici got a bank in Milan, and alliances were formed with France, Savoy, Naples, and Florence. The Sforza went bullheaded for peace and stability. Wars there could not fail to be, but Sforza wanted them local, petty, and circumscribed.

The dukes of Milan became an accepted fact in the major state-system of Italy as Francesco Sforza completed the work Gian Galeazzo Visconti had begun. No condottiere had won

such a prize as Francesco; and the tough captain who had once stood amazed by the luxury of Pavia and the splendor of its library now enjoyed the prosperity his sword had brought him. War or no war, the Milanese throve. Francesco settled his court at Milan, the heart of his dukedom, ruling his subjects until his death in 1466 as he had once led his troops—wisely, directly, decisively—always keeping within the limits of the possible. About him there was something of the inexorable single-mindedness of the long-distance runner. Unhappily, his children proved more devious, more extravagant, more brutal even than their Visconti ancestors. The Sforza brood would have done honor to the pages of the most bloodthirsty of Elizabethan dramatists. And the story of Milan and its Renaissance reaches a climax in the rule of Lodovico Sforza.

Francesco was a great warrior—in love as well as in war—and his brood of Sforza, legitimate and illegitimate (the difference in Renaissance Italy was scarcely remarked—Francesco himself was a bastard), numbered twenty. Lodovico was number six (legitimate), so his prospects of the throne of Milan were remote enough. He possessed, however, one card, spurious perhaps, but not without value: he was the first legitimate child to be born *after* Francesco had been acclaimed Duke of Milan. Its use, however, lay in the future, for his brother Galeazzo Maria Sforza had every intention of enjoying to the full the power and the riches which his father had bequeathed him. Indeed, his court left no doubt that the Sforza had arrived, that the wealth of Milan was vast, that neither the Doge in Venice, the Pope in Rome, the Medici in Florence, nor the Aragonese kings in Naples could outvie them in magnificence. The great Castello Sforzesco, built like the Tower of London on the verge of the city—a convenience which fulfilled both the needs of strategy and sport—witnessed some of the most remarkable spectacles of the fifteenth century. Galeazzo loved shows. He made St. George's Day the great military spectacle of the year; tournaments, pageants, processions gave his mania full rein, and he thought nothing of

ordering a thousand or more special liveries in costly velvet to put on his servants' backs. A greater pleasure still was to take a visiting prince or ambassador to his jewel house, Galeazzo's special pride and joy, where rubies, emeralds, sapphires, and diamonds lay in heaps—a treasure which King Christian of Denmark somewhat churlishly called "unbefitting a true and generous prince." Galeazzo, however, possessed a taste for more refined delights: his interest in music led him to comb Flanders, let alone Italy, for the singers who were almost the dominating passion of his life. Almost, but not quite: undoubtedly Galeazzo's greatest pleasures were drawn from the enjoyment of his courtiers' wives and the exercise of his personal power; and neither endeared him to his subjects. The latter, in fact, was his undoing. Rumors of his cruelty were inflated to the heights of a Gothic fairy tale, and rendered just as macabre by the Duke's pious, almost morbid, insistence on the strictest observance of religious ritual. So perhaps it was not entirely unfitting that his

assassins should have dispatched him in church. They were a typical Renaissance bunch—a penniless noble adventurer, a cousin who resented the rape of his sister, an old, very disreputable master of rhetoric who had preached too ardently, and practiced too publicly, the Greek way of life, and a youthful republican intoxicated by the concept of tyrannicide, who, as he was slowly and carefully torn to pieces, murmured, *"Mors acerba fama perpetua est."*

Galeazzo's wife was deeply troubled that her husband, whom she knew so well, should have been dispatched unconfessed. She made a list of his sins and was appalled. He was, she wrote, "Versed in warfare, both lawful and unlawful; in pillage, robbery, and devastation of the country; in extortion of subjects; in negligence of justice; in injustice knowingly committed; in the imposition of new taxes which even included the clergy; in carnal vices; in notorious and scandalous simony and innumerable other crimes." Obviously the torments of Galeazzo in Purgatory would be long and grievous,

The impressive Castello Sforzesco, shown in a sixteenth-century engraving (opposite), was fortified by Francesco Sforza despite the advice of one Milanese citizen who reminded him that princes should rely solely on the love of their subjects for protection. Francesco could trust his people, but his son Galeazzo Maria, whose portrait by Pollaiuolo appears at left, was beyond protection after ten years of misrule. A woodcut below shows his assassination by conspirators who had spent days stabbing each other with sheathed daggers to rehearse their crime. Galeazzo unwisely ignored comets, ravens, and other omens foretelling his death, and imprisoned a priest who had warned him that he would not rule eleven years.

so the Duchess implored the aid of the Pope. The Pope, moved by the distress of the widow, granted absolution in return for a considerable subsidy for the papal army.

Galeazzo left a child and five brothers; so the years after his death proved dramatic enough for Milan and Italy. Conspiracies in Genoa and Parma linked themselves with greater conspiracies, engineered by the Pope and the King of Naples, in Florence. Lodovico tried his utmost to kidnap the child Duke, but he failed until the ructions in Florence gave him the backing of the Holy Father and King Ferrante. With luck and good judgment, aided by the silliness of the Duke's mother and the misguided cunning of her lover, Lodovico became regent of Milan. He imprisoned the Duchess, ousted her favorite, and chopped off the head of Cecco Simonetta, the brilliant ducal secretary who throughout his long life had devotedly served the Sforza, for the crime of attempting to secure an undivided inheritance for the legitimate heir. Fortunately for Lodovico, his most active and ambitious

brothers had died during the struggle for power, and his nephew proved so weak in intellect and character that it was unnecessary to dispatch him. As soon as this internecine struggle was over, Milan settled down to such spectacular festivities that they pushed the memories of Galeazzo's junketings to the commonplace. The child Duke was betrothed to Isabella of Aragon, and Lodovico himself took Beatrice d'Este, the daughter of the Duke of Ferrara and granddaughter of the King of Naples, for his bride. Although their marriages were long delayed, the festivities celebrating their nuptials provided the hired chroniclers of the court of Milan, long practiced in rhetoric and panegyric, a subject worthy of their hyperbole. Men and women were dressed, or rather undressed, as pagan gods and goddesses; fabulous animals were wondrously contrived; knights jousted in Moorish costumes; wild men, dressed by Leonardo da Vinci, scared the ladies; dwarfs, giants, hunchbacks provided robust fun; sycophantic poets produced verse by the ream to give a sense of immortal oc-

casion; the best musicians of Milan, and they were certainly the best in Italy, played and sang through the day and night; masques with elaborate scenery and ingenious fireworks linked the intervals between Gargantuan banquets. The prodigious munificence of Lodovico naturally stirred the interest of painters, sculptors, engineers, historians, philosophers, and poets. Leonardo, frustrated and restless in Florence, was one of the first to seek his patronage.

Lodovico's extravagance was not mere self-indulgence. He wished to demonstrate not only the wealth and power of the Milanese state but also his own supreme control. He was a highly intelligent man with a deep sense of cunning, who realized acutely the insecurity of his realm as well as of his dynasty. Prosperity, he thought, would cure the former, diplomacy the latter. He cultivated the rich Lombard plain assiduously. He promoted canals. He encouraged new crops, particularly rice. He fostered trade and manufacture. And his interest in Leonardo da Vinci owed as much to the artist's in-

ventive genius in mechanics and fortifications as to his ability as a sculptor and painter. By such means he created the sinews of power, but its exploitation depended on his wit.

Milan's dangers were these: first Venice, secondly France, thirdly the Holy Roman Emperor, and fourthly the Swiss, who could be manipulated by the others. Milan had been intermittently at war with Venice since the Venetians decided to become a mainland power at the beginning of the fifteenth century. The problems represented by the Emperor and France were interrelated. For Lodovico's Visconti ancestors, the Emperor had been a safety factor, since they were his legal representatives in Lombardy. The Sforza were not, however, and the legal basis of their power had to rest on popular acclamation. To complicate the matter further, the Visconti had intermarried with the junior branches of the French royal family, and this had given the French certain dynastic claims on Milan. Furthermore, the French had always coveted Genoa, which was a linchpin of the Milanese economy; and

they supported the Anjou pretensions to the throne of Naples. To create some stability in this world fraught with danger, Lodovico, Lorenzo de' Medici, and Ferrante, the King of Naples, had enacted the Triple Alliance. Together they had been able to present the threat of sufficient force to make external or internal powers hesitate to attack them. War had not been abolished, but certainly the Triple Alliance diminished it, and Lodovico was the beneficiary. Milan had other reasons than the Triple Alliance for friendship with Naples. Ties between the two cities had been strengthened by the marriage of the young Duke and Ferrante's granddaughter, Isabella of Aragon. Or so it would seem. Reasons of state and reasons of strategy were at variance, however, with Lodovico's personal ambition. He wished to be Duke of Milan, *de jure* as well as *de facto*. That meant setting aside, or killing, the young Duke, whose wife already bitterly resented the anomaly of her position and the slights, real and imagined, from Lodovico's wife—the intelligent, formidable, and far

from discreet Beatrice d'Este. Behind the wronged wife, Naples could be arrayed; so might France, for the Duke of Orléans had better dynastic claims than Lodovico; so might the Emperor, who could bestow his Vicariate on whomsoever he wished. In so complex a situation Lodovico worked his astrologers hard, and the conjunction and combination of the stars became his daily concern. The point of desperation was reached when his nephew came of age and fathered an heir before Beatrice d'Este produced a son for Lodovico. The arrival of an heir to the dukedom was received with modest celebrations, and much to Isabella's fury the banquets, jousts, pageants, and *Te Deums* that celebrated the birth of Lodovico's son were as splendiferous as they were prolonged. No doubt remained as to how the Regent's mind was working.

Lodovico's opportunity came when Charles VIII of France, who had acquired the Anjou claims to the Neapolitan throne, having settled his quarrel with the Emperor, thought that he might exercise his nobility and seek honor and reward by in-

vading Naples. This seeming act of folly Lodovico encouraged; and in return for his benevolent neutrality Charles supported Lodovico's claim to the Emperor to be appointed Imperial Vicar of Milan—a legitimization of power never yet won by a Sforza. A further piece of luck—as no doubt the stars had foretold—took place. His nephew, the Duke, died. Lodovico proclaimed the infant Francesco duke. Not surprisingly, the Council would not have him; they begged Lodovico, at such a time of peril for the state, to assume the title with the power. Lodovico complied; the populace cheered. So Lodovico achieved his *coup d'état*—a bloodless one and timed to perfection. In his campaign against Naples, Charles VIII proved almost miraculously successful (as is common with military miracles, it was based on superior armament, particularly cannon). With Charles thus occupied and the imperial edict safe in his pocket, Lodovico suddenly changed sides, and when Charles began to withdraw from Italy, Sforza was one of those who harried and hurried him on his way. Then,

sensing the possible benefits, he seized the opportune moment to switch allegiance to Charles once again.

So Lodovico had his years of triumph. He could boast that the Pope was his chaplain, the Emperor his condottiere, Venice his chamberlain, and the King of France his courier. For a time Milan was prosperous, the court brilliant, the prince magnificent. And then death took a hand. Beatrice, who had done so much to bring Lodovico's subtleties to decisive action, died in childbed. Charles VIII of France also died; his successor, Louis XII, claimed Milan and regarded Charles VIII's failure to take it for him as a disgrace. Apart from Naples, which feared a fresh invasion, the powers of Italy leaped as rapidly as possible onto the French bandwagon (Venice alone bargaining hard for its ticket) and were overjoyed that the victim beneath the juggernaut's wheels should be Lodovico. The French won; Lodovico retreated to the Tirol; the French puppet outraged the Milanese; Lodovico returned; so did the French, and won again with consummate ease. This time they

Although his plumed helmet made him an easy target, the French King Francis I emerged unscathed from the Battle of Marignano in 1515 (opposite). His victory sent Massimiliano Sforza into exile and brought Milan under foreign rule for the third time in twenty years. In 1493 Sforza power had been at its zenith; Lodovico bribed the Holy Roman Emperor into marrying a Sforza princess, and capped the wedding celebration by exhibiting Leonardo da Vinci's monumental clay model of a horse, part of a statue planned in honor of Francesco Sforza. (At right is one of Leonardo's preliminary studies.) But by the time the huge horse was ready for casting, Lodovico could no longer afford the ten tons of bronze required for it.

packed Lodovico off to France, where his imprisonment was strict enough to titillate the most morbid humanist, obsessed with the fate of tyrants. He finally died in a tiny, lightless, underground cell in the dungeon of Loches.

It was not the end of the Sforza. They had become pawns in the battle between the great European powers who used Lombardy as their tilting ground. Sforza's son, Massimiliano, was brought back by the lances of the Swiss, and after a brief and extravagant career he was removed, after the Battle of Marignano, by Francis I and pensioned, not imprisoned, in France. These two wars, which devastated Milan, were soon followed by a third, when Charles V, who combined the formidable power of his Holy Roman Empire with that of Spain, decided to expel the French from Lombardy. This he did in 1525 outside the great Visconti capital of Pavia. It was a fitting place, for with that battle the last gleams of Milanese independence disappeared. The reason for this tale of blood is not far to seek. Although Milan possessed natural frontiers

and great wealth and an able ruling house, as a state it never acquired the stability of Florence or Venice or even Naples, simply because its class struggles went unresolved. The feudal nobility were never uprooted; they constantly quarreled with each other and provided a ready support for any adventurer, internal or external, who would favor their personal ambitions. This powerful aristocracy also thrived on the divisions and jealousies of the merchant class which hated it. Finally, Milan was hemmed about with cities almost as great as itself, all possessing rich, ambitious, jealous guilds of merchants who seesawed between wanting the stability which the leadership of Milan alone could bring and the gain that might accrue from its humiliation. In such an unstable world the abilities of the Visconti and the Sforza were largely wasted. The great horse designed by Leonardo for Lodovico in memory of his father seems curiously symbolic of their destiny— conceived in grandeur, executed in clay, never cast, ruined by the French, and destroyed by time.

A self-portrait, the only known likeness of Leonardo.

Leonardo da Vinci

by J. BRONOWSKI

Leonardo was born outside the small town of Vinci, near Florence, in 1452; the traditional date of his birthday is April 15. The birthday is hardly worth remembering, but the year is, for its remoteness remains a constant surprise. Leonardo's gifts speak so directly, his imagination is so immediate to us, that we have to remind ourselves with an effort that he was born more than five hundred years ago. He lived long before William Shakespeare and Rembrandt and Isaac Newton. Leonardo was dead before Nicolaus Copernicus felt sure that the earth goes around the sun; he was an old man, unhappy and full of regrets, when Martin Luther began the Reformation; and he had already passed the turning point of middle life when Christopher Columbus discovered America.

Leonardo was the illegitimate son of a lawyer and a woman who may have been a servant in the house of Leonardo's grandparents. The boy's father did take several wives—each a member of a good Florentine family—but not for over twenty years were there any more children. Leonardo was thus his father's only child during those formative years.

Italians in the Renaissance were not outraged by the thought that a bright child had been conceived out of wedlock. Illegitimacy was a commonplace of the time; men were proud of making their own way; and churchmen and condottieri, artists and statesmen, boasted that they were born out of wedlock. This was no stigma among the thrusting, self-made men of the Renaissance; indeed, as the historian Jakob Burckhardt wrote, "The fitness of the individual, his worth and capacity, were of more weight than all the laws and usages which prevailed elsewhere in the West."

Nevertheless, we get the feeling that Leonardo never walked easily in the houses of the great, and that this wariness goes back to his childhood. There is something hooded and withdrawn about his character which calls up a picture of a child made much of and yet not at home in the house of his birth. All his life he hated to see suffering. The story is told of Leonardo buying birds in the market place, holding them in his hand for a moment, and then setting them free. It is evident that in that rough, insensitive time he was one of the few men who could not bear to give pain to animals.

When Leonardo was about fourteen, his father apprenticed him to Andrea del Verrocchio, one of the foremost artists in Florence. The time was 1466 or thereabouts; Florence was aflower with wealth and splendor; its tone was set, its taste was led, by the great family of the Medici. Here the display of riches was more than a reward for success—it was almost a ritual, a public announcement of status and authority.

The *botteghe*, or workshops, of Verrocchio and other artists supplied this society with its beautiful treasures and trinkets. Verrocchio was a painter and sculptor, and was also a goldsmith and a decorator. His studio was, in an exact sense, a workshop, and it was Verrocchio's business to supply from it a picture or a chair, a statue or a goblet, a golden chafing dish or a ceremonial suit of armor. Verrocchio himself could turn his hand to all these things; however, he was a rather wooden painter, and he seems therefore to have turned more and more to sculpture.

One reason why Verrocchio could turn from painting was that his apprentice Leonardo was so good at it. The artist who ran his studio as a workshop had to conserve and to divide its labor intelligently and expediently; and when he had an apprentice who could paint, he gave him his head—and did something else himself. Tradition has it that Leonardo was still a boy when he painted an angel in one of Verrocchio's religious commissions, and made it more lifelike than his master could.

The story of the boy painter who outdoes his master is characteristic of the Renaissance; it is also told of Raphael and others. For this was an age in love with surprises, eager to discover genius, native and untaught. Yet the evidence is that the story is true of Leonardo. There is at least one picture by Verrocchio, *The Baptism of Christ,* in which one of the angels is unlike the rest, and has clearly been painted by a more sensitive and subtler hand. Moreover, the landscape of the *Baptism,* the detail of trees and grasses, has a vivid intimacy and an absorbed lucidness of vision which belong to no painter before Leonardo. There is at least one other painting by Verrocchio whose landscape shows the hand of Leonardo in the same way. Verrocchio must have known that the young Leonardo was not merely a better painter: he was a new painter.

Leonardo finished his training with Verrocchio about 1472, when he was twenty or so, and then went on working in Florence for another nine or ten years. He was good at other things besides painting. He is described as tall and handsome, graceful in all his actions, and apparently he had a fine singing voice, and the official records show that he was accused once of some homosexual scrape. (The evidence is that he lacked the usual sensual feelings for women, and tended rather to admire strong men.) He was interested in mathematics and mechanics, and particularly in the mechanics by which living things move: he constantly drew birds in flight, and he also made his first studies of human anatomy then.

These are odd interests in a painter, in the traditional sense; and yet they are inseparable from that desire to enter into the very structure of natural things which to Leonardo was the essence of painting. Later in life he wrote very simply about this:

And you who say that it is better to look at an anatomical demonstration than to see these drawings, you would be right, if it were possible to observe all the details shown in these drawings in a single figure, in which, with all your ability, you will not see nor acquire a knowledge of more than some few veins, while, in order to obtain an exact and complete knowledge of these, I have dissected more than ten human bodies, destroying all the various members, and removing even the very smallest particles of the flesh which surrounded these veins without causing any effusion of blood other than the imperceptible bleeding of the capillary veins. And, as one single body did not suffice for so long a time, it was necessary to proceed by stages with so many bodies as would render my knowledge complete; and this I repeated twice over in order to discover the differences.

This is an account of work in anatomy, but it carries no hint of a medical interest. For Leonardo did not want to cure men: he wanted to know how their bodies are made and work. He distrusted the doctors of his time, and indeed the whole of medical and chemical science then, which saw nature as an interplay of occult qualities. Leonardo looked at nature directly, not through the mind but through the eye. And his was a wonderful eye, sharp and abrupt as a camera, which could stop a bird in flight and fix the muscled movement of its wing. He wanted no speculation about the soul of the bird, which scholars were still repeating from Pythagoras; he wanted to understand the harsh mechanics of its flight:

A bird is an instrument working according to mathematical law, which instrument it is within the capacity of man to reproduce with all its movements, but not with a corresponding degree of strength, though it is deficient only in the power of maintaining equilibrium. We may therefore say that such an instru-

ment constructed by man is lacking in nothing except the life of the bird, and this life must needs be supplied from that of man.

These preoccupations with the structure of things, with the muscle under the skin and the bone under the muscle, seem to have grown on Leonardo from the time that he began to work for himself. They made him uninterested in, and perhaps unhappy with, the opportunities which Florence in the 1470's held out to artists who could display the warm beauty of the surface of things.

At this time Verrocchio was working on a statue of the great condottiere of Venice, Colleoni, and he left Florence to finish the work in Venice. Perhaps Leonardo felt that Florence was no longer the center of art it had once been. Or perhaps he could not resist the urge to create a statue better than Verrocchio's, for although he was not a sculptor, he wrote a long letter in 1482 to Lodovico Sforza in Milan, offering, among many other things, to make a statue of his father, the condottiere Francesco. In that same letter he described in detail his talents as a military engineer and inventor (two abilities likely to appeal to a Sforza), and soon after, at the age of thirty, he left Florence, carrying with him a silver lute that he had made in the shape of a horse's head, to spend nearly twenty years at the turbulent court of Milan.

Leonardo was in many respects self-taught, a self-willed man who did things almost truculently at times. Some of his paintings have perished as a result of ordinary bad luck, but others because of his insistence on mixing pigments with curious ingredients or on drying them in new and different ways. He was an innovator, an experimenter, a man never satisfied with the accepted or acceptable, and his decision to leave Florence was taken because Florence was a city of tradition, living on its golden dreams of the past.

We can only guess at the reasons for Leonardo's move from Florence to Milan. Yet if his reasons, intellectual and emotional, had any psychological coherence, it is clear enough what was the common strand in them. When Leonardo chose between Florence and Milan, he was not merely choosing between different cities: in a profound sense he was choosing between different cultures—between two different aspects of the Renaissance.

The Renaissance had begun, as its name implies, as a rebirth of a culture which had already been born once. It was, in the first place, a recovery of ancient learning, and the early Renaissance was not a revolution, but a revival.

Florence was above all the home of this classical revival. The medieval Church had leaned heavily on Aristotle, and had elevated him almost to the status of an honorary saint; now the Medici, in opposition, praised the work and the outlook of Plato. The pride of Florence was the Medici library of ancient manuscripts and commentaries on them, and the Platonic Academy. Florence in the 1470's, when Leonardo worked there, was dominated by the taste of the greatest of the Medici, Lorenzo the Magnificent, which was wholly classical and luxurious.

By contrast, Leonardo was one of the first men in whom the Renaissance expressed itself in a new way, not as a recovery but as a discovery. By the standards of Lorenzo, Leonardo was an unscholarly, unlettered painter: he did not even know Latin (he learned it later in Milan) and he never aspired to Greek. This is a subject to which he returned often and with heat in his notebooks:

I am fully aware that the fact of my not being a man of letters may cause certain arrogant persons to think that they may with reason censure me, alleging that I am a man ignorant of book-learning. Foolish folk! Do they not know that I might retort by saying, as did Marius to the Roman patricians, "They who themselves go about adorned in the labor of others will not permit me my own." They will say that because of my lack of book-learning, I cannot properly express what I desire to treat of. Do they not know that my subjects require for their exposition experience rather than the words of others? And since experience has been the mistress of whoever has written well, I take her as my mistress, and to her in all points make my appeal.

In this and other passages Leonardo is making two points. First, he is expressing his contempt for the new aristocracy of Florence, the moneyed men who lean on the talents of others, and whose taste, however authoritative, shows no mind of its own: "Whoever in discussion adduces authority uses not his intellect but rather memory." And second, Leonardo is setting up a new standard for the creation of works of art: the standard of the original mind that goes directly to nature, without intermediaries:

The painter will produce pictures of little merit if he takes the works of others as his standard; but if he will apply himself to learn from the objects of nature he will produce good results. This we see was the case with the painters who came after the time of the Romans, for they continually imitated each other, and from age to age their art steadily declined. . . . it is safer to go direct to the works of nature than to those which have been imitated from her originals with great deterioration and thereby to acquire a bad method, for he who has access to the fountain does not go to the water-pot.

In these quotations we have the crux of principle which divided Leonardo from his predecessors in the Renaissance. The medieval Church had taught that the universe can be understood only spiritually, as a God-given and abstract order; that the beauty of man and of nature is a snare which tempts us away from that stark understanding. The Renaissance denied these morose dogmas, holding instead that fleshly and natural beauty is not sinful, that it is, on the contrary, an expression of the divine order. Yet the form which this humanistic belief took was different at different times. The pioneers of the Renaissance found their ideal of man and nature in the splendid texts of the classics and in the works of art of antiquity. But the new men of the Renaissance, the self-taught and self-willed men like Leonardo, were not content with anything at second hand. They wanted to see, to understand, to enter into nature for themselves. Leonardo above all wanted not to recover, but to discover, his own humanity.

When Leonardo left Florence, he was, therefore, turning his back on the classical Renaissance, and looking for the kinship of other men who shared his thirst for a more popular Renaissance. It was natural that he should look for such men in Milan. Here was a city larger than Florence, less dependent on its rich men, less self-satisfied, and with a more cosmopolitan outlook toward the rest of Europe—particularly toward France and toward Germany. Printing had been invented before Leonardo was born, but hitherto had spread little into Italy; now in the 1480's it became important in Milan. Mathematics and mechanics, too, were more highly regarded in Milan than they were in the Platonic climate of Florence. Leonardo all his life was deeply drawn toward mathematics, and in Milan he drew the pictures for a book, *The Divine Proportion,* which the mathematician Luca Pacioli wrote and later printed. The divine proportion is that geometrical ratio which we now call the golden section, and it may be that this modern name was in fact first used for it by Leonardo da Vinci.

Intellectually, Leonardo was drawn to Milan because he was seeking a more downright and popular expression of Renaissance humanism than Florence offered. Emotionally, also, we sense that there was something about the brutal power of the court of Milan which attracted him more than the classical air of Florence. Lodovico Sforza was hardly a gracious man; yet something in the sinister directness of such a man, his naked drive to power, his simple and single will, plainly fascinated Leonardo. Like other sensitive men of the mind, he seems to have found a satisfaction in watching other men impose themselves ruthlessly on a world in which he himself was so ill at ease. We catch a hint of the same regard for male power in Leonardo's feelings for his model Giacomo Salai, whom he picked up in the streets of Milan, and whose endless misdeeds he forgave year in and year out with a tender and tolerant contempt.

This is another side of the search for the simplest, most rudimentary forces in man and in nature which took Leonardo to Milan. It made him accept the whims of Lodovico in a way in which he would not have accepted those of Lorenzo. Whatever his other faults may have been, Lodovico was an admirable patron. The fact that his patronage lacked the literary overtones of the Medici made it more attractive to Leonardo, and the variety of the work which Leonardo was called upon to perform at once appealed to his ingenuity, his curiosity, and his interest in experiment. In Milan, Leonardo became a busybody bending his great powers of invention to the trivial mechanics of court entertainment. He painted portraits of Lodovico's mistresses. He designed the costumes and devised the trick surprises of scenery for the court masques. To celebrate a visit of the King of France, he made an automaton shaped like a lion, which spilled a shower of lilies from its breast. He drew maps and proposed schemes of irrigation, he founded cannon and installed central heating, he planned engines of war and palaces, he designed a dozen schemes that Lodovico disregarded. And he went on making countless sketches of the most stupendous surprise of all, the statue of a rearing horse on which should sit Francesco Sforza, the soldier who had created the Milan that Lodovico now ruled. (It is interesting that he considered the animal the center of the monument, and that he should have referred to the statue simply as "the horse.") But like everything that Leonardo did for his patron, this also came to nothing.

Yet the years that Leonardo spent in Milan were not wasted. In an odd way, he could follow his bent here. The pageants and the plans that were expected of him can hardly have filled his time, and Lodovico was too busy with his ambitions to pester the court sculptor who had not finished his commission. In Milan, Leonardo did not have to work hard to earn his keep by doing the things that he knew how to do —above all, by painting. In one way this is a pity for us: we would have more great paintings, and fewer sketches, if Leonardo had had to deliver his work for cash during the years in Milan, when his gifts flowed most easily. But in another way we can be grateful that Leonardo in those years of his middle life did not have to do the things he could do so well, which somehow were becoming distasteful to him. Leonardo in Milan grew impatient with his own gifts; he did not care to paint, he disliked the likenesses that he could catch so swiftly, the tricks of light and shade, the surface appearances. His interest was more and more in the structure of things, and as a result his notebooks are now full of sketches which are always, as it were, taking nature to pieces. He did not want to copy: he wanted to understand.

An indication of how his mind was working during these years may be seen in the beautiful portrait of a mistress of Lodovico Sforza (see page 122), painted soon after Leonardo arrived in Milan. The sitter, who could have been no more than a girl when he painted her, was probably Cecilia Gallerani. The ermine which she holds in her arms was an emblem of Lodovico, and is probably also a pun on the girl's name. And in a sense the whole picture is a pun, for Leonardo has matched the ermine in the girl. In the skull under the long brow, in the lucid eyes, in the stately, beautiful, stupid head of the girl, he has rediscovered the animal nature; and done so without malice, almost as a matter of fact. The very carriage of the girl and the ermine, the gesture of the hand and the claw, explore the character with the anatomy. The painting is as much a research into man and animal, and a creation of unity, as is Darwin's *Origin of Species.*

The notebooks of Leonardo are as unexpected, and as personal, as everything about him. There are about five thousand pages of them which have been preserved. Each page is a wonderful jumble of drawings and notes, in which a piece of geometry, a horse's head, an astronomical conjecture, and a flower stand side by side. A photograph shows all this with Leonardo's transparent clarity, but it does not show the delicate scale on which Leonardo worked. Many of the pages in the notebooks, crowded with detail, are no bigger than a man's hand. This is perhaps another expression of Leonardo's withdrawn and indrawn character, and so, no doubt, is the mirror writing which Leonardo used, writing with his left hand. The shading in his drawings is left-handed also, but it is not certain that he painted with his left hand. It is possible that he had damaged his right hand in Florence, and that thereafter he still used it, but only for the most delicate parts of his pictures. The pocket notebooks, the left-handed shading, the mirror writing, express something else, too, in Leonardo's character: a determination to do everything for himself, in his own way, down to the smallest detail. Witness, for example, his anatomical drawings showing the hollows and blood vessels in the head—drawings so exact that they have been compared point by point with photographs made by X-ray or by radioactive tracers. It is not only the enormous scope of his researches that is impressive, it is the absorption, the meticulousness, and the intensity with which he looked for the mechanism behind what he saw. Leonardo was not merely an original man, in the sense that he had two or three profound and new ideas. He had a passion for looking afresh at everything that came into his life, no matter how trivial the occasion. In this sense, he was not merely an original but a perverse man; and perhaps all the oddities of his life reach back into the childhood of the lonely boy.

"Intellectual passion drives out sensuality," Leonardo wrote on a page of his notebooks. But perhaps his tragic and unfulfilled life proves that when the intellect becomes the subject of such a passion, it ends by being a kind of perversion.

Leonardo's notebooks from this time are full of the penetrating observation of nature, particularly in the anatomical drawings; and are full, too, of a springing invention which was fired by his observation. He had long been absorbed by the flight of birds, and now it led him to invent a parachute and a form of helicopter. The fact that the latter did not work may be blamed on the age in which he lived, which did not understand, and could not have commanded, the mechanical energy necessary for flight. He observed, one hundred years before Galileo, that the pendulum might be used to make a clockwork keep equal time. He saw that red light penetrates through mist and that blue light does not, and so devised practical rules for giving depth to the painting of landscapes. There are mechanisms on his pages here and there which he noted from others, but the bulk of what he outlined was original, and it included various types of bridges, a mechanical excavator, machines for grinding needles and mirrors, a rolling mill, an automatic file cutter, an instrument for measuring wind speeds, and a self-centering chuck. Here is a characteristic invention, which characteristically goes into every essential detail:

A Way of Saving Oneself in a Tempest or Shipwreck at Sea

It is necessary to have a coat made of leather with a double hem over the breast of the width of a finger, and double also from the girdle to the knee, and let the leather of which it is made be quite air-tight. And when you are obliged to jump into the sea, blow out the lappets of the coat through the hems of the breast, and then jump into the sea. And let yourself be carried by the waves, if there is no shore near at hand and you do not know the sea. And always keep in your mouth the end of the tube through which the air passes into the garment; and if once or twice it should become necessary for you to take a breath when the foam prevents you, draw it through the mouth of the tube from the air within the coat.

There is no wonder that, as Leonardo grew more absorbed in the mechanism of nature, the work which he had come to Milan to do was put off further and further. At last, in 1493, it could be put off no longer. Lodovico Sforza was arranging to marry his niece to the Emperor Maximilian. Leonardo made a full-sized model of the statue of Francesco Sforza on horseback in clay. The bronze to cast the statue was gathered, too, but that had to be sent off next year to make cannon for Lodovico's allies. Lodovico was now deep in intrigue, trying to marshal one group of the city-states of Italy against another. Finally he invited the French to come into Italy on his side, and they, as treacherous as Lodovico, entered Milan in 1499. Lodovico fled, but a year later they took him prisoner.

Leonardo also fled from Milan in that year, a defeated man now nearing fifty, who had given the richest years of his life to a second-rate tyrant with a passion for power. The French archers had used the clay horse and its rider as a target, and there remained in Milan little to show for Leonardo's spent years except a painting of the Last Supper which be-
gan to molder on its damp convent wall even before the artist died. The prior had complained that Leonardo had been dilatory in finishing even that, and Leonardo in revenge had said that he would paint the prior for eternity into the figure of Judas. Yet, characteristically, when it came to the point, Leonardo had done something more profound with the figure of Judas: he had moved Judas out of the place that the Middle Ages had assigned to him and had put him on the same side of the table with Jesus.

Leonardo lived for twenty years after the fall of Milan, wandering irresolutely from one city to another, and from one commission to another, without ever again settling down to any one. In 1502 he served briefly in the train of Cesare Borgia as military engineer. This was the same treacherous campaign on which Niccolò Machiavelli was present— the one which provided the Florentine diplomat with a portrait of undeviating ambition for *The Prince.*

Soon after, Florence commissioned two patriotic pictures of battle scenes, one from Leonardo and one from Michelangelo. Leonardo's drafts of the picture survive, but the painting itself deteriorated almost immediately. During this time Leonardo painted a portrait of the third wife of a local merchant named Giocondo. This is the *Mona Lisa,* which in its day was admired for the warmth of its flesh tones, and which time and varnish have now turned to the faint green of ice in a landscape of rocks.

Leonardo went back to Milan from time to time to make sketches, now, for another horse and rider. This time the rider was to be Gian Giacomo Trivulzio, that Italian condottiere who had fought on the side of the French in the battle for Milan and had overthrown his one-time master and Leonardo's patron, Lodovico. Once again, nothing came of this monument. Then, in 1513, the son of Lorenzo de' Medici became Pope Leo X, and Leonardo went to Rome, where Raphael and Michelangelo had been working for some years, and there received several papal commissions. The story goes that Leonardo began, upon his arrival, to make the varnish for one picture before he started to paint it, and that Leo X observed, sadly and wisely, "This man will never do anything, for he begins to think of the end before the beginning."

The King of France at last offered Leonardo a retreat without obligation near Amboise, and there he spent the remainder of his life, from 1516 until 1519. His self-portrait, drawn a few years earlier, shows him as a man looking much older than his sixty years, full-bearded and patriarchal, his eyes veiled against emotion and his mouth set bitterly, and the distress of an old age full of regrets for the wonderful things that he had planned and never finished now fills his notebooks. Once he had been so sure of his own gifts that there had seemed to be an infinity of time in which to fulfill them. In those confident young days he had written:

I wish to work miracles;—I may have less than other men who are more tranquil, or than those who aim at growing rich in a day.

Now he was conscious every day of the merciless erosion of time, which leaves nothing of the living vigor and beauty of a man if the man has not perpetuated them in his own creations. Leonardo is looking into his own face when he thinks of Helen of Troy and, borrowing from Ovid, writes:

O Time, thou that consumest all things! O envious age, thou destroyest all things and devourest all things with the hard teeth of the years, little by little, in slow death! Helen, when she looked in her mirror and saw the withered wrinkles which old age had made in her face, wept, and wondered to herself why ever she had twice been carried away. O Time, thou that consumest all things! O envious age, whereby all things are consumed!

The works of art that Leonardo left behind are indeed sadly few—not a whole statue, about a dozen finished paintings, some fine anatomical and mechanical drawings, and otherwise only the thousands of sketches. For some artists with one small gift, this might be enough; but when we consider the prodigious talent of Leonardo, the instant eye, the exact hand, and the penetrating mind, we understand why he scribbled desperately on page after page of his later notebooks: "Tell me if anything at all was done . . . Tell me if anything at all was done . . ."

And no doubt Leonardo was right to think that he had wasted his life; but he was wrong to think that he had wasted his gifts. At bottom, his true gifts were not those of a painter, for his painting, original as it was, was not out of the reach of his contemporaries. As a painter Leonardo was in the stream of the Renaissance tradition which Botticelli, Raphael, Michelangelo, and others were also helping to form. Leonardo's most profound gifts were of another kind, and make him seem modern to us today, five hundred years after he lived.

The first of the gifts which made Leonardo a pioneer was his absorbed interest in the structure and mechanism of nature. The science of his day has hardly a hint of this, because it was still dominated by a magical view of man. The alchemists of Leonardo's time believed that they would command nature only by breaking the natural order of things, by casting a spell over nature which made her function in a way contrary to her own laws. They wanted to bewitch the world, and to gain power by forcing it to obey them instead of the laws of nature. Leonardo realized, as his contemporaries did not, that we command nature only when we understand her, when we enter into her processes and give them scope to work naturally. He was full of contempt for those who wanted to force nature to do the impossible: "O speculators about perpetual motion, how many vain chimeras have you created in the like quest? Go and take your place with the seekers after gold."

Leonardo's second pioneering gift was to see that the structure of nature also reveals her processes, which are perpetually in movement and in development. The way a skeleton is hinged, the way a muscle is anchored, the way a leaf is veined—all such knowledge tells something about the functioning of the organism and therefore, in the end, about the whole cycle of its growth. Leonardo dismissed the easy appeals to vital forces and the spirits that inhabit living things with which his age fobbed off all questions; he looked for the strict mechanism by which living things move and act; and he saw that mechanism as something dynamic. This dynamic quality is present even in his simplest sketch of a machine, and in his old age it expressed itself in a growing preoccupation with the forms of plants and of flowing water. Leonardo did not think that a scientific analysis of the processes of nature deprived them of life; on the contrary, he wanted the analysis to express their changing and living movement.

Third, and most important, Leonardo understood that science is not a grand parade of a few cosmic theories, of the kind that Aristotle and Saint Thomas Aquinas had propounded. Until Leonardo's time a theory was expected to give a general explanation of some large phenomenon, such as the motion of the moon, and no one then asked whether the theory could also be made to match the precise times at which the moon rises and sets. The detail was not thought important, and any discrepancy between theory and fact was shrugged off as a point of detail. Leonardo for the first time elevated the detail so that it became once and for all the crucial test of a scientific theory. He was seldom misled by what the classical medicine of Galen said in general about the functioning of the heart or the way that the eye sees; he drew what his dissection showed him, and then asked how it could be squared with the vague medical beliefs which were then accepted.

Here we are at the center of Leonardo's pioneering mind. Because he had an exact eye, because he was a painter for whom nature lived not in generalities but in the very shape of a flower or a waterfall, he was at the opposite pole from the theorizing scientists of his own age. Leonardo did not therefore lose interest in science: he transformed it. Only a painter could have forced science to change its outlook, and to become as dedicated as his art was to the discovery of the natural order in the minute detail of its structure. Leonardo *was* that painter, who is the true pioneer of science as we practice it.

His interest in what was new made him unwilling to look back; his gaze was outward and forward into nature. His passion for the exact turned him toward mathematics, his passion for the actual urged him to experiment, and it is significant that these two dominant themes—logic and experimentation—have remained, ever since Leonardo's time, at the base of scientific method.

It was natural that, with these gifts, Leonardo should have quarreled with the classical and literary Renaissance in which he was brought up and should have turned to a more popular and naturalistic Renaissance. It was natural that he should give up pictures for machines, and that his machines should have that subtle quality of human intelligence, of one operation controlling another, which today we call automation. It was natural that these interests should take him from the rich merchant culture of Florence to the brutal thrust for power of the Sforza and the Borgia. And it was natural and inevitable that a life spent at the courts of such men should have about it the modern ring of our own age, the pointless planning of pageants and machines of war, the aimless postponement of every constructive scheme, and the final despair of a great mind that from childhood has been baffled by an alien world. At the end of his life Leonardo wrote constantly of his visions of the cruelty of man to man, and what he foresaw links his gangster age to ours:

Of the Cruelty of Man

Creatures shall be seen upon the earth who will always be fighting one with another with very great losses and frequent deaths on either side. These shall set no bounds to their malice; by their fierce limbs a great number of the trees in the immense forests of the world shall be laid level with the ground; and when they have crammed themselves with food it shall gratify their desire to deal out death, affliction, labors, terrors, and banishment to every living thing. And by reason of their boundless pride they shall wish to rise towards heaven, but the excessive weight of their limbs shall hold them down. There shall be nothing remaining on the earth or under the earth or in the waters that shall not be pursued and molested and destroyed, and that which is in one country taken away to another; and their own bodies shall be made the tomb and the means of transit of all the living bodies which they have slain. O Earth! what delays thee to open and hurl them headlong into the deep fissures of thy huge abysses and caverns, and no longer to display in the sight of heaven so savage and ruthless a monster?

A portfolio of drawings by

Leonardo da Vinci

A striking face—a model, perhaps, for one of the grotesques above—might lead Leonardo through the streets for a day. Whatever he observed, he recorded in his notebooks. Some five thousand pages survive, covered with drawings and comments (entered in his famous mirror-writing) on subjects as varied as perpetual motion, a deluge, the anatomy of a horse. It was his conviction that "those sciences are vain and full of error which are not born of experience, mother of all certainty." The drawings that follow represent inquiries into man, nature, and machines; the quotations, also from the notebooks, are Leonardo's own words.

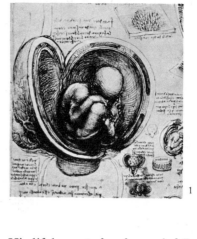

His lifelong study of man led Leonardo to strive for a noble ideal: "Would that it might please our Creator," he wrote, "that I were able to reveal the nature of man and his customs even as I describe his figure." Caption numbers on these seven pages refer, of course, to pertinent illustrations.

(1) "In the case of this child, the heart does not beat and it does not breathe because it lies continually in water. And if it were to breathe it would be drowned, and breathing is not necessary to it because it receives life and is nourished from the life and food of the mother."

(2) This drawing of a transparent female figure appears on a page of anatomy studies, with the words: "Your order shall commence with the formation of the child in the womb . . . and how it is nourished, learning in part from the eggs which hens make."

(3) Why study the shoulder? "The painter who has acquired a knowledge of the nature of the sinews, muscles, and tendons will know exactly in the movement of any limb how many and which of the sinews are the cause of it, and which muscle by

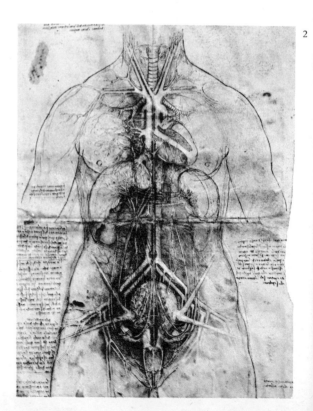

4

its swelling is the cause of this sinew's contracting, and which sinews having been changed into most delicate cartilage surround . . . the . . . muscle." (4) Leonardo might have been describing this detail study for the destroyed fresco, *The Battle of Anghiari,* in his *Treatise on Painting:* "Make the beaten and conquered pallid, with brows raised and knit together, and let the skin above the brows be all full of lines of pain; at the sides of the nose show the furrows going in an arch from the nostrils and ending where the eye begins, and show the dilation of the nostrils which is the cause of these lines; and let the lips be arched displaying the upper row of teeth, and let the teeth be parted after the manner of such as cry in lamentation." (5) Leonardo explained graphically the statement made by Vitruvius, in his work on architecture, "that the measurements of a man are arranged by Nature thus . . . The span of a man's outstretched arms is equal to his height."

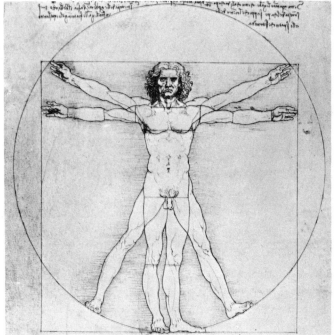

5

A thorough knowledge of nature, Leonardo asserted, was essential to the painter, who must render all of its forms "with equal facility and grace." Each of his finished works reflects his own unceasing inquiries, the discipline of countless sketches. In the background of the *Mona Lisa* are effects derived from studies of geology and air currents; a veritable botanical garden blooms in *The Annunciation;* thousands of drawings of horses, mostly lost, preceded the great Sforza monument. And alongside certain drawings in the notebooks, Leonardo wrote animal fables, vividly revealing the depth of his understanding of nature.

(1) To portray a deluge, "You should show how fragments of mountains, which have been already stripped bare by the rushing torrents, fall headlong into these very torrents and choke up the valleys, until the pent-up rivers rise in flood and cover the wide plains and their inhabitants."

(2) Leonardo was fascinated with horses, and on one occasion reminded himself to "represent the knee of a man bent like that of a horse."

(3) The artist's study of *lilium candidum.*

(4) A bramble proves his theory that "branches are found in two different positions: either opposite to each other or not opposite. If they are opposite to each other the center stem is not bent: if they are not opposite the center stem is bent."

(5) The story of a dog, a sheep, and a flea: "While the dog was asleep on the coat of a sheep, one of its fleas, becoming aware of the smell of the greasy wool, decided that this must be a place where the living was better and more safe from the teeth and nails of the dog than getting his food on the dog as he did. Without more reflection therefore it left the dog and entering into the thick wool began with great toil to try to pass the roots of the hairs; which enterprise however after much sweat it found to be impossible, owing to these hairs being so thick as almost to touch each other, and there being no space there where the flea could taste the skin. Consequently after long labor and fatigue it began to wish to go back to its dog which however had already departed, so that after long repentance and bitter tears it was obliged to die of hunger."

(6) The misfortunes of a crab: "When the crab had placed itself beneath the rock in order to catch the fish that entered underneath it, the wind came with ruinous downfall of the rocks, and these by rolling themselves down destroyed the crab."

2

3

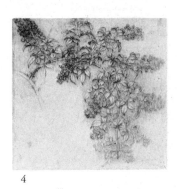

4

5

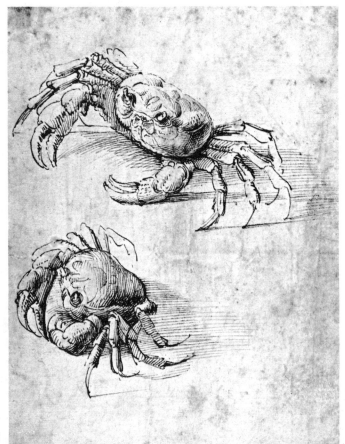

6

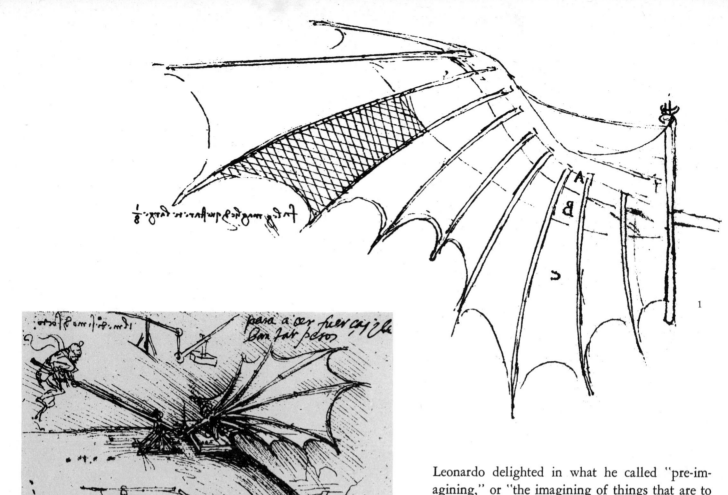

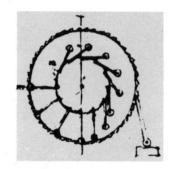

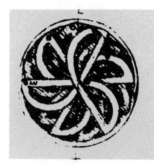

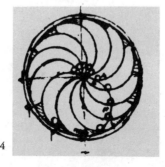

Leonardo delighted in what he called "pre-imagining," or "the imagining of things that are to be." And from his fertile mind came visions of winged flight, parachutes, and automobiles, of ideal cities, of laborsaving devices in staggering profusion. This was Leonardo da Vinci the theorist, "pre-imagining" the shape of the future.

(1) Detailed building instructions came with this drawing of a wing mechanism. "Make the meshes of this net one eighth wide. *A* should be of immature fir wood, light and possessing its bark. *B* should be fustian pasted there with a feather to prevent it from coming off easily. *C* should be starched taffeta, and as a test use thin pasteboard."
(2) This machine, operated by man and lever, demonstrates the lifting power of the wing.
(3) Long before modern aerodynamics, Leonardo designed the first parachute. "If a man have a tent made of linen of which the apertures have all been stopped up, and it be twelve *braccia* across and twelve in depth, he will be able to throw himself down from any great height without sustaining any injury."
(4) To prove the impossibility of perpetual motion, Leonardo made these three drawings. "No inanimate object will move of its own accord; consequently when in motion it will be moved by unequal power, unequal that is in time and velocity, or unequal in weight; and when the impulse of the first motive power ceases the second will cease abruptly."
(5) The lessons of history influenced Leonardo's schemes to control rivers with weirs. "There were

many of the chief towns . . . which, through being placed upon their chief rivers, have been consumed and destroyed by these rivers, as was Babylon, by the Tigris . . . and the science of water gives exact information as to their defenses."

(6) Leonardo hinted at submarine inventions more ominous than this early snorkel: "How and why I do not describe my method of remaining under water for as long a time as I can remain without food; and this I do not publish or divulge on account of the evil nature of men who would practice assassinations at the bottom of the seas, by breaking the ships in their lowest parts and sinking them together with the crews who are in them; and although I will furnish particulars of others, they are such as are not dangerous, for above the surface of the water emerges the mouth of the tube by which they draw in breath, supported on wineskins or pieces of cork."

(7) This dredge for marsh mud was particularly apt "for the saving of time, which saving springs from the fact that the instrument which conveys the earth up from below is always in the act of carrying it and never turns back."

(8) An ancestral automobile, propelled by springs.

(9) Architecture merged with city planning in Leonardo's design for a two-decker city. "The high-level roads are not to be used by wagons or vehicles such as these but are solely for the convenience of the gentlefolk. All carts and loads for the service and convenience of the common people should be confined to the low-level roads."

(10) "At every arch there should be a spiral staircase; it should be round because in the corners of square ones nuisances are apt to be committed."

OVERLEAF: This page has cats in every variety of pose, with a dragon thrown in for good measure.

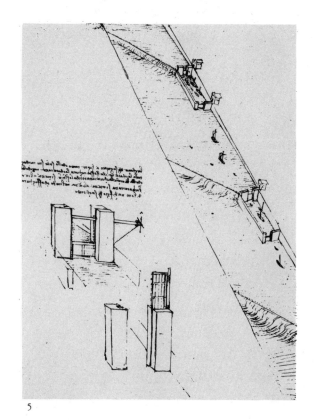

5

6

7

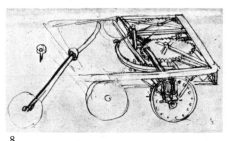

8

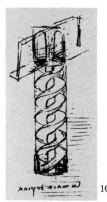

10

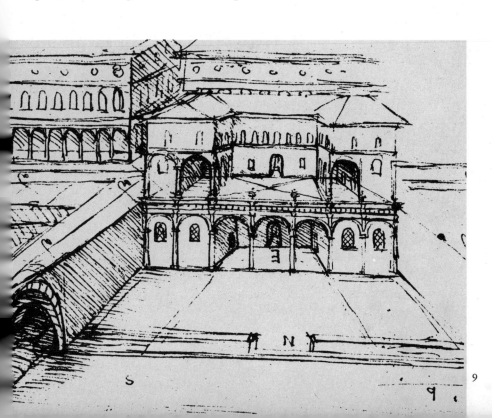

9

199

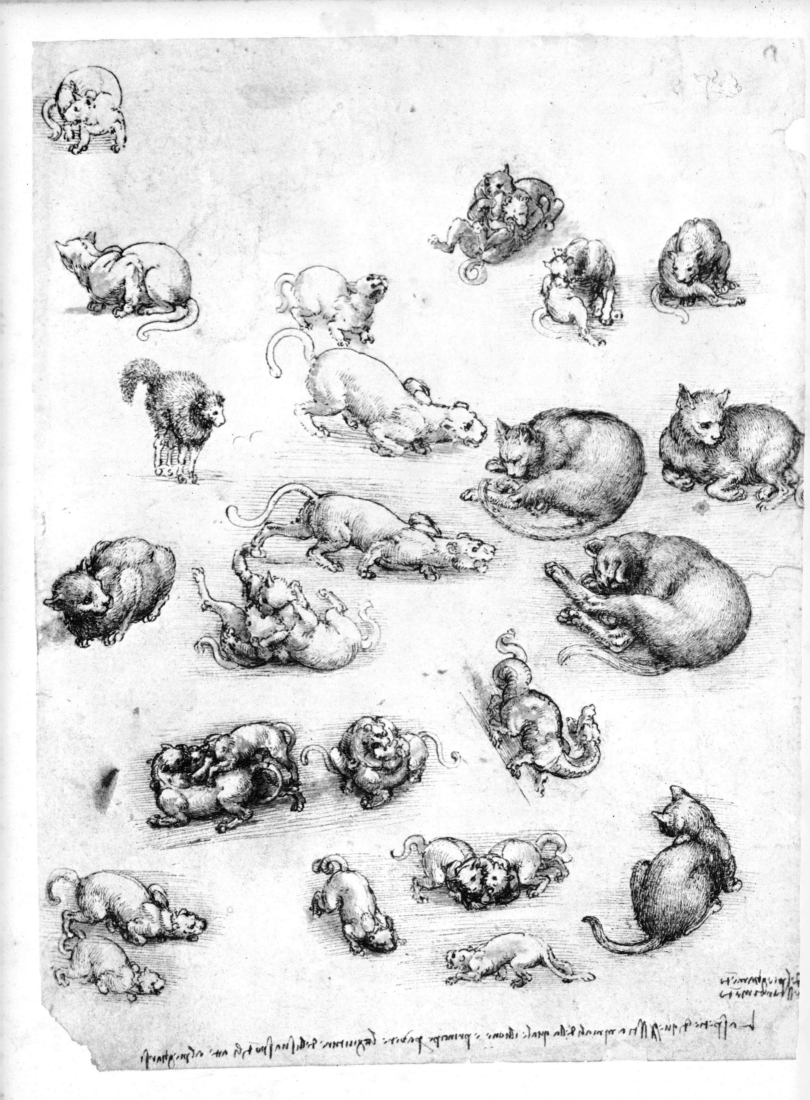

THE BUILDERS OF MILAN

At one time a rumor went the rounds to the effect that Galeazzo Maria Sforza had caused Florence's church of Santo Spirito to catch fire by eating meat every day during Lent while on a state visit to that city. In truth, Milan's dukes traditionally fostered the building of churches. Gian Galeazzo Visconti endowed a fund to pay for the great Duomo, and nearby, in the ancient Lombard capital of Pavia, he established an immense Carthusian monastery, the Certosa, to serve the Visconti dynasty as family church and mausoleum. Work on both buildings progressed whenever Milan could spare money from its wars, but a century later, when Borgognone painted the Certosa (above) as a detail of *The Carthusians Following Christ,* its marble façade had not been completed. By then the last Visconti duke had been dead for fifty years, and Sforza power was at its height. Francesco Sforza inherited no money from the Visconti, but he carried on their tradition of building. On the site of one Visconti palace he commissioned a new hospital, shaped like a cross so that all the patients could hear Mass being sung in the central chapel. He continued work on the Certosa (the Visconti now shared it with their successors) and built a castle where his children held court above the ruins of an old Visconti fort. A tithe of the castle's cost went to finish the towering Duomo, where jubilant crowds had borne Francesco on horseback when he first became duke.

THE MAKING OF A DYNASTY

Surrounded by heroes of antiquity, with Julius Caesar on his right and Hannibal on his left (above), Francesco Sforza was enthroned by admiring contemporaries among the immortals of history. Chronicling his deeds, a well-paid humanist at the court of Milan turned out a twelve-thousand-line epic, *The Sforziad,* and the visionary court architect Filarete honored him with plans for Sforzinda, the ideal city of the future. *The Sforziad* failed to rival Homer, and Vasari called Filarete's treatise "perhaps the most stupid book ever written," but the court of Milan did not judge them for aesthetic value alone. The Duke found their propaganda useful in raising the status of the Sforza name. Francesco's father was a substantial peasant who got his start in life by running off with a band of wandering mercenaries; the conquest of Milan made Francesco's sons equal to princes and one of his grandsons later became a king. Marrying the daughter of the last Visconti duke was Francesco's wisest move, for it provided a secure dynastic foundation. With his own claim to Milan confirmed by his wife's title, Francesco shrewdly set about strengthening his family's hold on the duchy. He made his brother Bishop of Milan and one of his sons a cardinal. He sent another son to live in Cremona, and named his heir Count of Pavia. But the Sforza gained most from Francesco's carefully planned program of dynastic marriages.

His own marriage had set the stage; the Visconti were allied to English and French royalty,

Ranked among heroes, Sforza chats with Caesar.

and by mixing their blood with the less exalted Sforza strain, Francesco vastly enhanced his children's eligibility. He married one legitimate daughter to the future King of Naples. His heir, Galeazzo Maria, was wed to a sister of the Queen of France; she had no dowry, but her royal connections were enough for the *nouveaux riches* Sforza. According to their legitimacy or rank, Francesco's other offspring were pledged to less imposing mates—a duke's second daughter, a minor Italian noble, the son of an untitled condottiere who might make good. There was an occasional misalliance— one daughter, who wed Sigismondo Malatesta, may have been strangled by her violent husband —but most Sforza marriages had more positive results. The best match came after Francesco's death, when the family purchased an emperor for his granddaughter Bianca Maria. Her first fiancé, a prince of Savoy, died before she was old enough to marry, and her second lost his appeal by failing to inherit the crown of Hungary. Bianca's prospects improved with her dowry, however. Originally it had been three hundred thousand ducats, but then the Sforza added one hundred thousand more; that convinced Maximilian, ruler of the Holy Roman Empire, that it would not be beneath him to marry a Sforza once he gave his new in-laws legitimate title to the duchy of Milan.

Both of Milan's dynasties are portrayed on marble portals of the Certosa at Pavia. Opposite, Visconti and Sforza dukes; at right, Milan's duchesses.

In a suit of armor enriched with gold, young Massimiliano posed for Ambrogio de Predis.

A HAPLESS PRINCE

Like his dynasty, Massimiliano Sforza had an auspicious beginning. At his birth in 1493 the bells of Milan pealed in celebration for six days, and the infant prince, secure under a golden quilt in a gilded cradle, was rocked to sleep against their din. As a mark of imperial favor, Emperor Maximilian endowed the boy with his own name, but Massimiliano was as ill-starred as most Sforza heirs. When he was seven, his father, Lodovico, was overthrown, and the boy was exiled to Innsbruck. There his careful Italian upbringing went to waste, and when he retrieved his duchy in 1512, Massimiliano returned with manners so shockingly Germanic that they dismayed his cultivated aunt, Isabella d'Este. The faithful Milanese had built triumphal arches to welcome him home from exile, but rain drenched their enthusiasm along with their decorations. At the welcoming ceremonies a youth costumed as Fortune promised Massimiliano success, but French cannon still in control of the Sforza castle provided a mocking echo. The new Duke had almost forgotten how to read or write; he overtaxed his subjects and spent money foolishly, and although Isabella tried to aid him, her diplomacy could not keep him on his throne. Three years of misrule brought another French army over the Alps, and, like his father, Massimiliano was exiled by the victors.

In miniatures painted to decorate little Massimiliano's schoolbooks, court artists showed him at some of his extracurricular activities. Above, he rides through the streets of Milan, impervious to a wide-eyed maiden admiring him from her window. Another triumphal progress (below, left) shows him upon a chariot, attended by his dwarf and pages bearing Sforza standards. Below, the prince pays homage to his cousin, the Emperor Maximilian. Beautiful schoolbooks made little impression on Massimiliano; once, when asked what he wanted most, the boy replied: "Not to go to school."

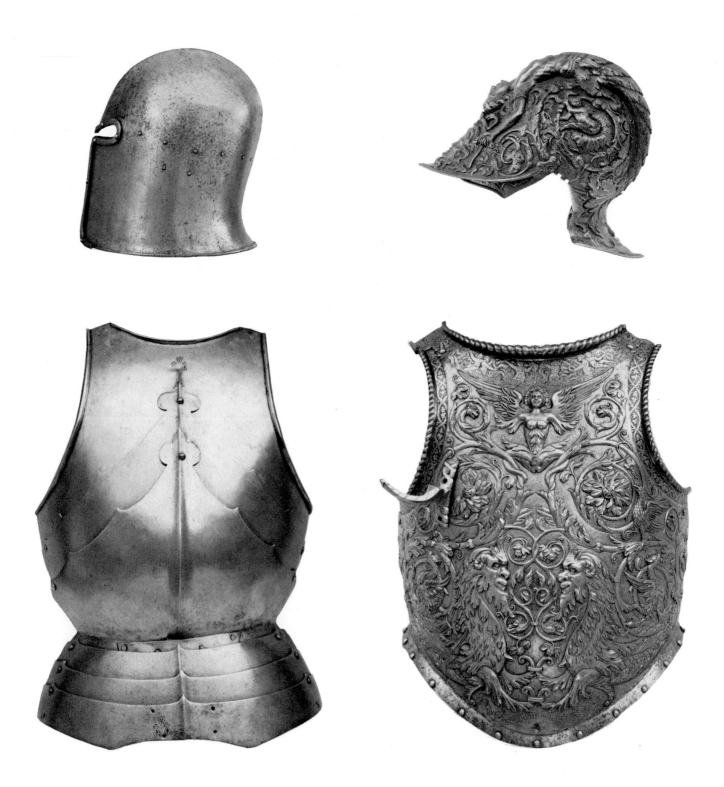

As armor became less functional it increased in beauty. The sturdy helmet and breastplate at left, fifteenth-century products of the Missaglia workshop, were forged for a belligerent age in which the only requirement was simple utilitarianism. But as war changed, the Missaglia hallmark (their divided crosses topped by a crown appear at the very top and bottom of the cuirass at left) gave way to the Negroli name, which is engraved at the bottom of the breastplate at right. Made a century later, after firearms had considerably decreased the effectiveness of battlefield armor, the Negroli breastplate is as showy as a Renaissance pageant. Mermaids and mermen sport upon the collar, and the surface is richly embossed with birds, twining branches, and monsters, above which a winged maiden sprouts from the foliage. On the equally elaborate parade helmet above it is a graceful reclining mermaid. Negroli armor became very fashionable, and one rival German armorer was so enraged by the family's success that he stooped to unethical advertising and embossed his armor with a defeated soldier, dying under a Negroli shield.

THE ARMORERS
OF MILAN

To celebrate the marriage of Lodovico Sforza in 1491, the Street of the Armorers in Milan was lined with a double row of figures—empty suits of armor ranged in ranks to look like a regiment on parade. Milan's major industry was the making of armor, and the Sforza, true to their military heritage, did their best to encourage it. Like the glassmakers of Venice, Milanese armorers were given special privileges. The city's leading workmen, the Missaglia family, were freed at times from taxes and were given a factory by the Duke for a token payment of one helmet a year. They were even ennobled, and they proudly added a crown to their hallmark and painted Sforza emblems upon their walls.

Armorers were more than craftsmen: the Missaglia operated mines, smelted ore, converted steel to plate in their own mills, in addition to fabricating suits and weapons. Even so, they were a small part of the industry. Milan could mass-produce armor, and after one fifteenth-century battle the city outfitted six thousand soldiers in a few days. As Lombard arms were exported all over Europe, guildsmen grew rich on the trade. Abroad, Milanese armor merchants peddled lace and ribbons as well (hence the English word *milliner*). As the richly embossed style of the Negroli, an offshoot of the Missaglia clan, came to dominate sixteenth-century armor, lavish decoration became fashionable, and military dandies found the appearance of a suit of armor more important than its protective strength.

Off the battlefield, knights prized armor for ceremonial occasions, and the Milanese catered to their tastes with suits designed to awe the audience rather than the enemy. The gilded suit of armor at right, designed for a pageant, is etched from head to toe with swirling arabesques. The finest complete example of Renaissance armor still in existence, it was constructed for a French soldier, the Master of the Royal Artillery, whose profession made battle armor obsolete. Renaissance armorers worked with tools as beautiful as their armor; at left is a vise ornamented with carved grotesque figures.

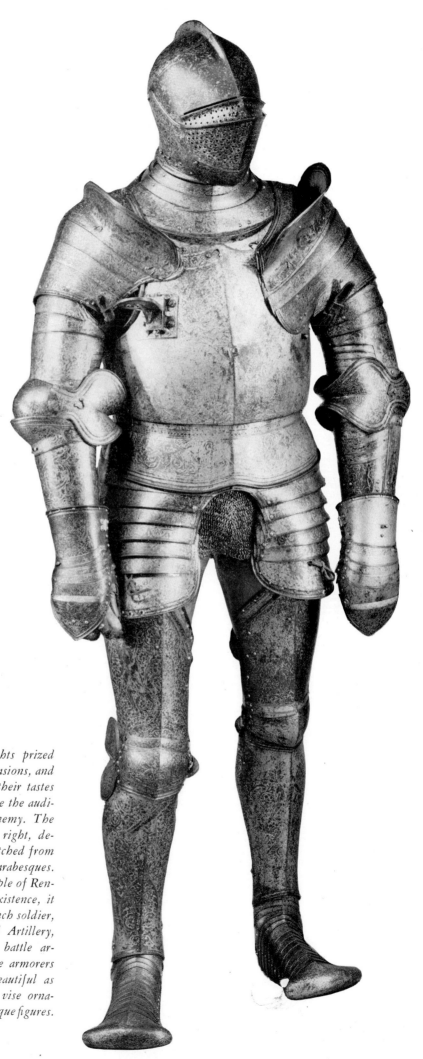

ROME

SPLENDOR AND THE PAPACY

Rome was a city caught, like an old man, in memories, delusions, and dreams. Even when fighting (and not too successfully at that) the little town of Tivoli, medals were struck bearing the proud title, *Roma caput mundi:* Rome, the world's ruler. By 1400, however, even the great days of the Middle Ages seemed remote to realistic men, and gone forever. For most of the fourteenth century the popes had lived at Avignon in France, in the great and luxurious Palais des Papes that looms above the Rhone, where the broken Roman bridge became a symbol of the Church's break with its own past. To Avignon went the clerics, lawyers, and merchants who harvested and spent the wealth which a pious Europe poured into the papal lap. It was to Avignon that Francesco Datini, the famous merchant of Prato, went to make his fortune as a small but ambitious boy of fifteen. And make it he did, in his determined, hardheaded, Tuscan way, selling silks, jewels, works of art, damasks, swords, silverware, cloth, even salt—anything that would make the money grow, although

the profits on his insurance and his banking interests nagged at his conscience. Through men like Datini, Avignon prospered and Rome lost; and, of course, the artists too went where the money was, and Sienese artists painted the frescoes that adorned the Palace's walls.

True, in Rome a few cardinals still flaunted their courtesans, and a few saintly men continued to dedicate themselves to the liturgical worship of God and the relief of the poor. Even the Curia functioned, although ever more slowly. But the absence of the Papacy was killing Rome as inexorably as a cancer. The vast ruinous buildings, combined with constant plague, stifled hope, depressed the spirit, bred despair. In this dark world the great, furious Roman tribes—the Orsini, the Colonna, the Frangipani—made their sport, and what a sport it was! They tossed each other into the Tiber, and when a pope ventured to enter Rome, they chased him into the fortress of Sant'Angelo or frightened him—like the aged Gregory XII—into the remoter corners of the Patrimony.

JOHN XXIII (1410-1415)   MARTIN V (1417-1431)   EUGENIUS IV (1431-1447)

PAUL II (1464-1471)   SIXTUS IV (1471-1484)   INNOCENT VIII (1484-1492)

PIUS III (1503)   JULIUS II (1503-1513)   LEO X (1513-1521)

They terrorized the citizens, raped the nuns, robbed the monks, pillaged the churches. To compound confusion, from 1378 to 1429 there was an antipope as well as a pope, and in 1409 even three authentic successors of St. Peter—a glorious opportunity for rebellion, riot, and plunder. King Ladislas of Naples prowled about the broken-down streets of Rome, extorting what he could and decapitating whom he dared. Popes and kings hired the toughest, most brutal condottieri —including Braccio, who, according to a chronicler, enjoyed the sufferings of others, and for his pleasure would throw a few men from the highest towers in Rome or drop a prisoner into a boiling cauldron. After years of anarchy the Romans were willing to believe anything and nothing. When John XXIII, afterwards struck from the list of the popes and accused of a huge catalogue of crimes, the least important of which were incest, sodomy, and murder, swore that he would defend them to the death, they replied that they would rather eat their children than surrender to his enemies. During the

same night John XXIII flew under the cover of darkness, taking all the portable wealth he could lay his hands on, and the Romans opened their gates the next morning, their children undevoured. Such a kaleidoscope of brutality, such a cascade of violence, broke the government of the city in pieces and reduced it to a poverty and a misery it had not known since the barbarian invasions.

No one in 1425 could have foreseen that Rome was about to be reborn (not spiritually—the Renaissance popes were not to prove men of the spirit—but physically, artistically, and politically). St. Peter's, the Vatican, the churches, the tombs, the squares, the great palaces and gardens of Rome which now entrance the eye and delight the heart, were brought into being and gave an impetus to the pursuit of beauty that the stern moralities of the Counter Reformation could not stop. For two hundred years the beauty of Rome became the pride of the Papacy. The downward plunge into anarchy and destitution and poverty was checked by Martin

NICHOLAS V (1447-1455)

CALIXTUS III (1455-1458)

PIUS II (1458-1464)

ALEXANDER VI (1492-1503)

A GALLERY OF POPES

During the Great Schism, from 1378 to 1417, popes in Rome struggled with antipopes in France and, for a while, with a third claimant as well. Unity was finally restored under Martin V, but not until the advent of the "political popes" in 1471 were affairs in Rome fully under control. The temporal ambitions of Sixtus IV and his successors saw papal power and extravagance rise steadily, reaching a zenith during the golden age of Leo X, but that trend ended abruptly with the catastrophic sack of Rome in 1527, and papal magnificence never again approached the same grandiose scale.

ADRIAN VI (1522-1523)

CLEMENT VII (1523-1534)

PAUL III (1534-1549)

V, himself a Colonna and a Roman. During his pontificate (1417–1431) the dreadful split in the Church was cured, if not quite healed. Furthermore, he proved a good administrator and such a fearsome personality that he secured peace for the city. He checked the robberies, violence, and murder, and stimulated the city's trade. With the papal court back in Rome, back came the pilgrims and supplicants, back came the merchants, and back came the lifeblood—the papal tax harvest that was reaped from Europe's peasantry. And so the Roman soil was fertilized again, for without wealth no Renaissance was possible. The next pope, Eugenius IV, had to flee down the Tiber in a rowboat, disguised as a monk, and eluded capture only by a hair's breadth. For years he kept his court at Florence, where he patronized the humanists and bided his time, while he left Rome to be pacified by a ferocious bishop, Vitelleschi, who razed cities, hanged and decapitated barons, slaughtered right, left, and center, and probably met his own end by poison (possibly with Eugenius'

connivance). By such murderous methods were the popes reestablished. The calculated savageries of Cesare Borgia, that were to astound a later generation, were unusual only in the beauty and dexterity of their timing.

To be secure in Rome, the Papacy needed to control the States of the Church which stretched in a broad diagonal across the long leg of Italy. During its residence at Avignon and the Great Schism (1378 to 1417), men and cities had naturally usurped papal rights and privileges, and what they had won by force they would not yield by persuasion. Excommunication, interdict, or anathema left them unmoved. These had been flung about so wantonly by rival popes at each other that they had lost much of their force. Indeed, it seemed to the popes that the Church could only get back its own by acting like any other power in Italy. By alliance, by diplomacy, by war, the Church might wrest its possessions from alien hands. Its wealth permitted it to hire the ablest condottieri, including the great Francesco Sforza as well as Federigo da

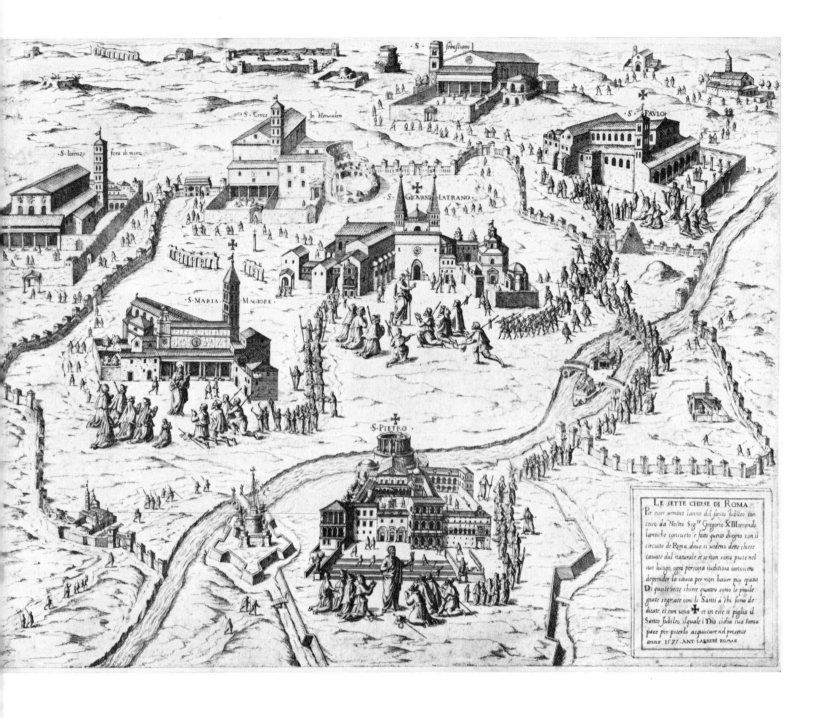

Montefeltro. Having been a plaything of the great powers, the leaders of the Church wished to secure independence by giving the Church great temporal and political strength. That being so, they looked for a leader not among the saints nor usually among the scholars (Nicholas V and Pius II were exceptions) but among the administrators and natural politicians. They looked for worldly men, men of powerful personalities, tough fiber, and quick decision. And again, as the power of the Papacy steadily grew through temporal measures such as war and diplomacy, so did the need for such qualities in a pope seem ever more necessary. This is the explanation of what so many now find difficult to understand—of popes such as Alexander VI or Julius II. Alexander VI, whose lusts repelled even the tolerant age in which he lived, was a very hardheaded diplomat and excellent administrator, whose policy undeviatingly pursued what was thought to be a necessity for the Church—temporal power, expressed in the overlordship of central Italy. Julius II, even as pope, loved war, loved

to get on his horse, to feel the weight of his armor and hear the blood-call of battle.

So, by and large, the Renaissance popes were worldly men, pragmatic, tough, concerned with power. And like many hardheaded, ambitious men they did not wish to be outshone by their rivals in the symbolic display of wealth and greatness. They were determined to build vast churches, huge palaces, magnificent fountains; to employ the finest painters, sculptors, craftsmen; to collect the loveliest antiquities, the most resplendent jewels, the most remarkable books, the most exquisite manuscripts. These things, like their armies, were necessities of state, and the cost irrelevant. So hand in hand with the resurgent power of the Papacy went the artistic Renaissance in Rome; and because the popes controlled more wealth, the result was more splendid than anywhere else.

Rome was full of priests, monks, nuns, churches, monasteries, convents, holy relics, miraculous shrines, healing images. Every year thousands of pilgrims from all corners of

the Western world made their way to it in penitence and in hope. Most were simple people to whom the sight of a piece of the True Cross or a saint's leg justified the dangers and tribulations of their journey. They cared nothing for the whispered rumors of the Pope's children, of his poisonings, murders, or even the alarming sensualities of the Borgia. Twenty thousand of them reverenced Alexander VI in the great Jubilee year of 1500—unmindful of his lusts. For them the mounting grandeur of Rome was a wondrous thing, a visible proof of the glory of their Church. Humanist criticism of the Church's venality, corruption, immorality, and obscurantism fell on deaf ears. A Savonarola or a Bernardino of Siena might momentarily stir this multitude with a sense of the world's unrighteousness, but the vast mass of the Western world was locked in an accepting piety, and the luminous sins of the popes and cardinals were a matter for gossip but not for radical rage. Throughout the Renaissance, with its political and personal immorality and its intellectual skepticism,

Rome remained the center of the Western world's religion. From this atmosphere of worship no pope could escape, and it became subtly interwoven in the Renaissance in Rome.

There is no need to follow the twists and turns by which the Papacy gradually re-established its dominion over the Patrimony or to describe how from time to time this was endangered by popes trying to create hereditary dominions for their children (Cesare Borgia, for example), a tendency which scores of Orsini and Colonna died bloody deaths to prevent. The treaties, battles, and plots have faded to near-oblivion; there remain, however, in all their greatness, the treasures of the Vatican, its library, its antiquities, its sculptures, its paintings. And the Vatican is but a fragment of Renaissance Rome; the *Laocoön* and the *Apollo Belvedere* belong to it as much as St. Peter's or Via Giulia, for a reverence for her own past grew with her new delight in beauty.

The revival of Rome began, like the Renaissance itself, with literature. The Italian Papacy, at the time of the Schism,

had many Tuscans in its service, among them Poggio, one of the luckiest of the humanists. After Petrarch's discovery of lost letters of Cicero the search for ancient manuscripts intensified, and Poggio's instinct seemed to lead him unerringly to his target like a pig to truffles. Perhaps he was more thorough, more remorseless than the rest; whatever the cause, his haul was prodigious. In the Swiss monastery of St. Gall he unearthed the entire works of Quintilian; other highlights of his discoveries were the poems of Lucretius, discourses by Cicero, treatises on architecture by Vitruvius and on agriculture by Columella. The rich patrons of Italy rushed to buy them or to have them exquisitely copied and illuminated, for the competition to possess first-rate classical manuscripts splendidly illuminated was as keen as that for French impressionists among present-day millionaires. Tommaso Parentucelli, the son of a surgeon, who became Nicholas V, was as addicted to books as the Borgia family was to women. "What was unknown to Parentucelli," said Pius II, "lay outside the sphere of human learning." He encouraged his secretaries to ransack old monastic libraries, and he employed an army of copyists. Terrified by the fall of Constantinople, he sent his emissaries scurrying to Greece and collected a few Greek codices at vast expense. He paid extravagant prices for the work of translation as well as for the books themselves: indeed, he offered ten thousand gold pieces for a fine translation of Homer. He employed the best of all classical scholars, Lorenzo Valla, who had proved some of the most hallowed documents in the papal Curia to be forgeries. As well as being a destructive scholar of genius, Valla was a satirist with the bite of acid, and his favorite targets were priests, monks, and cardinals. In fact, during the pontificate of Eugenius IV, Rome had been too hot for him. Nicholas V welcomed him and employed him. And, of course, the Pope created a fitting setting for his great library: the books were housed in the Vatican and exquisitely bound in red velvet with silver clasps. Philosophers, rhetoricians, poets, historians, philologists,

About 1534 a Dutch visitor drew the ruins of the Palace of Septimius Severus (above). The Laocoön *(far left), described by Pliny the Elder, was uncovered in 1506 near the Baths of Trajan and, with the Apollo Belvedere (right), formed the nucleus of a Vatican museum of antiquities begun by Julius II. The figures of Romulus and Remus were added to a bronze Etruscan wolf (left) during the Renaissance; the animal's statue may have been the one mentioned by Cicero as having been struck by lightning in 65 B.C.*

grammarians, and teachers of Latin and Greek all were welcome in the new palace of the Vatican that Nicholas was creating, whether their work fortified or undermined the authority of the Papacy. Only a few setbacks marred the triumphant development which Nicholas had started. As with so many aspects of the Renaissance, Sixtus IV was also involved in the extension and adornment of the Vatican library. Even Alexander VI added to it, although his interest in learning, and it was a genuine one, expressed itself in the patronage of the University of Rome. Between them Nicholas and Sixtus laid the foundations, and secured some of the rarest treasures, of the greatest library in the Western world.

Although the reverence of most popes for the literature of antiquity was profound, their attitude toward the visible remains of ancient Rome was more haphazard. The collection of coins, of bronzes, and of statuary had been the cult of a few cardinals even as early as 1400; and naturally, as the fashion for antiquity spread, so did the desire to acquire genu-

ine works of art of classical Rome and Greece. But the vast ruins of Rome were a different matter. The huge Palatine Hill, upon which had stood the immense palaces of the emperors, had become an incoherent mass of rubble—broken arches, paths, and masonry covered in sage and thyme and rosemary, crowned with olive trees, and grazed by sheep. It was a desolate, rural place—a paradise only for the meditative humanist brooding on the mortality of greatness. The Arch of Constantine was buried in ruins and covered by houses; the Colosseum was a mound of tumbled marble; everywhere there were broken columns, remains of theaters, circuses, stadiums; and medieval houses spread like weeds in and out and over this ruined city. These crapulous vestiges of a glorious past were harder to cherish, and although an occasional pope paid lip service to the need for their preservation and issued Bulls for it, the majority happily plundered them for building materials or razed them to the ground for their new projects. Nicholas V removed 2,300 wagon loads of marble

from the Colosseum in a single year, as well as quarrying from the Circus Maximus, the Forum, the Arch of Titus, and the Temple of Venus. Even that great patron and connoisseur Sixtus IV took stones from ancient buildings and built a bridge across the Tiber from the masonry of the Colosseum. A few dedicated men, like the great architect Brunelleschi, dug and measured and drew the ancient buildings; but most men were drawn to them, like the robbers of the pyramids, by the hope of a lucky find, for the search for antiquities had revealed masterpiece after masterpiece of ancient art, culminating in 1490 in the discovery of the *Apollo Belvedere* in a Roman villa. Even if the great plundered the ruins or ignored them, there were humble scholars whom they fascinated, and the best of these was Ciriaco de' Pizzicolli who wandered throughout the classical world, measuring, sketching, describing the visible remains of antiquity. Antiquarian studies, however, were largely confined to medals, coins, inscriptions, marbles, and bronzes, things which could be collected and

displayed: there were, of course, not enough, and forgeries soon abounded, to the confusion and despair of posterity.

Although the popes had little wish to preserve, as in aspic, the ruins of Rome, they dearly desired to restore its architectural supremacy. The popes recovered a ruined city shrunk to a tiny area of Imperial Rome, and fields and orchards and wild, overgrown places abounded. Nicholas V, fortunately, possessed a touch of megalomania; fortunately, because size and space are vital principles of architectural splendor. He not only dreamed, but also planned, a vast new Rome, dominated by a new St. Peter's, a new papal palace, and protected by an invincible Castel Sant'Angelo. The medieval popes had lived in the indefensible and oft-burned Palace of St. John Lateran, but on their return from Avignon it was so ruinous that they had taken up residence in the Vatican Palace, which had been the guest palace for emperors and kings. Nicholas V sent for the great Florentine architects Rossellino and Alberti, men totally hostile to the Gothic, and as addicted as the

The Roman Forum (left), plundered, half buried, used as a market, and partially leveled in 1536 to provide a triumphal entrance for Charles V, was known for centuries as the Campo Vaccino, or cow pasture. A few ancient monuments fared better. Castel Sant'Angelo (above, in a 1491 drawing), which was built as Emperor Hadrian's mausoleum, was fortified and used by various popes as a refuge from Roman mobs and the sack of Rome.

Pope to classical antiquity. All the gold and silver of the West would scarcely have been sufficient for the multitude of churches, convents, monasteries, palaces, theaters, gardens, piazzas, towers, walls, and fortifications which they planned. The cost did not daunt the Pope. He tore down the ancient Roman temples near St. Peter's and began slowly to lay the foundations of his new basilica. At his death the whole of what is now the Vatican City was scarred with trenches for the huge walls of his dreams. They were never fulfilled, but Sixtus IV, Alexander VI, Julius II, and Leo X completed the destruction of medieval Rome and created the new city of the Renaissance that was to prove worthy of him.

Sixtus IV, born in poverty, ruthlessly pursued greatness. Sensual, self-indulgent, decisive, an excellent administrator and generous patron, he is in many ways the most typical of Renaissance popes. He showered gold on his nephews (one of whom was to become pope as Julius II) and stopped short of no means to get his political ends. He helped to promote the Pazzi conspiracy and, in fury at its failure, placed Florence under the Interdict. His personal immorality gave rise to the wildest rumors; but the lack of restraint in the satisfaction of his appetites provoked an extravagance that was entirely beneficent for posterity. Not since the days of the emperors had Rome witnessed such junketings. Here is a description of the food at the banquet given by Sixtus when a bastard daughter of the King of Naples arrived in Rome to meet her future husband: "Before them were carried wild boars, roasted whole in their entire hides, bucks, goats, hares, rabbits, fish silvered over, peacocks with their feathers, pheasants, storks, cranes and stags; a bear in its skin, holding in its mouth a stick; countless were the tarts, jellies, candied fruits and sweetmeats. An artificial mountain was carried into the room, out of which stepped a liveryman with gestures of surprise at finding himself in the midst of such a gorgeous banquet; he repeated some verses and then vanished. Mythological figures served as covers to the viands placed on the table. The history

of Atlas, of Perseus and Andromeda, the labors of Hercules were depicted life size on silver dishes. Castles made of sweetmeats and filled with eatables were sacked and then thrown from the loggia of the hall to the applauding crowd. Sailing vessels discharged their cargoes of sugared almonds . . ." By such means, perhaps, Sixtus obliterated the memories of his hungry youth, but many of his indulgences were less transitory. His taste in building was as simple and as austere as his delight in food was riotous and fantastic. He widened streets, constructed bridges, built hospitals, erected churches, gave land to all who would build houses and palaces. He encouraged his cardinals to foster the splendor of Rome: the market was expelled from the Piazza Navona and the building of its churches and palaces begun. There was scarcely a ward of the city that Sixtus did not improve or adorn, but his greatest glory is the chapel in the Vatican that bears his name. Utterly simple in design, it served merely as a frame for its adornment, and for this purpose Sixtus brought the best art-

ists in Italy to Rome—Signorelli, Botticelli, Perugino, Pinturicchio, Ghirlandaio, Rosselli. Later, in the pontificate of Julius II, who wished to complete his uncle's work, these frescoes were dwarfed by the superb ceiling by Michelangelo, for which the Sistine Chapel is so famous. Such, however, was the galaxy of painters in Rome in the 1470's that they founded their own guild, that of St. Luke, which afterwards developed into the famous academy. Although painters and sculptors and architects had been patronized by the popes long before Nicholas V and Sixtus IV (Giotto had created mosaics and painted frescoes for the old St. Peter's, and Fra Angelico had adorned many churches), yet with their pontificates papal patronage moved into a new dimension. It touched all aspects of art and learning. Possessing great wealth and sublime authority, many of the popes rose to the enormous visions of Nicholas V. The Basilica of St. Peter's—the work not of one but of a plethora of geniuses: Alberti, Bramante, Raphael, Michelangelo, Bernini—is the most impressive Christian

monument in the world, yet it is essentially a product of the Renaissance. The treasures of the Vatican Palace—paintings, sculpture, antiquities, ancient manuscripts, and rare books— are incomparable, yet in 1420 the Papacy possessed no more perhaps than three hundred books, and scarcely any antiquities or pictures or statues of merit. To the sensual, warlike, popes who ruled from 1471 to 1521 Rome owes a great deal of its present beauty.

What a strange gallery these popes make, yet essentially they are as much creatures of the Renaissance as Michelangelo's *Adam* or Donatello's *David*. The strangest of all is doubtless Alexander VI, whose name has become a byword for lust and cruelty. Certainly he was a man of strong, animal passions, driven remorselessly by his instincts. His attachment to his mistress, Vannozza, who bore him the terrible Borgia brood, was profound and life-lasting, no matter what other temporary indulgence he permitted himself. He loved his children to desperation, with a fierce physical passion. When

one son was stabbed and thrown into the Tiber, probably by another son, Cesare Borgia, his grief astounded the cardinals whom he called to a consistory in order to bewail the loss of his child. So deep was his grief that, in tears, he swore not only to reform his own life, but also the Church's. His animal spirits, however, soon reasserted themselves, and his slavish devotion to his son Cesare became the bane of Italy when he resolved to create for him a great Italian kingdom. After spectacular victories in which, with French aid, Cesare overcame the great, seemingly impregnable fortresses of the Romagna, as well as Urbino, he seemed to Machiavelli to be the destined ruler of Italy. Machiavelli admired the way Cesare welcomed his enemies as friends and then neatly strangled them. By such stratagems were the Orsini obliterated. The speed, the decision, the timing of Cesare had an almost physical perfection. Yet, as in some Greek tragedy, the fates kept a bitter end in store. Before Cesare could consolidate his power, his father died; at the time he himself was prostrated with a loathsome

Michelangelo crowned his huge statue of Moses (left) with the two horns symbolic of the prophet since the Hebrew word for "rays of light" was mistranslated as "horns" in the Vulgate. It was intended as a central figure of the massive tomb planned for Pope Julius II, but the monument was finally set up on a much diminished scale thirty-two years after the Pope's death, and the frustrated Michelangelo declared, "I lost all my youth in bondage to this tomb." The fierce stare of the statue is echoed in Raphael's portrait of Pope Julius, on the facing page. A detail from The Mass of Bolsena *in one of the Stanze, this was so realistic a portrait that Vasari said, "it seems alive."*

and debilitating sickness. Stripped of power, he became a pawn of popes, kept on sufferance, banished to prison in Spain, and finally was killed in a brawl in Navarre. The life of Alexander's daughter, Lucrezia, was marked by a similar irony of fate. The Pope loved her with an almost incestuous passion. He heaped wealth on her; no delight was too sumptuous or too lascivious to be denied her. No husband was worthy of her charms: one was declared impotent by Papal Bull; one was assassinated. But Lucrezia lived on long after her father's death, her life threaded with tragedy and stultified by a wearisome piety that mocked her past. The depth and ferocity of the Pope's passion for his children have made him an ogre of history, making men forget his astonishing dignity, his overwhelming physical charm, and the immense presence as well as that animal vitality which made him as unwearying at work as at pleasure, and the bull his proper emblem. His irresponsible virility was scarcely in keeping with the tiara, but his pontificate was far from disastrous for the Papacy. He

brought its temporal possessions more firmly under its control, and even though his intention to transfer these temporalities to his own family would, if realized, have ruined the Church, yet the possibility that this could be achieved was so remote that the success of Cesare merely redounded to the advantage of the Papacy.

That advantage was brilliantly exploited by Julius II. Sixty years old when he was elected pope, he possessed the strength and decision of a man half his years. He loved action, hated the French, loathed the great Roman families, not one member of which he elevated to the purple, and detested the tyrants of Perugia and Bologna who usurped the temporal power of his Church. Defeat merely increased his energy, and in all his dealings this tough, thickset priest was bold, decisive, and single-minded. His aim was the absolute independence of the Papacy from emperors, kings, or Romans, for without that temporal independence its claims to universality in a world of national states, he realized, would be meaning-

less. As in politics, so in art, Julius never vacillated. Nor did he play safe. Hearing of the abilities of the young Raphael, he sent for him from Florence, ordered him to obliterate paintings by Piero della Francesca, Signorelli, Perugino, Sodoma, and the rest and to cover the walls of the rooms now known as the Stanze of Raphael with subjects of his own choice. The result is one of the great glories of Renaissance Rome. In architecture Julius showed the same sweeping vision, the same decisive action. He patronized Bramante, a man whose dreams were as grandiose as Julius could wish, accepted his colossal plans with alacrity, and taxed the faithful. Nor was it in any way surprising that Julius, who always stared life directly in the eye, should contemplate death with the same robust realism. Michelangelo's designs for his tomb entranced him; after all, it was the largest and most ornate mausoleum conceived in Europe since Theodoric's, but he could not bridle his impatience with the sculptor's slow progress, his creative doubts and endless reconsiderations, which

drove the Pope to such furious quarrels that Michelangelo left Rome in anger and the project came to a standstill. Nor did reconciliation speed it forward—long after his death, a part of Julius' tomb went up in the little church of San Pietro in Vincoli; his bones lie in an undistinguished grave in the Vatican. Julius' furious spirit did not always meet such adamantine opposition.

The triumph of the Renaissance Papacy received its most splendid illustration in the coronation of Julius' successor—the young Giovanni de' Medici, son of Lorenzo, who became pope in 1513, at the age of thirty-seven. Bull-necked, popeyed, red-faced, he totally lacked the presence and ferocity of an Alexander VI or a Julius II. The cardinals in conclave had decided to avoid aggressive, virile temperaments. They had had enough of them. Leo X belied his name. Subtle, intuitive, sophisticated, he charmed with his generosity, affability, and sweetness of manner. Discretion veiled his private life, and his character and his education gave him a range of

The Piazza del Campidoglio (right) designed by Michelangelo in 1538, crowns the Capitoline Hill, overlooking the city. The pompous humanist Baraballo did not realize he was the object of a joke as he rode there on Leo X's pet elephant, to be crowned poet as Petrarch had been in 1341. The hilarity of the crowd caused the elephant to throw him off, but the incident was commemorated by an inlaid door in Raphael's Stanze (left). A different sort of coronation is seen on the majolica plate below. Pope Clement VII, humbled by the sack of Rome, places the crown of the Holy Roman Empire on the head of his conqueror, Charles V, in 1530.

intellectual interests and sympathies not matched by a pope since Nicholas V. Bred in riches and nurtured in luxury, he had no compunction in using the wealth of the Church in splendiferous pageantry. Since the days of the emperors the Romans had never witnessed a procession comparable to his, as it made its way from the Vatican to St. John Lateran. Cardinals and bankers vied with each other in the display of artistic treasures or the construction of ceremonial arches. Agostino Chigi erected an eight-column arch and festooned it with his best pictures and sculpture. Apollos, Ganymedes, Bacchuses, Minervas, Venuses, nymphs and dryads, emperors and princes, the best antiquities that Rome had to offer lined the Via Triumphalis, sharing it with the newly painted apostles and prophets of Christendom. The procession itself equaled its setting. Two hundred and fifty abbots, bishops, patriarchs, and cardinals were matched by the representatives of Italy's great families. The Gonzaga, Este, Sforza, Bentivoglio, Colonna, Orsini, Baglioni, nobles of Florence, patricians from

Venice, knights from the Romagna, the Duke of Urbino in black velvet, Lucrezia Borgia's husband released from excommunication for the occasion, and the rebel Cardinal, Alfonso Petrucci, whom Leo, four years later, was to have executed, were set like jewels amidst chamberlains, standard-bearers, guards, and acolytes. On that day passions were buried, no stones were hurled, no angry shouts drowned the plainsong, no daggers flashed in the cruel sun. All paid homage to the fat, perspiring, red-faced Pope, clad in white, sitting sidesaddle on his white palfrey. Eighty years earlier no pope could have risked his life and throne in such a spectacle.

Although Rome steadily increased in splendor, and the Pope's authority waxed majestic, violence, turmoil, and chicanery still threaded the papal annals with the scarlet of battle and murder. Enemies of papal power abounded: the French, the Spaniards, and the Milanese had found no resolution to their dynastic ambitions, and the Venetians had not given up their belief that security could only be achieved by

raping the Church of its northeastern temporalities. What was more, the wealth of the Church proved insufficient for its needs. Taxes grew grievous, the sale of indulgences more blatant. Across the Alps criticism of clerical worldliness, of monkish foolishness, of papal avarice, of Roman decadence, had often been sharp and prolonged. Under the stimulus of national needs, criticism developed a political and social purpose. And Luther, who might easily have met his end at the stake like another Savonarola, became the founder of a reformed Christianity that came to see the Pope as Antichrist and Rome as the whore of Babylon. The tribulations of the Reformation dimmed the luster of the Papacy; yet the heretic Germans were remote and their future uncertain, and it was a more immediate tragedy that jolted the Romans and the Church out of the gilded sweetness of Medicean rule into a sterner, harsher world. In 1527 the soldiers of the great Hapsburg ruler Charles V, whose dominions embraced the Spanish as well as the German Empire, sacked Rome effi-

ciently, brutally, completely. After the death of Clement VII, another Medici who succeeded Leo X, the growing rift with Protestantism and the shock left by the devastation of Rome bred a sterner spirit in the Church and Papacy. The more flamboyant aspects of the Renaissance were suppressed: speculation went out of fashion; dogma was more sharply defined at the great Council of Trent; the Holy Office and the Index maintained its purity; the new order of Jesuits soon dominated the school and the confessional, and men of ruthless will and unbending morality sat on the throne of Saint Peter, marshaling and leading the resurgent forces of Catholicism. They deplored paganism; repressed the licentiousness of the Romans, religious and secular; insisted on sacred subjects in art and clapped fig leaves on the statues of antiquity. So great, however, was the impetus of the Renaissance that they could not stop it. For centuries Rome continued to grow in beauty, and became, as no other city, the embodiment of the arts, if not the spirit, of the Renaissance.

I P
FA
nih
Su
aut
lica
ria
qu
lar

perio conntinuitur. Quid
nominif gloriam querimuf
dulcedinem aliquam haur

Pope Pius II

by IRIS ORIGO

The road that winds up from the eleventh-century *pieve* of Corsignano—roughhewn in the golden stone of the region and containing the font in which Aeneas Silvius Piccolomini was christened—to the perfect little Renaissance city of Pienza—named after Pope Pius II—is a short one. But the ascent it symbolizes was one unusually swift and high even in a period in which able men quickly made their mark—the ascent which led a clever country boy from a humble secretary's desk to Peter's throne. A shrewd statesman, an elegant humanist, an inquiring traveler—keenly addicted to the learning of the past, but equally alive to any new ideas or discoveries of his own time—witty and urbane, skeptical and adaptable, he might be considered an entirely typical figure of the Renaissance, had he not, at the very summit of his career, devoted his last years to a vast and impracticable idea which was more closely in harmony with the spirit of an earlier age: the last Crusade. To carry out this plan, he cast aside every obstacle suggested by expediency or prudence and certainly hastened, though well knowing that his scheme had failed, his own death.

Aeneas Silvius Piccolomini, the son of an impoverished country nobleman who had been a soldier of fortune, was born in 1405 in the little Tuscan village of Corsignano, on the bare, dust-colored hills of the Val d'Orcia. A clever boy, he was sent by his father at the age of eighteen to Siena, the city which he called "sacred to Venus." There, while certainly not neglecting the charms of the beautiful Sienese women, he ardently pursued his legal studies with the celebrated jurist Sozzini, and later on continued his classical studies in Florence with Filelfo. Too poor to buy all the books he needed, he would sit up at night copying out long passages from the volumes lent to him by his friends—once even setting his nightcap on fire, as he nodded over his work. Cicero, Virgil, Livy, these were his first models, and among the moderns, when first he began to write verse, Petrarch. His first glimpse of the efficacy of eloquence, when he saw the whole congregation of Siena swept off their feet by the sermons of the famous popular preacher Saint Bernardino, excited him so much that he pursued him to Rome, to ask whether he, too, should not follow the same path. But Saint Bernardino firmly dissuaded him, telling the future Pope to return to the worldly pursuits for which he was apparently more fitted.

It was thus not as a priest but merely as a young scholar with some legal training that Aeneas' career began. Cardinal Capranica, passing through Siena on his way to Basle to claim redress from the Ecumenical Council in his quarrel with Pope Eugenius IV, took him with him as his secretary—and in Basle the young man at once found ample scope for his talents. The Council—which had recently reaffirmed its supremacy even over the Pope, and which had the support of both the King of France and the Emperor Sigismund—was confronting two vast tasks, the destruction of heresy and the reformation of the Church. There Aeneas made the acquaintance of most of the great European prelates and observed their intrigues and counterintrigues; he fostered the cynical detachment already inherent in his Tuscan blood; and he acquired the adaptability, the breadth of vision, and the persuasive eloquence which were to lead him to success. In his *Commentaries* he related, with disarming vanity, that he once held his audience so riveted by his words that for two hours no one even spat!

For twenty years he led a wandering life between Switzerland, Germany, and Austria. He was sent on missions all over Europe: to James I of Scotland—probably for the purpose of inciting fresh border-raids against England—to the Hussite heretics of Bohemia, and to the hermit-duke Amedeus of Savoy, whom he described as leading, in his luxurious hermitage on the Lake of Geneva, "a life of pleasure rather than of penitence." He became known in Germany as "the apostle of humanism." He accepted a post in the chancery of Frederick III, negotiated the marriage of the young Emperor to Eleonora of Portugal, and later went to meet the young bride and to escort her and her bridegroom to Rome. Ambition, he quite frankly admitted, was to his mind the chief spur to every human activity. But he also found time to make love to many pretty women (declaring chastity to be a philosopher's virtue, not a poet's, and sending home one of his bastards to be brought up by his father at Corsignano, "so that another little Aeneas may climb on your and my mother's knees") and to write some scurrilous tales and a little satirical treatise on the miseries of life at court, as well as the poems which caused him to be crowned as poet by the Emperor. To all this he added a formidable list of more serious works, which included treatises on education, on rhetoric, on the Holy Roman Empire, and even on horses; histories of Bohemia, of the Goths, of the Council of Basle, of the Diet of Ratisbon, and of the Emperor Frederick III; and some *Lives of Illustrious Men*—and finally, after becoming Pope, the famous *Commentaries*.

It was not until the age of forty that he returned to Rome, obtained the forgiveness of Pope Eugenius IV, and conducted the negotiations which led to the reconciliation of the Papacy with the Empire—and it was only two years later, in 1447, that he at last took orders. After this, the speed of his preferment was remarkable. Within a year he became Bishop of Trieste and resumed his travels between Italy, Austria, and Bohemia; in 1449 he was made Bishop of Siena; in 1456 Calixtus III nominated him Cardinal of St. Sabina; and two years later, in 1458, he was elected Pope.

Success comes most swiftly and completely not to the greatest or perhaps even to the ablest men, but to those whose gifts are most completely in harmony with the taste of their times. The Renaissance man admired versatility, scholarship, eloquence, diplomacy, and an inquiring and balanced mind; above all, he valued style, both in life and letters. All these were qualities possessed by the new Pope to a very high degree. *"Aeneam rejicite, Pium suscipite"* (Reject Aeneas and accept Pius), he wrote, with a harking-back to the Virgilian phrase which had also determined the choice of his new name—and it is certainly true that he abstained for good, after his ordination, from the loose living and scurrilous writings of his early years, and lived a life of great industry, sobriety, and benevolence. "I do not deny my past," he wrote to his friend John Freund, "but we are old, nearer to death . . . I have been a great wanderer from what is right, but I know it, and I hope the knowledge has not come too late."

He was not exempt from one fault of many other pontiffs: nepotism. Three members of his household (including his nephew Francesco) were given the cardinal's hat at the same consistory, another nephew, Antonio Piccolomini, was made commander of Castel Sant' Angelo, and his sisters were richly endowed with both money and palaces.

The fullest picture of his daily activities is to be found in the book which was the mirror of his times and of himself: his *Commentaries.* This is not only one of the most readable autobiographies ever written, but also a historical record of many of the important events of Pius' time, seen with a sharp eye and a ripe judgment, and enlivened by brilliant sketches of men and places, and by perceptive reflections on human nature. *"Nil habuit ficti, nil simulati"*—nothing was there in him of deceit or pretense, wrote one of his earliest biographers—and indeed this book carried these qualities so far that when it was first published in 1584 (during the Counter Reformation), it was thought necessary not only to prune it severely, but even to ascribe its authorship to its copyist, Gobellinus of Bonn, so that "matters which the heretics gladly seize upon" should not come from a pope's pen. Now that the full text is again available, however, we are afforded an unvarnished picture of the Pope's contemporaries. It is not always flattering. He described the Florentines as "traders, a sordid populace who can be persuaded to nothing noble." "When once Pius asked the Bishop of Orta what he thought of Florence and he replied that it was a pity that so beautiful a woman had not a husband, the Pope replied, 'She lacks a husband, but not a lover.' As though to say she had no king, but a tyrant, meaning Cosimo." Of the Bolognese he wrote: "They are cruel rather than brave at home, while abroad they are known to be cowards," and many pages were filled with attacks on the Venetians, who drew back from their promises of alliance against the Turks, while he said, "They favored the war against the Turks with their lips but condemned it in their hearts." "Glorious deeds," the Pope said, "are not embraced by democracies, least of all by merchants, who, being by their nature intent on profit, loathe those splendid things that cannot be achieved without expense."

The tyrants of the Italian states were described with an equally sharp pen. Cosimo de' Medici, indeed, was admitted to be "more lettered than merchants are wont to be," but Borso d'Este was depicted as "listening to himself when speaking, as though he pleased himself better than he did others," and as a man "whose mouth was full of flattery mixed with lies." And Sigismondo Malatesta, for all his brilliance of mind, artistic sensibility, and military skill, was described as "a man essentially pagan" and "so avaricious that he never shrank not only from looting

but from theft, so ruled by his passions that he raped his daughters and his sons-in-law. He surpassed all barbarians in cruelty." The Pope publicly declared that, just as some holy men are canonized, so Sigismondo should be "enrolled as a citizen of Hell." On the steps of St. Peter's his effigy was burned, bearing the inscription: "Sigismondo Malatesta, son of Pandolfo, king of traitors, hated by God and man, condemned to the flames by the vote of the Holy Senate."

It is when he is writing of the members of his own Curia, however, that Pius II's indictments are most startling. Shortly before his death he addressed a secret consistory of his cardinals: "Like businessmen who have failed to pay their creditors, we have no credit left. The priesthood is an object of scorn. They say we live for pleasure, hoard up money, serve ambition, sit on mules or pedigree horses, spread out the fringes of our cloaks and go about the city with fat cheeks under our red hats and ample hoods, that we breed dogs for hunting, spend freely upon players and parasites, but nothing in defense of the Faith. Nor is it all a lie!"

Yet when Pius met true saintliness or valor, he was swift to recognize it. It was he who canonized Saint Catherine of Siena and who, in describing the entry into Vienna of the humble Franciscan friar Giovanni da Capistrano—"with so tiny a body, so advanced in years, so dried up, exhausted, all skin and nerves and yet always serene"—at once recognized in him the attributes of a saint. He also gave a singularly detached and impartial account of the story of Joan of Arc, "that astonishing and marvelous maid," ending with the comment, "Whether her career was the work of God or a human invention we would not like to say."

But where his regard was not awakened, no figure was so eminent as to escape his darts. He described James I of Scotland as "smallish, hot-tempered, and greedy for vengeance," and said of his former master, the antipope Felix V, that when he appeared without his beard, he looked like "an unsightly monkey." Before the assembled Curia he referred to the Cardinal of San Marco as "the buffoon of your Order," and to the brilliant, unscrupulous French Cardinal d'Estouteville of Rouen as "a slippery fellow who would sell his own soul." And here is his account of another prelate, Jouffroy, Cardinal of Arras—a man "made mad by too much learning"

—"He wanted to seem devout and would say Mass, sometimes in the Basilica of St. Peter's, and sometimes elsewhere. By face and gesture he would show how much he was carried away, drawing sighs from the bottom of his chest, weeping and, as it were, conversing with God. But before he had taken off his sacred vestments and left the altar he had cuffed one or another of his servants who had made some slight mistake in his ministration . . ."

His description, too, of the conclave by which he himself was elected Pope is as cynical as it is convincing. "The men having most power in the College . . . summoned the others and demanded the Apostolate for themselves or for their friends. They implored, promised, threatened; some, even, without a blush and forgetting all modesty, spoke in praise of themselves . . ." Aeneas' chief rival was the Cardinal of Rouen, and many were the intrigues which took place in the latrines of the Vatican ("as being a private hiding place"). The French Cardinal openly distributed promises of honors and posts to those whose support he thought he could obtain, but the next morning Aeneas called in turn upon *his* friends —appealing to the loyalty of one prelate and the vanity or self-interest of another. In the end nine votes for him and six for the Cardinal of Rouen were dropped into the golden chalice. But still the required majority had not been obtained. For a while no man dared to commit himself. "All sat in their places, silent, pale, as though they had been struck senseless. No one spoke for some time, no one opened his mouth, no one moved any part of his body, except the eyes, which turned this way or that. The silence was astonishing, astonishing, too, the appearance of those men, as though you had found yourself among their statues . . . Then the Vice-Chancellor Rodrigo [the future Pope Alexander VI] rose and said, 'I accede to the Cardinal of Siena!' And his words were like a sword through Rouen's heart . . ." Another followed him, but still one vote was lacking, that of the old, fat Cardinal Prospero Colonna. As he rose he was seized by each arm by the cardinals of Nicaea and Rouen, who tried to hustle him out of the room. But before they could do so, he shouted, "I, too, accede to Siena, and I make him Pope!"

Pius II's *Commentaries*, however, will not now be read chiefly for their account of the intrigues of the Curia or of the politics of the Italian states. What gives them their peculiar flavor is their revelation of the point of view of a Renaissance man. "My spirit is an inquiring one," Aeneas wrote of himself in his youth, and in this he never changed. As an antiquarian, his curiosity embraced Christian and pagan monuments alike. In England he admired the stained-glass windows of York Cathedral and the shrine of Saint Thomas à Becket in Canterbury, "at which it is a crime to offer any metal less than silver," but he was no less interested in the translation of Thucydides in St. Paul's Cathedral, and in being told that Newcastle was founded by Julius Caesar. In Hadrian's Villa he tried to reconstruct the origins of the ruins. On his visit to Federigo da Montefeltro, the Pope and condottiere discussed not the politics of the day, but the arms used in the Trojan War. On his way to the Congress of Mantua he turned aside to search for the labyrinth of Clusium described by Pliny, and visited the house called Virgil's Villa. Even in his last years, crippled with gout, he was carried in his litter to Tusculum, Tibur, and Falerii; he examined "with great pleasure" the Roman ship recently dug up in the Lake of Nemi, and rowed down the Tiber to Ostia, speculating about the Latin name of the fine sturgeons he was given, and the site of one of the Roman palaces. At Albano he visited the old monastery of San Paolo, which its new owner, the Cardinal of Aquileia, had transformed into a fine villa surrounded by gardens, and the deserted church belonging to the Cardinal de Foix, which was "without roof, altar, or doors" and served only as a stable for cattle and goats. "These," he dryly commented, "are the Canons appointed by the Cardinal of Albano to perform God's service day and night." With regard to the preservation of ancient monuments, however, his own conduct was somewhat inconsistent. When, on the Appian way, he found a man digging up some stones of the Roman pavement, he sharply rebuked him, bidding Prince Colonna never again to allow the public road to be touched, and he even issued a Bull forbidding the use of ancient columns and statues for making mortar. But he himself used, to build the Loggia della Benedizione and the marble steps leading up to St. Peter's, many fragments from the Colosseum, the Forum, or the Baths of Caracalla, and he constructed most of the great new fortress at Tivoli with material from the amphitheater of that city.

He was in some ways singularly free from the superstitious beliefs of his time, rebuking Borso d'Este for "heeding the pagan folly" of his astrologers, and refusing, even after being racked with fever for seventy-five days, to summon a magician who was "said to have cured of fever two thousand men in the camp of Niccolò Piccinino." But he told a Saxon student who asked him whether he knew of a Mount of Venus in Italy, in which the magic arts were taught, that "in Umbria . . . near the town of Nursia [Norcia], there is a cave beneath a sharp rock, in which water flows. There, as I remember to have heard, are witches, demons, and dark shades, and the man who is brave enough can see and speak to the ghosts and learn the magic arts."

In his travels he always investigated eagerly, if skeptically, any local legend or tradition. In Scotland he was fascinated by the legend of the Barnacle Geese, which told "of a tree growing on a river bank, whose fruit rotted if it fell to the ground, but if it fell into water, it came to life and turned into birds; but when he [Piccolomini] went thither and made inquiries, eager for a miracle, he found that it was a lie . . ." When he visited the slopes of Monte Amiata, he looked for the herb called Carolina because, according to tradition, "it was once revealed by God to Charlemagne as a cure for the plague" and he succeeded in finding it—"a herb with prickly leaves which cling to the ground and are set around a flower similar to that of a thistle." He added, however, "Pius considered it a fable invented by Charlemagne's admirers."

He had an observant eye, too, for the different sorts of men and manners that he met upon his travels. In Scotland—where he spent one night in a rough farmhouse, with the goats picking the straw out of his pallet—he observed with interest that the white bread and wine that he had with him were such rarities that "pregnant women and their husbands drew near to the table, fingering the bread, sniffing the wine, and asking for a taste." He noticed, too, that "nothing gives the Scots more pleasure than to hear the English abused." In Basle he was impressed by the well-built stone houses and well-kept gardens, with fountains "as numerous as those of Viterbo," and in Vienna—according to his *Life of Frederick III* —by the comfortable dining halls with stoves and glass windows, where songbirds were kept, as well as by the fine churches and spacious cellars. He even

described a convent for the redemption of penitent prostitutes, "who sing hymns in the Teutonic language day and night. . . . But if one of them is caught sinning again, she is cast into the Danube." But he also complained of the rough German table manners, of a court in which any falconer or stableboy was more welcome than a scholar, and above all, of the gross drunkenness. He described how Heinrich, Count of Gorizia, would wake up his two little boys by a virtuous Hungarian lady in the middle of the night to pour wine down their throats. When the sleepy children spat it out, he turned upon his wife, shouting, "Strumpet, these brats are none of mine!"

Perhaps the most delightful passages in the *Commentaries*, as in Pius' letters, are those which reflect his passion for natural beauty. He might, indeed, be considered, with Petrarch, the first of the Romantic travelers. At Viterbo he went out almost every day at dawn "to enjoy the sweet air before it grows hot and to gaze at the blossoming sky-blue flax." At Bolsena he insisted on being rowed out to the islands in the lake, and whenever possible, he preferred to hold his consistories out of doors, especially in the great beech woods of Monte Amiata, "beneath this tree or that, and also by the sweetly running stream . . . Sometimes it happened that as the Pope was signing documents the dogs flung themselves upon some huge stag hiding nearby, which would drive them back with its horns or its hoofs and make off with all speed for the mountains." Often, too, he picnicked with his Curia in a meadow or poplar grove—though whether his cardinals, mostly elderly and urban gentlemen, enjoyed this habit is not related. One evening, as the Pope was returning home through some meadows, a cowherd, "seeing the golden litter carried by its porters and surrounded by horsemen . . . milked a cow that was near him and, full of joy, offered to the Pope the bowl which he used for eating and drinking, filled to the brim with milk . . . Pope Pius . . . was not too proud to put his lips to the black and greasy bowl."

One of Pius' most endearing traits was his simple enjoyment of homely pleasures: the cheese of Monte Oliveto, "which Tuscans consider the best in the world," the fresh trout which he saw caught on the Monte Amiata, and the engaging antics of his sister's baby. He even devoted a whole page to the misadventures of his poor little puppy, Musetta, who first fell into a cistern full of water and, when rescued at the last gasp, "was taken to the Pope, to whom she continued to whimper for a long time as if she wanted to tell him about her danger and stir his pity," but then was bitten by a large monkey, and finally, having climbed up on a high window sill, was seized by a violent gust of wind and dashed upon the rocks. The Pope sadly commented that, like some men, she was plainly foredestined to a violent end.

He described with relish the horse and foot races in Pienza, where a small and beardless grown-up slave inserted himself among the boys and defeated a little boy from Pienza, "with fair hair and a beautiful body, though all bedaubed with mud, who . . . bewailed his fortune and cursed himself for not having run faster. His mother was there, a handsome woman, comforting her child with gentle words and wiping off his sweat with a towel." "The Pope and cardinals"—so ends this chapter—"watched from a high window with no small merriment, though in the intervals they were busy with affairs of state."

The occasion of these events was the inauguration of the cathedral and palace which the famous Florentine architect Bernardo Rossellino had built at Corsignano—now renamed Pienza—as a summer residence for the papal court. The little city is still as perfectly harmonious a work of art as the early Renaissance has produced—the cathedral being flanked on one side of a little paved square by the papal palace, and on the others by the episcopal palace and town hall. Some smaller palaces were built nearby for the cardinals and their courts. The cost, however, was so much higher than the original estimate that everyone expected the architect to be cast into prison. But the Pope, after inspecting the buildings, sent for him and said: "You did well, Bernardo, to lie to us about what this undertaking would cost us. Had you spoken the truth, you had never persuaded us to spend so much money, and this fair palace and this church, the loveliest in all Italy, would never have existed. . . . We thank you, and we consider you deserving of special honor." And he issued a Bull forbidding the defacing of any of the church's walls or pillars, the building of any other chapels or altars, or any other change that might mar the church's perfect symmetry. "If any do otherwise, may he be anathema and absolvable only by the au-

thority of the Bishop of Rome, except in the hour of death."

This happy return to his native city was perhaps the last carefree incident of the Pope's life. His remaining years were obsessed by a single idea: the coercion of the reluctant princes of Christendom to fight against the Turks.

It is not difficult—even without attributing to Pius II the religious fervor of an Urban II or a Saint Catherine—to understand his motives. He was well aware of how closely Hungary and Austria, and beyond them Italy herself, were threatened by the rising ambition of that astute and designing sultan, Mohammed II. His historical imagination was intensely conscious of the ancient traditions of the Holy Roman Empire, and of the Papacy as the savior of Christendom. And as he himself would have been the first to admit, his sense of drama was fired by the image of himself as the central figure in the most significant of all wars, once again leading princes and peoples against the Crescent in the name of the Cross.

Long before his accession, Aeneas had tried to awaken the European princes to the Turkish menace. At the coronation of Frederick III he had pointed out that Hungary had become the last bulwark of Christianity, and when Constantinople fell he was among the first to realize that thenceforth the doors of Europe would always remain open to the Turk. "I see faith and learning," he wrote, "destroyed together." Aeneas implored both the Emperor and the Pope, Nicholas V, to convoke a European congress at which the princes would agree to a truce with each other, "and turn their arms instead against the enemies of the Cross." A Diet was actually held at Ratisbon, at which the few delegates who came voted for the Crusade, but only a few months later, when another congress was held in Frankfurt, most of them had already changed their minds. "They would not listen to the names of Emperor or Pope, but said they were deceivers and greedy men, who wanted to make not war but money." Aeneas was still struggling to persuade them to confirm their promises, when the sudden death of the Pope "rent the web that had been so long in weaving."

Immediately after his accession Pius returned to the charge. He summoned another congress at Mantua and, though crippled by gout and suffering from stone and bronchitis, decided to attend it himself. "It is all-important," he had written, "that a war should begin well, for the end of a war is often implicit in its beginnings." Certainly the beginning of this one foreshadowed its failure. The Pope set forth for Mantua with most of his cardinals, but when he arrived there, he found himself almost alone. His court implored him to go home again. Had they been brought here, they asked, to discuss a Crusade with the Mantuan frogs? Messengers from Thomas Palaeologus of the Morea (the southern part of the Peloponnesus) brought desperate appeals for help, but there were few to listen to them. The Duke of Burgundy now said that he was too old to come. The King of France, exasperated by the Pope's recent support of the accession to the Kingdom of Naples of Ferrante of Aragon, sent word that he could join no Crusade so long as he was still at war with England. England—torn by the Wars of the Roses—sent a similar message. Frederick III was engaged in invading the Kingdom of Hungary, while the envoys of that country—which alone, in the recent past, had defended Europe against the Turks—bitterly complained of this new menace. No single voice was raised to echo the old Crusading cry: "*Deus lo vult—* it is God's will!" Of the Italian rulers, Borso d'Este declared that his astrologers forbade him to attend; Malatesta suggested the employment of Italian mercenaries, but only to get their pay for himself. The Florentines and Venetians both feared the loss of their eastern trade, but Venice promised to furnish sixty galleys, if every expense was paid from the general treasury and she was given the supreme command of the naval forces and awarded the spoils of the war. "To a Venetian," the Pope commented, "everything is just that is good for the State; everything pious that increases the Empire."

Yet when at last he was in the presence of those envoys who did come, the Pope showed much of his old fire. He had learned to conceal his physical pain so well that it was only revealed by his yellow color and drawn features and by an occasional compression of his lips. The French, in return for their participation, demanded the re-establishment of the Angevin rule in Naples, and believed that the Pope's illness would at once cause him to yield. But he declared: "Though I should die in the middle of the assembly, yet shall I reply to that proud-stomached delegation!" Speaking with as much eloquence and energy as in

his youth, his cough ceased, and the color returned to his old cheeks. Even his most bitter opponents admitted that he had "spoken like a Pope." Moreover, in an attempt to shame the princes into following his example, he declared that he himself would lead the Crusade. "We can be borne in Our litter to the camp." On January 14, 1460, the Holy War was formally declared, and, discouraged but not defeated, the Pope started on his long journey home.

Before actually embarking on the Crusade, however, Pius II made one last curious effort to come to terms with the infidel—one which, if successful, might well have changed the course of European history. In a long and eloquent letter he attempted to convert the Sultan Mohammed II to Christianity. If he accepted baptism, the Pope wrote, a second Roman Empire might arise in the East, with Mohammed at its head. Pius reminded the Sultan that Clovis had brought Christianity to the Franks, and Constantine, to the Romans; he depicted a Europe once more united and, for the first time in centuries, at peace. The epistle—which now reads more like a fine literary exercise than a political document—was widely circulated in Europe, but whether it ever even reached the Sultan is not known. Certainly no reply was ever received in Rome.

It was now plain that the Turks could be conquered only by arms. In a last attempt to arouse the Roman people the Pope decided to display to them —in what Gregorovius calls "one of the most curious scenes of the Roman Renaissance"—a singularly precious relic: the skull of the Apostle Andrew, which the exiled Despot of the Morea, Thomas Palaeologus, had brought to him—"the symbol of the Empire of Constantine and Justinian, and of the Church of Origen and Photius." Three cardinals, who had gone to fetch the head at Narni, were met at the Ponte Molle by the Pope and the other cardinals, and after a solemn *Te Deum* they accompanied it in procession to St. Peter's. "It was a splendid spectacle," Pius wrote, "to see those old men walk on foot through the mud holding palms in their hands and wearing miters on their white heads . . . Some who till then had lived delicately and could hardly move a hundred paces except on horseback, on that day . . . walked two miles through mud and water with ease." All along the route, windows were hung with tapestries and lit up with torches and oil lamps;

altars were set up at street corners, branches of fragrant shrubs were set alight. "Any man who possessed paintings or a fine and lifelike statue displayed them in the portico before his door." Little stages were set up, on which children, dressed as angels, sang or played musical instruments.

Finally, on reaching St. Peter's, the Pope stood at the top of the marble stair before the church and displayed the head to the assembled crowd, renewing his own vow to the Apostle "to recover thy sheep and thy dwelling-place on earth," and calling upon God to deliver Christendom from the Turks. "Then there arose a great sound, like the murmur of many waters."

In the following spring, since the Turkish army was engaged in Bosnia, the Venetians, who had concluded an alliance with Hungary, decided that the moment was propitious to send off their own fleet to the Peloponnesus. "*We* are already at war," they declared. Pius had no illusions about the Venetian motives, but, as he pointed out to the Florentine envoys, even though the Venetians were "seeking the Peloponnesus and not Jesus. . . . if Venice is victorious, the Church will be victorious. . . . This war is our common war." Moreover, at just this moment, a most fortunate event had come to strengthen the Pope's hand. In the wooded hills of Tolfa, which were within the Patrimony, some mines of alum, the precious dye until then imported from Turkey, were discovered. This Pius declared to be a miracle, and at once set aside all its profits for the Crusade. On October 22, 1463, he issued the Bull *Ezechielis*, repeating his determination to lead the troops of Christendom himself. "In our spirit, old as it is, and in our sick body there is a determination to make war upon the Turks."

Already, however, he realized that many of his allies had failed him—in particular Francesco Sforza of Milan, Louis XI of France, and his vassal the Duke of Burgundy. The Venetian troops in the Peloponnesus had been swiftly defeated by the Turks, and their commander killed. The only troops to reach Ancona were a handful of unscrupulous adventurers, greedy for gain and loot. The Archbishop of Crete was appointed to weed them out, rejecting all those who had neither arms nor money.

Nevertheless, on June 14, 1464, in a solemn ceremony at St. Peter's, the Pope took the Cross, and four days later, so ill that he had to be carried onto his barge, he set forth. Turning back at the Ponte Molle for a last glimpse of Rome, he bade his city farewell, declaring, "You will never see me alive again." In all the history of the Crusades there are few episodes more pathetic than this journey of the dying Pope up the Tiber and across the Apennines—well aware that his enterprise was doomed. Often, as they drew near the coast, his attendants would draw the curtains of his litter, so that he might not see the bands of deserters who, scenting the prospect of defeat, were fleeing home before they had even begun to fight.

When the Pope reached Ancona, no Venetian ship was to be seen, and day after day, from the windows of the bishop's palace at the summit of the town, Pius scanned the Adriatic in vain for the galleys of Saint Mark. The city was now short of food and water and a pestilence had broken out, and the Pope himself was wasting away with dysentery.

When at last, on August 12, the Doge Cristoforo Moro sailed in with twelve ships, Pius was too ill to receive him. "Until now," he said, "it was a fleet that was lacking. Now the fleet has come, but I shall not be there." Two days later, feeling his end to be near, he summoned to his bedside the prelates who had come to Ancona with him, gave them his blessing, and told them that he was leaving them to finish what he had begun. Then, left alone with his nephew, his secretary, and his old friend Cardinal Ammanati, he once again exhorted the latter not to draw back. "Urge my brothers to go on with the Crusade . . . Woe befall you if you draw back from God's work." Asking for his friend's prayers, he lay back and died before the dawn.

On the next day his body was carried to the cathedral, where the Doge pronounced a long and insincere oration over it and then at once set sail for Venice, while the cardinals hurried back to Rome to elect a new pope. The last Crusade was over, with the death of the only man who had believed in it.

THE CITY OF POPES

Ninety years before Pius II became Pope, an exiled Florentine, Fazio degli Uberti, visited Rome. Inspired by its decaying grandeur, as were Dante and Petrarch before him, he wrote a poem eulogizing the ancient city. An illustration (above) from his manuscript personifies Rome as a widow forsaken by the popes in Avignon. Dressed in rags, she cries out her woe to the poet (upper left, with a friend), who listens as she points out the monuments of her past glories: the Colosseum lying at her feet; the equestrian statue of Marcus Aurelius partly hidden by an ancient aqueduct; the Baths of Diocletian (lower left) housing the cells of Carthusian monks; the Marble Horsemen standing on the Quirinal between the columns of Trajan and Marcus Aurelius; and the Pantheon (center), converted into a Christian church. All but forgotten during the reconstruction undertaken by the Renaissance popes, the aged ruins nevertheless affected nearly every artist from Alberti to Michelangelo, and humanists were inspired by their classical forms.

THE MAKING OF A POPE

A cycle of pictures, like an epic poem, may tell the story not only of a man, but of an epoch. The frescoes of the Piccolomini Library in the Cathedral of Siena—begun in 1502 by the Umbrian painter Bernardino di Betto, whose small stature earned him the nickname of Pinturicchio—are the work of an artist who was above all a decorator and storyteller, and who later went on to Rome, to fresco the Borgia apartments in the Vatican. His work, which had a strong influence on the young Raphael, reflects many of the tastes and values of the early Renaissance: a delight in pomp and splendor, in male beauty, vigor, and success, in the civilized pleasures of letters and the arts—a world without grotesques or the contortions of pain and grief, of well-planned spaces and clear transparent light. These frescoes tell the life story of a man who rose to the Papacy without being either a saint or a mystic, and also without the support of a great religious order or of powerful worldly connections, but entirely through his own gifts: a persistent ambition, a versatile mind, an eloquent and persuasive tongue—Aeneas Silvius Piccolomini, who became Pope Pius II. The pictures on these pages show him in his youth. On the left, a preliminary sketch for one of the paintings depicts him as an unknown young Tuscan clerk, riding forth in 1431 on a white horse from the harbor of Talamone, in the train of Cardinal Capranica, hoping to make his mark at the Council of Basle. This, in defense of his master, he swiftly did. "A mighty thing," he later wrote to a friend, "is eloquence . . . and to tell the truth, nothing so much rules the world."

On the right, Aeneas, now secretary to the Antipope Felix V elected by the Council of Basle, and sent as his envoy to the Emperor Frederick III, kneels before the Emperor to receive the poet's laurel crown—an award which, like Petrarch, he valued so much that until he became a bishop he signed all his letters Aeneas Silvius poeta.

At right is the jeweled miter worn by Piccolomini as Bishop of Siena. At left, Pius II presides, in 1459, at the Congress of Mantua, vainly attempting to arouse the enthusiasm of Europe's princes and his own cardinals to make war upon the Turks.

The dying Pius II, leading the last Crusade, arrives at Ancona (below). In the left foreground is the Doge Cristoforo Moro.

THE GOOD WORKS OF PIUS II

The subject of Pinturicchio's painting on the facing page was one of Pius II's most popular acts. This was the canonization of his fellow citizen, Saint Catherine of Siena, on the day of Saints Peter and Paul, 1461. Catherine, daughter of a humble Sienese dyer, was one of the most remarkable figures of the fourteenth century. Calling herself "the servant and slave of God's servants," she played a major part in the purification of the Church and—inspired by a divine command received in a vision—traveled to Avignon to persuade Pope Gregory XI to return to Rome, thus ending the exile of the Papacy. Her four hundred letters—written in the vigorous colloquial idiom of the Sienese poor, and addressed to such various people as the irascible Urban VI, the hesitant Gregory XI, the dissolute Queen Joanna of Naples, the excommunicated Bernabò Visconti, the arrogant condottiere John Hawkwood, the suspicious rulers of Siena, and to subtle theologians, or simple monks and nuns—show the ardor of a mystic and the intellect of a statesman, uniting spiritual authority and personal humility. In her daily life her extreme austerity was only equaled by her warm and immediate charity and by her disregard of all trivial conventions, since the time granted on earth for attaining perfection is "as small as a needle's point." She died in Rome in 1380, aged thirty-three. The two young men in the left foreground of the picture are Raphael and Pinturicchio, and the white Dominican on the right is Fra Angelico.

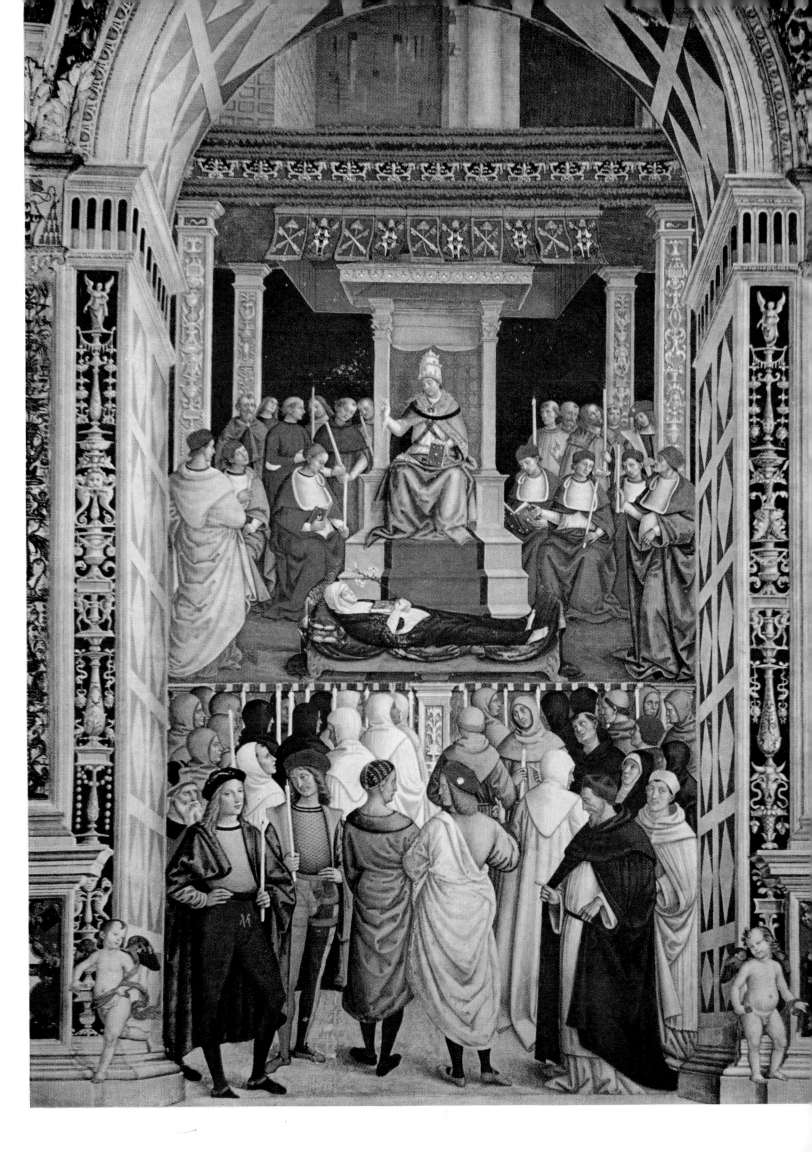

THREATS FROM ABROAD

The capture of Constantinople by the Turks in 1453 sounded the death knell for the Eastern Empire and removed the final buffer between Western Christendom and the Mohammedan world. It was up to Rome to unite Europe against the infidel, and there were popes such as Pius II who devoted all their energies to the task. But the majority were more concerned with their personal goals—rebuilding Rome, enriching their families, and maintaining lavish courts. Some even carried on diplomatic and trade relations with the enemy until forced to make war by some direct provocation. Alexander VI found the best means of all to hold off the barbarians and fill his treasury at the same time. The Sultan's rival, his brother Djem, became a prisoner of the Pope and, as a hostage, was a valuable tool with which to bargain. He was lodged in luxurious captivity in Rome

at the expense, ironically, of the Sultan himself, who paid vast sums to keep him out of the way. The threat to the Church came not only from the East, however, but also from the Christian monarchs of Europe, who were increasingly jealous of clerical power and independence within their borders. Resistance grew as the rulers of Spain managed to gain control over the potent forces of the Inquisition; the Pragmatic Sanction of Bourges severely limited papal jurisdiction in France; and in England growing hatred of clerical laws and distrust of the clergy paved the way for Henry VIII's revolt. The popes retaliated by entering more and more into the temporal conflicts of the day, but at the expense of their spiritual prestige. As Christian unity crumbled, the road was clear for Luther's denial of papal supremacy, the sack of Rome by Charles V in 1527, and the Reformation.

One of the few lasting results of the war against the Turks in 1501 was an early painting by Titian of the papal admiral, Jacopo Pesaro, who is shown (opposite) being presented to Saint Peter by Pope Alexander VI. An eyewitness recorded the Knights of Rhodes feeding the hostage Djem with their own hands (right) for fear that he might be poisoned. Below, Alexander VI's approval appears on a petition for religious indulgences from the German banking family of Fugger, who had loaned money to the Papacy.

Alexander VI made his nephew Giovanni Borgia a cardinal at his first consistory and this miniature is thought to commemorate that event. He also gave the red hat to the brother of the young and beautiful Giulia Farnese, his alleged mistress. The "petticoat cardinal," as Farnese was called, later became Pope Paul III and practiced his own nepotism. Titian portrayed him (below) with his grandsons Ottavio (right) and Alessandro (left), who was made a cardinal at the age of fourteen.

A Golden Rose is given annually by the Pope to a distinguished person, city, or church. Pius II gave the rose at right to Siena. Alexander VI presented one to Charles VIII (above) in a vain attempt to dissuade him from invading Italy.

INTERNAL DECAY

"Our churches, priests, altars, sacred rites, our prayers, our heavens, our very God, are purchasable," despaired an indignant contemporary scholar, bemoaning the calamitous state of the Church. To finance their pet projects and their lavish courts, the popes resorted to virtually any means to fill the papal coffers and their own pockets. Simony ran riot. Nearly every cardinal had purchased his red hat for a liberal amount of gold and was willing to sell his vote in the conclave for even more; Paul II left bishoprics unfilled so that he could collect the revenues himself; Innocent VIII seemed to spend most of his time financing the escapades of his profligate son; and Sixtus IV declared, "a pope needs only pen and ink to get what sum he wants." The sale of indulgences was another lucrative practice, and the appalling proportions it assumed under Julius II and Leo X gave Martin Luther the final provocation for his ninety-five theses. Those churchmen who had not obtained their positions by bribery were usually the favorites or relatives of popes. This practice of nepotism reached a nadir during the pontificate of Alexander VI, whose ultimate goal, some said, was to make the papal tiara a hereditary crown for his Borgia offspring. The Church could not help but suffer from such corruption; spiritual duties were neglected, monasteries lacked central direction, while ecclesiastical preferment and rewards were often given as bribes for services. Money, not salvation, seemed to be the preoccupation of these worldly pontiffs.

TEMPLA DOMVM EXPOSITIS: VICOS FORA MOENIA PONTES:
VIRGINEAM TRIVII QVOD REPARARIS AQVAM.
PRISCA LICET NAVTIS STATVAS DARE COMMODA PORTVS:
ET VATICANVM CINGERE SIXTE IVGVM:
PLVS TAMEN VRBS DEBET:NAM QVAE SQVALORE LATEBAT:
CERNITVR IN CELEBRI BIBLIOTHECA LOCO.

In 1440 Lorenzo Valla, the most erudite of all the humanists, wrote a discourse proving that the Donation of Constantine, upon which the Papacy based its temporal jurisdiction over Rome, was a forgery. It was followed by other pamphlets ridiculing the Latin of the Vulgate, denying the authenticity of the Apostles' Creed, and accusing Saint Augustine of heresy. Despite such attacks, Pope Nicholas V welcomed Valla to Rome in 1447 and appointed him Apostolic Writer. Other humanists received similar treatment: Poggio's indecent tales and scurrilous satires on the morals of the clergy did not prevent him from remaining a papal secretary for fifty years, and Filelfo, who despised the Church and attacked anything and anyone who neglected to pay him well for not doing so, was employed and entertained at Rome with great distinction.

Humanists were prized additions to every court and carefully nurtured their reputation as the only men qualified to fill the posts of secretaries and orators. They flourished in Rome under the patronage of such popes as Nicholas V, Sixtus IV, and even Alexander VI, as well as in the literary salons of rich and worldly cardinals. Under Julius II and Leo X, however, they gradually became less erudite and assumed a new elegance and stylistic sophistication. These later humanists did not indulge in the vindictive wrangles of Poggio and Filelfo, nor did they possess the scholarly thoroughness of Poliziano or the eloquence of Valla. But the greatest change lay in the fusion of pagan and Christian ideals in Rome. There no longer seemed to be any conflict between the two, and under Leo X the leading humanists—Bembo, Aleander, Sadoleto, and Bibbiena—nominally dedicated to the rebirth of classicism, were rewarded for their brilliance by being made princes of the Church.

Melozzo da Forlì painted Pope Sixtus IV (left) with his four nephews receiving Platina, the new Vatican librarian. The future Pope Julius II stands at the center. Raphael's portrait of Tommaso Inghirami (right) shows the humanist and papal favorite at work as secretary to the Lateran Council.

THE RESTORATION OF THE CITY

In 1377, when the Papacy returned from Avignon accompanied by its huge retinue of cardinals, courtiers, scholars, and artists, the glory of ancient Rome was slowly reborn. Spacious palaces were built amid the decaying ruins, churches rose in the ancient baths, gardens were laid out around the columns of the Palatine, and wide avenues swept over crumbling temples and arches. Much of the new building was at the expense of the old: Paul II used stone from the Colosseum to build the Palazzo San Marco; shops occupied the Theater of Marcellus; Sixtus IV destroyed the oldest bridge over the Tiber and built a new one in his name, using the old stone for cannon balls. Each pope strove to outdo his predecessors, and the coffered ceilings, collections of antiquities, magnificent paintings, and frescoes which adorned the interiors of the palaces made their handsome façades seem almost dull by comparison. The greatest monument of all, however, was the new Cathedral of St. Peter. The ancient basilica had been ordered destroyed by Pope Nicholas V, and in 1506 Julius II laid the cornerstone for a new church designed by Bramante. Successive popes poured money into the building as work progressed slowly under a series of architects, each with a new plan or addition. Finally the aging Michelangelo was put in charge. Ignoring the designs of Raphael and declaring that Antonio da Sangallo's plan would make the church so dark it would be dangerous for public morals, he returned to the original scheme, adding the great dome, which he modestly called "larger, but not more beautiful" than that of Brunelleschi in Florence. The master died before his work was complete, and later the plans were changed again, but the dome remained and rises today, the crowning achievement of the Roman Renaissance.

The anonymous sketch at left shows the huge dome beginning to rise over St. Peter's. Bramante's plan for the church, with two towers and a dome similar to that of the Pantheon, is on the bronze medal above.

PAPAL TREASURES
IN THE VATICAN

The worldly popes of the Renaissance were among the most lavish patrons of art in history, and the countless treasures in the Vatican —some of which are reproduced on the following nine pages—reflect their extravagant generosity. Their great wealth attracted to their court all the best artists of the age, who rebuilt, carved, painted, and decorated not only in the Vatican but in most of the churches and palaces of Rome as well. Sometimes working for popes and cardinals as individuals, sometimes for the Papacy as an institution, they were showered with money and rewards. Before, and in the early days of, the Renaissance, while the pontiffs were still struggling for political control, Pisanello, Gentile da Fabriano, and Masaccio were working in Rome. And the later popes, with a few exceptions such as Adrian VI, who walled up the pagan splendors of the Belvedere, outdid themselves in support of all the arts. They commissioned hundreds of jeweled objects, seals, chalices, monstrances, paintings, tombs, statues, and monuments, allowing the artists considerable freedom in order to retain their services. Raphael was apparently considered for the cardinalate despite his amorous adventures. Sodoma, so named as a result of his activities, was turned out of the Vatican by Julius II only to be recalled by Leo X, for whom he painted a nude Lucretia stabbing herself. He was rewarded for his efforts by being made a Cavalier of the Order of Christ.

The Vatican houses innumerable masterpieces from the hands of dozens of Renaissance artists who worked there: the Stanze and Logge where paintings by Piero della Francesca and Signorelli were plastered over to make room for those of Raphael; the Borgia apartments decorated by Pinturicchio; the huge library; the picture collection; the Cortile del Belvedere, housing such Renaissance discoveries as the ancient Laocoön; and, of course, St. Peter's Cathedral itself. The greatest treasure of all is unquestionably the Sistine Chapel (facing page). Begun in 1473 for Pope Sixtus IV with marble quarried from the ruined mausoleum of Hadrian, its simple interior was magnificently adorned by many talented artists. Botticelli was invited to plan and paint frescoes on the walls with scenes from the lives of Christ and Moses. He was assisted by Perugino, Pinturicchio, Rosselli, Piero di Cosimo, Signorelli, and Ghirlandaio, all masters in their own right. Mino da Fiesole carved the marble screen which divides the chapel; Verrocchio cast the silver statues of the Apostles which decorated the altar; the famed tapestries of Raphael at one time adorned the lower walls on ceremonial occasions; and in 1508 the greatest papal patron of them all, Julius II, commissioned Michelangelo, who covered the ceiling with scenes from the Old Testament. Years later the aging and infirm master returned, at the request of Paul III, to paint his last and most famous fresco on the altar wall—the *Last Judgment*. Its awesome beauty completed the room and makes the chapel as a whole the supreme creation of papal patronage.

Leonardo accomplished almost nothing during his short stay in Rome under the patronage of Pope Leo X's brother Giuliano de' Medici. His unfinished Saint Jerome (left) is therefore one of the prized possessions of the Vatican today. Fra Angelico was called to Rome in 1447 by Nicholas V to paint scenes from the life of Saint Lawrence in the Pope's private chapel. The fresco at right shows the saint distributing alms, with the flames of his martyrdom embroidered on his robes. According to Giorgio Vasari, Nicholas was so pleased with Fra Angelico that he offered to make him Archbishop of Florence, but the monk declined, "since he did not feel capable of ruling men." Below, a panel from the bronze doors of St. Peter's Cathedral shows Pope Eugenius IV, who commissioned the work, receiving the keys from Saint Peter. These doors, cast for the old basilica by Antonio Filarete to celebrate his patron's greatest goal, the expected reunification of the Greek and Roman churches, were incorporated into the new structure while it was being built.

OVERLEAF: *The Arch of Constantine bears a harsh Biblical warning against schism in Botticelli's* Punishment of Korah, Dathan, and Abiram, *from the wall of the Sistine Chapel. At the center Moses angrily calls down divine wrath on the rebels against his authority and sees them swallowed up by an abyss (left). The artist's self-portrait appears (second from the right) amidst a crowd preparing to stone the blasphemers.*

Jacopo Galli, a wealthy Roman banker, signed a contract with the French Cardinal of St. Denis in 1498, agreeing that a little-known sculptor named Michelangelo would carve a Pietà "that shall be more beautiful than any work in marble to be seen in Rome." The young artist amply fulfilled his task, and his famed statue (left), the only work he ever signed (his name appears on the band across the Virgin's breast), now rests in its own chapel in St. Peter's Cathedral. Critics complained that the Virgin seemed too young to be the mother of a grown man, but Michelangelo silenced them by replying that "chastity enjoys eternal youth." Twenty years later, Raphael and his pupils were hard at work decorating the Logge built by Bramante in the upper part of the Vatican. Raphael undertook so many commissions toward the end of his short life that he had to delegate much of his work to assistants, and it was Giovanni da Udine who covered the arches and pilasters of the Logge with their colorful stucco reliefs. The fanciful grotesque mask (upper right), a detail from his work, shows how greatly he was influenced by the decorations in the newly discovered Golden House of Nero, which had been buried for centuries under the Baths of Trajan. The word grotesque was applied to the Logge stuccos because their designs were first seen in the subterranean rooms, or grottoes, of Nero's palace. The two bronze reliefs at right come from the majestic tomb of Pope Sixtus IV. Antonio Pollaiuolo worked for ten years on the monument, which was commissioned by the Pope's nephew Giuliano della Rovere (later Pope Julius II). The sides of the tomb are divided into ten panels, each representing one of the liberal arts. At right center is the depiction of Geometry. Indicative of Italian interest in foreign learning is the inscription on the Perspective panel (lower right), which comes not from Italian authorities in the field, such as Alberti or Piero della Francesca, but from the Perspectiva Communis of Archbishop Peckham, an Englishman.

The frescoes in the Vatican Stanze, or rooms, of Raphael, commissioned by Julius II in 1508, represent the ideal combination of pagan and Christian themes in art. In the School of Athens (above) a number of ancient pagan philosophers and scientists, led by Plato and Aristotle (center), discuss their ideas within a huge basilica. On the opposite wall of the Stanza is the Disputation on the Sacrament, representing the triumph of theology and the Church Militant. The detail at right shows part of the assembly of theologians, saints, and churchmen. From left to right are Saint Augustine, dictating The City of God; Saint Thomas Aquinas; a martyred pope thought to be Saint Clement; Saint Bonaventura; and Pope Sixtus IV. In an adjoining Stanza the Mass of Bolsena honors Pope Julius. In the detail at left are four soldiers of the famous Swiss Guard, founded by the warlike Julius.

VENICE

THE GOLDEN YEARS

On Ascension Day, 997, Doge Pietro Orseolo stayed his galleon in the great sea-gateway that joins the Venetian lagoon with the Adriatic, poured a libation on the sea, and received the blessing of his Patriarch before he sallied forth to annihilate the Dalmatians. For eight hundred years that ceremony was repeated, growing in complexity and splendor as Venice herself grew rich and powerful, until it became one of the great ritual pageants of the Western world. The huge state barge of the doges, the *Bucentaur*, ablaze with crimson and cloth of gold, drew away from the Piazzetta to the chants of massed choirs. The Council of Ten, the Signory, the patricians and ambassadors, followed in their gilded gondolas. At the Porto di Lido the Doge, standing on the poop of the *Bucentaur*, cast a golden ring into the waters, declaring "O sea, we wed thee in sign of our true and everlasting dominion." The mixture of paganism, Christianity, and Oriental splendor was as symbolic of Venice as the marriage to the sea.

The sea linked Venice with Byzantium, the market for her goods, the protector of her liberties, the model of her state, the teacher of her crafts, the fountain of her arts. Under Byzantium's protecting wing Venice had grown to greatness, great enough to rend and despoil the Empire in the Fourth Crusade, yet not great enough to save the imperial city in its days of crisis when, in 1453, the surge of the Turkish hordes overwhelmed it. The loss proved grievous, but not disastrous, for by that time the sources of Venetian power were scattered throughout the seas of the Western world.

Venice lived by her ships. Thanks to them, the desolate mud flats had flowered in stone. To this strange water-borne city they brought riches, power, and security. Only twice in its history did enemy vessels sail into the waters of the Venetian lagoon, and both times the enemy was annihilated. To the landward its defenses proved equally inviolate. The Venetians made their ships in the great Arsenal that was the

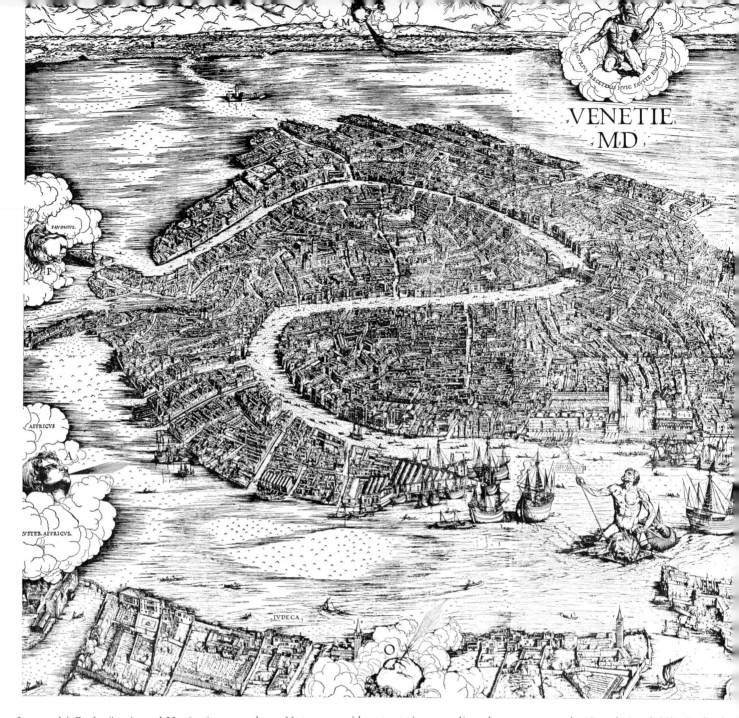

Within the image: VENETIE MD, FAVONIVS, P, AFFRICVS, A, VSTER AFFRICVS, IVDECA, O, M

Jacopo de' Barbari's view of Venice in 1500 shows Neptune astride a porpoise, guarding the entrance to the Grand Canal. The Rialto br.

wonder of Europe in the Middle Ages. Its two miles of forbidding fortifications enclosed the most formidable armory in the Renaissance world. Thousands of workmen toiled there, and a new galley was produced every hundred days. These ships could be commissioned with amazing alacrity. From the Arsenal to the lagoon the ships moved as on a conveyer-belt—masts, sails, oars, stores, and weapons were quickly loaded as the vessel slowly passed each storehouse. Most fittings on each galley were standardized, so that replacements could be stored in all Venetian warehouses, whether they might be in Southampton or Tyre; any crew could be moved to any ship without further training, or a fresh crew could be made up from survivors in battle. And every galley, whether used in commerce or in war, belonged to the state: no patrician, no matter what his wealth might be, could possess a Venetian galley. Such precise regimentation, such absolute control, gave Venice its pre-eminence over its rivals and

enabled it to ship a crusading army to the Holy Land without overstretching its resources. The other maritime powers of Italy hated the supremacy of Venice. Genoa ruined herself in a long and desperate war, which ranged from the Bosporus to the lagoon itself, in an attempt to crush Venice and despoil her of the riches which her great fleet carried for her merchants. By 1400 Venice had proved herself invincible; indeed, she had become the center of a sea-borne empire. Zara, Ragusa, Crete, and many Aegean Islands belonged to her absolutely: trading communities, enjoying extraterritorial privileges, had been established in Constantinople, Acre, Tyre, Sidon, Alexandria. Venetian merchants were as familiar with the Black Sea as the Adriatic; her ambassadors were to be found in Isfahan and in Cairo; her travelers, stimulated by the stories of Marco Polo, reached Sumatra and Ceylon long before Vasco da Gama rounded the Cape. And even though the Venetians never ventured to such far-flung

...sses the S-shaped waterway. At the eastern end of the city (far right) are the Arsenal's drydocks, shipwrights' workshops, and boat basins.

places as the Genoese at the height of their greatness, their contacts with the East were more stable, more secure, and made up in volume for what they might lack in diversity.

By 1450 Venice was the only power in Italy, save for the Papacy, that was truly cosmopolitan, one whose interests required not only a great fleet but also a complex intelligence system. Venice needed to know the intentions of the Shah of Persia, the Count of Flanders, the Sultan of Cairo, the King of France, or the Duke of Ferrara. And every merchant, every priest was expected to spy for his country's good. The Signory knew at once the deepest secrets of the most carefully guarded conclaves of the Papacy, for the patriarchs of Venice put loyalty to the state higher than the command of the Church. The carefully, beautifully written, well-informed, judicious reports of the Venetian residents in London, Paris, or Bruges now form some of the most reliable sources not only for the history of Venice, but also for the history of England, France,

and the Netherlands. In the great building of the Archivio Centrale, next to the Frari church, is the greatest collection of archives ever accumulated by a single city. There are a quarter of a million books, documents, and parchments, which if placed end to end would circle the earth eleven times. For the fourteenth and fifteenth centuries there is a multitude of papers, a plethora of facts, a pyramid of accounts, still awaiting the toil of the historian. The reason for it all lies in the attitude and methods of the famous, or infamous, Council of Ten who, throughout the Renaissance, were the absolute rulers of the most highly organized state west of Byzantium.

The Council of Ten believed in knowledge, in facts: nothing was too trivial, too remote. They were as interested in the words and actions of a shopkeeper in the Campo di Santa Maria Formosa as in the gossip of the harem at Samarkand. So voracious was their desire to pry that, throughout Venice, they set up the famous Lions' Mouths by which Venetians

259

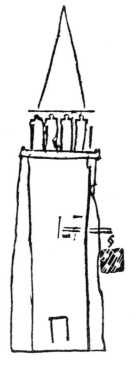

With jaws open to receive anonymous denunciations, lions such as the one below glared from the walls of Venetian buildings. If the malefactor were a cleric, he might be left to repent in the cheba *(left), a wooden cage hanging high above the Piazza San Marco. But Venice masked its cruelty with glitter; the Piazza was often the scene of tournaments as colorful as that painted by Domenico Morone (far left). The city's marble palaces and rich, brilliant costumes figure in the detail (facing page) from Carpaccio's* The Return of the Ambassadors. *Docked in the harbor is a trireme.*

could inform the Council anonymously of their suspicions of their neighbors. On this knowledge the Council acted swiftly and silently, for no public trials enlivened the Venetian scene, and there were no appeals. Once found guilty, the prisoner was sometimes quickly and efficiently strangled in the dungeons; or thrown into a part of the lagoon reserved for the purpose, where no fishing was allowed; or hanged by one leg from the pillars of the Doge's Palace; or quartered and distributed about the city; or buried upside down in the Piazzetta, legs protruding; or beheaded—as a public spectacle— between the great pillars on which stand Saint Theodore with his crocodile and the winged lion of Saint Mark. That was how the great condottiere Carmagnola met his end, when the Council discovered that he was prepared to sell Venice to her enemies. But most traitors went silently in the night, their broken bodies sending a shiver of horror through the waking city as dawn gilded the palaces and churches.

This formidable engine of government ruled with equal efficiency all departments of the state—finance, diplomacy, the navy, the army, the welfare of the city—and it would tolerate no real rivals. In the last resort the safety of the state, for which the Ten were responsible, overrode all other considerations. The powers of the Doge had been so ruthlessly suppressed (he could not even display his own armorial bearings) that he had become a mere ceremonial idol—a figure for pageants and formal acts of state. The Church, too, bowed to the state. No bishop, no parish priest, could officiate in Venice unless Venetian born. When placed under the Interdict by Pope Sixtus IV, the Patriarch fell discreetly ill, and the Council told the clergy that they would treat as a traitor any priest who refused to celebrate the offices of the Church. The clergy ignored the Interdict. During the most savage years of the Counter Reformation, the Council protected the historian Sarpi, whom good Catholics regarded as little bet-

ter than a Lutheran. In Venice there were no divided powers. Its immense wealth and its colossal maritime power were ruled with the iron will of a modern dictatorship. Unbridled capitalism might flourish on the Rialto, but the Doges' Palace was close cousin to the Kremlin.

The Council of Ten did not consist of permanent rulers. Its powers, if not its final authority, were partly shared by the Collegio or Cabinet; and beyond these there was a more numerous body still—the Senate or Signory from which the councils were appointed. No one, however, by a decree of 1297, could sit on these bodies unless his ancestor had been a member of the Great Council between 1172 and 1297. In 1319, in order to make certain that the purity of this oligarchy should be maintained, the heraldic officers of the republic drew up the famous Golden Book, the *Libro d'Oro,* as a perpetual studbook of Venice's aristocracy. This revolution, for it was nothing less, deprived the mass of Venetians of all the

political rights they had possessed. The murmurs and rebellions against it were quickly and ruthlessly suppressed, and, by the Renaissance, the patrician families of Venice were as secure in their political and social power as the English aristocracy of the eighteenth century. A patrician's life was not, however, one of gilded leisure. The aristocrats were expected to officer the fleets; trade was not regarded as ignoble; and the far-flung Venetian possessions required patricians for their government. Like the guardians of Plato's republic or the proconsuls of British India, these men were expected to lead lives dedicated to the state. Power and prestige might be theirs, but undeviating loyalty, exemplary courage, and unflagging generosity were the price they paid. If they aspired to the Doge's throne, they were aware of the risks, the dungeons, and the strangler's silent visit; if they sought glory in battle, their spirit was steeled by the grim epics of Venice's history—Admiral Dandolo, who bashed out his brains against

261

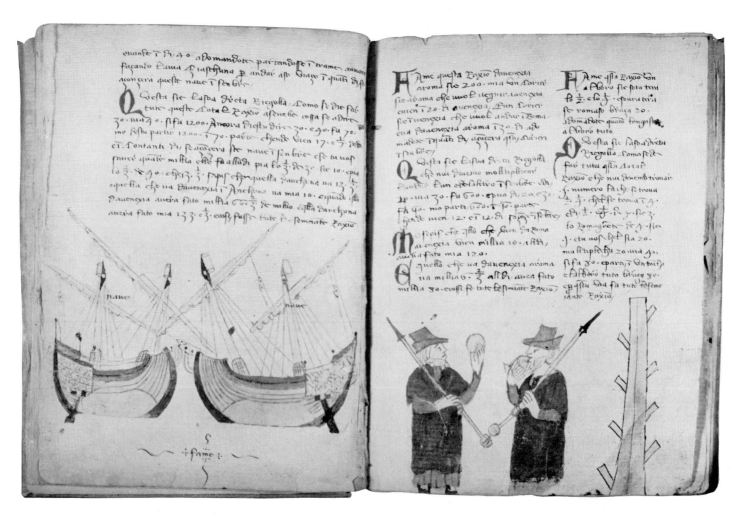

A decorated fourteenth-century trader's textbook includes insurance and cargo data and mathematics exercises. (Two merchants have met at the perennially problematical point between A and B.)

the timbers of his galley the night the Genoese defeated him, or the neatly folded skin of Admiral Bragadino, flayed from his living body by a sportive pasha. Such is the dulcet beauty of Venice, with its time-eroded buildings swathed in the opalescent light of the lagoon, that it is all too easy to forget the stern, unyielding, harsh, and dedicated spirit that inspired its rulers in their days of greatness.

Venice, however, was Janus-faced. Her commerce might be regimented, her aristocracy disciplined and controlled, her people subjected, yet she was cosmopolitan as no other city in Europe was. The crowded wharves of the Rialto and the Riva degli Schiavoni saw Gentile and Jew, Moslem and Greek, haggling over rich cargoes from the Orient. The Germans possessed a vast warehouse—decorated with frescoes by Giorgione—on the Grand Canal; the Turks, another, which had been the palace of the Pesaro family. Venice possessed the earliest ghetto in Europe, and the Armenians

followed their religion for centuries without fear of the Inquisition. All the nations of Europe mingled with the races of the Near East. They were brought together by the simple fact that Venice was the greatest market of the Western world. Anything could be bought and sold in Venice, but the principal commerce was in luxuries—in spices, slaves, gold, silver, glass, silks, damasks, jewels—cargoes that were small in bulk but huge in worth. Throughout the barbarian times, when Venice grew to greatness, Europe lacked the sophisticated skills and crafts that were commonplace in the Eastern Empire, or in Syria and Egypt; and in return for products from these places, Venice could offer the cheap raw materials that a primitive Europe produced—hides and tin from England, fine cloth from Flanders, raw silver from Bohemia, copper and steel from Germany. And there were the pilgrims. Decade after decade, century after century, in peace or in war, rich and devout Christians won their way

Venetian women developed an early form of lace by cutting away embroidery sewn on canvas (below), and Venice was famous for luxury fabrics, such as the velvet above, decorated with the Medici arms. But wool—an industry employing twenty thousand workers—was the city's most important textile product. The slave trade was of less economic value, since slaves worked mostly as domestic servants and were not used in industry. A sixteenth-century statuette carved of ambergris (right) shows an African girl at a moment of leisure, clothed only in fancy baubles.

to heaven via the Holy Places, to the great profit of the Venetians. For centuries the Crusaders warred in the eastern lands, and the Crusaders paid; paid for themselves, their armies, their horses, their necessities—and Venetians did not believe in bargains. In spite of their great wars—against the Genoese, the Greeks, the Turks—Venice waxed rich: rich on man's craving for luxury, for ostentation, for self-indulgence, on the pride of life and the lust of the eye. All the skills that she encouraged were luxury crafts rather than industries. The glass manufacture of Murano, based on secrets learned in the East, was guarded by the Council of Ten: for any workman with the knowledge of its manufacture to leave Venice was an act of treason. The Council hunted him down and killed him. Along with the monopoly in glass went another —the making of mosaic: this art, derived from Byzantium, was practiced only in Venice. Venetian jewelers had no rivals in the late Middle Ages, and emperors and kings sent there

for their crosses and scepters. Few Italian cities could rival Venice in the splendor of its silks, and none in the beauty of its lace. In Venice everything was for sale—love along with the rest. She boasted more courtesans than Rome. Their charges were carefully catalogued, and they were incomparable in skill as in price. They, too, had their rivals; the competition from homosexuals was so severe that the harlots complained loudly to the Council of Ten. As the wealth and prosperity of Europe lifted, so the riches of Venice soared.

On the threshold of the Renaissance, Venice possessed an unrivaled trade, and a stable and immensely powerful government firmly in the hands of its patricians. It was a city of hatchet-faced merchants. Jacopo Loredan entered in his great ledger: "The Doge Foscari: my debtor for the death of my father and uncle." After Foscari had been harried to death and his son killed, Loredan wrote on the opposite page, "Paid." In 1450 that was the spirit of Venice. By 1550

Glassmakers never made goblets, as some Venetians boasted, which shattered on contact with poison, but the delicacy of their work nevertheless seemed magical. The gilded bowl at right, which shows the triumph of fame, and the enameled goblet below are highly fragile; few like them have survived. Even more rare is opaque glass, such as the tumbler below; probably intended as a wedding gift, it may display a portrait of a bride.

a gentler, softer, more self-indulgent atmosphere had turned Venice to a city of carnival: still strong, still rich, still capable of sacrifice, but essentially an empire in defense, wishing for a secure isolation in which to enjoy her immoderate riches. And this change was brought about partly through a change in strategy—itself the result of the growth of the Renaissance state—and partly through the spirit of the Renaissance itself.

Safe in the security of the lagoon, the strategic problems of Venice had been largely distant and maritime. Her diplomacy had been directed solely to the pursuit of trade, and the acquisition of territory had been subordinate to these ends. Throughout the High Middle Ages the Venetians had excluded themselves from Italy (sometimes they hinted that they owed an allegiance not to the West but to the Greek Emperor at Byzantium), but when it suited their purpose they forgot the East and made a token gesture to the Emperor of the West. So successful had this policy been that many influ-

ential doges and patricians regarded it as the foundation of Venice's glory. They felt that any deviation would ruin the state, and the deviation that they most feared was that the government would succumb to those who demanded that Venice should extend her frontiers on the mainland and take her place as a great power in Lombardy. The problem was one that all expanding commercial empires were to face: Did the needs of commerce require the political control of its channels? So long as the plain of Lombardy was divided up between a multitude of petty powers, Venice had little to fear, but in the fourteenth century the dominant powers in northern Italy became fewer and fewer, and the danger of their enmity was brought home to the Venetians when Carrara, the despot of Padua, joined with the Genoese in the war that Venice saved on the very threshold of defeat by winning the great battle of Chioggia in the lagoon itself. The safety of the lagoon, let alone Venetian trade, depended upon the con-

With its shadow reflected in the water, a covered gondola glides across the Venetian lagoon (below), on a trip made even more romantic by the addition of imaginary mountains in the background. From the lagoon, Venetians could easily reach their sumptuous country mansions, which were located throughout the Veneto. One of the most beautiful of them all is La Rotonda (right), Palladio's architectural masterpiece in the temple-villa style, which stands atop a hill outside Vicenza. The devastating war waged against Venice by the League of Cambrai destroyed most of the great fifteenth-century villas, but decades later, in Palladio's time, peace had returned. His villas, with broad porticoes open to the countryside, reflect the wealth and security of his age.

trol of the great rivers—the Brenta and the Piave—that had cost the republic huge sums to canalize and divert from the lagoon. Beyond the rivers were the easy Alpine passes, particularly the Brenner, through which Venetian trade flowed to Northern Europe. And there were subtler motives at work —everywhere in Italy small city-states were going down like ninepins through the onslaught of Milan, Florence, Rome, Naples, and if the Venetians wished to be heard in the councils of Italy, they needed to acquire far more Italian territory than a few muddy islands and river mouths in a shallow lagoon. Finally, after the defeat of Genoa and before the collapse of Constantinople, Venice had plenty of money and plenty of young aristocrats ready for a venture.

Although the debate, particularly at the time of Doge Foscari, seemed bitter and prolonged, Venice was drawn inevitably into the vortex of Italian politics and war. Once embroiled, strategic needs forced her to push her frontiers ever westward and southward against Milan and Rome. Her vicissitudes were many, but her successes built up like a coral reef which, no matter how frequently it is submerged, continues to grow. There were years of danger, particularly when Venice struggled singlehandedly to keep the Turks confined to the eastern Mediterranean; there were even darker days when all the princes of Italy combined with her enemies in the League of Cambrai to ruin her. But Venice triumphed. Her frontiers stretched from Lake Como in the west to Trieste in the east, from the high Alpine valleys in the north to Ferrara in the south. And these rich territories were ruled with wisdom and restraint. No local customs were violated, no local law abrogated, no families uprooted. About all that the republic did there was a hardheaded, bourgeois realism. The possession of Verona, Vicenza, Padua, Bergamo, Brescia, Treviso, and the rest added enormously to Venetian wealth in spite of the cost of the wars their capture entailed.

The patricians found they could tap the riches of the *terra-ferma,* as they called the Lombard plain, far more easily than they could the Oriental trade, rich as it was. The Turks were in Constantinople, and the frequent, costly, and bloody struggles that resulted made eastern trade more difficult and more uncertain than it had been in the time of the Greek emperors. That trade had always entailed risks, from pirates, shipwreck, or the hazards of the sea, but money in farms on the rich alluvial plains of the mainland brought in a high, steady return. In addition, there were choice opportunities in the captured towns—real estate, banking, insurance, partnerships in trade and industry—yet it was the land that attracted the Venetians. For centuries their rich families had built their villas and landscaped their gardens on the Giudecca and Murano. There, in the summer evenings, they had escaped from the heat and stink of Venice for their *fêtes champêtres;* for the music and dalliance that are so brilliantly portrayed by Giorgione and Titian. But tenements and warehouses crept along the Giudecca; Murano was eaten up by the ever-expanding glass works, so the lovely sweeping curves and gentle slopes of the valley of the Brenta or the wilder hills of Cadore drew the Venetian aristocracy to the rustic but sophisticated life of the countryside. There Palladio built the most exquisite villas in the Western world, villas that were to inspire the architects not only of eighteenth-century England, but also the planters of Virginia. Their walls were painted by Veronese and by Tiepolo; their owners' portraits by Titian or Tintoretto. Here they created an indulgent Arcadian life that stood in harsh contrast to the battle-scarred days of Venice's heroic growth. As ever, the strength of merchants was sapped by the delight in being landed gentlemen.

The same spirit was at work in Venice itself; the city had become stuffed and bloated with possessions. Although it proved tenacious, still, in clinging to what it had, it grew ever

At Maser, forty miles from Venice, the patrician Barbaro family built a sixty-six room villa, designed by Palladio and frescoed by Paolo Veronese. In masterpieces of trompe-l'oeil *painting, Veronese decorated the walls with imaginary doors and windows, framing portraits and views of the rural scenery. The huntsman at left appears in one of the rooms, walking through a painted doorway. The Senate passed laws against the unrestrained use of luxurious wall hangings in Venetian palaces, but no restrictions were placed on these painted decorations.*

Venice's riches spurred building. The Foscari family commissioned Andrea Palladio to construct La Malcontenta *(right), a beautifully sited villa overlooking the Brenta Canal. Dwellings in the city were often as splendid, but rarely as fanciful, as Jacopo Bellini's imaginary palace shown at left. Its arcades are in pure Renaissance style, but its pointed windows, like those of many Venetian buildings, show Gothic influence.*

more indifferent to adventure. No Venetian galleys probed the secrets of the New World; no hardheaded merchants sought gold in tropical Africa. Perhaps it is not surprising that the early, exploratory, heroic phase of the Renaissance passed Venice by. Only, as it were, when the market in Renaissance goods was established did Venice enter it, but then she did so with a panache and a brilliance all her own. And furthermore, her proud independence and her utter indifference to the ideological strife of the sixteenth century enabled the spirit of the Renaissance to flourish long after it had been strangled elsewhere in Italy. Venetians, by the very nature of their experience in life, were quick to adopt technical improvements or to exploit the commercial possibilities of artistic development. The Flemish discovery in oil painting was quickly adopted by Venetian artists; the market for bronzes after the antique was flooded by Venetian craftsmen; family portraiture was a commonplace in Venice while it was un-

usual elsewhere. Whenever the calculating eye of the Venetian entrepreneur saw a main chance, he seized it. Printing, scoffed at in Rome and patronized in Milan, rapidly became a luxury industry with a growing mass market in the capable hands of Aldus Manutius and his family. The famous Aldine Classics were the first comprehensive, standardized sets of books produced. They lacked the beauty and rich ornamentation of the earlier books that attempted to ape the illuminated manuscripts, but about the Aldine Classics there is a spare and efficient functionalism. Elegant, not ornate, moderate in price, and easy to read, they were all that a book should be. Yet this was but one of over two hundred presses in Venice in 1500. Here the new printing trade, carefully nurtured and protected by the state, flourished as nowhere else.

Venice exploited with exceptional skill the bourgeois delights from which a growing public of increasing affluence derived intense satisfaction. Indeed, as her political and mili-

Music was often a theme in painting, and Giorgione made use of it in his Fête Champêtre *(opposite) to express life "as a sort of listening," to quote the English critic Walter Pater. The detail of Veronese's* Wedding at Cana *(above) shows Veronese himself with a cello, Bassano playing a flute, and at right, the aged Titian holding a bass viol.*

tary power gently, almost imperceptibly, ebbed, she became the symbol of self-indulgence and sensuous living—a city of extravagance, urbanity, and sophistication, an aristocratic Bohemia in which the future was forgotten in the day's delights. In the end, bereft of all but the pageantry of power, the Venetians, as hardheaded as ever, plucked their profits from the gaping provincial nobility of Western and Northern Europe. But between 1450 and 1570, the great years of the Renaissance in Venice, there was still vigor enough in Venetian commerce, achievement enough in Venetian arms, to create legitimate pride. The lords of Venice could still live in an aura of greatness without any sense of falsity. Yet the weakening, the softening, was spreading everywhere as decade followed decade, like the growth of self-indulgent fat on an old warrior. This atmosphere of transition was exceptionally fertile for Venetian art, even though it sapped its power.

The Signory had always believed in the value of art as propaganda. They were willing to pay high prices for huge frescoes in the Doge's Palace that celebrated the heroic deeds of the republic or the noble acts of its great men. Indeed, after the doges died, they might be willing to immortalize them in a splendid portrait. And when it came to a pageant, their hard fists opened willingly. They delighted in parading the might and splendor of the republic. Saints' days, the acquisition of a new relic, the anniversaries of notable victories, the solemnization of treaties, the visits of monarchs and princes, the presentation and dismissal of ambassadors—all provided opportunities for glorious display, a kaleidoscope of color in which the costumes of the senators were as glorious as those of the ecclesiastics. As they wound their way through the Piazza, or in and out of the Doge's Palace, the powerless populace became visually aware of the greatness of their masters. It was a lesson, the Signory thought, that could not be learned too often—and they commanded Venice's outstand-

ing artists to immortalize their pageants in paint and to embellish the walls of the Doge's Palace with the glories of the republic. Powerful guilds and rich patricians, with that quick eye for an opportunity, followed suit—and the life stories of Venice's favored saints in a peculiarly Venetian setting covered the charity schools and hospitals, the churches and monasteries of the city. Skilled craftsmen and painters had always been in demand in Venice, and the great personalities of Venetian art—the Bellini family, Giorgione, Titian, Carpaccio, Tintoretto, and Paolo Veronese—were surrounded by traditions that went back to the early Middle Ages. In Venice, because demand had been so heavy and the commissions so large, painting had to be a family affair, a workshop, almost a factory. The properties used for backgrounds were handed down generation after generation, some of Giovanni Bellini's reappearing in canvases a hundred years later. Every great Venetian painter was something more than an individual art-

ist at work; he was the director and inspiring genius of a studio of painters in which brothers, wives, sons, daughters, journeymen, and apprentices all worked together. Naturally, this increased output, and it enabled a painter like Tintoretto to cover acres of wall and roods of canvas in his long and active life; so, too, was it easy for the Bellini and Titian to produce hundreds of portraits and scores of pictures of pageants and religious mythology. Venetian art exists in abundance; indeed, in Venice the feast is almost surfeiting—every church, every monastery swarms with masterpieces. This abundance, this astonishing fertility, reflects the three strands in Venetian life, its vigor, its wealth, and its sensuous delight. Of all painting of Renaissance Italy, the Venetian is most alive to color, to the warm sensuous delight in flesh and clothes and landscape played upon by light and shade. The Venetian master could move with consummate ease from painting a vast wall glorifying the state to the representation

of the intimate enjoyment of physical love, yet whatever he might be painting there was warmth, and the reality that the Venetian knew. The huge *Paradise* of Tintoretto, the largest painting of its age, was peopled with Venetians. In Gentile Bellini's *Miracle of the Cross,* the canals, the gondolas, the roof tops and chimneys of Venice are all there. In Carpaccio's *Saint Ursula,* a Venetian girl sleeps in her bedroom; under the thin guise of a Christian story the rich, sensuous life pulsates, reflecting the splendor of the city.

Although the life of Venice was glorified in this way, individual men were not. An occasional doge, when dead, a patriarch or two, a brilliant condottiere, might be immortalized in a superb portrait or a statue—but the majority of portraits by Bellini or Titian have lost the names of their sitters, for they adorned the walls of those ordinary patricians who had no place in history—only the luck to be born in Venice at a time of artistic greatness. Yet how evocative are these portraits, how infinite their variety, and how sharp the sense of the transience of living and loving men that broods over them. Nostalgia emanates from things Venetian like miasma from the lagoon; the streets of Venice echo with a sense of loss. The poetry of existence, the sadness that veils a sensual life, informs not only the best Venetian painting but also the writing of its one outstanding literary genius—Aretino. In him were mirrored the conflicting images of man—the cosmic and the noble, the moral and the obscene—that were to hypnotize the creative writers of Europe for generations.

Venice at the crossroads of her destiny created a society of exceptional complexity. It was still the city of hardheaded merchants, still the city of enterprise and ingenuity, still the city of the all-pervading, all-powerful state, of the swift and terrible justice. Its claim to dominion over the sea did not ring hollow: the hieratic splendor of the Doge had not been reduced to a quaint old-fashioned pageant. Yet the Renaissance settled

on Venice like a golden haze, sweetening life, softening the edges. Venice had lost the future; from the city of commerce she was becoming the city of carnival. And this feeling of the future lost was already pervading much of the attitude to life of Venetian men and women, drawing them to the luxurious life which they could so easily afford, to the new delights in painting, music, architecture, and letters that the Renaissance produced in such abundance. Rome itself could scarcely vie with Venice in the splendor of its new buildings both public and private. The splendid façades of Sansovino had given the Piazzetta its permanent face, and scattered about the canals and islands of the lagoon were the churches and monasteries of Palladio. Its artistic luxuries were incomparable (so many craftsmen possessing such an ancient tradition were bound to throw up genius after genius in the visual arts), and its gold and silver, armor, jewelry, bronzes, glass, lace, printing, and bookbinding—indeed all the arts and crafts that adorn the life of man—were practiced not only with the highest skill but also in a profusion that made Venice, both in its lagoon and on the mainland, the most affluent state of Italy. The splendor of its new palaces of white marble, porphyry, and serpentine overwhelmed generations of foreigners, while the profusion of its merchandise bewildered them. Philippe de Comines, nobleman of France, ambassador of its King, rich, sophisticated, much traveled, was as entranced by the Grand Canal—*"la plus belle rue que je croy qui soit en tout le monde, et la mieulx maisonnée"*—as the merry, uncouth joker Thomas Coryate of Somerset, who walked all the way there and gaped, openmouthed with amazement, believing himself in paradise. Other cities might possess nobler paintings, statues, buildings; the spirit of the Renaissance maintained in Florence a more heroic aspect, in Rome its expression was more grandiose. But nowhere did it permeate more thoroughly the daily life of a city and its people than in Venice.

271

Francesco Foscari, wearing the Doge's pointed cap.

Doge Francesco Foscari

by H. R. TREVOR-ROPER

In 1423 the old Doge of Venice, Tommaso Mocenigo, lay dying. The prosperity of the city was now at its height; this indeed was the golden age of the republic. But for a generation grave problems had clouded the city's future, threatening not only its security and its carefully nurtured wealth, but its very survival. Now it seemed at the parting of the ways: should it concentrate on its empire abroad or on its base at home? For both were threatened.

The empire abroad was centered in the Aegean Sea, although it extended to the factories in Constantinople and on the routes to the Middle and Far East. Here the threat came from the Ottoman Turks, now settled in Europe, with their capital at Adrianople, and pushing into the Balkans. All the efforts of Venice were needed to keep them out of the Aegean, and for years that had been the prime object of Venetian diplomacy.

The threat to the home base came from closer quarters: from new powers which were rising ominously in and around Italy. Hitherto, Venice had been able to build up its empire abroad because its neighbors at home had given little trouble. Bishoprics, communes, petty princes—they could not be ignored, but equally they offered no temptations compared with the huge profits of the Levant. So the republic had practiced a policy of the balance of power, involving the minimum of direct intervention. But now these petty neighbors were becoming part or projections of greater powers, and these greater powers were threatening the very life of Venice. The rulers of Hungary and Naples were closing in on its Adriatic lifeline. Above all, a menacing new state was pressing down the valley of the Po. For this was the time when the free republics of Italy were gradually being converted into despotic princely states; and the greatest of these states was the new duchy of Milan, under the Visconti family. Having crushed the liberties of Milan, the Visconti were creating around it an even larger hinterland or *retroterra*. In the south they had absorbed the great mercantile republic of Genoa, which, being confined between the Ligurian Alps and the sea, lacked such a *retroterra* in which to fight. In the east the Visconti were pushing toward another great mercantile republic, which was squeezed between the lagoons and the sea—Venice.

How could the republic ensure its survival? The

answer, according to some Venetians, was to enlarge its own *retroterra*, the Venetian *terraferma*—a process which had already begun, with the annexation of Padua, Vicenza, and Verona. But there were others who distrusted this policy. Land wars, they said, were costly; they distracted the city from its real task, in the East; they created a new class of landed nobility and made the city dependent on condottieri; and was it not precisely out of the landed nobility and condottieri that the powerful new group of princes, which threatened the liberties of all Italian cities, was rising?

The Doge Mocenigo was one who argued thus. As he lay dying he summoned to his bed the ducal councilors and there delivered a famous speech. The war for the *terraferma*, he said, had shattered the finances of the republic. It could not be continued. The wealth of Venice lay in manufacture, trade, and shipping: only by keeping to these pursuits, and to peace, would the city master the wealth of Christendom. Therefore they must be careful to appoint a sound successor to himself. Then he went down the list of the possible candidates. Bembo, Loredan, Mocenigo, Contarini—the political members of the great mercantile families who formed the closed aristocracy of Venice—there was something to be said for them all. But at the end he warned them explicitly against one man: Francesco Foscari, he said, was proud, ambitious, unscrupulous. If he were Doge, it would mean war, war, war . . .

To us there may seem something unbalanced in such a warning. Already by that time the republic had achieved its perfect aristocratic form—a form which was to be final (in all essentials) for centuries. Gone were the days when the people had power of election; since 1297 the Greater Council, the legislature and electorate of the republic, had been "closed"—that is, confined to the nobility, who in turn kept careful control over their own membership. Gone, too, were the days when the Doge, however elected, had exercised personal power. By now successive "ducal promises"—the conditions which the nobility, after observing the faults of each Doge, imposed upon his successor—had reduced the Doge to a mere figurehead. If offered the dogeship, a Venetian nobleman was unable by law to refuse it. Once elected, his power was narrowly circumscribed. He was unable to travel outside Venice. Neither he

nor his sons could marry foreigners without permission. Neither his sons nor his personal officers could hold public positions under him (except as ambassadors or naval commanders, in which jobs they could not make trouble at home), and his official councilors, without whom he could do nothing, not even open a formal letter, could not be chosen by him. His income was fixed and his expenses limited, lest he should raise a party by bribery. His authority over the citizens was reduced, lest he should raise a mob in his support. He was not even allowed to give himself social airs. He could not set up his escutcheons in public places, nor answer to honorific titles. To foreigners, as representative of the greatest, richest republic in Italy, he might be *Serenissimo Principe;* at home, in that republic, he was only *Messer lo Doge.* And finally, he could not even lay down his office at will: except with the consent of his six councilors, ratified by the approval of the Greater Council, he could not even abdicate. Why then should an ambitious man want to be doge, and what could an ambitious man do, even if he were doge?

Nevertheless, Mocenigo's warning cannot have been entirely groundless. The Venetian constitution may have been completely aristocratic, and its aristocratic character may have been jealously preserved by a perpetual subdivision of authority, indirect elections, and a complex tissue of checks and balances. But even the most perfect constitution is operated by men with human passions, and the more complex a constitution is, the more certainly it falls into the hands of skillful politicians; and skilled politicians, even with the old rules, may play a new game. In the fifteenth century a new game was being played in all the republics of Italy. Faced by new problems, their old constitutions were crumbling, and new men —sometimes patricians rising out of their midst, sometimes condottieri in their service—were building up despotic rule. This had already happened in Milan, with the Visconti; it would happen again, with the Sforza. Soon it would happen in Florence, too. Cosimo de' Medici might begin as *pater patriae,* "the first citizen" of the republic. He would end by founding a dynasty that would last for centuries. Remembering this, no one can assume that even the Venetian constitution was proof against overthrow from above by an ambitious doge who, as a war leader, might build up a new form of patronage and power. Such at least may have been the fear which inspired the Doge Mocenigo to warn his fellow noblemen against electing, as his successor, Francesco Foscari.

Who was the man who aroused these fears? The great Venetian aristocrats are always somewhat impersonal figures. The very system, with its intense jealousy of individual power, tended to depersonalize them. For it was the essential character of the Venetian republic that all personality was ruthlessly subordinated to the state. Instead of the cutthroat private enterprise of Genoa, or the brilliant individualism of Florence, here we see only an impersonal state capitalism, an implacable reason of state, an official state culture entirely hostile to "the cult of personality." So the official records of Venice do not bring to life even a controversial personality like Foscari. And yet he certainly was a controversial character. His whole reign shows it—a fact which is demonstrated, first of all, by the battle over his election.

Foscari, it is clear, was determined to be doge. Moreover, from the point of view of Mocenigo and his friends, he was an outsider. That was why they so feared him. He was also young (at fifty he was the youngest of the candidates); he was regarded as poor by the great "nabob" families, although he had enriched himself by marriage; he was experienced (after sharing his father's exile in Egypt, he had held most of the great elective offices of the state); and above all—and this was what Venice particularly distrusted—he was ambitious and the head of a party. Moreover, this party was particularly suspicious to the great mercantile aristocracy, like the Mocenigo, that customarily ruled Venice, for it was a party of "the poor nobles," the lesser noblemen, the radicals, the "Westerners" who favored war by land—as distinct from the "Easterners" with their Levantine interests. We are told that, as Procurator of St. Mark's, Foscari had used the large cash balances in his hands to create his following; he had relieved the wants of poor noblemen, given portions to their daughters, and made himself dangerous by their support. No doubt he had won other support by his merits, too. And finally, as was soon to be shown, he was a consummate election manager.

When the forty-one electors met, Foscari was not the favorite. He was too impulsive, too controversial, too committed to a policy. The favorite was Pietro Loredan, the admiral of the republic, who was also determined on office. But Loredan made the mistake of speaking confidently on his own behalf, which lost him votes. Foscari was much more prudent. Although his rivals did not know it, he had already nine ballots safely in his pocket. These voters acted as a bloc, but they did not reveal themselves until they had quietly contributed to the defeat of all the other candidates. Instead, they allowed it to appear that they, too, were opposed to Foscari. Then, suddenly, at the tenth ballot, they all plumped for the outsider and carried him into the ducal chair.

Thus began the longest ducal reign in the long history of the Venetian republic. Foscari, who always liked panache, hastened to celebrate his victory. For a whole year he dazzled the city with feasts and pageants. The new Sala del Maggior Consiglio—the Hall of the Great Council—was opened with splendid ceremony. He fetched his wife, the Dogaressa, in triumph to the Palace in the ducal galley, the *Bucentaur*, attended by the noblewomen of Venice. These spectacles, incidentally, were something of a sop to the non-noble citizens of Venice who in that year lost their last vestigial rights in the government of the republic; but it is doubtful if their personal emphasis pleased the aristocracy. Then the Doge settled down to the business of government.

The character of Foscari's reign can be described in three words—pageantry, war, and dissension. There were feasts and spectacles of unexampled magnificence. There was also—as Mocenigo had prophesied—constant war for the *terraferma*. And thirdly, there was the undying jealousy and hatred of those whom Foscari had defeated—particularly of the Loredan family, whom he had pipped to the post. The pageantry gave his reign its outward splendor; the war its real content; and the hatred of the Loredan brought it to a tragic end.

The outward splendor was shown in many ways. New palaces, public and private, rose by the Grand Canal and the lagoon. The Rialto bridge was rebuilt. Paolo Uccello worked on mosaics in St. Mark's, Antonio Vivarini painted in San Pantaleon. Famous visitors were received with ever greater pomp and show. In 1428 it was the Prince of Portugal whom the *Bucentaur*, escorted by a fleet of boats, fetched in to a banquet attended by two hundred and fifty ladies dressed in cloth of gold and silk and jewels. In 1438 the Emperor of Byzantium himself, in his great time of trial with the Turks, condescended to come in person to Italy, with his brother the Despot of the Morea and the Patriarch of Constantinople, ready to accept the supremacy of the Roman Church in return for Western aid. When the *Bucentaur*, covered with red silk and golden emblems, carried the imperial party from the Lido, the whole lagoon was full of boats, flying banners and playing music, with oarsmen clad in cloth of gold. In 1452 even this event was eclipsed when the Holy Roman Emperor followed the Emperor of the East to Venice, and was drawn in triumph by the *Bucentaur* and the gaily colored boats up to the Grand Canal. By the next year the last Emperor of the East had perished in the sack of his capital, and the Doge Foscari would receive in Venice the fugitive scholars and salvaged treasures of Byzantium.

In Byzantine eyes, the fall of Byzantium was due to Venetian indifference. All through the reign of Foscari, it was said, the military resources of Venice had been turned too exclusively to the West. But this was hardly a fair judgment. The threat from the West was a real threat, as the fate of Genoa showed. And besides, in the first year of Foscari's reign there had been a great success in the East. In that year the Greek governor of Salonika, the emporium of Thessalian grain (Venice lived on imported grain) and the northern watchtower of the Aegean, gave or sold his city to Venice rather than lose it to the Turks. So the East, it seemed, was safe. Meanwhile, the republic had obtained an invaluable ally for war in the West. It happened that at this time the greatest condottiere in Italy, the man who had himself recreated the power of the Visconti in Milan, now, on some slight, deserted his master and offered his services to Venice. This was Francesco Bussone, known as Carmagnola. The Venetians could hardly resist such an opportunity. It was against a background of this double security provided by Salonika in the East and Carmagnola in the West that the republic, in 1425, made a league with Florence and declared war on the revived, aggressive power of the Visconti.

Thus, within three years of his accession, Foscari was carrying out the policy that had always been associated with him. There can be no doubt that it was

his policy: there exists the speech with which he persuaded the republic to make war. Of course, given the Venetian constitution, one can be sure it was not his policy alone, for he had only influence, not authority. Nevertheless, it seems that it was his influence, combined with circumstances, which weighted and held the scales. Even twelve years later, in 1437, that personal prestige was extraordinarily powerful. In that year the Doge sat, day after day, at the bedside of his son Domenico, who was dying of the plague. Foscari's supporters feared that he, too, would catch the infection, and then what would they do? The lives of many, they said, depended on his: if he were to fail, the fortune and the forward policy of the state would be in peril. Clearly, if men could say this, the Doge was no mere chairman. The forward policy of the state depended particularly on him in 1437, when those initial advantages which had made the western war popular a dozen years earlier had disappeared.

In fact neither Salonika nor Carmagnola lived up to their promise. Salonika was the first to go. In 1430 the Turks captured and sacked it; the slaughter was terrible, the loss final. From now on the Aegean Sea lay open to the Turks, with the wealth of Venice in it, scattered among subject islands whose Greek inhabitants preferred (or thought they preferred) Turkish conquest to Venetian exploitation. In the same year an attempt was made to assassinate the Doge. And as for Carmagnola, like so many condottieri, he proved thoroughly unsatisfactory. At the head of one of the greatest armies that had been seen in Italy, he somehow failed to be as victorious in Venetian as he had been in Milanese service, and he remained suspiciously familiar with his former employer and present enemy, the Duke of Milan. The Venetians offered to make him lord of Milan if he would only conquer it, but still he consumed time and money in mere parades or took cures at the baths of Abano. Finally the Venetians lost patience. With their usual circumspection, they did nothing rashly or openly, but invited Carmagnola to Venice to meet the Doge and discuss future strategy. He never saw the Doge. Instead, he was whisked from the palace to prison, tortured, tried, and condemned. When his sentence was discussed, the Doge voted for mercy, but was overruled, and Carmagnola was sentenced to death and beheaded. That was in 1432. After that the republic employed other, less dangerous condottieri.

So by 1432 Foscari's policy was faced with difficulties on all fronts. He sensed the obstacles, and next year asked to resign his office. It is said that he asked again in 1442 and again in 1446, and this suggests that he was an impulsive man, impatient of obstruction, easily discouraged by defeat. But the Venetian aristocracy, or perhaps his supporters in it, would not allow him to give up his office. On each occasion they reminded him that, by the constitution, he could not resign except with the assent of the six councilors and the Greater Council. It was an answer which he was later to remember and to use against his enemies.

Meanwhile the forward policy continued. The war for the *terraferma* went on. It was very long, lasting, with brief interludes, for thirty years. It was also very costly; the first ten years alone cost seven million ducats. It had its dramatic incidents—among them the bringing of Venetian ships over the mountains from the river Adige to Lake Garda; it had its disappointments, too—the most bitter being the gradual slide of the Florentines, out of commercial rivalry, toward the side of Milan. But in the end the war was successful. It carried the westward frontier of the *terraferma* to its furthest and final limit, to incorporate the provinces of Brescia and Bergamo, and the Doge solemnly received them as imperial fiefs. He also obtained Ravenna as a papal fief. And before his death he inspired and signed a new treaty —a league with Florence and Milan, Rome and Naples, which was to preserve the liberty of Italy. It would have been a great triumph had it lasted: all we can say is that at least it outlasted Foscari.

So the pageants and the war went on. But meanwhile what of the third feature of Foscari's reign, the enmity of his rivals? This, too, was very long— long and bitter, as Venetian enmities always were. For if Venice, with its exaltation of state service, was free from the strife of parties which ruined every other Italian republic, it was enlivened, even more than the others, by fierce personal and family feuds. In particular, the Doge Foscari never escaped the bitter hatred of the Loredan family. He had defeated them in 1423. They remembered their defeat, and in after years, with their allies the Donà and the Barbarigo, mercilessly persecuted him at his weakest point—his family.

At the time of his election, one objection to Foscari had been his large family, whose members, it was suggested, would feed on the resources of the state. This danger did not materialize, for of his five sons, four died young of the plague. The last survivor, who alone had heirs, and to whom the Doge was devoted, was Jacopo, a young man of cultivated tastes—a Greek scholar and collector of manuscripts —but indiscreet ways. In 1441 his marriage to Lucrezia Contarini had been one of the most magnificent of the many spectacles which the Doge gave to the city. There had been boat races, feasts, and illuminations, with the city adorned in scarlet and cloth of gold, a great tournament before thirty thousand people in the Piazza San Marco, and two hundred and fifty horsemen had ridden in cavalcade over the Grand Canal on a specially built bridge of barges. But in 1445 Jacopo Foscari was secretly denounced for receiving gifts from Filippo Maria Visconti, the Duke of Milan. At that time Francesco Loredan, the nephew of the defeated candidate, was one of the three chiefs of the Council of Ten, the secret political police of the republic. His ally Ermolao Donà was another, and the Ten decided to act at once. They ordered the arrest of Jacopo and excluded the Doge and his kinsmen from all their deliberations on the matter. Then sentence was pronounced: Jacopo was exiled to Nauplia in Greece, and all his goods were confiscated. In vain the Dogaressa begged to see her son; the orders were given, and the name of the Doge himself was placed, with ruthless, impersonal irony, at their head. Before they could be executed there was a hitch, and then, on grounds of health, the place of exile was changed to Treviso, which was both nearer and more comfortable; but the humiliation to the Doge was no less. It was after this bitter defeat that Foscari made his third attempt to resign; but he was forced to remain in office and drink the dregs of the cup.

Before long, however, the Doge was able to score a point. In 1447 he made a moving appeal to the Ten, and the Ten consented, not on grounds of humanity but (a typically Venetian reason) "because it is necessary at this time to have a prince whose mind is free and serene, able to serve the republic," to remit the exile of Jacopo, now sick in body and mind. But the reunion of the Jacob and the Benjamin of the house of Foscari did not last long. In

A RESOLUTION CALLING FOR THE DOGE'S ABDICATION,
VOTED BY THE COUNCIL OF TEN, THE PRIVY COUNCIL,
AND THE GIUNTA, A BODY OF TWENTY-FIVE NOBLEMEN.

There is no one who does not thoroughly comprehend how useful and altogether how essential to our State and to our affairs is the presence of a Prince, without which, as becomes manifest from the results, the greatest inconvenience and detriment are apt to arise to our State which, since it has by the infinite clemency of our Creator been bequeathed to us by our forefathers hereditary and fair to look upon, we are bound to preserve with all our power and to hold dearer to us than our very life. And although this our city is furnished with holy laws and ordinances, it is of little avail if they be not executed, if the observance of the same be relaxed. The presence of the Prince besides in the councils, at audiences, in the transaction of affairs of state—how desirable it is, how glorious it is, it would be superfluous to point out. All are aware that our most illustrious Prince has vacated his dignity for a great length of time; and from his advanced age it is not at all to be expected that he will be able to return to the exercise of the functions appertaining thereto. How pernicious his absence and incompetence are is more easily understood than explained. Wherefore: it is proposed that by the authority of this most excellent Council and the Giunta the resolution be agreed to that the Privy councilors and the chiefs of the council shall repair to the presence of the most illustrious Prince and declare to him our opinion "that the government of our city and State (which as his Highness knows very well is excessively arduous) cannot be carried on without the constant presence and cooperation of a Prince; also considering how long his Excellency has for personal reasons renounced all share in this government, and that there is no hope that he will be able at any time hereafter to discharge his duties according to the exigencies of this state; and [considering] that his absence is threatening to involve consequences such as we are assured from his affectionate patriotism, he can never desire to witness;—on these grounds which his Excellency in his supreme wisdom will readily appreciate, we with the aforesaid council of Ten and the Giunta have decided upon exhorting and requesting his Serenity, for the evident and necessary welfare of our State—his native land—freely and spontaneously to abdicate, which on many accounts he ought to do as a good Prince and a true father of his country, and especially as we provide that he shall have for his support and proper maintenance from our Office of Salt 1,500 gold ducats a year for life as well as the residue of his salary due to the present day. Also that if it happen that the same most illustrious Prince, on this declaration being made known to him, shall demand time to consider, he may be told that we are content to wait for such answer till tomorrow at the hour of tierce."

1450 the Loredan family found another pretext, and resumed their attack.

That year one of Jacopo Foscari's judges, Ermolao Donà, was murdered, and Jacopo was at once suspected. Again the Doge's son was arrested; he was even tortured; and although nothing was proved and he was probably innocent (it is said that another man afterward confessed to the crime), the Ten, having gone so far, were afraid to go back. They sentenced him, without proof, to exile, and this time there were no second thoughts; he was carried off to Crete. Even in Crete his movements were watched, his indiscretions observed; and in 1456 it was reported to the Ten that he was planning, or at least discussing, revenge with foreign help. The Ten (of whom Jacopo Loredan was now one of the chiefs) immediately decided that the matter was "of the greatest importance"; and once again the Doge's son was fetched back for a trial.

Now began the final tragedy of the Doge's reign, the tragedy which Byron converted into his drama *The Two Foscari*. Before this third trial it was admitted that Jacopo's projects were entirely academic, and that being in Crete, he could do little or nothing to harm the republic; but that made no difference. He was tortured and judged guilty, and the remorseless Jacopo Loredan urged that he be publicly beheaded as a traitor between the columns of the Piazza. Even the Ten drew the line at this, and the prisoner was sentenced to renewed exile in Crete, this time in prison. Before returning to Crete, he was allowed to see his father, now eighty-four years old. He begged the Doge to intercede for him. "Jacopo," replied the old man, "go and obey your country's commands, and seek no more." But when his son had gone, he threw himself upon a chair, weeping and crying, *"O pietà grande!"* Within a few months he was shattered by the news that his last son was dead in Crete.

The Doge's distress was his enemies' opportunity, and they now decided to complete their victory. The Doge, they said, was too old; he was distracted by grief—the grief they had caused him; he could no longer attend to business. Therefore he must go. The Council of Ten met and decided to demand his abdication (*see* opposite). Their message was brought to the Doge by Jacopo Loredan. But now the old man had his revenge. He turned on them the argument they had used against him in the past: by the law, he said, he could not abdicate unless the councilors proposed and the Greater Council agreed. Here, too, he obeyed his country's laws. Baffled, the Ten consulted again, reinterpreted the law to suit their convenience, and told the Doge of their reinterpretation; but still he kept to the old interpretation and would not move. Finally they sent him an order: he was to resign and clear out of the ducal palace within eight days. If he did so, he would receive an adequate salary and a doge's burial; if not, he would be driven out and all his goods confiscated.

It was a completely illegal demand, but the Doge was powerless. He gave in. The ducal ring was taken from his finger and broken, the ducal cap from his head. He promised to leave the palace. Then, seeing pity in the eye of one of his visitors, he called to him and, taking his hand, said, "Whose son are you?" "I am the son of Messer Marin Memmo," was the reply. The Doge said, "He is my old friend. Ask him to come and visit me so that we may go in a boat for solace; we will visit the monasteries." The next day he left the palace. Wearing his old scarlet robe of state, he stepped forth, bent but unaided except by his staff. As he went to the stone steps leading down to the water his brother Marco urged him to go to his gondola by the covered stair. "No," replied the Doge, "I will go down by the same stair by which I came up to my dukedom." A week later he died— of rage, it was said, on hearing the bells announcing the election of his successor.

The people of Venice were indignant at the indecent deposition of the Doge who had reigned so long, who had enjoyed all the honors and prestige of government, whose figure and personality were so striking, whom the emperors of East and West had visited, and who had given them such splendid shows. There was much murmuring against the usurpation of the Ten, and even the Doge's enemies were now a little ashamed that they had not waited another week for a natural death. When Foscari was dead they gave him a splendid funeral, in spite of the protests of the former Dogaressa at this solemn humbug. He was buried in the church of the Frari, and a majestic Gothic-Renaissance monument commemorated his achievement—the conquest of the *terraferma*. Meanwhile the Ten withdrew from the invidious limelight, until the furore over their indecent treatment of the old Doge had abated somewhat. But there was no denying that they had won a notable victory. From now on the constitution was not only clearly oligarchical; it was also clear where the center of oligarchical power lay. It lay with that inner ring of self-elected councilors who could mobilize, even against the Doge, the Council of Ten.

Thus ended the long reign of Francesco Foscari. It ended, as it had begun, in bitter personal controversy, and even today historians dispute its significance. It has been said that it was Foscari who diverted the attention of Venice from East to West, sacrificing Salonika and Constantinople to Bergamo and Brescia. This diversion, it is added, led to disastrous consequences fifty years later, when the powers of Europe united against "the insatiable cupidity of the Venetians and their lust for power." And yet, one may answer, could any other doge really have acted differently? Before Foscari's time the dilemma had been there: if the land powers of Europe would not unite against the Turks, a sea power could not defeat them alone; and could Venice ignore the western threat, or the ominous example of Genoa? Other historians have dwelt on the fear of princely despotism; they have represented the Loredan as incorruptible republicans, Catos inexorable in the cause of the constitution. But is there in fact any evidence that Foscari ever entertained thoughts of altering the constitution? Perhaps in his early years he did (though we can only judge from the suspicion he inspired); but how seriously could an old man of eighty have threatened the established power of the oligarchy? In the end it was not he but his enemies who broke the constitution. He submitted to its most humiliating rules, malevolently applied; his foes broke through its last restraints in order to humble him.

Nevertheless it must be admitted that Foscari's reign was crucial in Venetian history. Whatever his personal aims, they were in the end subordinated and absorbed by the impersonal Venetian system. During his term in office the last Milanese republic was converted into the duchy of the Sforza, the great Florentine republic into the domain of the Medici, but the jealous republicans of Venice, whatever their motives, and whether they were right or wrong in their personal suspicions, positively strengthened their republic. They accepted the policy, and then crushed the personality, of the one man who might conceivably have recreated the old ducal power, so long undermined. And their victory over him was final. After 1457 the republic no longer feared the Doge. Before that date seven doges had been assassinated, nine had been blinded and exiled, twelve had abdicated, one had been sentenced to death and beheaded, two had been deposed. But after that date all is peace inside the republic. The Venetian constitution survived intact through the era of the native princes. It kept its independence when the other Italian states fell under foreign rule; it resisted the Papacy during the Counter Reformation; and it was to be praised, in the seventeenth century, as the most perfect model of government for any mercantile state which aspired to be free, effective, and independent.

VENICE OF THE DOGES

"*Stupendissima!*" exclaimed Beatrice d'Este when she was welcomed to Venice in 1493 by one of the colorful naval pageants with which the republic dazzled its distinguished guests. Venice was "the most triumphant city in the world," she declared, and the Venetians agreed with her completely. The city itself was the greatest spectacle of all, but its unique splendors were mirrored elsewhere, too—in the precious glass of Murano, in the villages and gardens of the Veneto, in official paintings commissioned to foster the worship of the state (above, a detail of Carpaccio's *Lion of St. Mark* shows the Doge's Palace and the domes and campanile of St. Mark's). But Venice did more than admire itself, for this was a city that faced outward. Its banner flew over thousands of ships, its traders were seen from Greenland to China. The republic's fate was intertwined with the life of Byzantium, a city almost a thousand miles away, where Venice not only borrowed traditions of government and art, but plundered treasures for the Cathedral of St. Mark. Venice inherited Byzantium's enemy, too, and the inexorable advance of Turkish power finally threatened to strangle her empire as it had ruined the empire of the Greeks.

A solemn Corpus Christi Procession, *by Gentile Bellini, crosses the Piazza in front of St. Mark's and the Doge's Palace (right rear).*

THE PIAZZA SAN MARCO

The center of Venetian life was the Piazza San Marco. In this spectacular setting, guilds and religious brotherhoods paraded before the Doge, bearing banners and jeweled reliquaries, and censers to perfume the salt air. Each new Doge celebrated his election there, scattering coins to the cheering crowd as he was carried past by a band of Arsenal workers. During the Renaissance, many of the Piazza's eyesores—the fish market opposite the Doge's Palace, and the barbers' and dentists' shops huddled around it—were cleared away, and a new border of colonnaded state buildings made the square a more splendid stage for Venetian pageantry. The focus of state ceremony was the eleventh-century domed Basilica of St. Mark, whose gold mosaics seemed to reflect the glory of Venice as much as the glory of God. It was the private chapel of the Doge and displayed, high above its central portal, the symbols of the state—four bronze horses stolen from Byzantium's ancient hippodrome, and the winged Lion of St. Mark.

Beside a great
of Venetian co
the porticoes
cious Eastern
nearby, and alo
fruit and fish.
Europe's busie
bawdy house—
eign merchants

The Rialto,
ninth century,
life. Its merch
their risks care
ventures to de
or the Turks. 1
of the great sta
the Mediterran
return 40 per c
that rate, trader
on the walls of
chant's law be j

Under the c
merce flourishe
coming to pick
cargo at the po
netian merchan
foreign traders.
superiority, the
and shipwrights
tian territory. Ev
The lagoon wa
chants who took
houses demolish

SCENES ALONG THE WATERWAYS

On a loggia over
a piece of the Tru
nous painting, Th
cession crosses th
gondola ride pro

Preparing to attack each other with eggshells filled with perfumed water, masked carnival revelers (bottom right) walk past a pair of street jugglers. Like the peddlers fiddling to attract trade (left) and the dueling bravoes (below), they are from a souvenir book of Venetian scenes purchased in the sixteenth century by a honeymooning French couple and published here for the first time. On the facing page are other city sights: top, the Doge's Bucentaur, its figurehead bearing scales and a sword; below, hooded members of a religious fraternity and an aristocratic lady peering demurely from a sedan chair.

Dance pavilions floating on the Grand Canal, galleys decked with flowers, and regattas in which beautifully dressed women rowed were but a few of Venice's tourist attractions. A hundred thousand visitors came each May to attend the springtime trading fair and see the symbolic ceremony of the Doge marrying the Adriatic. Others came for the annual carnival, to stroll the streets in masks and watch harlequins perform in the piazzas. Masquerades were popular (maskmakers formed a separate branch of the painter's guild), and until the Senate restricted the use of disguise to carnival season, they were held throughout the year, with elaborate costumes copied from the dress worn by Venice's famous street actors, the forerunners of the Commedia dell'Arte. The actors in turn took Venetians as models; one of their stock characters, Pantaleone, caricatures a typical bearded merchant, such as the man (above right) whose bravoes defend him from robbers.

COUNTRY

LIFE

"Away with melancholy!" proclaimed one Venetian gentleman, preaching the joys of rural life. In the country, he said, the sun shines brighter, the sky is bluer, the stars are clearer, and bellyache is unknown. His fellow patricians agreed with him. In mainland villas, built in a classical style ordained by the architect Palladio, merchants devoted their leisure to hunting, concerts, card games, and to reading Latin poets who had inspired the fashion for country living. Frescoes on villa walls pictured their diversions, and gardens, sometimes designed by the same painters, provided a setting for their banquets and theatricals. Palladio had recommended that villas overlook the water, and the Venetians followed his advice as faithfully as their builders copied his models. Marshes were drained, farms irrigated, and a network of canals constructed throughout the Veneto. One river, the Brenta, with scores of luxurious villas built along its banks, became a mainland Grand Canal, crowded with boats carrying merchants in from the Rialto, and farm produce to city markets from the foothills of the Alps.

Rural life held simple pleasures, like the duck hunt (facing page) painted by Carpaccio, but in ornate mansions such as Villa Trissina (Palladio's plan for it appears below), luxury was usually unrestrained. A picnic could be as lavish as Pozzoserrato's Banquet of Epulon (below, left), and gardens elaborate as that of the Maggi family (left) were common, with mazes, banqueting loggias, and curiously clipped arbors. Attributed to Veronese's studio, the painting of the Maggi estate shows the rich merchant clan under a shower of jewelry and flowers, to symbolize the honors heaped on Carlo Maggi after his return to Venice from Turkish slavery.

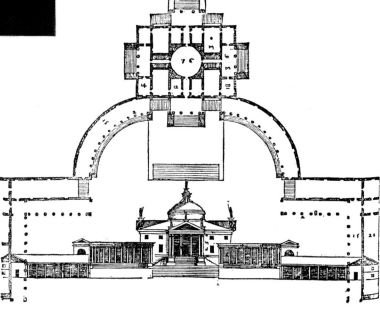

NAVE·DEL·ARMER·

With its two thousand workmen, the Arsenal of Venice was probably the largest industry in the sixteenth-century world. Its great sheds extended over sixty acres, and in them shipwrights could build and repair more than a hundred galleys at a time. Throughout the trading fleet, Arsenal standards prevailed, and even vessels constructed privately were identical with those built in the government shipyards. Thus every sailor (and all citizens were liable for naval service) knew his post on any galley in the fleet, and merchant vessels could be converted quickly to warships. Until 1500 galleys were the mainstay of the republic's navy. Equipped with both sails and oars, they were exceptionally swift, were never becalmed, and rarely ran aground. Their freight rates were high, but cargoes on them needed little insurance. But as cannon became more common, the galleys were gradually replaced with round ships, such as those that fought in the Battle of Zonchio (left), which could resist a cannon broadside and, with improved rigging, could maneuver just as well.

At the Battle of Zonchio in 1499 arrows, rocks, and cannon balls greeted Turks trying to board Venetian ships. But the Turkish leader Kemal Ali, or Chmali as the artist calls him at left center, still managed to capture one Venetian vessel (labeled "Nave del Armer" after its captain) and burn the Loredan ship ("Nave Lordana").

The republic's lucrative trade with Egypt was safeguarded by Venetian ambassadors in Cairo (painted by a follower of Gentile Bellini).

TRADE WITH THE EAST

Venice faced eastward with both eyes open. She rented her fleet to the Crusaders once, at 85,000 marks a year; then persuaded them to leave her Saracen customers in peace and attack Constantinople instead. The Crusaders obliged, sacked the city during Holy Week, and gave a lion's share of the loot to the Cathedral of St. Mark. Venice grabbed the choicest quarter of Constantinople and the best ports of the empire; her merchants enjoyed trading privileges that even their Byzantine rivals did not have. The republic grew rich on Byzantine gold, and when Emperor John Palaeologus came to the Doge in 1369, pleading for help against Turkish attacks, Venice blandly imprisoned him for debt. This shortsighted, greedy action only helped the Turks, and the city soon faced a foe far stronger than Byzantium had been.

Traditionally, Venice's commerce depended on five great sea routes which her official trading convoys sailed each year; by 1517, when they conquered Egypt, the Turks controlled all but one. The republic remained strong enough to charge toll to every foreign vessel that sailed the Adriatic, but now she was subject to tribute herself, and had to pay 10,000 ducats yearly for the right to trade with ports under Turkish control.

Perched atop a galley, John Palaeologus (left, in a painting by a Florentine artist) sails to beg for Western aid. Venice refused help, and when Mohammed II seized Byzantium a century later, sent Gentile Bellini to portray him (opposite).

THE SPLENDORS
OF VENETIAN ART

Richly hued velvets and gleaming silks model the patrician figures of merchants and aristocrats in the immense gallery of portraits left by the Venetian artists. Nudes from the brush of Titian and Giorgione shimmer with all the subtle tones of the flesh; religious scenes that decorate the walls of churches and guildhalls are set in a blaze of luminous splendor. With their tastes molded by the treasury of Byzantine icons and mosaics displayed in the Basilica of St. Mark, Venetian artists became masters in the use of rich color. Foreigners, observing their work, were overwhelmed. If Titian had only drawn as well as he colored, Michelangelo proclaimed, "he would have produced works which none could surpass."

Venice's tradition of color was an ancient one. Early paintings had been encrusted with gold, in an attempt to imitate such Byzantine icons as the image of the Archangel Michael (opposite), guardian of the true Church, which had been stolen from the heretical Greeks in 1204 and deposited in Catholic Venice. Later painters never abandoned their love for lavish Eastern colors, but they muted their intensity, and transformed their predilection for painting with gold into a taste for hard cash which was well attuned to the atmosphere of Venetian society.

For the republic's painters achieved more than a mastery of color. Titian managed to garner pensions from the treasuries of Naples, Spain, and the German merchants trading at Venice. When a church which had commissioned a painting failed to meet his price of five hundred crowns, he judiciously presented the work to the Emperor Charles V instead, who gratefully gave him two thousand crowns for it. Giovanni Bellini reputedly put on a disguise and posed for a portrait in order to discover the lucrative secret of oil painting. His brother Gentile, repaying Venice's artistic debt to Constantinople, was sent as court painter to Mohammed II and there, despite the Koran's stern moral stand against painting, so gratified the Sultan with his erotic pictures that he returned to Venice with a golden chain around his neck and a patent of knighthood packed in his baggage.

Profits were high, but painters worked hard for their money. The Senate decreed that Giovanni Bellini and his assistant Carpaccio were to labor "continuously and every day" on their decorations for the Doge's Palace. Despite their prodigious output, artists sometimes spent years embellishing one building, covering acres of wall with paintings so immense that Carpaccio once advertised a picture as unequaled "not only for excellence and perfection, but also for size." Venice's concentration of great works of art was increased by the longevity of her artists. Giovanni Bellini lived to be eighty-six, and Titian was still painting industriously after he had passed ninety. The sea air eroded frescoes on palace walls, and frequent fires destroyed the vast murals of Venetian history in the Doge's Palace, so that each Renaissance generation had to do them over again, but the great body of work that remains in the city today constitutes one of the major monuments of Western art.

"The satisfaction of seeing the effigies of his ancestors," Vasari wrote, "is of the greatest value to any man and awakens in him the love of glory." Venetian artists were quick to take advantage of society's demand for portraits, and to quote Vasari again, there was "hardly a noble of high rank, scarcely *a prince or a lady of great name* whose portrait has not been painted by Titian." That artist portrayed the youthful Ranuccio Farnese *(left)* in a doublet of gleaming silk with a gold cross emblazoned on his cloak; he also painted the unknown woman above him, and the bearded nobleman at far left, whose ballooning blue sleeve rests on a parapet bearing Titian's initials. The sober Young Man in a Red Cap *(right)*, attributed both to Carpaccio and Lorenzo Lotto, apparently did not possess such luxurious clothing, and other portraits of humbler folk were done occasionally. For example, Fra Teodoro posed for Giovanni Bellini as Saint Dominic *(below)*, holding a lily and a book, the saint's sacred emblems. Bellini ignored traditional descriptions of Dominic, and, happily for posterity, decided to paint the monk exactly as he saw him.

Fresh from the studio of Giovanni Bellini, the young artist Giorgione
rented a house near the Rialto and covered its outer walls with figures of
musicians, poets, and cupids to advertise his genius. These pictures, like
all of his frescoes, have now disappeared, for the south winds of Venice,
as Vasari reported, "bear a most noxious saline humidity"; but they lasted
long enough to win the artist an enviable commission to fresco Venice's
newest trading warehouse. Giorgione covered the façade with allegorical
figures which baffled his contemporaries, just as his surviving works have
puzzled later generations. The meaning of the masterpiece at right, The
Tempest, has never been clear, but the artist's feeling for the harmony
between man and nature is evident in the relationship among the detached figures, the poetic landscape, and the approaching storm. It was
begun as a picture of two women bathing; then the figure of the man in
red was painted over one of them, and the fantasy grew as the work
progressed. Like Giorgione's other canvases, this has the dramatic intensity,
the evocative use of light, and the perceptive observation which set a
standard for other artists to imitate. Titian, his friend and later his bitter
rival, copied his style; his drawing of two figures in a landscape (above)
integrates figures and scenery with a natural ease learned from Giorgione.

Newly risen from the sea, Titian's magnificent Venus Anadyomene *(opposite)* wrings water from her flowing hair. This is probably an easel copy of a figure which the artist painted on the walls of the German merchants' warehouse near the Rialto in Venice. The theme was an ancient one (Emperor Augustus had placed a picture of the same subject in the temple of Julius Caesar), but Titian's treatment of it, with its spare and simple design, is unique. The reclining female nude, another motif which was to preoccupy painters for centuries, is represented by Titian's Venus of Urbino *(below)*. Her pose was copied from Giorgione's painting of Venus in a landscape, which Titian completed after his colleague's death; but Titian placed his nude in a luxurious Renaissance room instead, with two servingmaids in the background rummaging through a clothes chest. To meet the new fashion for classical nudes, of which the anonymous sixteenth-century bronze dancer at right is an example in another medium, Titian painted a series of Dianas and Venuses. His best customer for them was Philip II of Spain. Philip's father had made Titian his court painter; he so admired the artist that he once stooped to pick up a paintbrush which Titian had dropped, declaring that a Titian might well be served by a Caesar.

In 828, when patriotic Venetian merchants performed one of the proudest feats in the city's history by stealing Saint Mark's body from its sarcophagus at Alexandria, the saint himself, it was said, helped speed his departure by stirring up a tempest. Tintoretto, commissioned to paint the story for the School of St. Mark, one of Venice's five major charitable guilds, set the dramatic scene in a Renaissance piazza (left), under a stormy sky blazing with red light. Another charitable society, the School of St. Rocco, named after the patron saint of plague victims, also called on Tintoretto to decorate its guildhall, and promised him an annual pension of a hundred ducats in exchange for three pictures yearly. His masterpiece, a vast panorama of the Crucifixion, stretches for forty feet across the wall of one of their great assembly rooms; above is a detail from it, showing Nicodemus and the youthful Apostle John kneeling in grief before the Cross. Venetians rendered Saint Rocco the same compliment they had paid to Saint Mark. His remains, too, were stolen from their resting place in southern France and brought back to the city to serve as a talisman against the plagues which periodically attacked the Venetian republic.

Michelangelo's statue of David *might be said to symbolize Renaissance man: to the classical ideal, a new force and vitality have been added.*

THE IMAGES OF
MAN

Venice, Rome, Milan, and Florence were, physically speaking, new cities—cities in construction littered with scaffolding, scarred with half-realized plans. The villas, the taverns, the lounging places in the piazzas and gardens were filled with earnest argument about the new cathedrals and palaces. The statues that adorn the Piazza della Signoria at Florence gleamed with an almost raw whiteness. The Piazza San Marco at Venice shook itself free from the clutter of stalls, bakers' shops, and latrines to acquire the beauty that we see. In Milan the new citadel of the Sforza drew a wondering crowd of enthusiasts. In Mantua, Parma, Naples, Perugia, Viterbo, Genoa, indeed in all the towns of Italy, it was the same story —a new physical world was being built that buried or obscured the old barbarisms. In the churches and monasteries scarcely a year passed without a new masterpiece being painted on the walls. Today the blackened surface and faded pigments baffle the imagination and make it difficult to recapture

the sharp impact that these pictures had on the eyes that first saw them, and the same is true of statues and bronzes staled by centuries of reproduction and plagiarism. Impossible, too, to recapture the novelty of books, the miracle that it must have seemed to scholars to possess their own Virgil, their own Cicero, or to see their own poems and plays and familiar letters stacked by the hundreds in printers' shops. To this fresh, lavish, and splendid world were being added new horizons, and old certainties were dissolving as rapidly as the old scenes. Stories from Portugal and Spain, tales from Genoese sea captains, the gossip of the Venetian Cabots, told of a wondrous world of continents before undreamed of. Soon speculation became certainty, and the fables of Marco Polo and Mandeville gave way to the sober statements of mariners. The discoveries of Columbus, of the Cabots, of a whole generation of Portuguese in the Eastern Seas—"such great adventures as Fate had to no former age allowed"—confirmed

305

the belief, already held by many men and women, that the age to which they belonged was original and new, and that the immediate past was dead. Undoubtedly such convictions bred a sense of liberation and encouraged a belief in the unique quality of personal destiny. Men began to create new images of themselves—a habit as old as man himself, but always fresh and entrancing.

"Men," wrote Alberti, "are themselves the source of their own fortune and misfortune." "O supreme generosity of God the Father," apostrophized Pico della Mirandola, "O highest and marvelous felicity of man. To him it is granted to have whatever he chooses, to be whatever he wills." Man was heroic, destined by his own nature to greatness or to failure, but eternally alone, eternally himself. If born wise, then he might of course benefit by the wisdom of the past; if sensitive, he would gain from philosophy and religion; if apt, he could acquire the education of a gentleman. In the last resort,

however, all rested on himself—on his nature and on his luck, that curious personal destiny, controlled of course by God, but a mystery that could never be unlocked except by time. Portents and the conjunction or combustion of the stars might, as in a riddle, hint an answer, but essentially man was alone with fate. This attitude was deeply bound up with the growing capitalism of society, in which the merchant sought a profit by gambling on his own ingenuity, but there lay between these ideas a barrier of unawareness, like that which lies between the unconscious drives of a man's personality and his rational self. To the men who lived in the fifteenth century, this view of man—his individuality, his lonely destiny, his isolation—had nothing whatsoever to do with the active world or its expanding horizons. For them it was a new truth, self-evident, eternal, inescapable. As this attitude to man gathered momentum, it spread to places and communities that were unripe for its reception. Also it became entangled in the

Leon Battista Alberti, the universal genius whose self-portrait appears on the plaque at right, once wrote a play in such perfect Latin verse that it was published by the scholarly Aldus Manutius as a newly discovered Roman classic. During the Renaissance all classes delighted in the drama, especially the farcical comedies of Terence. A setting for one of them is seen at far left, on the facing page. Next to it (top) is a woodcut illustration from the Canzoni *of Lorenzo de' Medici, a group of poems written for the youthful street singers of Florence. The gay and frequently bawdy humor of the times is also reflected in the numerous satires written on a wide variety of subjects. Below is an engraving which is a broad contemporary spoof on cuckoldry.*

strong, clinging, wayward tendrils of the past. Men were still priests, monks, scholars, soldiers, aristocrats, and merchants, and each profession, each community, each class possessed rules, regulations, beliefs, and attitudes already centuries old. On these the new conception of man worked, but, in working, suffered its own sea change.

Yet the concept of man, untrammeled, as a creature of destiny, but with his destiny provoked by his own self, enthralled most of the sensitive spirits of the Renaissance. Its fascination is beautifully illustrated in the growth and development of drama and the theater. Plays there had been in medieval Europe, but they were a looking glass of morality, not a mirror of man. They had concerned themselves, often in an intensely human way, with God, Christ, the Virgin, with the Creation or the Flood, or with personified moralities —vices like Lust and Sloth, virtues like Chastity and Humility. The humanists and their circle found these plays bar-

barous. They took delight in Plautus and in Terence, in the obscenities and the jokes, the brave declamations and fateful tragedies of individual men and women, crude as they were, two-dimensional as they might now seem; to us they are caricatures rather than living men, yet the change from the immediate past was very great. So, too, in history, the humanists looked for heroes, not men, looked for the individual life lived on a scale of intensity and drama beyond the range and experience of common mortals. And this spirit spread through literature like a dye. All aspects of a personal life—birth, love, marriage, ambition, defeat, senility—were blown up, endowed with an excess that in the hands of a genius, a Tasso or an Ariosto, acquired a heroic and universal significance. If the dramatists, poets, rhetoricians, and novelists were often second rate, if their creations now seem bombastic and ridiculous, they entranced their contemporaries. Nothing was more fashionable at any court than plays, masques, the declamation of

set speeches, the recitation of poetry, or even the reading of familiar letters between humanists. Of course, these fashionable literary banquets were concerned with more than the heroic nature of man. They provided a setting for the display of ancient learning, for the parade of the esoteric, for the language of concealment that all literary coteries delight in cultivating. And they also gave an opportunity for display—a physical setting was required, and all Renaissance man's delight in ostentation and sumptuous adornment was given full rein. The masques, poetic entertainments, and dances were produced regardless of cost; the drama itself created its own special theater, with scenery as spectacular and as realistic as the world was ever to know. Yet overlaid as the setting might be with a distracting luxury, time and time again the theme of poem or play or philosophic oration harked back to the lonely plight of man, to his capacity for heroism and for tragedy. Sometimes this was threaded with comic realism,

with the sense of man's absurdity; at other times a portrayal of his vigorous instinctive life flashed over both the comedy and the tragedy. But always the writers were drawn back, as indeed were the painters and sculptors, to man—enlarged, ennobled, romanticized.

This attitude toward man did not remain merely a theme for the arts; it spread into society, modifying customs, penetrating politics and changing them. The belief—often unconsciously adopted—that man's instincts and abilities must find their own destiny, be it what it may, influenced sexual practices more profoundly than any other social conventions. In the Middle Ages there had been sinners galore, priests, cardinals, popes who could not resist the itch of concupiscence; novices had been thrust into monasteries at too hectic a period of their adolescence; nuns found that the time of waiting for their heavenly groom lay heavily on their hands. And the laity, as ever, found the desires of the flesh pushing them

through the barriers of accepted morality. But in the Middle Ages these things were wicked, a matter for penance and sorrow; matters to be suppressed and eradicated. A wandering scholar might glorify the sins of his flesh in a lyric, but medieval society condemned them. Not so in the Renaissance. Sex was par excellence the expression of the individual man. Nor were the humanists confined by Christian or Hebraic morality: they had read their Plato; they knew of the lives and loves of the gods. Jove had his Ganymede, why could not they? So Aeneas Silvius sends his bastard to his mother and father so they will have something of him to love. Pietro Aretino asks the Duke of Mantua to send him a boy that struck his fancy. Lorenzo Valla spends the leisure from his exacting scholarship in the Vatican library writing some of the most brilliant, and certainly the most obscene, familiar letters, a literary activity which Machiavelli, too, enjoyed with relish. The follies of Alexander VI provided no more gossip for Rome than did the follies of Aretino in his old age for Venice. Not since the days of Petronius had public men indulged themselves in such unmeasured erotic fantasy.

Untrammeled by convention, dominated by instinct, swept along by his nature, fulfilling his fate with the agility of an acrobat, yet true to his inner essence, his mysterious *virtù*— this was the compulsive image which Renaissance man created for himself. Instead of the stage being the mirror of life, it seemed rather as if the characters of melodrama had usurped the true characters of men. In no other man of this age is the image more sharply mirrored than in Pietro Aretino—the first Bohemian.

"I am a free man," Aretino wrote, "I do not need to copy Petrarch or Boccaccio. My own genius is enough. Let others worry themselves about style and so cease to be themselves. Without a master, without a model, without a guide, without artifice, I go to work and earn my living, my well-being, and

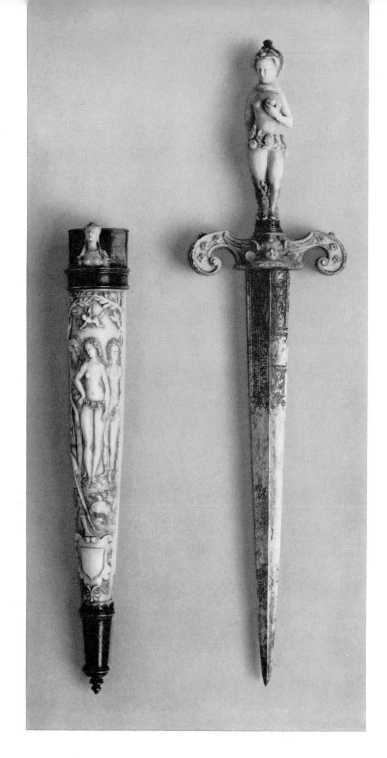

my fame. What do I need more? With a goose quill and a few sheets of paper I mock the universe." And he did, riotously, splendidly, until in his vigorous sixties he roared too vehemently at a bawdy joke, had apoplexy, and died. But what a life he had lived—shameless, selfish, magnificently free from humbug and splendidly creative.

Born the legitimate son of a poor shoemaker of Arezzo, Aretino passed himself off as the bastard of a gentleman until a fellow citizen, in a moment of rage, blew the *gaffe*; then Aretino boasted the truth as vehemently as he had paraded the lie. He received no serious education. He turned up for a time, in his late adolescence, at Perugia, probably living as a painter's apprentice. Already he had started to scribble sonnets. He next appears in the household of the great Roman banker Agostino Chigi (as a domestic servant, his enemies said, who was quickly dismissed for pinching the silver). Aretino claimed Chigi, however, as patron, not master. What-

ever his situation, Chigi's household gave him a lifelong taste for luxury, feasting, and pomp. Rome also offered him a golden opportunity for his natural literary genius.

At the corner of the Piazza Navona, a worn antique statue had become a curious sort of notice board. Learned lampoons of the Pope's government and the leading personalities of Rome were stuck to it. It was called Pasquino after a bitter-tongued schoolmaster. Later another statue in the Campus Martius was used in a similar way, and then the two statues took to having dialogues. These were known as pasquinades. Most of them were dull and pedantic, but risky in a mild way because of the freedom of their criticism. Aretino changed all that—his opportunity came on the death of Pope Leo X. To press the claims of his candidate, Cardinal Medici, afterward Clement VII, Aretino launched a series of unbridled lampoons against the cardinals. Every vice they may have practiced (and Aretino's imagination was rich), every dishon-

orable event in their own lives or their families', was widely and mercilessly pilloried. To make it worse, these verses were printed and sold as handbills. Rome rocked with laughter; princes asked their ambassadors for copies. No one believed that such impudence could go unpunished, but it did. Aretino demonstrated the power of the pen; he became the "scourge of princes." However, when an old Dutchman was elected Pope, Aretino thought he would cool his heels in Mantua. There the Gonzaga enjoyed his talents and boasted of his presence at their court, but with the election of Cardinal Medici as Clement VII, Aretino was summoned back to Rome to regale the papal court with his wit and license. At Rome he began to write his superb comedy *La Cortigiana;* of course in Italian, and with complete disregard for the models of Terence and Plautus that were thought sacrosanct. His reputation for wit and daring soared to new heights. His fancy, however, became powerfully stimulated by sixteen remarka-

bly obscene drawings by Giulio Romano that an enterprising publisher was about to have engraved. For each, Aretino provided a sonnet as explicit and as indecent as the picture. This did not endear him to his patron the Pope, who lacked the temperament and interests of the Borgia. At the same time Aretino was cuckolding as many husbands as he could. After a bad brawl in which he was nearly killed by an irate husband, the Pope's protection abruptly ceased. So off went Aretino to join the famous condottiere Giovanni delle Bande Nere. In that great captain, Aretino saw a mirror image—a man compelled like himself to follow his star, to fulfill his own life on his own terms, outside society, beyond custom, a man of destiny. With Giovanni he rejoiced in the freedom of military life, whose sweetness and pain were heightened by the dark presence of death. For a man of Aretino's powerful imagination and strong instincts, the grandeurs and miseries of war proved deeply enriching. The death of Giovanni acted

Federigo da Montefeltro's most prized possession was his great library at Urbino, established with the aid of Vespasiano da Bisticci. Later stolen by Cesare Borgia, it now forms part of the Vatican collection. The Duke's portrait (facing page), probably by Pedro Berruguete, shows him in his knightly robes, the Order of the Garter at his knee, reading to his son from one of the beautifully bound volumes. Symbolic of the intense interest generated during the Renaissance in the image of man is the Venetian painting reproduced below, frequently called The Three Ages of Man.

as a traumatic experience which Aretino described in one of the most remarkable letters that he ever wrote. In it he depicted, in language that was simple, grave, and noble, the last hours of a heroic man, triumphing over pain, accepting death, making his own terms with God as he had done with man. After Giovanni's death, Aretino felt more keenly his isolation from society; in his bitterness he poured his acid scorn on popes and princes. However, he had to live, and with his usual journalistic flair he brought out an almanac in which he flayed men and affairs by predicting the year's events. Its vast success enabled Aretino to settle in Venice— free, secure, rich from his pen: princes tumbled over themselves either to obtain a few flattering lines of prose from him or to avoid mention altogether; even the Pope forgave and pampered him; everything he wrote sold handsomely. He lived like a prince on the Grand Canal, his *palazzo* full of women and boys—the Aretines, he called them. There he of-

fered profuse hospitality, gargantuan banquets and feasts of love, orgies of literary gossip. Titian was drawn to him like a moth to a candle. He painted him over and over again, and in return Aretino pushed Titian's paintings on his patrons. They drank together, rioted together, lived the Bohemian life of the writer and artist that became one of the most seductive and compelling images of man, at once creative and destructive, and one that still had the power to hypnotize long after they were dead. Aretino's life gave great impetus to the idea that the artist was beyond morality, outside society, a spirit dedicated only to the compulsive needs of his art. At the same time he invested this image with a nobility, a certain grandeur, and the possibility of tragedy. The end of a free man could be brutal, harsh, and black with pain; in the midst of a riotous life those shadows were with him. Titian saw them in his face, and painted them.

Of course there were men who were alarmed by Aretino,

shocked by his life, disgusted by his writings, who condemned him roundly. Christian morality and the precepts of the Church were to the majority of men not shackles on the instinctive life but principles by which it should be lived. Yet in spite of themselves many were drawn to the image that Aretino or men like him presented. And some were honest enough to admit it. True, they tended, like Machiavelli, to discover man as a free agent more in princes and in captains of war, in the life of decision and action, than in writers and the writers' life. In war and politics, if anywhere, man was solitary, alone, without friends, and of necessity, they believed, without principle. To survive, to succeed, to kill before being killed, such were their destined lives. And this image artists evoked in painting as Machiavelli did in prose; the profiles, the faces of the Renaissance princes, have a terrible majesty, an aloofness, a dedication beyond the reality of common men.

So complex a society, of course, created many images that expressed its needs and hopes and aspirations, and not all mirrored egotism and the pursuit of fame. To some, Aretino or Cellini with his "Men like Benvenuto . . . stand above the Law" were tedious. Men yearn to belong, to be secure, to be accepted. At a time when the courtly graces were being practiced in London, Paris, Dijon, or Avignon, the rocky fortresses of Urbino, Rimini, or Orvieto were full of raw robber barons, uncouth, scarcely literate. Few despots could boast a long ancestry: within a mere three generations the Sforza rose from peasants to princes; even the Medici had modest origins. Rich Italy might become, but many of its prosperous men felt insecure in the luxury they could afford. Yet there existed, for them, antique patterns of behavior. The knights of the late Middle Ages had developed chivalry into a code of manners, a complex dance of love as intricate as a tarantula's; Greece and Rome offered guides to gentility and

sophistication. Above all there was Plato to teach them the efficacy of education; human nature, they hopefully believed, could be molded to what men might desire it to be.

This attitude was formulated most effectively by two men —Vittorino da Feltre, who ran an academy for boys and girls at Mantua, and Baldassare Castiglione, who became the arbiter of taste for the western world. Education, they both maintained, was more than learning: it was breeding, which might give what the heritage of blood had conferred on the nobles of the Middle Ages. Those knights had been required to learn the manners as well as the skills of the warrior's trade, to be "a verray parfit gentil knight," but the training did not confer *gentility*. That they inherited or, more rarely, won on the field of battle. The men of the Renaissance were concerned, however, to turn sow's ears into silk purses, peasants into princes.

The rough soldier of fortune and the uncouth merchant from the counting house wished to appear as men of breeding, as connoisseurs of taste, as representatives of antique virtue. Even though they spurned the fortune of birth, cared not a rap for legitimacy, they could not bear to be considered barbarous. Barbarity was shown in a man's deportment, in his attitude to women, in his pleasures, and, of course, in his possessions. Some things were easier to eradicate than others. Giovanni della Casa thought no perfect gentleman would thrust stinking fish under the noses of his friends, or closely examine the contents of his handkerchief, or sit so that the more intimate parts of his person were revealed, or pick his nose, or spit, or break wind. The fact that della Casa found it necessary to expatiate on such things in his handbook of gentlemanly behavior indicates the rudeness, the roughness, and the untutored nature of much of Renaissance society. But della Casa wanted more than behavior free from physical offense. He also stressed that no man could be a gentleman

without modesty, without being "very desirous of beautiful things, well-proportioned and comely," and squeamish of all that was not. To achieve this, Vittorino da Feltre and his imitators thought that all activities of the child should be directed to that end. Gentility, they maintained, was not an attribute of correct conversation or well-chosen clothes, on the contrary, it was the whole being of man; indeed, the highest perfection a man could achieve was to be immediately recognized as a gentleman.

The qualities of soul, the aspects of refinement and sensibility, which marked off the perfect gentleman were, of course, subject to endless debate, in which the classics were ransacked for precepts. Vittorino established a certain canon of requirements: the body as well as the soul needed to be brought to perfection. Exercise, quickness of eye, control of the muscles, and grace of movement were linked to moral qualities which the proper use of the body promoted—cour-

age, hardiness, stamina, indifference to pain and discomfort. Intellectual exercises, like physical ones, were aimed at building character, developing moral qualities, and for this purpose classical antiquities and mathematical knowledge had special merits: the former was full of the most excellent precepts, the latter revealed the harmonies of man and nature. Although many of the qualities which Vittorino sought in his pupils had been qualities of knightly perfection in earlier times, his attitude to boys and girls and to their educational needs was nearer far to Plato than to Aristotle. Above all, he believed that a gentleman should be literate and his aesthetic senses refined by teaching. Nor did he believe gentility to be conferred by birth; he educated the poor with the rich.

With the growing leisure and the growing secularization of life in the Renaissance, social pleasures became a pursuit in themselves. As ever with an emerging class, opulent but insecure, many yearned for the aristocratic distinctions of a

previous age—long genealogies, emblazoned arms, the somewhat archaic extravagance of the joust and tourney. Some humanists, however, would have none of this hankering after the trappings of feudal nobility. "The longer the line of bold miscreants," wrote Poggio, "from which a man traces his descent, the further he is removed from true nobility." For him nobility lay in the individual heart and cultivated mind, in a man's nature and education—not in his birth. There was endless debate—snobbery, a desire for exclusiveness, drawing one way; a pride in the freshness and strength of their own world and times pulling another. In drawing rooms of courts, in the lounging places of the piazzas, in tents on the battlefield, in the country houses of bankers, men discussed over and over again the nature of men and the way of perfection. Or they argued on how they should act in love or in war, or what attributes they should cultivate, or which passions they should despise and suppress. Naturally men arose who be-

came by common consent arbiters of such matters, and the greatest of these was certainly Baldassare Castiglione, who was, as might be expected, the son of an ancient, noble, but very poor family, a man whose birth drew him toward the old, but who lacked any future except with the new and emerging world of his own time.

His long, grave, handsome face with its expression of almost careless elegance became the image of what an aristocrat and a gentleman should look like. Everyone—kings as well as commoners—immediately recognized his quality. His presence at court was eagerly sought, and he conferred immortality on Urbino by writing of the conversations about the nature of a gentleman in which he had participated under the aegis of its blue-stocking Duchess. And in his *Book of the Courtier* there is portrayed another image of Renaissance man, distinct from Aretino's man of destiny; for Castiglione's man was a social being.

Belonging though he did to the knightly class, Castiglione was open-minded about birth. It was better to be born noble, easier to become a true gentleman if one were, but it was not, he reluctantly conceded, essential. Knightly virtues were, however, a necessity, for fighting, the pursuit of arms, the cult of honor, were the life of action to which a gentleman must dedicate himself. So courage and strength were prime virtues, and the exercise of the body a necessity. Horsemanship, fencing, wrestling, swimming, tennis—all things which gave the body suppleness and grace and power were proper pursuits for a gentleman. Naturally he must excel, but should avoid seeming to do so; above all he must cultivate grace of movement, and this Castiglione thought could only be achieved by the practice of *sprezzatura,* nonchalance, "so as to conceal all art and make whatever is done and said appear to be without effort and without almost any thought about it." Polish was as necessary as prowess, in exercises of the mind as well as the body. The gentleman was, of course, literate, knowledgeable about the classics, and eloquent. Learning must be lightly, negligently worn. Of course he should be quick in conversation but never thrusting, amusing but never mocking, humorous but never coarse, learned but never pedantic. And he must avoid being precious: eschew archaisms, never fear to use accepted colloquial speech, nor even bits of French and Spanish if they were in use in the society he frequented.

After the mind and the body came sensibility, connoisseurship. According to Castiglione, a gentleman might even be taught to paint—as, indeed, the Greek and Roman aristocrats had been. Music and its appreciation were necessities: music composed the mind, directed thought to gentle pleasures, inculcated a love of harmony. Music was essentially *right.* The lighter expressions of art as well as the weightier were proper pastimes—dances, masques, the parade of rhetoric, and, naturally, the pursuit of love (love, however, not

lust). The conquest of the heart, the possession of the mind, were a courtier's targets: the consolations of lesser delights were not altogether to be despised, even though they were improper subjects for conversation. A certain hypocrisy made for social ease.

About all activities, from the discussion of philosophy to the tilt of a hat, there must be ease, grace, and nonchalance; nobility must shine through. The princes of Italy might be murderers, adulterers, traitors, violators of boys and girls, but Castiglione depicted them as they desired themselves to be, just as Titian painted them as they wished to look—distinguished, set apart by their *virtù* and destiny from other men, yet full of ease, grace, nobility, and charm. The image created by Castiglione and his imitators, for his book enjoyed a vast success, increased the civility of Italians, made their courts a byword for sophisticated living. The cleanliness of their homes, the decorum at their tables, the beauty of their clothes and furnishings, the elegance of their manners, became models for the rude provincial gentry of the northern countries. Indeed for many generations Italy became an obsession for the less sophisticated nations of Europe, for it provided Europe not only with images of men, but also with a mirage of aristocratic and courtly life. Of course between image and reality there was frequently enough of a chasm. Most men could not live like Castiglione. Crude manners, vulgar habits, coarse pleasures, the instinctive life of which Aretino sang, lurked even in the Courtier. The importance of Castiglione lies in the fact that men thought they *ought* to be like his Courtier, and valued men who seemed to achieve it.

In the High Renaissance, aristocratic attitudes triumphed over the rough bourgeois spirit of its earlier days. Certainly in so doing the idea of what an aristocrat should be suffered a profound change. The armed knight, chivalry itself, became, as in *Don Quixote,* a pathetic joke. Much of the world

in which the new aristocracy moved with such elegance grew, after all, out of the activity of merchants, bankers, and seafarers, not out of feudalism. But the code of manners which evolved was not a merchant's code; it had little to do with the traditional attitudes of the middle class. By 1530 much that Alberti had written about the family in the fifteenth century wore an old-fashioned air, and lives devoted to the pursuit of gain were regarded as vulgar. Castiglione and others like him had helped to define the terms by which men were included in or excluded from gentility. It was essentially a private world with its own scale of values, but one that twinkled with recognition symbols. Style in the turn of a phrase or the cut of a cloak; fields of knowledge, of taste, even of sport, that a gentleman might know or practice; attitudes to love, to religion, to the prince—all these things marked off the gentleman from the man. The rich could achieve this exclusive world only by leaving the countinghouse behind and getting away from the rattle of the loom.

This, as we shall see, had profound consequences, and still has, for Western society. But the importance of the dominating image of man created by the Renaissance lies in this: it arose after the heroic age of Italy's commercial and industrial expansion was past. It belonged to the gilded twilight world of a luxurious but defeated society—defeated not only by the discoveries of the outer world which had given Western Europe the future, but also by the exceptional resilience of its traditional class structure which triumphed over the pragmatism, the disorder, the violent economic and political changes, of Renaissance Italy.

It was against this world of Castiglione—a society at once charming, elegant, inbred, and effete—that Aretino and his followers had to rebel, and so present the image of a genius for which conventions are but naught. Castiglione taught men how to belong, Aretino how to live.

The humanist Duke of Urbino, a famous painting by Piero della Francesca.

Federigo da Montefeltro

by DENIS MACK SMITH

For a brief fifty years, a little hill town in the northern Marches was one of the great cultural centers of Europe. Urbino was the birthplace of Raphael and Bramante. Sculptors were drawn there from Milan and Florence, architects from Siena and Dalmatia, painters from Spain and tapestry workers from Flanders. Paolo Uccello worked inside its hospitable walls; so did Piero della Francesca and Melozzo da Forlì. Baldassare Castiglione emigrated from Mantua in order to live there, and was sent as the special envoy of Urbino to England, taking with him a painting commissioned from Raphael as a present for the English King. And as a result of Castiglione's much-translated *Book of the Courtier,* people all over the Western world heard of this remote mountain town, and learned from the standard of Urbino a code of manners, a way of courtesy and refinement, which became the norm of polite behavior.

The duchy of Urbino and its standards of taste in art and manners were created by Federigo da Montefeltro, whose unforgettable broken-nosed profile portrait by Piero della Francesca has helped to make him one of the best known of Renaissance personalities. Earlier Montefeltro princes had won no special reputation either in politics or culture. For three centuries they had governed no more than a few dozen square miles in the Apennines, sometimes as feudatories of the Holy Roman Emperor, but usually owing nominal allegiance to the Pope. The soil and climate were indifferent, but the precipitous hill villages were easily defensible, and their hardy mountaineers fought well, with the result that the rulers of Urbino remained independent, even though they never owned a port on the Adriatic and never penetrated far down the alluvial valleys into the fertile coastal plain of Ancona. Federigo, who ruled from 1444 to 1482, was the greatest of the Montefeltro dynasty. He consolidated several scattered mountain fiefs and extended them into a state three times larger than his original inheritance. His duchy, which reached from the environs of San Marino in the north to beyond Gubbio in the south, was about sixty miles each way at its longest and broadest, and included perhaps four hundred villages and 150,000 inhabitants. Its independence was maintained by playing off one potential enemy against another—Rome against Venice or Florence against Rome—and luckily two of the strongest Italian states, Naples and Milan, were sufficiently remote from Urbino and sufficiently threatened by Rome or Venice to be generally friendly.

Like many prominent contemporaries, Federigo was born illegitimate. As a boy he spent a year as a hostage in Venice and then went to Mantua, where he was taught by Vittorino da Feltre, the greatest edutor of Renaissance Italy. Vittorino ran a boarding school where princes mixed with poor scholars and were given a severe classical education based on Latin and mathematics. The aim was to form character as well as mind and body. Federigo was taught frugal living, self-discipline, and a high sense of social obligation. He was made a connoisseur of literature and the arts, and also had to practice the manly sports, riding, dancing, and swordsmanship—all the accomplishments, in fact, which Castiglione later prescribed for the perfect courtier. Religion and scholarship were equally cultivated, but with a practical application: philosophy was made a guide to the art of living, and gracefulness and self-possession were inculcated as training for public life. As Federigo himself said later, Vittorino had instructed him "in all human excellence."

Few details are known about Federigo's early life. In 1432, at the age of ten, he was knighted by the Emperor, and five years later, after returning from Mantua to Urbino, he was married, after an engagement which dated from his early childhood. A few months later he set out for Lombardy with a company of eight hundred men to learn the art of war under a professional condottiere who was fighting against Gattamelata. Fighting was the occupation to which most contemporary princes were dedicated, and especially so in Urbino, where the Montefeltro family compensated for the poverty of the land and their remoteness from any significant trade routes by selling their services and their army to one side or other in most Italian wars. This was to be Federigo's chosen career. While his half brother Oddantonio succeeded their father as ruler of Urbino in 1443, Federigo himself seemed doomed to the traditionally subordinate life of the poor, illegitimate relation. But in 1444 the young Oddantonio, because of violent indignation against his debaucheries, was assassinated and his body torn to bits by the town mob. At first Federigo seems to have been refused entry to Urbino, but eventually he was chosen to succeed "by the voice of the people" after promising not to revenge the murder.

Probably the chronicler who called this an election by popular acclaim was not romancing, for contemporaries unanimously praised the young Federigo, and later generations looked back to his reign as a golden age. Any patron as generous as he could no doubt buy adulation from that narrow but important group of writers which handed down what was likely to become the verdict of history, but with Federigo there were no dissentient voices even among commentators who did not benefit from his generosity. Unlike many Renaissance rulers, he avoided the accusation of cruelty and extravagant self-indulgence. He was magnanimous to his foes, and was rewarded handsomely when they preferred to surrender to him rather than run the risk of sack. He was also exceptional for his time in never deserting his allies for gain, and never was he known to break his word, not even when urged to do so by a papal legate. This honesty and trustworthiness were unusual in such a treacherous and brutal age. Federigo's great enemy, Sigismondo Malatesta, was in this respect more typical. Sigismondo was no less picturesque, no less refined and tasteful a patron, and equally fierce a fighter, but his atrocious cruelties were legendary; his dishonorable treatment of allies and his brutality toward subjects were common knowledge, and so was his failure to withstand such a prince as Federigo, who possessed the trust of ordinary people.

The biographers of Federigo (Raphael's father was the first of them) were concerned mainly with military exploits, and consequently there is little information about other aspects of his reign. We know, however, that he had to grant a charter of liberties at his accession. Taxes were to be reduced, some kind of public educational and medical service was promised, and the populace was to have some say in electing magistrates. Probably we should have heard further about this charter if he had governed harshly. According to one chronicler, "revisers" were sent round the country to investigate grievances and relieve poverty, and grain from Apulia was stored away so that prices could be kept steady when the harvest failed. Certainly Federigo was more generally accessible than most Renaissance rulers. Vespasiano da Bisticci described how at mealtimes the doors would be opened so that anyone might address him between courses. Furthermore, "When he rode out he met none who did not salute him and ask how he did. He went about with few attendants; none of them armed . . . He would often go afoot through his lands, entering now one shop and now another, and asking the workmen what their calling was, and whether they were in need of aught. So kind was he, that they all loved him as children love their parents. The country he ruled was a wondrous sight." This affability and accessibility were remarkable at a time when assassination was a common form of political behavior. The benevolence of Federigo's despotism was famous throughout Italy. Where his brother was said to have burnt a page alive for some minor lapse, Federigo was merciful to all offenses save blasphemy. The few recorded instances indicate a man who was just and humane, who prudently considered the welfare of his subjects. A ruler who was so often away on campaign could not afford serious discontent at home.

An important reason for this unusual domestic tranquillity was the profits of successful war, which kept taxes low. Federigo's salary, together with the wages of his army, and perhaps not least the booty they captured, were the means by which a poor country for a while became rich, civilized, and content. His employers included two kings of Naples, two dukes of Milan, and three popes, and even in winter, when not fighting, he insisted on a substantial retainer fee from them. He commanded a good price particularly because of his tried loyalty, for Federigo never kept up relations with both sides simultaneously and never surrendered an allegiance until the end of his stipulated *condotta*. His income also reflected the fact that for many years no other general possessed quite his prestige. Less brilliant than many previous condottieri, he was nevertheless more successful than any in avoiding defeat, and both Castiglione and Vespasiano proudly, if not quite accurately, boasted that he lost not a single battle even when heavily outnumbered.

Federigo was known for keeping exceptionally good discipline among troops. When he met the enemy, his usual technique was to be prudent in the early stages of a battle and impetuous and daring the moment he observed some weakness in his foe's deployment. As a young man he had lost an eye in a tournament, but otherwise he was fit and tough. People admired his swift unexpectedness, the mastery and modernity of his complicated siege works, his skill in carrying heavy guns through difficult mountain country, and his tested ability to endure fatigue, hunger, and wounds. Others admired his charity and the pains he took "to mitigate the horrors and miseries of war." Machiavelli derided the safety-first tactics of professional condottieri, and incorrectly asserted that not a single man was killed when Federigo fought the great Colleoni at Molinella in 1467. The two captains certainly met after this battle to exchange civilities, for chivalry was not extinct, but Machiavelli wrongly assumed that wars were necessarily going to be more decisive and more justifiable in the sixteenth century, when they became less humane and more destructive. Federigo had to satisfy his employers, or he would have been without a job. Wars of independence and imperialism were as real in the fifteenth century as later, even if they were smaller and less lethal.

Federigo's first regular patron was the powerful Sforza family, for whom in 1445 he helped to win Pesaro at the same time that Fossombrone was acquired for Urbino. This earned him an excommunication because it was at odds with papal ambitions, and it also increased the enmity of the Malatesta. Sigismondo Malatesta controlled a large stretch of coast above Ancona. His state and Federigo's were too close to avoid friction, and they shared an insecurity and lack of natural frontiers which led to quarrelsomeness and aggression. In between his struggles with Sigismondo, Federigo in 1448 raised an army for the Florentines. Several years later he contracted to serve the Aragonese dynasty in Naples, and this arrangement lasted almost all his life. The throne of Naples was at this point contested by the French Angevins, who found considerable support among the Neapolitan baronage, but Federigo in 1460 helped the Aragonese to resist the invaders, and in the following year he captured the important town of Aquila.

While Federigo was preoccupied in southern Italy, a Malatesta army invaded Urbino and papal territory. The ferocious Sigismondo was therefore "canonized to hell" by the Pope and burnt in effigy before St. Peter's, while his excommunication for heresy, uxoricide, incest, and other crimes was pronounced by Cardinal Nicholas of Cusa. Federigo, as captain general of the Church's forces, seized this opportunity to destroy his rival's power for good. Sigismondo's heir was taken prisoner when Fano fell after a difficult and damaging siege, but Federigo released him without ransom despite the fact that contemporary practice made such hostages a legitimate and profitable asset. In addition to Fano, Senigallia was captured, and all that remained to the Malatesta was Rimini. Sigismondo, on his knees, publicly recanted his atheistical beliefs. Most of the Malatesta empire was claimed by the Pope and the papal nephews. Federigo, however, was allowed some fifty townships, which made him more powerful than any other ruler throughout the Marches and the Romagna. Although still a pigmy among the giant states of Milan, Venice, and Naples, he sometimes held the balance of power in Italy.

At this time the Papacy was trying to enforce its suzerainty and taxation rights over the seignorial families who ruled in central Italy. Pius II had exploited the rivalry between Montefeltro and Malatesta, employing one to subdue the other, and in 1465 his successor, Paul II, appointed Federigo *gonfaloniere,* or captain, of the Church's forces, in order to extend papal power still further. The condottiere from Urbino was now a famous man in Italy. In 1467 he was made commander of a league of states alarmed at the aggressive imperialism of Venice. The Venetians, retreating before the Turks on the far shore of the Adriatic, were attempting to compensate for these losses by pushing their empire westward and southward in Italy, to the consternation of their neighbors and the Pope. Federigo's own state was among those upon which both Rome and Venice might have ambitions, and this dual threat increased in direct proportion to his general political success.

In 1468 Sigismondo Malatesta died, and the Pope tried to annex Rimini. At this point Federigo, who had hitherto been more frightened of Venice, recognized the danger of further papal aggrandizement. He was a devout and loyal son of the Church, but not without qualification, for he could see that Venice and Rome between them were gradually swallowing up the Romagna. Even more alarming, the popes were trying to conquer principalities for their sons and nephews before another family succeeded them in their sacred office. Against this danger Montefeltro and Malatesta made common cause out of self-preservation, and instead of renewing his lapsed *condotta* with the Pope, Federigo supported the claims of Roberto Malatesta to Rimini. The ruler of Urbino, as captain of a league which included Naples and Milan, as well as other Romagnol *signori,* routed the papal army at Mulazzano.

Federigo's first wife, Gentile Brancaleoni, had died in 1457 leaving no children. He then married Battista, daughter of Alessandro Sforza of Pesaro. Battista's face is almost as well known to us from Piero's portrait as her husband's. Married at thirteen, she died at twenty-five, leaving one son, many daughters, and the reputation of being a formidable bluestocking who had governed the state in her husband's absence and could extemporize publicly in Latin. Federigo's half sisters had married into the neighboring dynasties of Sforza, Gonzaga, and Malatesta; two of his daughters were bestowed upon papal families, the Colonna and della Rovere, and a third upon Roberto Malatesta, the illegitimate son of his old enemy. The circle of appropriate families being limited, there was an inevitable tendency to inbreed.

In 1472, the year Battista died, Federigo was asked by Lorenzo de' Medici to raise an army against Volterra in Tuscany. (Lorenzo was defending the mining interests of Florentine citizens against nationalization in Volterra.) The military task was easy, but after the town had surrendered, Federigo could not restrain his soldiers from a terrible sack. Discipline in mercenary armies was always a problem, especially since the prospect of loot was an inducement for enlisting recruits, but this was a solitary lapse on Federigo's part. For himself he seized only a polyglot Bible of great rarity and beauty, and he was then escorted in triumph to a civic banquet in Florence and given a helmet adorned by Pollaiuolo. Another distinction received soon afterward was the Order of the Garter from England, and this emblem became a common motif in the decoration of his palace. Such was his reputation outside Italy that special embassies arrived not only from England and Hungary but from Persia and Trebizond. A further triumph came in 1474, when Sixtus IV, solemnly receiving him in St. Peter's, changed his traditional title of Count to Duke. This acknowledged that Urbino had now reached a special position of independence and strength that distinguished it from other small city-states. It also acknowledged the Pope's need for military support for his nephews, and the formal concession of the title was designed to seal the alliance.

Federigo served Sixtus well. He tamed the insubordinate ruler of Città di Castello in Umbria, and in 1479 he campaigned against Florence after the Pope had tried and failed to assassinate Lorenzo de' Medici. Papal ambitions, however, soon became dangerous again when Sixtus began planning a conquest of Ferrara for yet another nephew. Federigo wrote to the Pope, urging him to turn against the Moslems who had just won a foothold in southern Italy; but the head of Christendom was more anxious to establish his family than to oppose the Turkish advance. As a result, war broke out over Ferrara, and Federigo aligned himself against papal aggression with Naples, Florence, Milan, Mantua, and Bologna, while his son-in-law, Roberto Malatesta, led the opposing papal forces. In the malarial swamps of Ferrara the rival commanders were stricken with the fever which was the greatest scourge of Renaissance Italy, and Federigo and Roberto died on the same day, September 10, 1482.

For a time Federigo's son and successor, Guidobaldo, was able to maintain the model state of Urbino, continuing his father's lavish patronage of the arts until his lack of success as a general lessened the profits of warfare upon which the economy depended. Then, in 1502, Pope Alexander VI persuaded Guidobaldo to loan the papal army his artillery, and at this crucial moment the Pope's son, Cesare Borgia, swept down on Urbino, forced its ruler to flee, and appropriated the priceless art collection, much of which he sold to pay his troops.

Perhaps Federigo himself would have fared no better. He had been the last of the great condottieri, and lived at a time when defense was much easier than attack. Shortly after his death that day had passed; heavy artillery became more common and more efficient, and when it did the fortified hill towns and castles were suddenly vulnerable. The superiority of new weapons spelled ruin for the small Renaissance princedoms. A decade after his death, the perennial conflicts between Italian cities and families led to an invasion of the peninsula by France and Spain, and it was these new, large nation-states which were to dominate the next period of European history. For three centuries Italy was a convenient location where foreign armies could fight each other; and whereas Federigo had taken care to conduct his wars abroad, Urbino itself now became a battleground. By 1530 a series of invasions and counterinvasions had sacked Rome and Florence and desolated that world of small city-states which had engendered the Renaissance. Much of the surplus wealth which enlightened princes had once used for endowing culture and the arts was dissipated, and in this strange new world Urbino was too small and too awkwardly situated between rival empires to survive.

Federigo da Montefeltro is not remembered for his battles; he made no notable contribution to the art of war; his dynasty and dukedom disappeared. The one thing which survived intact was the memory of Federigo and his court of humanists and artists. In retrospect he and his son were spoken of alongside the magnificent Lorenzo. They were children of their time in a love of lavish display, in their burning drive for self-expression and a competitive urge for prestige. These instincts without doubt contributed in part to their devotion to art and learning, though both of them showed well enough that they also possessed a disinterested love of all things beautiful. Certainly they were far above all other contemporary rulers in character and intellectual refinement. Through them Urbino became a celebrated center of culture which attracted men of talent and renown from all of Europe; it was the place to which the Doria, Orsini, and Farnese families, as well as wealthy parents in other countries, sent their children to be educated. Castiglione, nostalgically recollecting that Federigo, in his day, was "the light of Italy," described life at Urbino in his delightful book *The Courtier,* in which he recorded a portrait of the model gentleman. As Vittoria Colonna wrote to him, "I do not wonder that you have depicted the perfect courtier, for you had only to hold a mirror before you, and set down what you saw there." The conversations recorded in *The Courtier* took place in the palace which Federigo had built at Urbino.

Books of all kinds were Federigo's greatest joy, and Vespasiano described his efforts to build the great library in Urbino: "We come now to consider in what high esteem the Duke held all Greek and Latin writers, sacred as well as secular. He alone had a mind to do what no one had done for a thousand years or more; that is, to create the finest library since ancient times. He spared neither cost nor labor, and when he knew of a fine book, whether in Italy or not, he would send for it. It is now fourteen or more years since he began the library, and he always employed, in Urbino, in Florence, and in other places, thirty or forty scribes in his service . . . There are numerous Greek books by various authors, which when he was not able to get them otherwise, he sent for them, desiring that nothing should be wanting in any tongue which it was possible to acquire. There were to be seen Hebrew books, all that could be found in that language, beginning with the Bible, and all those who have commented upon it, Rabbi Moses and other commentators. Not only are those Hebrew books the Holy Scriptures, but also on medicine, on philosophy, and in all branches, all that could be acquired in that tongue.

"His lordship having completed this worthy task at the great expense of more than thirty thousand ducats, among the other excellent and praiseworthy arrangements which he made was this, that he undertook to give to each writer a title, and this he desired should be covered with crimson embellished with silver. He began, as has been noted above, with the Bible, as the foremost of all, and had it covered, as was said, with gold brocade. Then beginning with all the Doctors of the Church, he had each one covered with crimson and embellished with silver; and so with the Greek Doctors as with the Latins. As well philosophy, history, and books on medicine, and all the modern Doctors; in such a manner that there are innumerable volumes of this kind, a thing gorgeous to behold.

"In this library all the books are beautiful in the highest degree, all written with the pen, not one printed, that it might not be disgraced thereby; all elegantly illuminated, and there is not one that is not written on kidskin. There is a singular thing about this library, which is not true of any other; and this is, that of all the writers, sacred as well as profane, original works as well as translations, not a single page is wanting from their works in so far as they are in themselves complete; which can not be said of any other library, all of which have portions of the works of a writer, but not all; and it is a great distinction to possess such perfection."

Vespasiano had helped to collect this library. "Some time before," he wrote, "I went to Ferrara, being at Urbino at his lordship's court, and having catalogues of all the libraries of Italy, commencing with that of the Pope, of St. Mark's at Florence, of Pavia—and I had even sent to England to obtain a catalogue of the library of the university of Oxford —I compared these with that of the Duke, and I saw that all were faulty in one particular; that they had numerous copies of the same work, but they had not all the works of one writer complete as this had; nor were there writers of every branch as in this." Virtually the whole corpus of known classics was in the library, as well as Avicenna, Averroes, and medieval texts. Federigo was also a patron of contemporary literature. Ficino, Landino, Poggio, and Piero della Francesca dedicated writings to this man whom the humanist Piatti eulogized as *oraculum totius Italiae.*

The Duke was a competent Latinist in an age when close attention to the example of olden times was recommended for statesmen and generals. He was also an early enthusiast for Greek and hired instructors to teach it. He was able to discuss the Trojan war with Pius II and dared to contradict that learned scholar about the geography of Asia Minor. He liked to have Livy's histories read aloud at mealtimes, and was especially fond of Tacitus and the *Commentaries* of Caesar. "To return to letters," Vespasiano wrote, "the Duke of Urbino was well versed therein, not only in history and in the Holy Scriptures, but also in philosophy, which he studied many years under a distinguished teacher, Maestro Lazzaro, afterwards for his merits made Bishop of Urbino. He was instructed by Maestro Lazzaro in the *Ethics* of Aristotle, with and without comments, and he would also dispute over the difficult passages. He began to study logic with the keenest understanding, and he argued with the most nimble wit that was ever seen. After he had heard the *Ethics* many times, comprehending them so thoroughly that his teachers found him hard to cope with in disputation, he studied the *Politics* assiduously . . . Indeed, it may be said of him that he was the first of the *Signori* who took up philosophy and had knowledge of the same. He was ever careful to keep intellect and virtue to the front, and to learn some new thing every day."

With all this, the Duke was devoutly religious. He heard Mass daily, and delighted in discussing religion with the abbot or mother superior of the monastic houses which he had endowed. He not only knew the Scriptures well, but was familiar with the great Doctors of the early Church and possessed an extensive theological library. He developed "a strong predilection" for the works of Saint Thomas Aquinas. He was no puritan, yet despite his four illegitimate children he was a moral man and, as befitted a pupil of Vittorino, recognized no dichotomy between humanist and Christian ideals.

Federigo's taste and qualities of mind were embodied most obviously in his famous palace at Urbino, for to him architecture was not only queen of the arts but the very summit of intellectual as well as aesthetic activity. Beginning around 1450 and building slowly, Federigo gradually amplified his ideas, and in 1468, after searching and failing to find an architect in the Tuscany which he so admired, he chose Luciano Laurana as chief architect. After Laurana there arrived Francesco di Giorgio, the foremost engineer in Italy, who dedicated to the Duke a celebrated treatise on architecture and gratefully acknowledged an indebtedness to his employer for many technical hints about fortification. Five architects and engineers are mentioned in a surviving list of palace officers.

The same list reveals the royal scale of life in the great palace. There were five hundred people in the court: in addition to knights and men-at-arms, these included two hundred servants, four teachers, an astrologer, five "readers aloud at meals," four men who transcribed manuscripts, two organists, the keeper of the bloodhounds, and a man who tended the camel-leopard.

But it was the buildings which struck people most.

Lorenzo de' Medici admired them, and they were to astonish Montaigne and a long succession of travelers. Federigo had furnished his palace, Castiglione wrote, "so well with every suitable thing that it seemed not a palace but a city in the form of a palace; and furnished it not only with what is customary such as silver vases, wall hangings of the richest cloth of gold, silk, and other like things, but for ornament he added countless ancient statues of marble and bronze, rare paintings, and musical instruments of every sort; nor did he wish to have anything there that was not most rare and excellent." Vespasiano da Bisticci was even more enthusiastic. (As a Florentine, Vespasiano judged by the highest standards.) "As to architecture it may be said that no one of his age, high or low, knew it so thoroughly. We may see, in the buildings he constructed, the grand style and the due measurement and proportion, especially in his palace, which has no superior amongst the buildings of the time, none so well considered, or so full of fine things. Though he had his architects about him, he always first realized the design and then explained the proportions and all else; indeed, to hear him discourse thereanent, it would seem that his chief talent lay in this art; so well he knew how to expound and carry out its principles."

Vasari was another Florentine who commented admiringly on the commodious apartments of Urbino's palace, and its stairways which were "more convenient and agreeable than any that had existed previously." Windows and doorways in admirable proportion, a graceful court with slender columns, a hanging garden, the great library, and room after room with splendid decorations in stucco and marble relief—all testifying to the sensibility as well as the munificence of the Duke. Intarsia, marquetry, polychrome marble, and *trompe-l'oeil* work on the walls represented what was best in current fashion all over Italy. Ambrogio da Milano and Domenico Rosselli of Pistoia were employed to design ornamental motifs on jambs, pediments, and chimney pieces, upon which the garter of England and the eagle of Montefeltro were frequently found. Typical of Federigo was that alongside his religious chapel, and with the same proportions, was another chapel dedicated to the Muses; and in his study were twenty-eight portraits of famous men in world history, among whom Homer was alongside Aquinas, Ptolemy with Saint Ambrose, and Seneca with Solomon. Typical also of this Renaissance prince was an inscription round the interior court which told how the great Federigo had raised this palace for his own glory and for his posterity.

In all respects, Federigo had represented the best in his age, and his example endured long after he had passed away. Through his practice the teachings of Vittorino inspired a small but noble society which, even when conquered politically, made a conquest of all Europe. At Urbino could be found an intellectual elite which believed that an integrated and disciplined education would result in proper behavior and a proper sense of duty toward God and man. Federigo's classical upbringing and intellectual curiosity in no way undermined, but rather reinforced, the teachings of orthodox religion. Nor did he tend to that all too common form of humanism which despised science; on the contrary, Vespasiano praised the Duke's skill in geometry and arithmetic. As for the arts, Federigo was enthusiastic about more than architecture. His musical tastes perhaps show the influence of contemporary Flanders, the same influence which brought Justus of Ghent and Flemish savants and textile artisans to his court. "He delighted greatly in music," Vespasiano noted, "understanding vocal and instrumental alike, and maintained a fine choir with skilled musicians and many singing boys. He had every sort of instrument in his palace and delighted in their sound, also the most skillful players. He preferred delicate to loud instruments,

caring little for trombones and the like."

Anything loud and harsh was anathema at the court of Urbino. Dress had to be sober, demeanor quiet, conversation lively but gentle. Women were given an active and respected place in this world, setting new standards for polite society. Vittorino's educational goal had been to create the complete all-round person who was courteous, upright, sensitive, but at the same time active. Federigo himself was such a man. He possessed a robust physique which resisted wounds and great hardship, yet the rough practice of war left his finer feelings unimpaired. Everyone knew him to be a man of honor as well as courage. His official portraits show him not so much as a warrior but as an intellectual, either reading, contemplating, listening to a lecture, or at prayer. Unlike many Renaissance princes, he lived without excess, "eating plain food and no sweetmeats," and the five hundred people who composed his court followed as orderly an existence as in a monastery: "Here was no romping or wrangling, but everyone spoke with becoming modesty."

What little we know about this court of Urbino gives us a precious insight into the civilization of the Renaissance in Italy at its most admirable. Piero della Francesca's work has partially perished, the superb ducal library was swallowed up by the Vatican, and Federigo's portraits were scattered to Florence, Milan, and Windsor. But time cannot easily erase his memory and example. Had he been more representative of his class, the course of the Renaissance might have followed a still more brilliant path.

Rules for Gentlemen

Intense self-consciousness marked the Renaissance man. Increasingly aware of his new importance as expounded by Pico della Mirandola and other humanists, he strove continually to prove himself worthy in the eyes of his fellows. In the open society in which he lived, where genius and character, rather than birth, were the measures of excellence, the highest goal of the educated man was to be considered a gentleman at first sight. Every detail of behavior and deportment was analyzed and discussed, and countless treatises were written on education, conduct, politeness, and good usage, as those who had risen to wealth and power through commercial or military means searched for gentility and acceptance. An example of their quest for perfection was the *Fior di Virtù,* a compilation of maxims and mores from ancient and Biblical sources, which went through sixty-six editions in less than thirty years. The most important book on the subject, however, was Castiglione's *The Courtier,* written about the court of Urbino and published in 1528. It set the pattern for gentlemanly conduct not only for its own time, but for later generations of European society and for modern times as well. With a few exceptions, its standards of propriety concur with those in general usage today. The excerpts on the following pages are taken from various Renaissance writings on behavior, and the woodcuts used in illustration are all from contemporary sources. The picture above appeared originally in a 1493 Florentine treatise on the game of chess.

The Dignity of Man, *excerpted below, was written by Giovanni Pico della Miran-dola in 1486 and reflects man's new importance. At left is the frontispiece to a 1490 edition of* Fior di Virtù, *and below, a 1523 illustration for a play by Terence.*

Now the Highest Father, God the Architect, according to the laws of His secret wisdom, built this house of the world, this world which we see, the most sacred temple of His divinity. He adorned the region beyond the heavens with Intelligences, He animated the celestial spheres with eternal souls, and He filled the excrementary and filthy parts of the lower world with a multitude of animals of all kinds. But when His work was finished, the Artisan longed for someone to reflect on the plan of so great a creation, to love its beauty, and to admire its magnitude. When, therefore, everything was completed . . . He began at last to consider the creation of man. But among his archetypes there was none from which He could form a new offspring, nor in His treasure houses was there any inheritance which He might bestow upon His new son, nor in the tribunal seats of the whole world was there a place where this contemplator of the universe might sit. . . . Finally the Great Artisan ordained that man, to whom He could give nothing belonging only to himself, should share in common whatever properties had been peculiar to each of the other creatures. He received man, therefore, as a creature of undetermined nature, and placing him in the middle of the universe, said this to him: "Neither an established place, nor a form belonging to you alone, nor any special function have We given you, O Adam, and for this reason, that you may have and possess, according to your desire and judgment, whatever place, whatever form, and whatever functions you shall desire. . . . I have set you at the center of the world, so that from there you may more easily survey whatever is in the world. We have made you neither heavenly nor earthly, neither mortal nor immortal, so that, more freely and more honorably the molder and maker of yourself, you may fashion yourself in whatever form you shall prefer. . . . O supreme generosity of God the Father! O highest and marvelous felicity of man! To him it is granted to have whatever he chooses, to be whatever he wills.

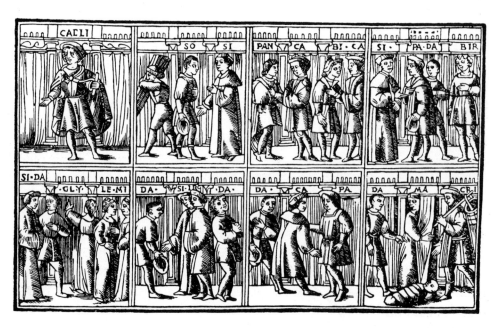

This selection, from a biography written shortly after 1460 by Leon Battista Alberti, indicates many of the attributes considered worthy in men of his time. Apparently modesty was not one of them, however; the subject of the biography was Alberti himself. At the upper right is a woodcut from a 1485 Neapolitan edition of Aesop's Fables; the one below comes from a 1499 book on Roman perspectives.

In everything suitable to one born free and educated liberally, he was so trained from boyhood that among the leading young men of his age he was considered by no means the last. For, assiduous in the science and skill of dealing with arms and horses and musical instruments, as well as in the pursuit of letters and the fine arts, he was devoted to the knowledge of the most strange and difficult things. And finally he embraced with zeal and forethought everything which pertained to fame. . . . he strove so hard to attain a name in modeling and painting that he wished to neglect nothing by which he might gain the approbation of good men. His genius was so versatile that you might almost judge all the fine arts to be his. Neither ease nor sloth held him back, nor was he ever seized by satiety in carrying out what was to be done. . . . to him letters, in which he delighted so greatly, seemed sometimes like flowering and richly fragrant buds, so that hunger or sleep could scarcely distract him from his books. . . . when letters began to be displeasing to him, he turned to music and painting and exercise. He played ball, hurled the javelin, ran, leaped, wrestled, and above all delighted in the steep ascent of mountains; he applied himself to all these things for the sake of health rather than sport or pleasure. As a youth he excelled in warlike games. With his feet together, he could leap over the shoulders of men standing by; he had almost no equal among those hurling the lance. An arrow shot by his hand from his chest could pierce the strongest iron breastplate. . . . he could throw an apple into the air so high that it would go far beyond the top of the highest roofs. . . . He delighted in the organ and was considered an expert among the leading musicians. . . . at the age of twenty-four he turned to physics and the mathematical arts. He did not despair of being able to cultivate them sufficiently, because he perceived that in them talent

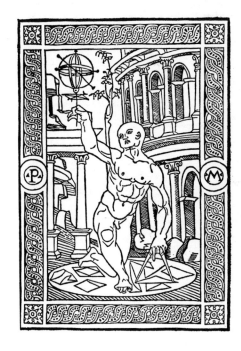

rather than memory must be employed. . . . When he heard that a learned man of any kind had arrived, he would at once work his way into a position of familiarity with him and thus from any source whatsoever he began to learn what he was ignorant of. . . . He wholly despised the pursuit of material gain [and] he always served genius rather than fame. His mind was never free from meditation and deliberation. He rarely stayed at home out of the public eye without deliberating upon something, and also pondered at dinner between courses. . . . even when he was discussing serious matters, he always showed himself agreeable, and though maintaining his dignity, even gay. . . . He could endure pain and cold and heat . . . showing by example that men can do anything with themselves if they will. . . . He took extraordinary and peculiar pleasure in looking at things in which there was any mark of beauty or adornment. . . . When his favorite dog died he wrote a funeral oration for him. Whatever was done by man with genius and with a certain grace, he held to be almost divine; and he so respected anything achieved that he insisted even poor writers were worthy of praise. The sight of gems, flowers, and especially pleasant places more than once restored him from illness to good health.

In 1489 Pope Innocent VIII, seeking an alliance between the papal see and the republic of Florence, made Giovanni de' Medici a cardinal. Since Giovanni (who later became Pope Leo X) was only thirteen, it was only natural that his father, Lorenzo, should write him a letter of advice, portions of which are printed here. The illustration is from a book of Lorenzo's canzoni, *published in Florence in 1533.*

You, and all of us who are interested in your welfare, ought to esteem ourselves highly favored by Providence, not only for the many honors and benefits bestowed on our house, but more particularly for having conferred upon us, in your person, the greatest dignity we have ever enjoyed. . . . The first that I would therefore suggest to you is that you ought to be grateful to God, and continually recollect that it is not through your merits, your prudence, or your solicitude, that this event has taken place, but through His favor, which you can only repay by a pious, chaste, and exemplary life. . . . Endeavor therefore to alleviate the burden of your early dignity by the regularity of your life and by your perseverance in those studies which are suitable to your profession. . . . I well know, that as you are now to reside at Rome, that sink of all iniquity, the difficulty of conducting yourself by these admonitions will be increased. The influence of example is itself prevalent; but you will probably meet with those who will particularly endeavor to corrupt and incite you to vice . . . To these difficulties you ought to oppose yourself with the greater firmness, as there is at present less virtue amongst your brethren of the college. . . . To give you particular directions as to your behavior and conversation would be a matter of no small difficulty. I shall therefore only recommend that in your intercourse with the cardinals and other men of rank, your language be unassuming and respectful, guiding yourself, however, by your own reason, and not submitting to be impelled by the passions of others, who, actuated by improper motives, may pervert the use of their reasons. . . . You are not only the youngest cardinal in the college, but the youngest person that ever was raised to that rank; and you ought therefore to be the most vigilant and unassuming . . . With those of less respectable character converse not with too much intimacy; not merely on account of the circumstance in itself, but for the sake of public opinion. . . . Silk and jewels are not suitable for persons in your station. Your taste will be better shown in the acquisition of a few elegant remains of antiquity, or in the collection of handsome books, and by your attendants being learned and well-bred rather than numerous. . . . Let your own food be plain, and take sufficient exercise, for those who wear your habit are soon liable, without great caution, to contract infirmities. . . . Be attentive therefore to your conduct, and confide in others too little rather than too much. There is one rule which I would recommend to your attention in preference to all others. Rise early in the morning. This will not only contribute to your health, but will enable you to arrange and expedite the business of the day . . . You will probably be desired to intercede for the favors of the Pope on particular occasions. Be cautious, however, that you trouble him not too often; for his temper leads him to be most liberal to those who weary him least with their solicitations. This you must observe, lest you should give him offense, remembering also at times to converse with him on more agreeable topics; and if you should be obliged to request some kindness from him, let it be done with that modesty and humility which are so pleasing to his disposition. Farewell.

The excerpts below, by Aeneas Silvius Piccolomini, later Pope Pius II, were addressed to the young king of Hungary and Bohemia, who had sought his advice on education. At the upper right is a woodcut from the Rime *of Bernardo Bellincioni, published in Milan in 1493. Below is an illustration from a spelling primer.*

As regards a boy's physical training, we must bear in mind that we aim at implanting habits which will prove beneficial during life. So let him cultivate a certain hardness which rejects excess of sleep and idleness in all its forms. . . . Too much importance can hardly be attached to right bearing and gesture. . . . A boy should be taught to hold his head erect, to look straight and fearlessly before him, and to bear himself with dignity, whether walking, standing, or sitting.

Every youth destined to exalted position should further be trained in military exercises. It will be your destiny to defend Christendom against the Turk. It will thus be an essential part of your education that you be early taught the use of the bow, of the sling, and of the spear; that you drive, ride, leap, and swim. These are honorable accomplishments in everyone, and therefore not unworthy of the educator's care.

As regards the use of wine, remember that we drink to quench thirst, and that the limit of moderation is reached when the edge of intellect is dulled. A boy should be brought up to avoid wine, for he possesses a store of natural moisture in the blood and so rarely experiences thirst.

Birth, wealth, fame, health, vigor, and beauty are, indeed, highly prized by mankind, but they are one and all of the nature of accidents; they come and they go. But the riches of the mind are a stable possession, unassailable by fortune, calumny, or time. . . . Literature is our guide to the true meaning of the past, to a right estimate of the present, to a sound forecast of the future. Where letters cease, darkness covers the land; and a prince who cannot read the lessons of history is a helpless prey of flattery and intrigue.

In conversation kindness and courtesy are always attractive; pertinacity or pretentiousness are odious; a turgid, affected style arouses contempt. Insincerity or malice are, of course, not mere defects in form but positive sins. So let your address be frank, outspoken, self-respecting, manly.

We must . . . insist upon the overwhelming importance of memory, which is in truth the first condition of capacity for letters. A boy should learn without effort, retain with accuracy, and reproduce easily. Rightly is memory called "the nursing mother of learning." It needs cultivation, however, whether a boy be gifted with retentiveness or not. Therefore, let some passage from poet or moralist be committed to memory every day.

Castiglione's The Courtier, *from which the idealistic and often snobbish excerpts on these pages are taken, became the handbook of proper behavior for generations of European gentlemen. The woodcuts at left are from a 1491 Florentine edition of the* Fior di Virtù. *On the facing page are a scene from* The Story of Two Lovers *(right), and an illustration from a 1523 edition of Boccaccio's* Decameron *(bottom).*

I would wish the Courtier . . . endowed by nature not only with talent and with beauty of countenance and person, but with that certain grace which we call an "air," which shall make him at first sight pleasing and lovable to all who see him.

I would have him more than passably learned in letters, at least in those studies which we call the humanities. Let him be conversant not only with the Latin language, but with Greek as well, because of the abundance and variety of things that are so divinely written therein. Let him be versed in the poets, as well as in the orators and historians, and let him be practiced also in writing verse and prose, especially in our own vernacular; for, besides the personal satisfaction he will take in this, in this way he will never want for pleasant entertainment with the ladies, who are usually fond of such things.

He should also know how to swim, jump, run, throw stones; for, besides their usefulness in war, it is frequently necessary to show one's prowess in such things, whereby a good name is to be won, especially with the crowd (with whom one must reckon after all). Another noble exercise and most suitable for a man at court is the game of tennis which shows off the disposition of body, the quickness and litheness of every member, and all the qualities that are brought out by almost every other exercise.

When dancing in the presence of many and in a place full of people, I think he should maintain a certain dignity, though tempered with a fine and airy grace of movement; and even though he may feel himself to be most agile and a master of time and measure, let him not attempt those quick movements of foot and those double steps which . . . little befit a gentleman.

A man ought always be a little more humble than his rank would require; not accepting too readily the favors and honors that are offered him, but modestly refusing them while showing that he esteems them highly, yet in such a way as to give the donor cause to press them upon him the more urgently. For the greater the resistance shown in accepting them in this way, the more will the prince who is granting them think himself to be esteemed, and his benefaction will appear the greater the more the recipient of it shows his appreciation and how great he considers the honor done him by it.

The method that the Courtier ought to follow in making his love known to the Lady would be to reveal it to her by actions rather than words, for it is certainly true that more of love's affection is sometimes revealed by a sigh, by a reverence, by timidity, than by a thousand words; next, by making his eyes be faithful messengers in bearing the embassies of his heart, since they often reveal the passion within more effectively than the tongue itself, or letters, or messengers; and they not only reveal thoughts but they often kindle love in the beloved's heart.

Our Courtier will not indulge in foolish presumption; he will not be the bearer of unpleasant news; he will not be careless in speaking words which can offend, instead of trying to please; he will not be obstinate and contentious, as are some who seem to delight only in being troublesome and obnoxious like flies, and who make a profession of contradicting everybody, spitefully and indiscriminately. He will not be an idle or lying babbler nor a boaster or inept flatterer, but will be modest and reserved, observing always (and especially in public) the reverence and respect that befit a servant in relation to his master . . .

I am not satisfied with our Courtier unless he be also a musician, and unless, besides understanding and being able to read music, he can play various instruments. For, if we rightly consider, no rest from toil and no medicine for ailing spirits can be found more decorous or praiseworthy in time of leisure than this; and especially in courts where, besides the release from vexations which music gives to all, many things are done to please the ladies, whose tender and delicate spirits are readily penetrated with harmony and filled with sweetness.

[Chess] is certainly a pleasing and ingenious amusement . . . but it seems to me to have one defect, which is that it is possible to have too much knowledge of it, so that whoever would excel in the game must give a great deal of time to it, as I believe, and as much study as if he would learn some noble science or perform well anything of importance; and yet in the end, for all his pains, he only knows how to play a game. Thus, I think a very unusual thing happens in this, namely, that mediocrity is more to be praised than excellence.

Giovanni della Casa, a papal nuncio and great friend of Cardinal Bembo, wrote the
Galateo between 1551 and 1555, probably for a young nephew, Annibale Rucellai.

To help you understand how to behave I must first teach you that your conduct should not be governed by your own fancy, but in consideration of the feelings of those whose company you keep. . . . For this reason it is a repulsive habit to touch certain parts of the body in public, as some people do. . . . Again, when you have blown your nose, you should not open your handkerchief and inspect it, as though pearls or rubies had dropped out of your skull. Such behavior is nauseating and is more likely to lose us the affection of those who love us than to win us the favor of others. . . . It is not polite to scratch yourself when you are seated at table. You should also take care, as far as you can, not to spit at mealtimes, but if you must spit, then do so in a decent manner. . . . We should also be careful not to gobble our food so greedily as to cause ourselves to get hiccups or commit some other unpleasantness . . . It is also bad manners to clean your teeth with your napkin, and still worse to do it with your finger, for such conduct is unsightly. It is wrong to rinse your mouth and spit out wine in public, and it is not a polite habit, when you rise from the table, to carry your toothpick either in your mouth, like a bird making its nest, or behind your ear. . . . It is also unmannerly to sprawl over the table or to fill both sides of your mouth so full with food that your cheeks are bloated. And you must do nothing to show that you have found great relish in the food or the wine, for these are the customs of the tavern and the alehouse. . . . I do not think it right to offer food from one's own plate to anyone else, unless the person who offers it is of much more exalted rank, in which case it would be a mark of honor for the other. If both are of the same rank, it is rather a presumption of superiority for one of them to offer his food to the other, and sometimes the tidbit might not be to his taste. . . . No one must take off his clothes, especially his lower garments, in public, that is, in the presence of decent people, because this is not the right place for undressing. . . . You should neither comb your hair nor wash your hands in the presence of others, because—except for washing the hands before going in to a meal—such things are done in the bedroom and not in public. . . . Again, you must not appear in public with your nightcap on your head or fasten your hose when other people are present. . . . Anyone who makes a nasty noise with his lips as a sign of astonishment or disapproval is obviously imitating something indecent, and imitations are not too far from the truth.

RENAISSANCE MEN

The individual and his aspirations became the new focus of thought during the Renaissance. And the liberal arts, pictured above in a fifteenth-century manuscript, symbolized this new goal of universality. Educators such as Vittorino taught men to be well-rounded individuals; Castiglione set forth the many skills necessary for the ideal gentleman; and Leonardo's catholicity was an example which many sought to imitate. In every field of endeavor and in all classes of society, individuals, inspired by wider freedoms and wider learning, realized new goals: doctors were polished humanists; artists excelled in the sciences; monks created artistic masterpieces; and aristocrats became accomplished musicians. The following pages suggest a few of the areas in which individuals achieved new heights of creativity.

Franchino Gafori (1451–1522) was a member of Lodovico Il Moro's brilliant circle of scholars and artists, a teacher at Il Moro's famous music school in Milan, and the most eminent Italian theorist of his time. Woodcut frontispieces from two of his many books show him (left) teaching a class in principles of harmony and (below) demonstrating the hexachord system on the organ.

THE MUSICIAN

The growing enthusiasm for popular music during the Renaissance typified man's new desire for freedom and pleasure. Music played an essential part in the great pageants and festivals of the Medici and other princes; street singers serenaded the Florentines on summer nights; crowds flocked to hear the famous cathedral organists of Milan and Florence; and the Sistine and Julian choirs in Rome attracted the best singers in Europe. The spirit of humanism which inspired poets also affected such musicians as the blind Francesco Landino, whose graceful and emotional *ars nova* compositions fill the pages of one of the loveliest of all musical manuscripts, the *Squarcialupi Codex*.

Despite its new popularity, however, music was the only art in which the Italians lagged behind in technical achievement. There were, of course, a few outstanding individual contributors: Franchino Gafori, the choirmaster of Milan, wrote several books on theory which revolutionized the rules of composition and harmony; and the works of Ottaviano de' Petrucci, the first musical printer, have rarely been matched for beauty or accuracy. But by and large most new developments up to the mid-sixteenth century were fostered by the French. Italy's principal contribution was to free music from the bonds of religious supervision. Princely salons became the centers of music during the Renaissance and vied with each other for the services of leading musicians. Humanist poems were now set to music, new and beautiful instruments were designed, and Castiglione made musical ability a requisite for his ideal courtier. In the gay and worldly atmosphere of the courts, music was able to free itself from the fetters of ancient form and began to develop along new and melodious lines.

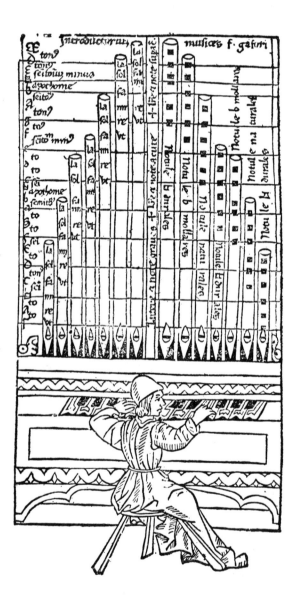

Fra Luca Pacioli and a student, thought to be Guidobaldo, the young Duke of Urbino.

THE MATHEMATICIAN

The classical ideals of proportion and perspective espoused by Alberti and Piero della Francesca made a lasting impression on one of their young students, Fra Luca Pacioli. Instilled with a desire to see their theories put to use in everyday life, Pacioli wrote numerous mathematical books, the most important of which was a huge volume, published in 1494, which laid the foundation for most modern study of the subject. Fra Luca was the head of his monastery in his later years, as well as an inspiring teacher and author. He spent most of his time, however, in the intellectual circles of Urbino and Milan, where he was a friend of Leonardo's and tried to persuade the artist to publish his scientific drawings. But Pacioli's greatest fame came from his publication of the double-entry bookkeeping system, which was of vast importance to Italy's merchants and affected the entire business world. It was that masterwork which earned him the title, "Father of Bookkeeping."

Jupiter with two signs of the zodiac

THE ASTROLOGER

Whatever the advances in scientific thinking, there remained a widespread belief that every human action and natural occurrence was ultimately directed by the stars. Astrologers abounded, they were employed by nearly every court, and throughout Italy they busily prepared horoscopes, advising rich and poor upon the most propitious timing for everything from declaring war to planting trees. Nearly all learned men conceded the power of the planets. Even though he relegated stargazers to hell, Dante admitted the influence of cosmic forces on the soul; Pico della Mirandola wrote a treatise against astrologers, but when he died on the day they had predicted for him, his arguments lost their cogency; and even in the Church, which frowned upon the occult as bordering on heresy, Pope Julius II set the time of his coronation according to astrological calculations. In the universities, too, astrology was accorded high importance, and was regarded both as a major science itself and as the basis for all the natural sciences.

A detail from the astrological tables of G. Bianchini (left) shows the author presenting a copy to his patron, the Emperor Frederick III.

Madonna and Child *by Fra Filippo Lippi*

THE MONK

Within the monasteries of Italy were some of the brightest talents of an exceptional age—men of the caliber of Fra Angelico, Fra Filippo Lippi, Fra Luca Pacioli, and Fra Bartolommeo. And beyond the works of art produced by members of their orders, priors commissioned some of the masterpieces of the Renaissance. The monasteries continued their traditional sponsorship of schools, hospitals, and charitable institutions, but in this worldly era their secularism and immorality—tales of which fill the pages of Boccaccio's *Decameron* and other contemporary writings—were often more apparent than their virtues. Scandals and concubinage were common, and Filippo Lippi, a Carmelite, shocked even that lusty age when he ran off with a young nun. (When offered freedom from his vows to marry her, he refused, since matrimony was more binding than the monastic life.) Savonarola and other reformers fought to stem the moral laxity, but it continued to engulf all but a few of the strictest orders.

The model for Lippi's Virgin (above) was the young nun with whom he eloped. The artist's portrait, in a detail from his tomb, is at right.

THE DOCTOR

The superstitions, nostrums, and miracle cures of medieval medicine began to give way during the Renaissance to many new advances. Artists spurred on the study of anatomy, effective quarantine had controlled leprosy, hospitals multiplied, and laws restricted quack doctors. The greatest challenge to Renaissance medicine was an epidemic which broke out in Naples in 1495. The "love pestilence," as it was called, necessitated new treatments—among them city hygiene laws prohibiting mixed public baths, and a mercury cure which improved on traditional herbal remedies. A wealthy and brilliant physician, Girolamo Fracastoro, wrote a long Latin poem on the causes, symptoms, and care of the disease. Fracastoro was extremely acute in most of his observations and later won great fame for his advanced studies of other contagious infections (he was the first to recognize typhus), but in his poem he bowed to the universal belief in astrology, naming the disease syphilis after a mythical shepherd, Syphilus, who was supposedly stricken with it for offending the god Apollo.

Above is a portrait of Girolamo Fracastoro. A Fifteenth-century manuscript (below) shows doctors caring for hospitalized patients.

Cellini's portrait (by Giorgio Vasari) appears at far right. The ornate gold cup above, with its sphinx handle and brilliantly enameled dragon and tortoise base, reflects his elaborate work as well as the sumptuous taste of the time. At the right is a study for his famous statue of Perseus which still stands in the Loggia dei Lanzi in Florence. Cellini spent nine years completing it and the remainder of his life trying in vain to collect his payment.

THE CRAFTSMAN

"Men like Benvenuto, unique in their profession, stand above the law," said Paul III of Cellini, and the craftsman took him at his word. His brawls, love affairs, violent tempers, and escapades resulted in numerous enmities, eight children (one of whom was legitimate), and a bevy of dead men. But as an artist he was hard-working, tremendously talented, and his services were in demand by pope and princes alike. Michelangelo called him the "greatest goldsmith of whom the world has ever heard," and although few of his innumerable ornate works survive, the still-extant saltcellar made for Francis I and the portrait medal of Bembo amply justify the egotism which fills his *Autobiography*. That account gives a vivid picture not only of its famous author, whose seventy-one years saw countless adventures and endless wrangles over his many commissions, but also of the life of a Renaissance craftsman par excellence.

343

A fifteenth-century marble figure, portraying an unknown Italian matron, evokes the proud and intelligent spirit of Renaissance woman.

WOMEN

OF THE RENAISSANCE

François Villon, the vagabond poet of France, wondered, as he drifted through the gutters and attics of fifteenth-century Paris, where were the famous women of the days long past? Where Héloïse, for whom Abelard had endured such degradation? Where Thaïs, Alis, Haremburgis, where the Queen Blanche with her siren's voice, where were these fabled, love-haunted, noble women, of more than human beauty? Gone, he thought, gone forever. Even the rough Viking bards sang of their heroic women, of Aud the Deep-minded who "hurt most whom she loved best." The lives of these fateful, tragic women, medieval heroines of love and sorrow, became themes of epic and romance which were told in the courts of princes; yet even as Villon bewailed their loss, men were growing tired of them.

The age of heroes was dying. The unrequited love of Dante for Beatrice, the lyrical attachment of Petrarch for Laura, and, in a different mood, the agreeable pleasantries of Boccaccio, had domesticated love, making it more intimate. The dawn of a carefree, less fate-ridden attitude to woman was gentle, undramatic, and slow, beginning way back with the wandering troubadours and scholars who moved from castle to farm, from monastery to university, singing their light-hearted lyrics to earn their keep.

Down the broad way do I go,
Young and unregretting,
Wrap me in my vices up,
Virtue all forgetting,
Greedier for all delight
Than heaven to enter in:
Since the soul in me is dead,
Better save the skin.

Sit you down amid the fire,
Will the fire not burn you?
Come to Pavia, will you
Just as chaste return you?
Pavia, where Beauty draws
Youth with finger-tips,
Youth entangled in her eyes,
Ravished with her lips.

So sang the nameless Archpoet, young, consumptive, in love, as he wandered down to Salerno to read medicine. The time was the twelfth century—three hundred years before the haunting love poems of Lorenzo de' Medici were written. Yet the sentiments of both men were a part of the same process, part of the lifting tide of Southern Europe's prosperity, of its growing population, of the sophistication that wealth and leisure brought: for in leisure lies dalliance. The wandering scholars were few; their mistresses, chatelaines or girls of the town: yet they were the naïve harbingers of a world that was to reach its fullness in Italy in the fifteenth century.

It was the new prosperity that influenced the lives of women most profoundly. It brought them fresh opportunities for adornment; it increased their dowries and their value. It emancipated many from the drudgery of the household and from the relentless, time-consuming demands of children. Women entered more fully into the daily lives and pursuits of men. And, of course, the new delights of the Renaissance world—painting, music, literature—had their feminine expression. Much of the artistic world was concerned with the pursuit of love in all its guises. Women were a part of art.

Except for the very lowest ranks of society, women were inextricably entangled in the concept of prosperity, and their virtue was a marketable commodity. They were secluded from birth to marriage, taught by women and priests, kept constantly under the closest supervision in the home or in the con-

In a square outside the Baptistery of Florence, richly dressed couples parade under a striped canopy in celebration of the Adimari wedding, which took place in the middle of the fifteenth century. At far left, pages carry serving vessels of gold, while musicians play a fanfare on trumpets decorated with the lily of Florence. Both visitors and servants wear bright colors, but those in the wedding party are dressed mainly in black and gold. Paintings such as this often decorated the bride's cassone, *a wedding chest designed to contain her trousseau.*

vent. Marriage came early: twelve was not an uncommon age, thirteen usual, fifteen was getting late, and an unmarried girl of sixteen or seventeen was a catastrophe. Women conveyed property and could often secure a lift in the social scale for their families. Even more important was the use of women to seal alliances between families, whether princely, noble, or mercantile. The great Venetian merchants interlocked their adventures overseas with judicious marriages at home. The redoubtable Vittoria Colonna was betrothed at the age of four to the Marquis of Pescara to satisfy her family's political ambition. Lucrezia Borgia's early life was a grim enough reminder of the dynastic value of women. Her fiancés were sent packing, her husbands murdered or declared impotent, so that Alexander VI could use her again and again in the furtherance of his policies. In less exalted ranks of society women were still traded. It took Michelangelo years of horse-trading to buy a young Ridolfi wife for his nephew and so push his family up a rank in Florentine society. Marriages so arranged were symbolic of power and social status as well as of wealth, and their celebration, in consequence, demanded the utmost pomp and splendor that the contracting parties could afford. Important Venetian marriages were famed for an extravagance that not even the Council of Ten could curb. The festivities began with an official proclamation in the Doge's Palace. The contracting parties and their supporters paraded the canals *en fête.* Gondoliers and servants were dressed in sumptuous livery; the façades of the palaces were adorned with rare Oriental carpets and tapestries; there were bonfires, fireworks, balls, masques, banquets, and everywhere and at all times—even the most intimate—serenades by gorgeously dressed musicians. Of course, such profusion acted like a magnet for poets, dramatists, rhetoricians, painters, and artists of every variety. For a few ducats a wandering humanist would pour out a few thousand words, full of recon-

dite references to gods and heroes; poets churned out epithalamiums before they could be asked; and painters immortalized the bride, her groom, or even, as Botticelli did, the wedding breakfast. And they were eager for more mundane tasks, not for one moment despising an offer to decorate the elaborate *cassoni* in which the bride took her clothes and linen to her new household. Indeed, the competitive spirit of both brides and painters in *cassoni* became so fierce that they ceased to be objects of utility and were transformed into extravagant works of art, becoming the heirlooms of future generations.

The artistic accompaniment of marriage became the height of fashion. When the Duke and Duchess of Urbino returned to their capital after their wedding, they were met on a hilltop outside their city by all the women and children of rank, exquisitely and expensively dressed, bearing olive branches in their hands. As the Duke and Duchess reached them, mounted choristers accompanied by nymphs *à la Grecque* burst

into song—a special cantata which had been composed for the newlyweds. The Goddess of Mirth appeared in person with her court, and to make everyone realize that jollity and horseplay were never out of place at a wedding, hares were loosed in the crowd. This drove the dogs insane with excitement, to everyone's delight. No matter how solemn the occasion, marriage always involved coarse farce, usually at the climax of the wedding festivities, when the bride and groom were publicly bedded. Although there was no romantic nonsense about Italian weddings, certainly few marriages for love, everyone knew that the right true end of the contract was the bed. The dowager Duchess of Urbino, something of a bluestocking and a Platonist, and a woman of acknowledged refinement, burst into her niece's bedroom on the morning after her marriage and shouted, "Isn't it a fine thing to sleep with the men?"

Marriage for the women of the Renaissance gave many

their first taste of opulence, leisure, and freedom. They were very young, the atmosphere of their world was as reckless as it was ostentatious, and furthermore, they had not chosen their husbands, who frequently were a generation older than themselves. Their men, who were frequently soldiers or courtiers who lived close to the razor edge of life, fully enjoyed intrigue, so the young wife became a quarry to be hunted. As she was often neglected, the chase could be brief. Even Castiglione, who was very fond of his wife, treated her somewhat casually. He saw her rarely, and made up for his absence with affectionate, bantering letters. Of course, she was a generation younger than himself and therefore hardly a companion. Such a situation was not unusual: a girl of thirteen might excite her mature husband, but she was unlikely to entertain him for long. She fulfilled her tasks by bearing a few children and running a trouble-free household, and neither matter was too onerous for the rich. Nurses took

over the children as soon as they were born; a regiment of servants relieved wives of their traditional housewifely duties. So the leisure which had previously been the lot of only a few women of very high birth became a commonplace of existence for a multitude of women.

The presence of these leisured women in society helped to transform it. It created the opportunity for personality to flourish, for women to indulge the whims of their temperaments—free from the constraining circumstances of childbirth, nursery, and kitchen. There were men enough to adorn their vacant hours. Italy was alive with priests, many of them urbane, cultured, and idle, whose habit acted as a passport, hinting a security for husbands which their actions all too frequently belied. Nevertheless, they were the natural courtiers of lonely wives, and they swarmed in the literary salons of such distinguished women as Elisabetta Gonzaga at Urbino, the Queen of Cyprus at Asolo, or Vittoria Colonna at Rome.

Poets and their allegories were high on the list of feminine interests.
On the facing page is a strange, mystical allegory, The Maiden's Dream,
painted by Lorenzo Lotto, whom Titian called "as good as goodness, and
as virtuous as virtue." Above, a maid crowns a poet with a laurel wreath.

Soldiers as well as priests needed the sweetness of feminine compassion to soften their tough and dangerous lives. Fortunately, military campaigns in Renaissance Italy were short and usually confined to the summer months, and so the horseplay, the practical jokes, and the feats of arms which were as essential to the courtly life as literary conversations or dramatic performances were provided by the knights. In addition to soldiers and priests, there were the husbands' pages, all in need of the finer points of amorous education. For a princess, further adornment of the salon was provided by an ambassador—often, true enough, a mere Italian, but at times French or Spanish, which gave an exotic touch that a woman of fashion could exploit to her rivals' disadvantage. Naturally, these courts became highly competitive: to have Pietro Bembo sitting at one's feet, reading his mellifluous but tedious essays on the beauties of Platonic love, was sure to enrage the hearts of other women. In fact, the popularity of

Bembo illustrates admirably the style of sophisticated love that the extravagant and princely women of Italy demanded.

Pietro Bembo was a Venetian nobleman, the cultivated son of a rich and sophisticated father who had educated him in the height of humanist fashion at the University of Ferrara, where he acquired extreme agility in bandying about the high-flown concepts of that strange mixture of Platonism and Christianity which was the hallmark of the exquisite. Petrarch, of course, was Bembo's mentor, and like Petrarch he lived his life, as far as the pressures of nature would allow him, in literary terms. He fell verbosely and unhappily in love with a Venetian girl; his ardent longings and intolerable frustrations were committed elegantly to paper and circulated to his admiring friends. This experience provided him with enough material for a long epistolary exchange with Ercole Strozzi, who was as addicted as Bembo to girls in literary dress. Enraptured by the elegance of his sentiments, Strozzi invited

Bembo to his villa near Ferrara, doubtless to flaunt his latest capture, Lucrezia Borgia, as well as to indulge his insatiable literary appetite. However, the biter was quickly bitten, for Bembo was just Lucrezia's cup of tea. A mature woman of twenty-two, thoroughly versed in the language as well as the experience of love, she was already bored with her husband, Alfonso d'Este, and tired of Strozzi. Soon she and Bembo were exchanging charming Spanish love lyrics and far larger homilies on aesthetics. After a visit by Lucrezia to Bembo, sick with fever, the pace quickened. Enormous letters followed thick and fast. Bembo ransacked literature to do homage to Lucrezia; they were Aeneas and Dido, Tristan and Iseult, Lancelot and Guinevere—not, however, lover and mistress. For a time they lived near each other in the country, while Ferrara was plague-ridden. Proximity and the furor of literary passion began to kindle fires in Bembo that were not entirely Platonic, and, after all, Lucrezia was a Borgia. Her

tolerant but watchful husband, however, had no intention of being cuckolded by an aesthete, and he rattled his sword. Bembo did not relish reliving the tragedy of Abelard; he might love Lucrezia to distraction, but he cherished himself as only an artist can, so he thought it discreet to return to Venice (he had excuse enough, as his brother was desperately sick). There he consoled himself by polishing his dialogue, *Gli Asolani,* which already enjoyed a high reputation among those to whom it had been circulated in manuscript. Resolving to give his love for Lucrezia its final, immortal form, he decided to publish it with a long dedication to her. To present her with his divine thoughts on love was a greater gift by far, of course, than his person. Doubtless both Lucrezia and her husband agreed; whether they read further than the dedication is more doubtful.

Bembo had written these highfalutin letters—informal, mannered, obscure, and so loaded with spiritual effusions on

love, beauty, God, and women that they are almost unreadable—during a visit to that tragic and noble woman Caterina Cornaro, Queen of Cyprus. The daughter of a Venetian aristocrat, she had been married as a girl to Giacomo II of Cyprus for reasons of state and declared with infinite pomp "daughter of the republic." Bereaved of both husband and son within three years, she had defied revolution and civil war and maintained her government for fourteen years until, to ease its political necessities, Venice had forced her abdication and set her up in a musical-comedy court at Asolo. There she consoled herself with the world of the spirit, about which Bembo was better informed than most, and he was drawn to her like a moth to a candle. Her court was elegant, fashionable, and intensely literary. *Gli Asolani,* published by Aldus in 1505, made Bembo the archpriest of love as the *Courtier* was to make Castiglione the archpriest of manners. Indeed, Bembo figures in the *Courtier,* and Castiglione adopted his

literary techniques. These two subtle and scented bores were destined to turn up together, and nowhere was more likely than the court of Elisabetta Gonzaga at Urbino, for her insatiable appetite for discussion was equal to their eloquence; her stamina matched their verbosity; and night after night the dawn overtook their relentless arguments about the spiritual nature of love. Neither, of course, was so stupid as to think that even the high-minded Caterina or Elisabetta could live by words alone, and Bembo, at least, always interlarded the more ethereal descriptions of Platonic love with a warm eulogy of passion in its more prosaic and energetic aspects. Indeed, he was not above appearing (not entirely modestly disguised) as an ambassador of Venus, in order to declaim in favor of natural love. After six years of this excessively cultured refinement at Urbino, Bembo became papal secretary to Leo X in Rome. Appropriately, at Rome the word became flesh, and Bembo settled into the comfortable arms of

a girl called Morosina who promptly provided him with three children. It is not surprising, therefore, that Bembo's interests became more mundane, turning from Platonic philosophy to the history of Venice. After the death of his mistress, the life of the spirit once more claimed him, and he entered the College of Cardinals in 1538. More than any other man of his time, he set the pattern of elegant courtship, so that the flattery of the mind, combined with poetic effusions on the supremacy of the spirit, became a well-trodden path for the courtier. It possessed the supreme advantage of passionate courtship without the necessity of proof—a happy situation, indeed, when the object was both a bluestocking and a queen.

Even though the great ladies of Renaissance Italy cultivated the heart and mind so ardently, some of them did not wish to neglect entirely the more commonplace forms of love. They liked their flattery to be carnal, even though love was pure. They insisted on being admired for their physical charms, and they were prepared to listen, as Lucrezia Borgia was, to a lengthy eulogy not only about the charms of their spirit but also on the beauty of their dress, upon which they spent as profusely as any women in the history of mankind. The jewels of the Este girls at Ferrara came in for almost as much praise as their intellects. The extravagance of their fashions, like their predilection for poets, was eagerly imitated in less exalted circles. Blonde hair became so much *de rigueur* that a brunette was not to be seen in Venice except among the working classes. Venetian women spent hours dyeing and burnishing their hair until they achieved the harsh metallic glitter that was considered a necessity. But in these things the women of the Renaissance were no different from women of any age: the only change from the immediate past was that their wealth permitted them greater luxury, giving them greater opportunities of self-indulgence; and the fact that there were, at this time, more wealthy women than ever

*In long blonde curls, a young Sienese maiden,
the grandniece of Pius II, posed for her portrait.*

before meant that the jealous competition between them was intensified.

Yet it would be wrong to think that the gilded lives of Renaissance princesses were merely elegant, sophisticated, and luxurious, or that flirtation took place only in the most refined language. Few could concentrate their thoughts year in, year out, on the nobility of love like Vittoria Colonna. She, who inspired some of Michelangelo's most passionate poetry even as old age was ravaging her features, could and did live in an intense world of spiritual passion, in which the lusts of the flesh were exorcised by an ecstatic contemplation of the beauties of religion. The miracle was that she retained her charm, avoided the pitfalls of hypocrisy, and secured without effort the devotion of Castiglione and Bembo as well as Michelangelo. Even the old rogue Aretino attempted to secure her patronage, but naturally she remained aloof. In her the Platonic ideals of love and beauty mingled with the

Christian virtues to the exclusion of all else. Amazingly, no one found her a bore. However, few women could live like Vittoria: they sighed as they read Bembo, became enrapt as they listened to Castiglione, but from time to time they enjoyed a quiet reading of Boccaccio and, better still, Bandello.

Matteo Bandello had been received as a Dominican and spent many years of his life at the Convento delle Grazie at Milan, which seems to have been a more exciting place for a short-story teller than might be imagined. He acted for a time as ambassador for the Bentivoglio and so came in contact with that remarkable woman Isabella d'Este Gonzaga, whose court at Mantua was as outstanding for its wit, elegance, and genius as any in Italy. There Bandello picked up a mistress, which put him in no mind to hurry back to his brother monks. At Mantua, too, he laid the foundations of his reputation for being one of the best raconteurs of scandal in all Italy, Aretino not excepted. How true Bandello's stories are is still a

matter for fierce warfare among scholars, but this they agree on: they did not seem incredible to those who read them. That being so, they give a hair-raising picture of what was going on at courts, in monasteries, in nunneries, in merchant houses, in the palaces and parsonages of Italy. The prime pursuit, in the vast majority of Bandello's stories, is the conquest of women, and to achieve success any trick, any falsehood, any force, is justifiable. His heroes' attitude to success in sex was like Machiavelli's to politics—the end justifies any means. The aim of all men is to ravish other men's wives and daughters and preserve their own women or revenge them if they fail to do so. Vendettas involving the most bloodcurdling punishments are a corollary to his major theme. In consequence, Bandello's stories, cast in a moral guise, nevertheless read like the chronicles of a pornographer. Here are the themes of a few that were thought to be proper entertainment for the lighter moments of court life or for quiet read-

ing by a bored wife—the marriage of a man to a woman who was already his sister, and to his daughter; the adultery of two ladies at a court and the death of their paramours, which is a vivid record of sexual pleasure and horrifying punishment; the servant who was decapitated for sleeping with his mistress; the death through excessive sexual indulgence of Charles of Navarre; Gian Maria Visconti's burial of a live priest; the autocastration of Fra Filippo—and so one might go on and on, for Bandello wrote hundreds of short stories and they were largely variations on a single theme. The women of the Renaissance loved them, and few storytellers were as popular as Bandello (such abilities did not go unmarked, and he finished his career as Bishop of Agen). Nor was Bandello exceptional: there were scores of writers like him. Malicious, distorted, exaggerated as these tales were, they were based on the realities of Italian life. Undoubtedly the increased leisure of men and women released their ener-

Beauty substituted for comfort in the wooden chair shown on the facing page, which was made in the fifteenth century for the Strozzi, a Florentine family rivaling the Medici in culture and wealth. More often, Renaissance craftsmen succeeded in combining beauty with convenience, as evidenced by the beautifully wrought silver service below, made by a Roman artisan (the substitution of forks for fingers was a recent innovation). The rigors of housekeeping were eased for many rich ladies by slaves, two of whom are illustrated here in charming silhouettes. Pope Innocent VIII once received a gift of one hundred Moorish slaves, whom he distributed as a gratuity to cardinals and friends.

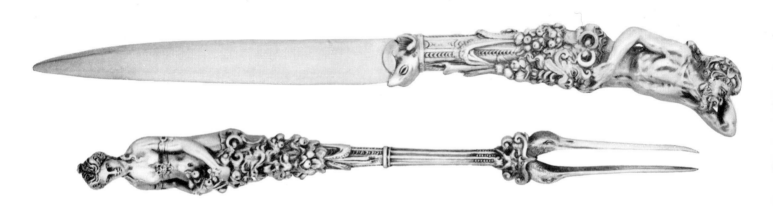

gies for a more riotous indulgence of their sexual appetites.

However daring the Italian males of the Renaissance were, the prudence of wives and the vigilance of husbands prevailed more often than not. The Emilia Pias, Elisabetta Gonzagas, Isabella d'Estes, Lucrezia Borgias, Costanza Amarettas, and Vittoria Colonnas were all too rare—particularly for cardinals and bishops ravenous for Platonic love. So in Rome, in Florence, in Venice, and in Milan there developed a class of grand courtesans, more akin to geisha girls than to prostitutes, to the extent that the *cortesane famose* of Venice despised the *cortesane de la minor sorte* and complained of their number, habits and prices to the Senate (they felt they brought disrepute on an honorable profession). Grand as these Venetian girls were, they could not compete with the great courtesans of Rome, who not only lived in small palaces with retinues of maids and liveried servants, but also practiced the literary graces and argued as learnedly as a Duchess

of Urbino about the ideals of Platonic love. Imperia of Rome, for example, held a salon for priestly humanists and gratified their spiritual as well as their carnal lusts with a delicacy and grace that made her name legendary. Her virgin daughter had been brought up so immaculately that she even threatened suicide to escape the amorous advances of a randy cardinal. Such a quean did honor to Rome, and her death was celebrated as a day of public mourning.

Even Imperia, however, could scarcely hold a candle to Tullia d'Aragona, the authoress of *On the Infinity of Perfect Love,* a subject for which her profession, perhaps, gave her special insight. Certainly she drove the aesthetes crazy. She was rhapsodized on her arrival at Ferrara in June, 1537, in these terms: "There has just arrived here a very pretty lady, so staid in deportment, so fascinating in manner, that we cannot help finding in her something truly divine. She sings all sorts of airs and motets at sight; her conversation has

Leisured Florentine women might devote their time to studying Latin, but Venetian ladies, like the one shown at right, were apt to spend hours on a rooftop with their hair spread out in the sun to bleach. Wide brims protected their skin, since a white complexion was prized as highly as blonde hair. Washing in a liquid distilled when a dove was cooked in its feathers was guaranteed to make skin beautiful; to keep it that way, Venetian ladies usually wore veils in the streets. This custom gave them an appearance of modesty not usually associated with the Renaissance, but the effect was diminished by the décolletage then in fashion, which reduced the illusion of decorum to a bare minimum.

matchless charm; she knows everything and there is nothing that you cannot talk to her about. There is no one here to hold a candle to her, not even the Marchioness of Pescara" (*i.e.,* Vittoria Colonna!). Tullia actually preferred her clients to be philosophers or historians. After Leo X had chased her and her sisters from Rome, she settled in Florence, where the reigning Duke insisted that all whores should wear yellow as a mark of their infamy. Her admirers, however, protested so vehemently on Tullia's behalf that she was publicly excused by the government on the grounds of "literary talents that are found in her to the great joy of noble minds."

Italy during the Renaissance was a country at war, plagued for decades with armies. A well-versed condottiere might battle with skill even in the wordy encounters of Platonic passion, but the majority wanted a quicker and cheaper victory. For months on end the captains of war had nothing to do and money to spend; they needed a metropolis of pleasure

and vice. Venice, with its quick eye for a profit, provided it and plucked them clean. There girls were to be had for as little as one *scudo,* well within the means even of a musketeer. And it was natural that after Leo X's purge, the majority of the fallen from Rome should flow to Venice. That city, with its regattas, *feste,* and carnivals, with its gondolas built for seclusion and sin, became a harlot's paradise. The trade in women became more profitable and extensive than it had been since the days of Imperial Rome. The Renaissance recaptured the past in more exotic fields than literature or the arts.

Life, however, for the noble women of the Renaissance was not always cakes and ale; it could be harsh and furious: the male world of war, assassination, and the pursuit of power frequently broke in upon their gentle world of love and dalliance. Indeed, Caterina Sforza, the woman whom all Italy saluted as its *prima donna,* won her fame through her dour courage and savage temper. Castiglione tells the story

of the time she invited a boorish condottiere to dinner, and asked him first to dance and then to hear some music—both of which he declined on the grounds that they were not his business. "What is your business, then?" his hostess asked. "Fighting," the warrior replied. "Then," said the virago of Forlì, "since you are not at war and not needed to fight, it would be wise for you to have yourself well greased and put away in a cupboard with all your arms until you are wanted, so that you will not get more rusty than you are." Violent, sensual, inexhaustible, contemptuous, and credulous, she is more a figure of a saga than a woman of the Renaissance. Three of her husbands were assassinated. At one time she defied the French, at another Cesare Borgia, who caught her and sent her like a captive lioness to the dungeons of Sant' Angelo. She told her frantic sons that she was habituated to grief and had no fear of it, and as they ought to have expected, she escaped. Yet tough and resourceful as she was,

Caterina could be a fool in love—much more of a fool than the Duchess of Urbino or Vittoria Colonna. Time and time again her political troubles were due to her inability to check her strong sensual appetite, which fixed itself too readily on the more monstrous of Renaissance adventurers. So eventful a life induced credulity, and like the rest of her family, Caterina believed in the magical side of nature, dabbled in alchemy and mysteries, and was constantly experimenting with magnets that would produce family harmony, or universal salves, or celestial water, or any other improbable elixir that the wandering hucksters wished on her. At any age, at any time, Caterina would have been a remarkable woman, but the Renaissance allowed her wild temperament to riot.

Certainly the women of the Renaissance were portents. Elisabetta Gonzaga and Isabella d'Este are the founding sisters of the great literary salons that were to dominate the fashionable society of Western Europe for centuries. But the courts

Gardens were a proper setting for dalliance. When Lorenzo de' Medici planted a myrtle, sacred to Venus, in his botanical garden, he made the spot an appropriate setting for scenes such as the one on the facing page—a Florentine engraving depicting the Garden of Love. Milan had no great botanical garden, but Leonardo da Vinci made one room of the Sforza palace into a verdant bower by painting branches on its ceiling. The interlaced pattern on the sleeve of a girl thought to be Lodovico Sforza's daughter (right) was probably designed by Leonardo, too, but the lovely portrait is now attributed to Ambrogio de Predis.

of Italy were few, the families that were rich enough to indulge the tastes and pleasures of sophisticated women never numerous. The lot of most women was harsh; they toiled in the home at their looms or in the fields alongside their men. They bred early and died young, untouched by the growing civility about them, save in their piety. In the churches where they sought ease for their sorrows, the Mother of God shone with a new radiance, a deeper compassion, and seemed in her person to immortalize their lost beauty. Even the majority of middle-class women knew little of luxury or literary elegance. Their lives were dedicated to their husbands and their children; their ambitions were limited to the provision of a proper social and domestic background for their husbands; and they were encouraged to exercise prudence, to indulge in piety, and to eschew vanities. Yet their lives possessed a civility, a modest elegance, that made a strong contrast to the harsher experiences and more laborious days of medieval

women. Their new wealth permitted a greater, even if still modest, personal luxury. They could dress themselves more finely, acquire more jewels, provide a richer variety of food for their guests, entertain more lavishly, give more generously to charity. Although circumscribed, their lives were freer, their opportunities greater. It might still be unusual for a woman to be learned or to practice the arts, but it was neither rare nor exotic. And because they had more time, they were able to create a more active social life and to spread civility. After the Renaissance, the drawing room becomes an integral part of civilized living; indeed, the Renaissance education of a gentleman assumed that much of his life would be spent amusing women and moving them with words. As in so many aspects of life in Renaissance Italy, aristocratic attitudes of the High Middle Ages were adopted by the middle classes. Courtesy and civility spread downward, and the arts of chivalry became genteel.

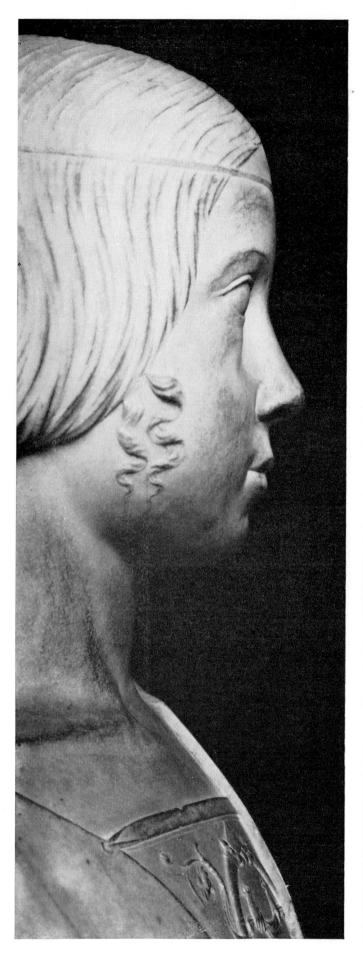 

The bust of Beatrice is by Gian Cristoforo Romano, Isabella's portrait by Leonardo.

Beatrice and Isabella d'Este

by MARIA BELLONCI

The stories of the two sisters, Beatrice and Isabella d'Este, are not easily interwoven in a single brief account, nor would either of them have relished such a thing, for they were lively, even peremptory individualists. Then, too, the span of their lives was very different. Of Beatrice, who died when she was twenty-two, we know only the transports, the vehemences, the proud and ambitious passions of adolescence. On the other hand, we know, step by step, Isabella's magistral development from youthful potential to the maturity that unfolds and reveals the meaning of a human life. They were born in Ferrara one year apart, Isabella in 1474 and Beatrice in 1475, thus preceding their four brothers—Alfonso, Ferrante, Ippolito, and Sigismondo.

The Este, one of the most ancient dynasties in Italy, had dominated Ferrara—a strategic area between Lombardy, Venice, and Emilia—and the broad luxuriant valley of the Po since the thirteenth century. They belonged to the Guelph party and for centuries had fought the Ghibellines in defense of the Church—and even fought the Church on those occasions when the popes had sought to meddle unduly in their affairs. These struggles, added to embroilments with neighboring powers or within the Este family, had forged a race of men who, no matter what their individual temperaments, were bold statesmen. In proof of this, the Ferrarese, a people proud to the point of arrogance and brave to the point of temerity (a Ferrarese proverb states that no man is too poor to own a dagger), never, not even when sorely provoked, rebelled against their masters.

It was Niccolò III, coming to power in 1402, who with the unsparing energy of his forebears consolidated the domain on a grand scale. Niccolò III was a resolute soldier, an astute manipulator of circumstance, and a man of constructive intelligence, who founded a university and was so solicitous of the people's welfare as to stipulate in his will that the monies allocated for his own funeral should be donated instead to public charity. Variously magnanimous and cruel (he ordered his son Ugo and his second wife, Parisina, beheaded when he discovered that they were lovers), Niccolò had exceptional sons who reigned in succession after him, the first two illegitimate, the third legitimate. Leonello, a levelheaded, shrewd politician, sowed the seeds of the flowering of humanism in Ferrara; Borso, also a statesman of peace, was equally devoted to the arts. The first legitimate son to rule was Ercole, a man whose temperament was so icy that it won him the nicknames "North Wind" and "The Diamond."

In 1473, two years after he ascended the throne at the age of forty, Ercole made the most political of marriages, wedding Leonora of Aragon, the daughter of King Ferrante of Naples, who was at the time a very powerful sovereign. The bride was beautiful —indeed, more than beautiful. Naturally regal, endowed with sound bourgeois sense and queenly courage, she was a sensitive, warm woman in whose company even the chilly nature of her husband was somewhat thawed.

Into this noble house and into a court traditionally cultivated and schooled in all the humanistic sciences, Isabella and Beatrice d'Este were born. From birth their destinies seem both divergent and parallel, patterned in counterpoint. Isabella, the first child, was born in May, 1474. She was welcomed with enthusiasm by parents, court, and populace, who saw in the blonde, softly rounded, comely infant girl the herald of the male, the heir to come. Beatrice was born a year later, in June, 1475, and the arrival of this second girl aroused no joy whatever. For her there were no celebrations, royal or popular, and no sign of love except perhaps the slightly humiliated tenderness of a mother who was beginning to feel marked by the most mortifying attribute of a princess —that of being "the mother of females." Both infants were given the names of queens, Isabella being called after her grandmother, the Queen of Naples, and Beatrice named for her aunt, who was wife to Matthias Corvinus, King of Hungary. One year passed and, fortunately, a son was born; Alfonso was received with noisy jubilation and festivities by all Ferrara. The next year another son, Ferrante, arrived. The girl infants had been redeemed.

Ferrante was born in September, 1477, in the Neapolitan palace of the grandfather whose name he took. That year the King, who was even less old in feeling than in fact, had married for the second time, taking as wife the delicate, elegant Giovanna of Aragon. Leonora was bid to pay her respects to her father and stepmother, and she went to Naples carrying with her not Alfonso—the heir had to remain in Ferrara—but the two girls and the still unborn child. The King of Naples, a dissipated man, richly endowed with ambiguous charms and a taste for the grandiose, took an immediate fancy to Beatrice. He recognized in her the long face and heavy cheeks, the jet-black hair and eyes, and the sulky, heavy-lidded

glance of the true Aragon. His marriage was duly celebrated, and Leonora's second son was born shortly thereafter, whereupon she was recalled in haste to Ferrara by Duke Ercole, who sniffed the scent of war in the air. She took only Isabella with her, leaving Beatrice and Ferrante in Naples, where they stayed for eight years. The little Este children played with their cousins, among whom was Isabella of Aragon, betrothed to Gian Galeazzo Sforza, who would one day clash with Beatrice in a mortal match.

In her grandfather's court in Naples, Beatrice learned that pride is vital and splendid, that every gesture of King and nobles was governed by an etiquette compounded equally of pomp and fantasy, and she realized, too, that power must be deserved. Accordingly, she began then to develop the intrepid patience that would stand her in such good stead when she returned to Ferrara to find herself in a position secondary in every respect. There was no doubt about it; the child who reigned in the Este palace was the elder sister, the gay and witty and wise Isabella. Everyone adored Isabella. No one had ever seen such an intense and vivacious feminine intelligence, such a felicitously inventive art in arranging things to her own liking while capturing the consent of others. Even the judicious Leonora was beguiled into calling her "my dearest and sweetest of daughters." Perhaps Isabella was not as beautiful as they say: she was not very tall and her features were not perfect, but she had a clear, rosy-cheeked complexion and a bearing of incomparable elegance. And her intelligence was prodigious. Her teachers were stunned when she translated smoothly and rapidly a selection from Virgil's *Bucolics* or a letter of Cicero; she mastered Greek and Latin grammar, committed Terence and Virgil to memory, learned to perform songs and madrigals on the lute, was first in perfecting the steps of a new dance, embroidered faultlessly, conversed —and held her own—with ambassadors.

The year 1480 was a year of engagements in the Este house, and it brought Isabella the worst bit of sheer bad luck that she was to suffer in her whole life. In April a marriage contract was signed between her and Francesco Gonzaga, heir of the neighboring Marquis of Mantua. Scarcely a month later, an ambassador arrived from Milan to ask for Isabella's hand on behalf of Lodovico Sforza. Il Moro, as he was called, was the guardian of his young nephew, the Duke of Milan, but in actuality Lodovico was master of both his nephew and half of Italy. Since

Duke Ercole would never offend the Marquis of Mantua, who was his friend and ally, by reneging on agreements already signed, he took advantage of Il Moro's suit to marry off both of the pawns he held in the game of alliances. Let the first daughter go to the Marquis of Mantua, and let the second, who was the equal of her sister—legitimate, healthy, intelligent, and cultivated—go to Il Moro. (Alfonso d'Este, his eldest son, was already affianced to Anna Sforza, the Duke of Milan's sister.) Lodovico was not enthusiastic, and he accepted this engagement of expediency with perceptible disappointment.

Happily, a fresh and quite unusual relationship developed between Isabella and Francesco; the innocent and touching charm of the girl surprised and beguiled her fiancé, a vigorous and already experienced fifteen-year-old youth, even before it made him fall in love with her. But between Beatrice and Lodovico there was nothing of this sort. He who was judged the first man in all Italy, and who was certainly one of the richest, scarcely remembered the dark-haired girl, twenty-five years younger than he, who awaited him in Ferrara. On the contrary. Surrounded by the elaborate pomp of his court, he was flaunting his passion for the beautiful, exquisitely mannered Cecilia Gallerani (*see* page 122), the unofficial queen of Milan. It is not certain whether Beatrice knew of her rival or not, for contemporary accounts record only the silences of the young Este girl in this period.

In February of 1490, ten years after her engagement, Isabella went as a bride to the castle in Mantua, her resolute, slim sixteen years transported there in the triumphal carriage designed by Ercole de' Roberti; his, too, was the hand that painted the thirteen chests that followed her, in which her elegant trousseau was packed. She was followed also by her father, mother, sister, her three brothers, the whole band of her Este relatives, and the acclamations of seventeen thousand spectators. Isabella was going to a youthful court, since her delightful parents-in-law, Federigo and Margherita, who so warmly wanted her in their family, had died while still young. Her husband was twenty-five, his two brothers twenty-one and sixteen. Her new eighteen-year-old sister-in-law was Elisabetta Gonzaga, a woman of pale and heraldic beauty, who was the wife of Guidobaldo, Duke of Urbino. (For a time no one suspected the burning secret of the unconsummated marriage which Elisabetta endured with love and shame and a pas-

sional exhaustion which bordered on despair.)

That February, the most gloomy, foggy month in the year for lacustrine Mantua, was for Isabella a period of acquisition, confirmed by a whole series of new possessions beginning with her husband. She served no novitiate as daughter-in-law, but came at once into both title and power, rising to the demands of her role with the sparkling glance and lightness of step that lent wings to her sixteen years. Isabella realized that her marriage had the rigorous political significance of an alliance between reigning families, for on this score she had learned her father's lesson well, and she responded to her husband's passion like a woman who appreciates the quality of being warmly involved in marriage without being swept away or losing her own identity thereby. As for her young husband, one of the most ugly and fascinating men in Italy, he was the brave soldier, the complete gentleman, a graceful and entertaining conversationalist in the Lombard style, a lover of gentle sensuality—and so delightfully ingenuous as to have his humanists compose poems that he sent to his literary-minded wife as his own. He, too, was overcome with admiration for Isabella, but this admiration, which perforce grew greater day by day, was destined to alter in kind. Francesco Gonzaga scarcely realized it, but presently he began to lose confidence in this wife who was like no one else, and who, while obedient to his smallest wish, seemed always to protect a growing independence of her own. Yet she was so loyal, so adroit in sensing whatever could benefit the little Mantuan state and the Gonzaga family, that it was difficult to find cause for reproach. The new Marchioness of Mantua was clearly the pride of the city; her praises were sung, indeed, throughout Italy.

In Ferrara, Beatrice was awaiting her husband. She should have married immediately after her sister, but Lodovico Il Moro was bound to his Cecilia Gallerani and showed not the least concern about joining his betrothed. However, Ercole d'Este was not a man to accept even a small affront, and at a certain point he allowed a hiss of irritation to reach Lodovico's ear. Il Moro, knowing that he needed Ferrara to protect Lombardy against the threat of its centuries-old enemy, the republic of Venice, and further pressured by the marriage pact between his niece Anna and the Este heir apparent, finally brought himself to a decision. And once he had decided, he threw the gates of the Lombard palaces wide, opened the coffers of his treasury, and set in motion the mighty machinery of the Milanese court, which teemed with artists, poets, mathematicians, scholars, and a spirited nobility well disposed toward any courtly enterprise. The wedding date was set for January, 1491, and the place chosen was the castle in Pavia. Whereupon not a day passed without messengers arriving in Ferrara from Milan; they brought gifts, like the famous necklace of pearls strung with flowerets of gold and embellished with splendid drops of rubies, pearls, and emeralds; the masters of ceremonies came to arrange for the bride's journey —and to recommend that Beatrice bring many embroidered and bejeweled gowns; artists came, like Gian Cristoforo Romano, sculptor and engraver, accomplished lute player, and a man of wide literary attainments, who did the bust of Beatrice that is now preserved in the Louvre (see page 360).

With an intent, childish frown, Beatrice set about preparing herself for her unknown future, and she scarcely noticed the fearsome and memorable trip, as the ice-encrusted bucentaurs passed between the snowy banks of the canals. They arrived, finally, in a Pavia blanketed in snow, but inside the castle everything exuded warmth, wealth, and ease. Lodovico led his bride and her entourage through the princely dwelling, judged the most sumptuous in the world. At the last, he showed them its greatest treasure, the library begun by Gian Galeazzo Visconti and now rich in illuminated volumes and Greek and Latin manuscripts that Sforza had had copied in the most remote sanctuaries where they were preserved. In the face of all this splendor Beatrice appeared reserved, which everyone took to mean that she was timid. She had, in any case, no time to recover her self-possession after the wedding (which took place on January 17, the day chosen by the astrologers as propitious), for the next morning Il Moro left for Milan, to arrange, he said, for the celebrations, on which a legion of artists captained by Leonardo da Vinci and Bramante from Urbino were assigned to work. Yet how could one forget that Cecilia Gallerani was living there in the castle?

Eventually, the whole company moved on to Milan, and the spectacle in the great Lombard city surpassed belief: imaginatively staged tournaments, elegant dances, theatricals, masquerades, concerts of rare music, and fantasies of every kind. Energy, grandeur, verve, intelligence, and beauty joined to compose around the bride—who until yesterday had been quite obscure—a magnificent show of which she was the sole heroine. She could, it seemed, be sure even of her husband, from the moment she realized that her youth attracted him. She led him on to fondle her, used every charm to beguile him into kissing her before everyone; she offered him an olive-toned, girlish face that was flushed and alight with happiness; everything she did expressed her joy in having been called to so full a life. Before the eyes of her startled mother and sister, Beatrice let go; this was her moment, and it was as if she cut herself off from all else in a frenetic drive to seize it.

Once back in Mantua, Isabella saw to it that she was kept informed daily of what was going on in Milan. The accounts that reached her told of a whirl of amusements; of a morning, Beatrice, Galeazzo di Sanseverino, and Diodato the jester would set out in a carriage, singing three-part songs. They fished, they lunched, they played ball and fished again, and returned home in the evening deliciously exhausted. Beatrice won quick ascendancy over her husband, and if she did not succeed in dislodging Cecilia Gallerani from the castle, she did manage to break off, officially at least, that lady's relationship with Il Moro. In 1491 Cecilia married Count Bergamini, shortly after she gave birth to a son by Lodovico.

Beatrice never wearied of thinking up masquerades, jokes, or expeditions, with herself and her ladies dressed like commoners and spoiling for a squabble with some plebeians. His wife's exploits were irresistibly amusing to Il Moro, who laughed and applauded the girl. In Milan, Beatrice had found her cousin again—that Isabella of Aragon with whom she had played at the court in Naples some years before. From the day Beatrice arrived, she had had to concede first place in the city to Isabella, acknowledging the unchallengeable primacy of her position as wife of the actual Duke, Gian Galeazzo Sforza. However, Isabella of Aragon's greatness of spirit, her courage, and the exquisite refinement of her nature (later, her court was considered an incomparable school for pages and courtiers) did not suffice in her efforts to support her husband, given his weaknesses. The young Duke of Milan appeared to combine the vices of his Visconti and Sforza forebears, although in him they were enfeebled by a congenital frailty that enervated both his physical and intellectual capacities to the point of decay. The courageous daughter of King Alfonso took an unblinking view of her present and her future. The desire for power that she had recognized in Gian

Galeazzo's uncle and guardian was now increased by Beatrice's appetite, which had all the fierceness of youthful passion. And the moment was propitious for the ambitious couple. The French King, Charles VIII, was girding himself for the conquest of the kingdom of Naples; the Borgia Pope, Alexander VI, was unable to dissuade him; and Il Moro favored the foreigners' coming, calculating that in this way he could be quit once and forever of all difficulties with the Aragons, who were the natural protectors of Isabella and her children. Without a thought for her grandfather, King Ferrante, who had so doted on her, Beatrice abetted her husband ardently. When in January, 1493, Beatrice's first son was born—Ercole, later called Massimiliano—and royal celebrations were held in his honor, the unfortunate Duchess Isabella of Aragon wept her eyes out.

But her protests accomplished nothing. Late in 1494, Charles VIII was in Italy, received with a whirlwind of festivities by Lodovico and by Beatrice, who dazzled the King, even if she could not prevent some of his French followers from maliciously evaluating her and her displays of costume and charm with the observation that "the husk is worth more than the kernel." At Pavia the tragic colloquy between Isabella of Aragon and the French King took place, in which Isabella fell to her knees before him, in tears. With a vague promise of protection for the Sforza children, Charles VIII left. While the French King was on his way to the easy conquest of Naples, the ailing Gian Galeazzo succumbed to tuberculosis; the young Duke's last request was to see his horses and his greyhounds.

Lodovico quickly set in motion the plan he had long since prepared, and had himself proclaimed master of Milan by his fellow citizens. Shortly thereafter Emperor Maximilian granted the title to the dukedom to him and to his direct heirs, disregarding Gian Galeazzo's son. The fame and fortune of Beatrice, now crowned Duchess of Milan and applauded and sung and glorified by all, glowed brilliantly above the downfall of Isabella of Aragon.

But the Italian states quickly realized that the French King was not a guest to be taken into the house so casually, and they hastened to repair the damage already done. Even Milan joined the league established among Venice, Mantua, the Pope, and other principalities, for Il Moro had come to see that if foreign invasions were dangerous for all, they were most dangerous for him, since Charles made no secret of his wish to annex the duchy of Milan, which, he said, was his by right of inheritance. The armies gathered, and to avoid being captured in the kingdom he had just conquered, Charles VIII withdrew rapidly up the peninsula, and at Fornovo di Taro met the allied armies of the league in a battle from which he managed, as a result of the Italians' incompetence, to escape and to return to France. Italy rejoiced in her recovered liberty, and in Mantua, Isabella rejoiced to see her husband, Marquis Francesco Gonzaga, captain general of the league, the hero of Italy's liberation.

As the characters of the Este sisters became more differentiated, a disquieting rivalry gradually unfolded; it was in no sense petty, for both were women of noble spirit and bound by family loyalties, but it was perceptible, nevertheless. Beatrice's accent on luxury was too loud, verging on the satanic. Everyone found her eighty-four new dresses, heavily embroidered with gold thread, jewels, and pearls, excessive; they hung in a great room that, as her mother, Leonora, observed with graceful irony, resembled a "sacristy hung with all the canonicals." Too many rooms were too full of silver, ivories, precious glass, paintings, perfumes, lutes, clavichords, in quantities sufficient to "fill all the shops." Her unchecked imperiousness, her inconsiderate way of treating people about her, her cruel little games (she used to terrify ladies in waiting by pretending to set her horses upon them at an unbridled gallop), were in the same measure her way of vindicating her humiliated adolescence. When Isabella realized that the festivities and gifts that always awaited her in Milan were contrived to oppress her with honors, she found excuses to accept no further invitations. The immense wealth and the traditional magnificence of the Sforza court allowed Beatrice to have about her men like Bramante and Leonardo; she made her presence felt even in politics, and could engage in well-informed arguments with heads of state.

Another source of bitterness for Isabella was their relative maternal status. In the Sforza household there were two sons, Ercole and Francesco; in the Gonzaga household there were two daughters, Eleonora and Margherita. When Beatrice sent her congratulations on the birth of Eleonora, there was a hint of self-satisfaction in her including the greetings of her little son to the newborn girl. Isabella was so infuriated that when she bore her second daughter, she insisted that the infant be removed from the sumptuous cradle which had been prepared for a boy. But the fabulous life story of Beatrice hung suspended by the thread of fortune that had created it. Something had already gone wrong when, around 1495, Il Moro had fallen in love with an exquisite lady of the court, Lucrezia Crivelli, and had refused to give her up. Wounded in her feelings and in her pride, Beatrice had pretended to see nothing in order to preserve her own happiness intact, and she had mastered her pain with great strength of spirit. She was pregnant for the third time, and by dint of will power she managed to save appearances, laughing, singing, arranging, commanding. On January 2, 1497, she held a ball in her apartments, with the whole court present. Toward evening she was taken ill; she was carried to her bedchamber; at two o'clock that morning she gave birth to a stillborn son, and within an hour and a half she died.

The chronicles of all Italy were filled with accounts of Lodovico's immoderate, theatrical, and romantic grief, of his repentant self-reproaches, his passionate lamentings, of the funeral at Santa Maria delle Grazie in the midst of a thousand flaming torches and thousands upon thousands of wax tapers, and of the final appearance of Beatrice robed in gold upon her bier. The blinding suddenness of the misfortune had moved everyone; and those twenty-two years consumed with such intensity and fervor had, it seemed, upheld not only the fortunes of the Sforza family but also the destiny of the duchy. From the moment of Beatrice's death, the future of Milan began to cloud; soon after followed the French invasions, the fall of the Sforza, and the imprisonment of Lodovico, who was fated to die in exile, in the castle of Loches.

Isabella's sorrow, like her character, was genuine but controlled. Having shed her tears, she kept assiduously in touch with her brother-in-law, feeling for Il Moro—powerful and superstitious, fanciful and realistic, indecisive and stubborn as he was—the attraction that strong, clear-headed women feel for men who are full of self-contradictions and, when all is said, are weak. She recovered quickly from her grief, for she had to ward off the perils represented by the French flanking her to the north, Cesare Borgia threatening from the south, papal interventions, and the bitter hostility of the Venetians. With disdainful patience she endured a family tie with the Borgia when, in 1501, with the Borgia star in full ascendancy, Lucrezia married her brother Alfonso d'Este, the widower of Anna Sforza, and came to reign in Ferrara as its Duchess.

To Cesare Borgia she sent masks, perfumes, and compliments to hold him at bay; at the same time she exulted when the troops of Faenza successfully withstood the Borgia forces, which led her to formulate her clear concept of domestic policy: the prince must deserve to have the people make his cause their own by making their cause his. This was the traditional Este idea of good government and, joined with a feminine nature, it was now translated into a series of sustained, sensitive political moves. All Mantua acknowledged the efficacy of Isabella's policies during her regency in 1509, a period when the League of Cambrai united Europe in an alliance against the excessive power of Venice. It so happened that Francesco Gonzaga, commander for the league, was taken prisoner while he was sleeping, to the anger and disgust of his allies. The little Mantuan state faced a grave danger then, but Isabella demonstrated her courage and the growth of her personality by calling the people together, offering her young son for the public's acclamation, and enjoining the strictest orders upon the army—forbidding the garrisons of the fortresses bordering Venice to open their gates even were the Venetians to lead Marquis Francesco to the foot of the glacis and murder him before their eyes.

And so Francesco Gonzaga, languishing and ill in Venetian prisons, waited to be liberated, while, in Mantua, Isabella played a most artful hand. Caught in a fearsome vise between venomous foes and suspicious friends, she succeeded in keeping the Mantuan frontier free not only of enemy assaults but also of allied garrisons. But because she had governed too well and ably, she found in 1512, the war ended, that she had lost the love of her husband. Shortly after his return from prison, Francesco Gonzaga wrote her in these words: "*We are ashamed* that it is our fate to have as wife a woman who is always ruled by her head." Not at all intimidated, Isabella replied with icy pride: "Your Excellency is indebted to me as never husband was to wife; nor must Your Excellency think that, even did you love and honor me more than any person in the world, you could repay my good faith." Day after day she watched as her husband became increasingly alienated. When she sensed that she had fallen from power, she protested in a way all her own—not in words but in action. She traveled, and one of her destinations was Rome.

Isabella arrived in Rome like a reigning sovereign who was securely established in her own kingdom.

No one suspected her real situation. In the splendid company of the papal court of Leo X, surrounded by a continuous thunder of acclamation, amid all the banquets and theatricals and the penetrating, brilliant talk, she permitted no one to guess the contrast between such homage and her true vagrant isolation. She was buoyed up by her taste for experimentation, and the thought of her children helped her—the sons, that is, who must be guided toward great futures. (Her daughters she cared very little about—at least at this time. When two of them, Ippolita and Paola, entered a convent, she did not weep, but with a license verging on blasphemy, declared herself content, since this son-in-law would cause her no trouble.) Her sons, Federigo, Ercole, and Ferrante, were educated and watched over with daily, unremitting attention. The first was destined to the throne, the second to the Church, the third to the army. But Federigo was clearly her favorite; her affection for him was the supreme expression of her maternal love, her pride, and even a kind of hope in the future. This explains how she should separate from the husband who had stripped her of all authority, for she knew that in Federigo she had a future, and she planned her own vindication in that future. When Francesco Gongaza died in 1519, worn down by illness, Isabella's tears paid tribute only to the memories of her youth. Since her son was far away in France, the one urgent and essential thing for her to do was to rule.

It was 1519, Isabella was forty-four, and to reign was the natural expression of her nature. "She trusts no one and will know the motive of everyone," observed the Mantuans, who were never displeased to have power exercised by a woman of her sort of matriarchal nobility.

Federigo, the nineteen-year-old Marquis, was at first overwhelmed by his mother and lived in a state of admiring subjugation, with little more than the occasional restiveness of an unruly colt. She governed well; she maintained a difficult equilibrium among the great powers that divided Italy, and she was the first to foresee that Charles V would prevail over the French King, Francis I. But Federigo presently discovered that his life was partitioned into two roles: one, that of the submissive son, and the other his own, that of an independent, effective man. It was only natural that the second seemed to him the good and true self, all the more so since he had the support of a young and extremely beautiful woman in proving it. The young Marquis was so in love with

Isabella Boschetti, called La Boschetta, that he refused to marry to ensure the continuity of the dynasty. The young woman fueled Federigo's idea of his total independence, and he responded by surrounding her with every royal honor, costly and magnificent gifts, courtiers, artists, and literary figures, while by sly, imperceptible moves he eliminated his mother little by little from direct participation in the government. He asked her advice, but privately —and gradually Isabella was relegated to the role of an elderly woman.

No moment in her life had been so serious as this, and once again she bided her time, waiting for her son's mistress to fall from favor. Isabella was coming to recognize bitterly that her beloved Federigo was a weak man, and worse. "The Marquis of Mantua is not good for much," Guicciardini wrote with terse accuracy in 1527, when Federigo and the Duke of Urbino opened the way by their betrayal for the German mercenaries to march south to sack the city of Rome.

Isabella d'Este had returned to Rome in 1525, and so shared in the final days of that tempered, cultivated, Christian paganism that was to be shattered by the brutal impact of the Lutheran gangs from Frundsberg. Rome had received her gloriously in the time of Leo X, and now, under another Medici, Clement VII, it welcomed her again. And again Isabella stood firm in her loyalty to Mantua and to the Gonzaga who had so often betrayed her. Thanks to her subtly modulated tactics, she succeeded in securing the red hat for her second son, Ercole, only a few days before the dreadful pillage of the city began. Federigo was writing her from Mantua meanwhile. He had seen the imperial hordes at first hand, and found them crude, fanatical, blasphemous, and innately hostile to the soil and civilization of Italy. Again and again he begged his mother to return to Mantua, but these entreaties had the opposite effect: they suggested a strengthening of her position that might restore her to an ascendancy over her son far above the poor physical expedients of La Boschetta. And then the terrible day, May 6, 1527, arrived. From within Palazzo Colonna, where she was securely housed, she heard the mercenaries howling through the streets, bent on robbing, killing, and torturing. Isabella remained steadfast; she took in gentlewomen, princes, ambassadors, priests, and friars who were seeking shelter; she encouraged them, shared her meager food with them, and with them trembled and hoped. Only when they were out of danger did she leave the ravaged city and make her way northward to Mantua without undue haste. Fired by the evidences of her courage, the populace was all for her and against La Boschetta. And gradually La Boschetta had to give in, retreat, and remove herself, allowing Federigo to marry Princes Margherita Paleologa—the wife chosen for him by Isabella.

Margherita was gentle, sensible, and in love; she had just the right degree of native shrewdness; and as her dowry she brought with her nothing less than a whole region—Monferrato. She bore her husband numerous sons, gave him constant, discreet support, and got along extremely well with her great mother-in-law, who gladly placed full confidence in her. Federigo's political future was a limited one, subject as it was to the will of Charles V, but within the sphere of his large and splendid court he was active, buying painting and sculpture, building extensively with his Giulio Romano, quarreling with his Aretino. Toward the mother to whom he owed so much, including his title of Duke, which Charles V granted to the rulers of Mantua, he continued to behave courteously and even affectionately, but he persisted in keeping her isolated. Her greatness of spirit was truly tried, yet her response was a gesture generous to the point of scorn; in effect, she offered to be his accomplice against her own interests, helping him to conceal her humiliation so that no one could suspect him of an unworthy action.

The futures of the other sons had been secured. Ferrante, the future Viceroy of Milan, would be a good general. Ercole would be a great cardinal, a major figure at the Council of Trent, and would come very near to wearing the triple crown; and when his elder brother died at barely forty years of age, leaving an infant heir, he would assume the regency of the duchy of Mantua and perform his duties with the prudence, the severity, and the awareness of his mother.

Although no one needed Isabella now, as she moved into her sixtieth year, she was stronger and more animated and gay than ever, always ready and eager to go to the heart of a problem. Respect and consideration were paid her in abundance; her court was, as always, exemplary and, as always, crowded with literary figures, courtiers, and beautiful and witty young women whom she formed and trained in her own school according to her own bold and modern moral concept—allowing them freedom but in-sisting that they be virtuous. In her new apartments on the ground floor of the ducal palace, she collected about her the noblest and finest creations that her age was producing. The famous rooms, the *Studiolo* and the *Grotta* with the celebrated door by Tullio Lombardo, were the talk of all the courts of Italy. Poems, songs, travel memoirs, writings of every description, flowed into Mantua from all over to satisfy her ever livelier curiosity. Nor did the heavy traffic in elegant luxuries diminish—the gowns, jewels, perfumes, cosmetics, adornments, and extraordinary objects like the doll "dressed inside and out exactly like her [Isabella]," which Francis I requested and received to send to his wife in France. But above all this, Isabella's inner life was fortified by a secret. This secret was called Solarolo.

Solarolo was a tiny possession in Romagna that belonged to her. This was all Isabella needed. She received secretaries as if they were ministers; she directed and adjudicated and enforced her own methods of management with almost affectionate ease, since here she was legitimately fulfilling her true nature and was finally giving expression to the passion for ruling that could have made her a magnificent queen. As she listened to her secretaries' reports, with the maps of Solarolo spread before her, and around her her collections of paintings, marbles, bronzes both ancient and modern, her crystal and her alabaster and her ornate clocks, she was expressing her personality fully and harmoniously.

Most rare Phoenix, the humanists called her, reviving the worn image to honor her—but more than that, a most rare woman. Yet why does posterity remember her? In both her marriage and her maternity she was sorely disappointed; emotionally hers was a wintry life. She has survived thanks to her individuality, to the awareness of self that she sustained with all the force and conviction of a style. It was a style fashioned by the mind; it was the effective alliance of idea and action; and it characterized Isabella's life until her death on February 13, 1539. It is impossible to say whether Beatrice would have been able to develop in the same way, had she lived to the same age. But both these princesses, these creatures of lucid and resolute intelligence, had understood one thing—the necessity of living according to an inner order that vibrates in continual response to the external world, and by which we surmount the error of facts, the harshness of circumstance, and the inertia of our surroundings.

Translated by Adrienne Foulke

THE NEW WOMAN

In a world which idolized beauty, princesses, courtesans, and housewives spent hours enhancing their charms. "Neither Giotto nor any other painter uses color better than the Florentine women," one critic complained, but the monk Angelo Firenzuola gallantly announced that "The beautiful woman is the loveliest object of contemplation, and beauty is the best of God's gifts to the human being." His enthusiasm exemplified the age's new liberalism, which gave woman the time and the freedom to display her beauty as well as the opportunity to write sonnets and rule duchies. Venus was the symbol of beauty and womanhood, and it was under her sign that astrologers located the Garden of Delight, which is illustrated in the charming miniature above, depicting men and women bathing in a fountain of love, while musicians, singers, and a pair of ardent lovers echo their harmony.

THE BRILLIANT
ESTE COURT

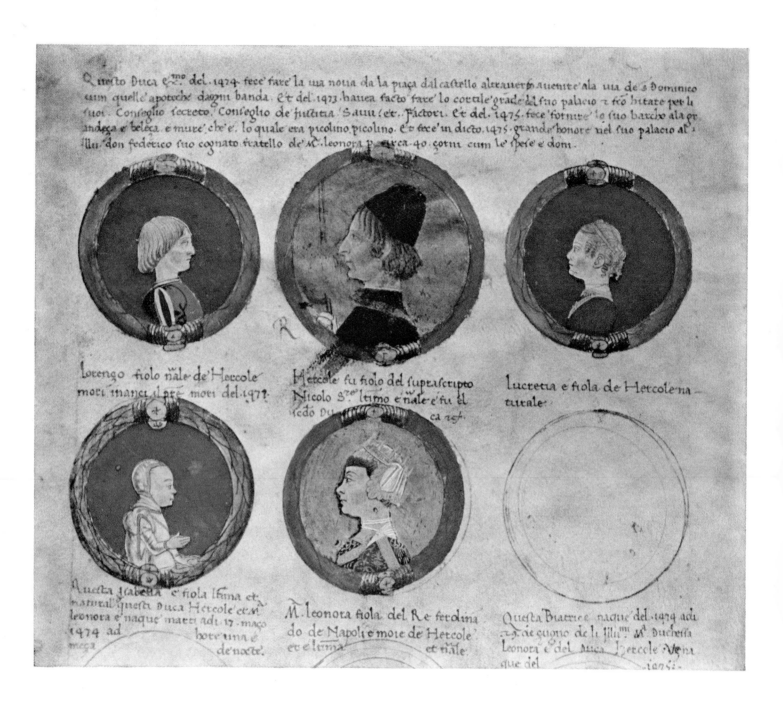

*An unfinished Este family tree shows Isabella as a
baby, dressed in a white gown and a tightly fitted cap.
Her mother, the Duchess Leonora, is shown next to
her, beside a frame left empty for a picture of Beatrice,
whose name and birth date are written under it. Duke
Ercole appears in the top row, under a list of his accomplishments; on either side are his two illegitimate
children, Lucrezia (at right) and Lorenzo, whose
early death in 1471 is recorded beneath his portrait.*

When Borso d'Este (below) died of malaria, his brother Ercole became Duke of Ferrara. He wed a Neapolitan princess, the beautiful Leonora (left), and their daughters married well, too. Above are Isabella's and Beatrice's husbands, the bearded Francesco Gonzaga and Lodovico Sforza.

The aunt of the Este sisters, Bianca, "The Virgin of Este," was famous for her writings; they displayed a Latin style rivaled in purity only by her virtue. The girls' mother, the Duchess Leonora, was an accomplished harpist, and the future Duke Alfonso, their brother, performed on the violin in public, with talent inherited from an Este uncle, the late Duke Leonello, who had been a virtuoso at the guitar. Duke Ercole, the father of the girls, translated Latin plays and staged them in the palace courtyard, while their cousin wrote pastoral dramas and composed musical settings of sonnets for Isabella to sing.

The sisters' talents equaled those of their relatives, and they were notable as well for their generous patronage of artists. The masque, which mixed comedy with dancing and music, developed at Ferrara, and the first permanent theater in modern Europe was constructed there. Piero della Francesca and Francesco Cossa frescoed rooms in Este palaces, and Cosimo Tura earned four golden florins when he painted a portrait of ten-year-old Beatrice to be sent to her fiancé as a Christmas present. The Duchess Leonora brought to Ferrara embroiderers from Spain and tapestry makers from Florence and Milan, and her collection of jewelry was considered the most artistic in all Italy (although it was often pawned to raise money for her husband's wars). With these female paragons of culture and virtue, the court of Ferrara provided a congenial shelter for the poets Boiardo and Ariosto, whose romances of chivalry, based on an idealization of women, established a new tradition of courtly poetry.

CHILDHOOD

Curious but shy, the little girl at right (a detail of the Crivelli Annunciation *on page 383) peeks from behind a wall to inspect an angel. Above, a boy of the same age looks trustingly at his grandfather, a Florentine merchant painted by Ghirlandaio.*

Despite the antics of his schoolfellows and a dwarf, Beatrice d'Este's son Massimiliano (right) briefly heeds his tutor's lesson. With fewer distractions, the boy below studies Cicero, whose initials M. T. C. are inscribed on the bench behind him.

Man's happiness, wrote Agnolo Pandolfini, lay not in public office or fame, but in his wife and children, his financial success, his reputation, and his friends. To ensure a happy marriage, he ought to wed a woman sufficiently young to be malleable, since he would have to teach her the obligations of motherhood and the art of managing the home. Paternal authority was supreme in the Renaissance household, but in all normal circumstances the mother was expected to supervise the day-to-day routine.

High on the list was the children's education, which began early, under the aegis of a tutor. Prodigies of ten or eleven wrote Latin letters, memorized pages of poetry, and entertained state visitors with eloquent and prolonged recitations from the classics. When it came to learning, there was little distinction between the sexes. "A little girl ought to learn Latin," Cardinal Bembo wrote. "It puts a finishing touch to her charms." They were also taught to embroider and to dance, and to supervise servants, but most of their domestic training was postponed until after marriage, when the real molding process began.

In a detail of Botticelli's The Birth of Venus *(left), the goddess, riding the waves on a gleaming shell, is wafted toward shore by zephyrs amid a shower of roses. The painting illustrates part of a long poem which Poliziano wrote in commemoration of Simonetta's tourney. Years after Simonetta's death, Piero di Cosimo, in a memorial portrait (right), symbolized her fatal illness by painting an enamel serpent coiled around her neck.*

GODDESS OF LOVE

Born at Porto Venere, the legendary site of Venus' rising from the sea, the lovely Simonetta Vespucci came to Florence and dazzled the city with her beauty. Giuliano de' Medici, falling in love with her, ordered a lavish tourney held in her honor, and commissioned Botticelli to paint her portrait on the banner which he carried into the lists. With that exception, all of the supposed portraits of Simonetta were done after she had died from consumption at the age of twenty-three. Sandro Botticelli recalled her loveliness years later when he used her likeness in the *Primavera.* "It seemed impossible," Lorenzo de' Medici said, "that she was loved by so many men without any jealousy and praised by so many women without envy," yet it seems to have been true. Faithful to her husband (a cousin of the navigator Amerigo Vespucci), Simonetta became a symbol of beauty for artists and poets, an embodiment of the Renaissance belief that perfection was possible.

OVERLEAF: *With her hand raised in blessing, Venus welcomes the advent of spring in Botticelli's allegory,* La Primavera. *The artist is thought to have painted Simonetta Vespucci as Venus, as the three Graces, and as the flower-decked nymph standing at the right.*

In a series of water-color miniatures, an anonymous Venetian artist recorded scenes of a courtesan's life. Above, a harlot leans provocatively out of her window to dicker with two prospective customers dressed in carnival costume; below, another entertains a bearded guest within her sumptuous chamber, while a pet dog looks on.

THE COURTESAN

Standing nude at their windows to entice customers inside, the harlots of Venice enjoyed the busiest professional practice in all Italy. Rome had a more distinguished collection of learned courtesans, whose intellectual attainments rivaled their other skills, but when the popes periodically expelled all harlots from the city they gravitated to Venice. Even there, however, they found professional hazards. They could be punished with a flogging for trafficking with Turks or Jews, and the prevalence of the dreaded French disease daily jeopardized their careers, if not their lives. Harlots had to take a holiday to celebrate religious festivals, even though the republic lost tax revenues when the profits of their trade decreased. Still, almost 12,000 registered prostitutes managed to eke out a living at a time when Venice's total population was only 300,000. One catalogue, listing the city's most notorious harlots, names 215 who were especially accomplished, but warns the enterprising tourist, who might be interested in striking up friendship with all of them, that his curiosity would cost a total of 1,200 scudi.

Prices were high, but the more cultivated courtesans provided their customers with intellectual refreshment, too. Despite clients' complaints that conversation was as expensive as love, salons held by famous courtesans often rivaled those of the great princesses like Isabella d'Este. Open to the public for a fee, the salons attracted the greatest men of the age to listen to music, to dance, and to engage in philosophical conversations. Courtesans were trained to be intelligent company; and in studying for their profession they took lessons in singing, dancing, Latin, letter-writing, painting, and deportment, and one earned immortality by memorizing everything that Petrarch and Boccaccio ever wrote. In tribute to their unsurpassed command of the courtly graces, humanists coined the euphemism *cortigiana* to distinguish these talented ladies from their less fortunate sisters toiling in ordinary brothels.

In décolleté finery, a pair of Venetian courtesans (right), in a painting by Carpaccio which Ruskin called "the best picture in the world," take the air on a balcony, surrounded by their pet birds and dogs, a peacock, and a page. The Senate tried to limit the splendor of harlots' costumes, but its efforts were in vain; to keep pace with honest women, prostitutes flaunted costly dresses, bleached their frizzed hair, and tottered about on high clogs like the red ones in Carpaccio's picture (beneath the peacock's tail). Dressed as elegantly, if more sparsely, another Venetian courtesan appears above, wearing richly jeweled headdress, earrings, necklace, and opulent red cloak.

THE FACE OF REALITY

Painters, poets, and courtiers chattered endlessly about beauty, but beauty faded quickly in fifteenth-century Italy. Brutal wars racked the countryside, plague raged in the cities, and the image of love, like Dante's Beatrice, Petrarch's Laura, and the adored Simonetta Vespucci, perished quickly. Brides were often widowed while still young, for Renaissance men preferred to marry late in life; and remarriage was frowned upon, for it was considered a disgrace to the memory of a dead husband. In Perugia second marriages had to take place after dark, and they were often disrupted by rioters, hooting derisively outside the wedding chamber. Maidens without dowries were even less fortunate than widows; with no prospects of marriage, they were sent off to finish their days virtually imprisoned in a convent. Theorizing about ideal proportions and the spiritual value of beauty, artists painted idyllic scenes of life as they wished it to be, but there were some who preferred to portray it as they saw it. Mary Magdalen, weeping over her sins in the desert, only made Titian see another plump Venetian nude with long ringlets and a fresh complexion, but Donatello, treating the same austere theme, had chosen instead to carve a haggard, repentant Magdalen (opposite), whose gaunt face and deep-set eyes reflect her suffering.

Pointing to herself as an example, a worn and aged woman (right), painted by Giorgione, displays the motto COL TEM-PO, *to warn that "with Time" everything meets destruction. The ravages of both sin and time show in the deeply moving face of Mary Magdalen (opposite), Donatello's last statue.*

In contrast with the calm beauty of Antonello da Messina's Virgin Annunciate *(above), Crivelli's* Annunciation *(opposite) shows Mary in a scene of splendor. Curiously, neither artist was in the main stream of the Italian Renaissance. Antonello was a follower of the Van Eycks; Crivelli worked in Padua, only lightly touched by the surge of culture.*

THE IMAGE
OF MARY

When workmen digging on the Appian Way in 1485 unearthed the perfectly preserved corpse of a Roman maiden, thousands of pilgrims filed by to marvel at her unequaled beauty. It seemed to prove what humanists had claimed—that the ancient world was superior to the Christian era. But most Italians of the time never lost sight of another, far more compelling ideal of incorruptible beauty—the Virgin, whose image protected every house, church, and wayside shrine. Despite the inroads of paganism, the Church kept a firm hold on Renaissance Italy. Whatever the signs of corruption in the Church, the great mass of the people retained their genuine devotion. Even the warring factions of Siena, once they had placed the keys of the town before the image of Mary and vowed to maintain civil peace, faithfully kept their promise for years. And for every woman acclaimed for her beauty or her wit, the Renaissance produced its saints. Many of them were simple women, like the Genoese matron, Caterinetta Fieschi, who established shelters for incurables who had been expelled from hospitals to die on the streets. Housewives gave their time and money to orphanages, nursed the sick, and distributed alms, and when they died, asked to be buried in the habit of a nun. Even Martin Luther, who deplored most Italian practices, found himself admiring the good works of Italian women.

· LIBERTAS · ECCLESIASTICA ·

Built in 1529 on the banks of the River Indre,
the château of Azay-le-Rideau was one of the
first masterpieces of Renaissance art in France.

THE SPREAD OF THE
RENAISSANCE

In the autumn of 1511, Erasmus, the most distinguished scholar of Northern Europe, took up his lodgings again in Queens' College, Cambridge—a cold, bleak room that overlooked the marshes of the fens. He was poor, he was frightened of the plague that raged about the University, he was very lonely. He had been swept to England by the tide of the Italian Renaissance, not for the first but for the third time. For five wearisome years Erasmus moldered in Cambridge until he could stand the poverty and the ignorance no longer, and off he went on his journeys again, to the Netherlands, to Switzerland, to Germany, always carrying with him the memory of those years in Italy when he had discovered himself. The new learning had filled him with such hope that not even the sorrows and hardships of his personal life could eradicate it. In 1517 he could still write, "Immortal God, what a world I see dawning! Why can I not grow young again?" Nor was Erasmus unique. In London one of the most

gifted, yet wayward, of Florentine sculptors, Torrigiano, was modeling, under the soaring Gothic arches of Westminster Abbey, the first Renaissance tombs of Northern Europe, built to immortalize Henry VII and his wife, Elizabeth of York. For decades the currents created not only by cataclysmic events such as the invasion of Italy by the French kings, but also by the excitement of the new learning, had been drawing such men as Erasmus and Torrigiano into or out of Italy. And that sense of wonder, of a new world and a new dawn of the spirit, touched less sensitive men than Erasmus. Edward IV conferred the Garter, the highest order of English chivalry, on the Duke of Urbino, and the court of Windsor witnessed the embassy of Castiglione who came to receive it for his master. So profound was Henry VII's respect for the Italian scholarship that he asked Polydore Vergil to write what became the first serious and dispassionate study of England's history. Indeed, the presence of Erasmus in England

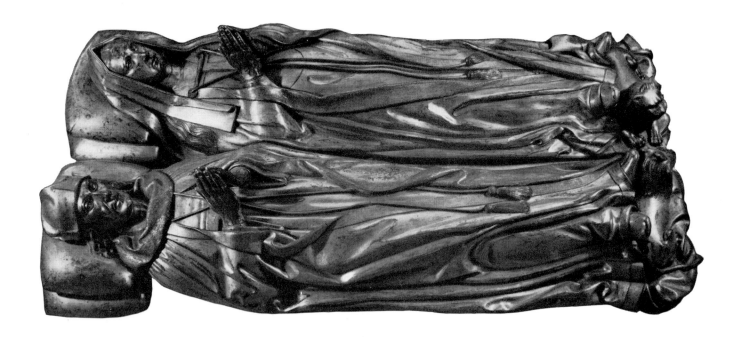

The bronze figures of King Henry VII of England and his Queen, Elizabeth of York, rest atop their elaborate Renaissance tomb in Westminster Abbey. Made by an Italian sculptor, Pietro Torrigiano, who had the dubious distinction of having broken Michelangelo's nose in a youthful brawl, the tomb is one of the earliest monuments of the Tudor style. Francis Bacon later commented that the penny-pinching King Henry "dwelleth more richly dead than he did alive in any of his palaces."

was due entirely to a devoted band of humanists—Linacre, Grocyn, and Colet—who had studied in Padua, Florence, and Rome, seeking to acquire facility in Greek and a knowledge of the old as well as the new philosophies. Their attitude was deeply Christian, and their aim was to perfect their theology through a more exact knowledge of the early Fathers. The employment of Pietro Torrigiano was also due to the same band of humanists, which included Lord Mountjoy as its patron and John Fisher as its chaplain, both of whom were intimately connected with the English royal family. What was true of England was also true of the Netherlands, of Germany, and of Spain.

As the Renaissance spread beyond the Alps, it was checked in Italy. In 1495 Charles VIII invaded Naples and in so doing unleashed thirty years of carnage. In the Lombard plain battle followed battle, draining away wealth, disrupting trade, heaping up taxes, destroying conditions favorable to art and

learning. Furthermore, the riches of the New World, so recently discovered, poured into Spain, the Netherlands, France, and England, but not into Italy; wealth went west, and with it art. And then came Luther, who in 1517 hammered his Protestant theses to the church door of Wittenberg. To hold off the Reformation, the Papacy needed a sterner spirit; the luxurious and wanton times of the Borgia and Medici were brought to an end, and a militant asceticism replaced the self-indulgence of Renaissance Rome. No wonder Vasari regarded the venerable Michelangelo as a relic of the age of heroes. This lonely, solitary artist had become the symbol of a time that had passed.

By 1500 Italy exerted a hypnotic influence, and just as the princes of the Western world wished to acquire the services of Italy's great painters and sculptors, so, too, did the artists of this outer world feel themselves drawn to Italy. The great Flemish school of painters might be secure within its own

great tradition and therefore possess little or no sense of
inferiority when confronted with the brilliance of the Italian
achievement; and in fact it contributed as much in technique and originality as it derived from Italy. The same
was not true, however, of the French or the German artists.
They had been ravished by the books of engravings of Italian
pictures that had begun to circulate after 1470. Crude as
these were, they sufficiently hinted the beauties of the masters
they copied to excite an overwhelming curiosity. Albrecht
Dürer, as a young apprentice at Nuremberg, somehow acquired engravings of Pollaiuolo and Mantegna. Already in
a tentative, schoolboyish, and rather shocked manner he had
begun to draw from the nude, but these engravings helped
to release his spirit from the harsh, moral, and cruelly realistic
treatment of naked women that had become traditional in
Gothic Germany. Engravings were not enough, however, and
try as he might the secret of the Italian painters seemed to
elude him. He believed that the formula for successful painting of the human figure, like some ancient mystery, was kept
hidden by Italian artists. He sought the magic formula in
Italy itself, deepened his imagination, improved his technique, but never found what he sought, and to his death the
Gothic tradition into which he had been born held him in
thrall. Yet without his Italian experiences and without his
preoccupation with Italian art, his own achievement would
have been less noble. As with Dürer, so with scores of artists
great or small over the next four hundred years. They came
to Italy as on a pilgrimage, for here was the source of their
art. The painting of El Greco is as idiosyncratic as any artist's
of Western Europe, yet his art is indelibly stamped with the
years that he spent in Venice. The way he draws, the glitter-
ing light that runs along the edge of his figures, derives from
Tintoretto, as his color does from Titian. The two greatest
French artists of the seventeenth century—Nicolas Poussin

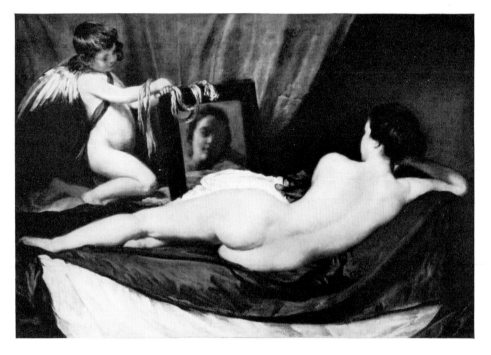

Giorgione's dreamlike Venus *(upper left) was one of the first classical reclining nudes in Venetian art, and was the model for many great paintings in the succeeding four centuries.* Titian's Venus of Urbino *(see page 301) is almost a direct copy. Although a great admirer of Titian, Diego Velázquez took a different and unusual pose for his* Rokeby Venus *(lower left), portraying her with her back discreetly turned. As paintings of the female nude were all but forbidden in inquisitorial Spain of the seventeeth century, it was perhaps the artist's way of appeasing the puritans.*

and Claude Lorraine—spent most of their working lives in Rome. Titian—his color, his atmosphere, even his figures—entranced Poussin. Again and again, artists of the highest genius—Velázquez, Rubens, Rembrandt, Goya, Renoir—paint the same themes, sometimes even copy the same pictures, that the artists of the Renaissance had first conceived and executed. Giorgione's reclining Venus haunts European painting like a dream. All who aspired to greatness in painting needed to make the long journey to Italy. Some, like Sir Joshua Reynolds, went in great comfort under the patronage of the rich; others, like Richard Wilson, went on foot and in poverty, painting for their bread. Until the twentieth century, the traditions created by the Italian Renaissance were those in which all Western European artists worked.

The French kings and their courtiers during their invasions of Italy were delighted by much that they saw in Milan and Venice: the Certosa of Pavia especially caught their imagina-tion. On the other hand, the austere and more truly classical buildings of Florence left them unmoved. So at first Italian influences on the new luxurious hunting lodges that the French nobility were building along the Loire combined, as at Chambord, the basic plan of a traditional medieval castle with the sophisticated elevation and greater comfort of an Italian palace. For a time this marriage of the old and the new satisfied Western Europe, but in the end, no matter how much inspiration might twist and turn within its national traditions, or frolic in the riotous decoration of the Baroque, it was drawn back, time and time again, to the purity of classical achievement, to Brunelleschi, to Bramante, to Palladio, and, finally—just before the Gothic revival destroyed architectural taste throughout Western Europe—to the Greek. In the visual arts, in its themes as well as its techniques, the achievements of the Italian Renaissance permeated Europe like an indelible stain. They expressed the world in which

"*If my head would win him a castle in France it should not fail to go,*" the humanist chancellor Sir Thomas More (left) said of Henry VIII, and lose it he did when he refused to support the King's divorce. Both he and Sir Thomas Cromwell (below), another chancellor who died on Tower Hill, are portrayed here by Hans Holbein, the German artist who was Henry's official court painter.

men wished to live—their dreams, their aspirations, as well as their actualities.

The arts of the Renaissance were not the only achievements that seeded themselves throughout the countries of the Western world. Changes that had taken place in Italy generations earlier were happening in Western Europe in the sixteenth century, with the result that a similar sort of society grew up with similar needs. Its basis, like Italy's, was mercantile and urban; and it was ambivalent toward the old feudal nobilities—longing for their grace, their courtliness, and their sense of privileged destiny, yet hating their special rights, their selfish and jealous independence that could cut so savagely across the needs of society as a whole, to the detriment of trade and profit. The new men longed for professional government, for a powerful person who could secure order and inculcate into a barbarous and anarchic society the *civilitas* of the ancients. For them the fountain of this politi-

cal knowledge was Italy: there the wisdom of the classical world, of Plato, of Aristotle, of Cicero, had been sifted and refined and adjusted to modern necessities. Even more importantly, the University of Padua could teach them the secrets of Roman government through the study of its laws. Again, the Italians had made a profession of diplomacy in Europe of the fifteenth century which had come to be regarded as essential to good government as statistical analysis is in the twentieth. Men of affairs in London, in Paris, in Brussels, in Madrid, in the towns and states of Germany, thought that they could only manage their new and baffling societies if they or their subordinates had studied in Italy. Most of Henry VIII's ministers of state—Wolsey, More, and Thomas Cromwell—were fascinated by the new learning, and they encouraged scholarship whenever they could. Wolsey endowed Christ Church, Oxford, in order to establish the study of the new humanities in England. Thomas More became the

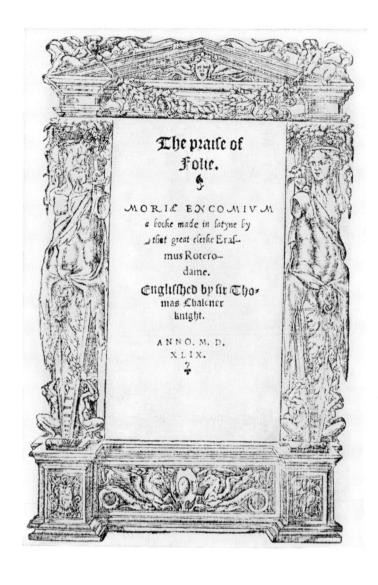

life-long friend of Erasmus. Cromwell lent his rare and precious Italian books to his friends and encouraged young men such as Thomas Starkey, who had spent years studying civil law at Padua in the household of Reginald Pole. (Pole, who was a Plantagenet and a kinsman of Henry VIII, maintained a small court of English scholars at the University of Padua.) This interest in Italian learning certainly had its practical aspects, but it captivated them all—even Cromwell, that hammer of the monasteries—at a deeper level than practical usefulness.

This new learning seemed to hold the secrets of life itself for most of them and, for the more sensitive, some of the secrets of eternity. More and his friends—Colet, Linacre, Grocyn—were deeply religious men. So were Lefèvre d'Étaples and his colleagues in Paris; so were Ulrich von Hutten and Reuchlin in Germany. They reverenced Italian scholarship, for it took them, via a knowledge of Greek, to the

purest texts of the New Testament. Here, they felt, they would find a faith cleansed from the impurities and evasions created by centuries of comment and explanation. By applying the new skills of philology and textual criticism which the Italian humanists had perfected, they would, they hoped, lay bare Christianity in its purest and most historical form and thereby strengthen the Church. This attitude toward religion fused with another, equally serious, but Flemish rather than Italian in origin. Before Renaissance influence had touched Northwestern Europe there had been a strong revival of religious mysticism, led by the Brethren of the Common Life, which had been given literary and devotional form by Thomas à Kempis in his *Imitation of Christ*. This mysticism stressed the importance of the individual's direct relation with God, and, by implication, lessened the importance of the priesthood and the Church. The search for historical truth, through scholarship, became linked with

As the alma mater of Pico della Mirandola and Bembo, the University of Padua (opposite) was one of the chief
centers of Italian humanism, and
throughout the sixteenth century its
famous teachers (Galileo was one) attracted students from all over Europe.
Among them were youths who were to
become kings of Sweden and Poland,
scholars who were to spread the Renaissance throughout Northern Europe.
Erasmus, shown at right in a portrait by
Hans Holbein the Younger, never studied at Padua, but did work at the library
of the University of Bologna. During
his lifetime, his satirical masterpiece
The Praise of Folly was printed forty
times; at left is the title page of an English edition published posthumously.

this search for truth in the exercise of the individual's religious conscience; and both became the seeding ground of
Protestantism.

No one is more typical of the linkage between Italian humanism and reformed Christianity than Erasmus, who prepared the ground for Luther. A bastard son of a priest, half-
tricked into monastic life, sensitive, excluded both by his habit
and temperament from an active life of the instincts, he concentrated his heart and mind on friendship with scholars of
like tastes. A man of formidable intellectual ability and exquisite literary gifts, his vast reputation was built up not only
by personal contact and familiar letters, but also by the new
invention of the printing press. His sharp satire—*The Praise
of Folly*—exploited the sensationalism which only the press
can give, and his Latin translation of the Greek Testament
established his reputation as a scholar with a rapidity that no
one could have achieved in earlier centuries. For Erasmus, the

institutions of the Church and its learning were encrusted
with silliness, stupidity, and barbarity. Christian faith could
never regain its pristine clarity until this dross of centuries
was cleared away. Yet he was no Protestant, no revolutionary,
and he retreated rapidly from the position toward which
Luther with his furious denunciations and precipitate actions
seemed to be dragging him. Naturally he refused to listen to
Albrecht Dürer's ardent plea: "O Erasmus of Rotterdam,
where wilt thou tarry? . . . Hear, Christian knight, ride
forth with the Lord Jesus . . . defend the right, obtain the
martyr's crown!" He preferred to die in his bed: scared of the
new age whose coming in 1517 he had welcomed with such
joy. But for Dürer the reformation of religion was an inspiration greater and deeper than any experience of his life, greater
even than his artistic experience in Italy.

Undoubtedly the scholars and critics had undermined, by
their sharp attack on contemporary religious practices, the

institutions of the Church; they mocked priests, bred resentment against papal taxation, and held the popes themselves up to the ridicule many deserved. Although some like Erasmus drew back, others such as Melanchthon and Peter Martyr, the Italian humanist, were prepared to go forward with Luther, feeling that he was leading them to the true dawn of a new age, to the rebirth of Christianity as Christ preached it. So the spirit of the Italian Renaissance, once it crossed the Alps, was diverted into new channels, plunging from the broad, sunlit meadows of secular delights into the dark ravines of religion.

Yet this political and religious twist to Italian influence was, for the early part of the sixteenth century, largely, if not entirely, confined to England, the Netherlands, and Germany. In France there were men like Erasmus, friends of his, deeply concerned with theology, deeply distrustful of scholasticism, as ardent as he was for pure religion. Yet they were not typical of French society as More and Colet or even Thomas Cromwell were typical of England. French society was more sophisticated, more secure, readier far to pursue that language of personal expression which lies at the heart of the Italian Renaissance. Much of Italian civilization—the gardens, the clothes, the furnishings and decoration of houses and palaces, the general civility of life, had entranced Philippe de Comines and many another noble Frenchman with the invading armies of Charles VIII and Louis XII. But it was Francis I who really fell in love with Italy and things Italian in spite of the fact that the greatest humiliation of his career —his defeat by the Emperor Charles V—took place at Pavia. He was the first prince outside Italy to begin a collection of paintings and sculpture by the great Italian masters. He persuaded Leonardo da Vinci to spend his last years at Amboise, close to his great hunting lodges at Blois and Chambord. He did everything he could to entice Michelangelo to live in

France and nearly succeeded. (He had to be content with a *Hercules* his agent bought.) With Benvenuto Cellini he was more successful. This fabulous rogue, a boastful, swashbuckling liar yet a craftsman of genius, entranced Francis, who tolerated his extravagance and forgave his bad temper for the sake of the embellishments (among them Cellini's superb gold saltcellar which is so justly famous) with which he was adorning his châteaux.

Francis I was not merely a collector; he wanted his court to outshine in literature and in manners, as well as in art, the most famous courts of Italy, and he flung his cloak of patronage on all who might bring distinction to his country. In this he was aided by his remarkable sister, Marguerite of Navarre, who can claim, perhaps, to be one of the most outstanding women of the Renaissance. She wrote the *Heptameron*, a bawdy collection of stories, after the style of Boccaccio; a mystical tract called *The Mirror of the Sinful Soul*, and a number of outstanding spiritual hymns. She corresponded with Erasmus, befriended Protestants, was accused herself as a heretic by the Sorbonne, and patronized Rabelais. Her court contained the whole world of letters, as complex and as strange as her own temperament. Indeed, many of the contradictions in her own self-expression reflected the contradictions of French artistic and intellectual society as it struggled to assimilate the achievements of Italy not only with its own Gothic traditions but also with those new horizons—intellectual as well as geographical—which the great discoveries had disclosed to the Western world. For Italian humanists, discovery lay in the past, in the art and history of their ancestors or their country's ancestors, the Greeks. With Frenchmen and with Englishmen, discovery also meant new worlds that knew neither Christianity nor Christian government nor Christian morality. To men such as Rabelais, Montaigne, Marlowe, Shakespeare, or Bacon, in-

Est donc a vous ma cousine et maistresse
Que mon labeur et mon honneur s'adresse
Vous requerant comme amye parfaicte
Que vous tenes ceste oeuure par moy faicte

PLVS·VOVSQVE·MOY

Es grandes et ineftimables Cronicqs: du grant τ enorme geant Gargantua: Contenant fa gcnealogie La grãdeur τ force de fon corps. Auffi les mcrueilleuσ faictσ darmes quil fift pour le Roy Artus: cõme Verrez cy apzes. Imprime nouuelfemẽt. 1532

---

security, anxiety, and elation mingled haphazardly and fused into art. Reverence for the past, a yearning for the safety of tradition, alternated with the intoxicating sense of the capacity of man, the uniqueness of his experience, and the splendor and freshness of the world about him.

In Rabelais, the greatest writer of the French Renaissance, this conflict was apparent both in his restless, troubled life and in his writings. Like Erasmus, he was a rebel monk who hated the ignorance and immorality of monastic life. He sought truth in the world. "Abandon yourself," he wrote, "to Nature's truths, and let nothing in this world be unknown to you." Rabelais followed his own dictum and it led him to strange places—to alchemy, to astrology, to the mysterious exoticism which seemed to offer new truth in the intellectual chaos of sixteenth-century Europe. And his great work *Gargantua and Pantagruel* is as odd and as moving as Rabelais' own quest for self-knowledge. Gargantua, Panta-

gruel, and Grangousier, the chief characters of this extraordinary fantasia, have the twisted extravagance of Gothic gargoyles. They are gross representatives of the instinctive life, yet full of satire and wisdom, capable of nobility and understanding. Above all they are in search of life and truth. And in the midst of their fantastic adventures comes the description of the Abbey of Thelema, a Utopian world that might have been dreamed by Castiglione. The turmoil and confusion of real life is stilled by the contemplation of realized ideals; men and women achieve the noble life. The whole book is written in a fabulous style, by a man utterly drunk with words. It is almost as if Rabelais had himself discovered language. This mixture of barbarity and civility, of satire and sincerity, entranced the French court. The Church might be scandalized, the Protestants outraged, but Pantagruelism became chic, the fashion of the aristocracy. It was original, it was in tune with the medley and confusion of contem-

A contemporary drawing (right) shows Marguerite of Navarre, beloved sister of Francis I, fondling her pet dog. Marguerite was equally protective toward artists, and Rabelais gratefully dedicated one volume of Gargantua and Pantagruel *to her. Although his chronicle of the lusty giant (left), a figure borrowed from French folklore, was condemned as obscene, Rabelais retained the royal patronage. Marguerite's own novellas were hardly less bawdy, but she composed devotional poetry as well. The miniature at far left shows her dressed in mourning for her son, giving Francis' mistress, the Duchess d'Étampes, a copy of one of her works.*

porary life, and above all, it was French.

As soon as a literary renaissance begins to flourish either in France or in England or in Spain, a strong nationalist sentiment rapidly infuses it, and the delight that writers and artists took in the Italian achievement led not only to emulation but also to envy. In 1549 Joachim du Bellay published his pamphlet *La Défense et illustration de la langue française* (cribbed almost entirely from Speroni's defense of Italian) in which he exhorted Frenchmen to challenge in their own language the triumphs of antiquity. The same court circle that patronized Rabelais took du Bellay's exhortation as a battle cry. Fortunately, du Bellay could practice what he preached. He and his friend Ronsard and their group, *La Pléiade,* produced excellent lyrics. They, too, were preoccupied with the loneliness of men and their dependence on love and affection to save them from unbearable solitude. In Marguerite of Navarre, Ronsard, Rabelais, du Bellay, and the rest,

the court of Francis I possessed a galaxy of talent that would have been a credit to any court of Italy. Owing vast debts to the Italian Renaissance, they nevertheless achieved a style, an idiom, and a theme that were distinctly French.

The same was to be true of the great efflorescence of literature that took place in England shortly afterwards. Plots, characters, in fact entire plays were lifted wholesale from Italian authors. The intentions of Edmund Spenser would have drawn from Castiglione nothing but his entire approval, and Spenser's debt to Ariosto's *Orlando Furioso* is as obvious as it is large. Yet there is no plagiarism: all is transmuted, Englished. Like Rabelais, the Elizabethans grew drunk on the discovery of their language. At the same time they were even less confined by tradition than the French, and their sense of achievement was far sharper, for the English were closer in time to barbarity and to anarchy. The great promise of the days of Chaucer, Langland, and Wycliffe had been checked

by the maelstrom of the fifteenth century. The Wars of the Roses had ripped apart the fabric of English life. The violent class turmoil of the early Tudor period which followed, which had led men of affairs to seek guidance in politics and diplomacy in Italy, had begun to settle by the reign of Elizabeth I into a new pattern of society in which gentlemen—but not noblemen—predominated. The break with the Church, combined with increasing knowledge of the worlds beyond Europe, intensified this sense of a new age, of an original time. Yet the very dissolution of the past created anxiety, insecurity, a sense of isolation, and a longing to discover standards. The dramatists held up a looking glass to this society in conflict. The violence, the rapacity, the passion of their age was more acceptable to the audience that thronged to see their plays if they were cast in Italy, in ancient Rome, or more daringly in their own historic past. For their crude audience, the crimes in the *Duchess of Malfi* or the *White*

Devil possessed a further dimension of evil and horror if set in the criminal splendor of an Italian court where incest, riot, poison, and murder were, everyone believed, commonplaces of life. As well as stimulating the poetic imagination of a Webster or a Tourneur, however, Italy and its Renaissance still possessed a serious purpose for Englishmen. Long after politicians had given up expecting to find the secrets of their craft there, and long after dramatists had exhausted the plots of its authors, Italy continued to exert the deepest influence.

Profoundly important as the influence of the Italian Renaissance might be on art and literature and learning, it was greater still in education, using that word in its widest possible sense. This possessed two aspects—one for the narrow circle of intellectually creative men, the other for the world at large. How far the intellectual skepticism of the Renaissance, with its search for truth in the evidence presented by men and events rather than in dogma and authority, stimu-

*Quentin Matsys was the dean of Flemish art dur-
ing the early sixteenth century, and such paintings
as* The Moneylender and His Wife *(facing
page) illustrate the transition from religious preoccupation to an interest in the common man
and his surroundings. The mirror in the foreground reflects what is probably the artist's self-
portrait. In England, the influence of Italy is
most clearly seen in Elizabethan drama. William
Shakespeare, whose portrait (below) appeared as
the frontispiece of his first folio, used numerous
Italian scenes, names, and tales in his plays. His
dramas were enthusiastically received in such
London theaters as the Swan (right), sketched
in 1596 by Johann de Witt, a visiting Dutchman.*

lated the growth of a rational attitude to the world is difficult to know. Certainly without the greater stimuli of the discovery of the world beyond Europe and the revolutionary achievements of science in the seventeenth century, it might easily have come to naught. However, to belittle the importance of those first broad cracks that were made in fifteenth-century Italy in the all-embracing dome of dogma is to falsify history. Ideologies were still to rage in the heart of man and haunt his destiny, but for Western man never again could there be two opposed worlds of Christians and heretics. Important though this impetus was to the habit of truth, to the growth of a scientific and skeptical spirit in the world of learning, it is of minor significance compared with the influence which the Italian Renaissance had on the social patterns which Western Europe adopted.

Italy, with Flanders, had been the first country in Europe to grow really rich on commerce, to throw up a middle class which could challenge the economic, political, and social power of the aristocracy. These merchants, bankers, craftsmen, found their first real security in economic life. This they knew; this they controlled. And so they organized their political and social life about their economic activity—in guilds —and ignored as far as they could the structure of the world about them. But the pressure of their wealth and the needs of their professions forced them from their exclusive habits, forced them into contact (and at times into conflict) with the aristocracy, whose sources of wealth, invigorated by the rise of commerce, remained large enough to maintain their privileged place in society. In the end a linkage was made between the aristocracy and the middle class: they remained distinct but joined by paths that men could traverse, and this mingling wrought a profound change in social customs, in manners, in education, in the images of man that seemed socially valuable. In its search for standards, Italy could look where

the Flemish could not—into its highly sophisticated past, to the days of Rome and Greece when life had also been urban, rich, and aristocratic, yet commercially minded. Although antiquity could provide some ingredients, it could not provide all, and the merchants' hunger to belong drove them to accept readily many of the concepts of feudal aristocracy.

By 1530 or so, however, Italian society had brought into being an idea of a gentleman that was neither classical nor feudal, neither noble nor bourgeois, neither rural nor urban, but a fusion of all of these. The projection of this image acquired such intensity because Western Europe had begun to undergo the same sort of violent social revolution that Italy had undergone between 1300 and 1450. In the sixteenth century commercial wealth poured into Cadiz, Lisbon, Bordeaux, Nantes, London, Antwerp, Hamburg. It raced through the veins of rural society, erupting, creating, destroying. The new men of this age—and there were thou-

sands of them—felt great social insecurity. They had to learn to be gentlemen, to move at ease in the aristocratic world which they could not or would not eradicate. They adopted the pattern of compromise which the Italians had established. They wolfed down the courtesy books—della Casa as well as Castiglione. They adopted Italian clothes and Italian manners. They educated their children according to Italian precepts. A knowledge of a great deal of Latin and a little Greek became an absolute necessity for anyone who aspired to gentility, from the North Cape of Norway to the Strait of Gibraltar. And a gentleman was not only delineated by his education, he also required breeding—those aristocratic airs, that easy nonchalance, that assumption of privileged position lightly borne, which Castiglione had emphasized over and over again. A taste in the visual arts, or connoisseurship, was as essential a part of breeding as skill in sitting a horse. As Europe assimilated its vast wealth,

and society became more ordered, so this image of a gentleman became more tenacious. It represented, as it did in
Italy, the triumph of the aristocracy at the expense of the
middle class, whose own merits—prudence, reticence, professional education—came to be regarded as either boorish
or comic, from which the young not only wished to escape
but were encouraged to do so. This is why the possession of
land achieved such sanctity in Western Europe—it was the
way to salvation, the route by which a merchant's children
might become gentlemen and gentlewomen. Excluded from
true social power, hypnotized by the snobbery and sophistication of aristocratic life to which the Italian Renaissance
had given such vivid definition, the merchant classes of Europe lost much of their dynamic and creative energy, and it
took nearly two centuries of frustration before they challenged, in the age of Napoleon, the aristocratic foundations
of European society.

During this period from the Reformation to the French
Revolution the spirit of the Italian Renaissance pervaded
Europe. It taught the rough and very raw provincial aristocracies of the West how to live, how to move at ease
through a world of bourgeois delights, without being con-
taminated by it. Certainly it intensified snobbery, hardened
the stratification of classes of men, and checked the scientific imagination by insisting on the education of character
rather than of aptitudes. In return it gave much. It taught
the new men of Europe that the purpose of art, the call of
learning, were an essential part of the use of wealth. And it
projected a theme—the uniqueness of personal experience,
the idea of man caught in the jaws of Time—that has given
rise to the world's greatest art and literature. The spirit of
the Italian Renaissance broods over these centuries which
link the age of feudalism to modern times, and makes them
a part of itself.

ITALY'S RENAISSANCE MOVES NORTHWARD

Federigo da Montefeltro called upon a painter from Flanders to decorate his new palace at Urbino. King Alfonso urged Jan van Eyck to emigrate to Naples, and when Rogier van der Weyden came to Rome for the Jubilee of 1450, Italian painters crowded around him like rustics gawking at a king. Flanders, along with the other domains of the Duke of Burgundy, was the only part of Europe which could claim to rival Italy's own Renaissance. Combining the trappings of knightly life with rich commercial activity, the Burgundian realms produced schools of painting which were to impose a lasting influence on European art. Italy was in constant commercial and artistic contact with the triple capitals of Ghent, Bruges, and Dijon, as indicated by Jan van Eyck's famous wedding portrait (opposite) of a Tuscan merchant and his bride. The painting, which reveals the passionate attention to detail for which Flemish artists were famous, is an example of the crosscurrents which flowed between the two lands.

Burgundy, which rivaled Italy's progress, was soon to foreshadow Italy's fate. With the death of Duke Charles the Bold in 1477, Burgundian territory fell prey to the battling powers of France and the Empire. Seizing most of the French-speaking hinterland, France established a national power which was to set the stage for the splendid reign of Francis I. Imperial Spain and the Flemish lowlands were less fortunate; they inherited each other, and soon were locked in mortal combat. Burgundy and Flanders, lands which Charlemagne had envisioned as part of a middle kingdom between France and Germany, became mere satellites of Paris and Madrid; yet those capitals, despite their political supremacy, looked to Italy for rules of art and diplomacy, manners and education. Italian universities lured students and visitors from all over Europe, who returned to implant Renaissance ideas in lands as distant as Sweden and Poland. But it was where political power was centered—in Spain, France, and later England— that the Renaissance flourished most brilliantly.

The pages that follow, briefly summarizing the spread of the Renaissance beyond the Alps, barely hint at the richness of the age, for merely a list of the men who reflected the Renaissance spirit would be an awesome one. In its heyday Spain boasted of Cervantes and Lope da Vega, El Greco and Velázquez. England gave birth to no great painters, but where Italy a century before had found its noblest expression in painting and sculpture, Elizabeth's kingdom had its poets —Spenser and Shakespeare, Marlowe, Jonson, and the translators of the Bible—who produced what is one of the few bodies of work in history which can stand beside the art of the Italians. Nevertheless, it was France which gained most from Italy: except for Rabelais and Montaigne, there were no great native names to equal the giants of Spanish or English literature, but France assimilated the Renaissance experience so thoroughly that in the centuries which followed she succeeded Italy as the light of Europe.

Once the King had an actor whipped for satirizing his court, but behind his back contemporaries still called Francis "Le Roi Grand Nez." Despite his long nose, the King was very vain of his good looks. Clouet's portrait shows him splendidly arrayed in a feathered bonnet and a robe of gold brocade with immense puffed sleeves.

THE RENAISSANCE
IN FRANCE

Louis XII, invading Milan in 1499, was so impressed by Leonardo's fresco of the Last Supper that he proposed cutting it down from the wall and carrying it back to France. His courtiers finally dissuaded him, and the King was forced to appease his hunger for Italian art by commissioning a group of minor Italian craftsmen to work for him in France. Louis' successor, Francis I, was more fortunate; he managed to employ the great Leonardo himself by promising him 7,000 pieces of gold and "a palace of his own choice in the most beautiful region of France." Francis also brought in other Italian painters to decorate his palace walls with frescoes celebrating royal patronage and power. This was not hollow symbolism; the King's devotion to art and letters almost equaled his notorious enthusiasm for philandering.

During Francis I's reign, Paris was the largest city of Western Europe; the population of his kingdom was five times that of England and more than twice as large as Spain's. As the King traveled with a retinue of thousands from one castle to the next, his court consumed wealth as industriously as the country produced it. Along the valley of the river Loire, Francis and his nobles built splendid châteaux, designed by Italian architects and adorned in Renaissance style. One of the earliest was Azay-le-Rideau (*see* page 384), which was erected by the royal treasurer, who devoted ten years to its construction, only to have Francis quickly requisition the château for himself.

Château life recreated the ideal courtly society envisioned by Castiglione. Catherine de' Medici, whom Francis had imported from Florence as a wife for his son, brought with her the tastes of the Medici as well as some of their cash. Under her aegis the French court achieved a splendor which foreshadowed Versailles. A circle of poets attached to the Valois dynasty reflected its Renaissance spirit. Led by Ronsard and du Bellay, they proposed a rigid set of rules to make French poetry classical (Ronsard followed them so closely that his countrymen sometimes needed a guide to understand him). When Mary Queen of Scots, the wife of Francis' grandson, persuaded Ronsard to publish his odes, he became so famous that students in Paris fought to touch his robes as he passed by. The royal women—Mary, Catherine, Marguerite of Navarre, and Henry II's mistress, the fascinating Diane de Poitiers—gave the courts of Renaissance France much of their luster, and artists looked to them for patronage almost as much as to the kings themselves.

"This is a hundred times more divine a thing than I had ever dreamed of," Francis I exclaimed when Benvenuto Cellini showed him a wax model of the golden saltcellar shown above. When the work was finished, the King was even more effusive. "He uttered a loud cry of astonishment," Cellini proudly reported, "and could not satiate his eyes with gazing at it." The female figure on the saltcellar symbolizes earth, while the male opposite her, holding a trident, represents the sea. Cellini earned the same salary which Leonardo da Vinci had received at the French court, but Francis gave Leonardo 4,000 additional crowns when he purchased the famous Mona Lisa portrait (below).

With the English Channel visible in the distance, Henry VIII (left) rides out of Calais on a white palfrey to meet Francis I. Their famous encounter took its name from the cloth of gold which covered the pavilion (top, center) where the kings met. The monarchs jousted and wrestled; after Francis won one of their matches, he showed his chivalrous nature by venturing into Henry's camp unarmed.

THE FIELD OF
THE CLOTH OF GOLD

The meeting between "those suns of glory, those two lights of men," Francis I and Henry VIII, on the Field of the Cloth of Gold near Calais in 1520, was the last splendid display of the age of chivalry. Shakespeare described the fortnight of celebration: "Today the French All clinquant, all in gold, like heathen gods, Shone down the English; and tomorrow they Made Britain India: every man that stood Show'd like a mine." Both Henry and Francis were heirs of kings who had suppressed nobles to unify their countries. Both were young and chivalrous. Both were patrons of the arts, and the accession of each promised his kingdom a new age of gold. "What may we not expect," rhap-

sodized Sir Thomas More, "from a King who has been nourished by philosophy and the nine Muses!" Henry gave England far more than the utopian Sir Thomas had anticipated; the King's break with Rome, which cost More his life, strengthened the doughty national spirit that kept England alive during the century's titanic battle between France and Spain. With the decline of medievalism, Europe's nation-states began to emerge. Enriched by the wealth of the New World and the expansive spirit of the Renaissance, they forged affluent new cultures which were to clash with each other far more ferociously than their small Italian counterparts had done a century before.

A panorama of the sack of Rome, probably painted by Pieter Brueghel the Elder, shows a horde of German and Spanish troops pouring into the city. The biggest contingent storms the palace of the popes at upper right (twin towers); below, its triple bastions overlooking the river, is Castel Sant' Angelo, where Clement took refuge. The invaders even massacred refugees who sought shelter in St. Peter's.

THE SACK OF ROME

All Italy agreed that the iniquities of papal Rome merited punishment, but no one imagined the extent of the catastrophe that befell the city in 1527. Emperor Charles V, warring with Francis I, had signed a treaty with Henry VIII undoing the results of the Field of the Cloth of Gold, and sent a German army into Italy. Reaching Rome, thirty thousand uncontrollable troops slaughtered hospital patients, raped nuns, stabled horses in shrines, and kindled campfires with precious manuscripts. Many were Lutherans who had joined the army to pillage Rome: convinced that the city's wealth came from milking Christian nations dry, they sought revenge by requiring every citizen to pay a ransom for his life. Pope Clement VII was impotent; imprisoned in Castel Sant' Angelo, he let his hair grow as a sign of mourning and roamed about repeating Job's lament to God: "Wherefore then hast thou brought me forth out of the womb!" When he was finally restored to power, only one-fifth of the city's houses were inhabited. Diplomats forced the Emperor to abandon his resolution to strip the popes of temporal power, and soon the Papacy, with characteristic elasticity, was as splendid as ever. Rome was lavishly rebuilt, and Michelangelo was called on to design a dome for St. Peter's, but Clement was the last of the great Renaissance popes. With the sack, his humanist scholars had fled, and in succeeding decades theologians took their place. Reacting to the forces of nationalism unleashed beyond the Alps, Rome now belonged to the Counter Reformation.

Longleat.

THE ENGLISH RENAISSANCE

The Renaissance in England was an age of new men. Within two decades after Henry VIII's dissolution of the monasteries, one-fifth of the country's land came up for sale, and merchants and lawyers, their purses fattened by trade and the burgeoning legal profession, acquired as much of it as they could. Many, like Shakespeare after his first success in London, commissioned heralds to design a coat of arms. "As for gentlemen," one observer complained, "they be made good cheap in England." Not as cheaply as he imagined, however; it took a fierce spirit to rise in that dangerous age. Still the list of gentry swelled with England's wealth, and as poets and population eagerly

borrowed foreign words and ideas, England's language changed too. The verbal extravagance of Elizabethan poetry reflected an age of extremes, in which men fanatically pursued riches or power, learning or gentility, with texts provided by Italy. Scholars tapped the wealth of Renaissance humanism, playwrights requisitioned the plots of Italian *novelle*, the new aristocracy found its pleasures in fanciful country houses built in the Italian style. For the ambitious, there was "the murderous Machiavel" to study, and for those who were yearning to be gentlemen, there was *The Courtier* and the dozens of imitative tracts which it had spawned.

A SON OF THE RENAISSANCE

When a generous Venetian colleague revealed the mathematical secrets which would enable Albrecht Dürer to draw a perfectly proportioned human body, the German painter declared that his new-found knowledge was more precious than a kingdom. He had first come to Italy in 1494 on a pilgrimage to see for himself "what had been hidden for a thousand years." The Renaissance was at its height, and young Dürer soon was converted by it. He copied the classical nudes of Mantegna and studied mathematics, read Poliziano's Latin poetry and later made an engraving inspired by it. In Nuremberg after a second trip, he wrote a treatise on painting and a book on human proportions which, along with his paintings, were to revolutionize German art. Despite his wife's nagging, Dürer refused to leave his books and attend strictly to his trade as an artisan-painter. He found his cronies among humanists and scholars, not in the painters' guild. Although he assimilated Italian ideas, Dürer still retained his own intensely northern character, alien to the flowing rhythm of Italian art. In this his painting reflects the fate of the Renaissance in Germany, which soon abandoned the easy acceptance of life inherent in the humanism and art of Italy. Like Dürer himself, Germany was overwhelmed by the Reformation, and its artists, scholars, and princes were dominated by the towering figure of Martin Luther. Aroused by his cause and prey to fanatical religious life, that country had little room for the spirit of humanism.

Dürer's watercolor of the landscape at Arco (upper left) is a memento of his Italian journey. Although The Four Witches *(left) is based on Italian studies of the nude, and* The Nativity *(opposite) uses a sophisticated perspective scheme learned in Venice, both retain Gothic touches, such as the tiny foreground figures in* The Nativity.

IMPERIAL SPAIN

Charles V ruled an empire that stretched from Prussia to Peru, and the heart of its power was Spain, where the gold of the New World had built a kingdom which was to dominate Europe for a century. Charles collected paintings as he collected provinces; his successor, Philip II, inherited dozens of Titians and Tintorettos to hang in the Escorial, his new royal palace near Madrid. Yet even that great collection was dwarfed by the immense palace, so Philip called on the artists of Spain to decorate it with paintings worthy of his royal taste and their country's new role in the world. Despite his challenge, the rooms devoted to Spanish art remained half empty, and most Spanish paint-

ings only imitated, but could not equal, Italian art. El Greco, who had studied with Titian and worked with Tintoretto, was unsuccessful in his efforts to attract royal notice. When he sent a canvas to the King, it failed, as one contemporary noted, "to find favor with His Majesty." "That was natural enough," the critic added, "for it finds favor with few people." El Greco left Philip to his empty rooms, settled in Toledo, and there, in the ancient capital of Spain, he continued painting, surrounded by the poets and scholars who inaugurated the Spanish Renaissance. Another generation went by before Velázquez again gave Spanish royalty the chance to patronize a painter as great.

El Greco painted The Adoration of the Shepherds *(right) to hang over his tomb in Toledo. The dramatic movement of figures recalls Tintoretto's painting, but the unique style of his remarkable pupil is evident in the immensely elongated forms of the shepherds. Velázquez deeply admired El Greco and owned some of his paintings. In* The Surrender of Breda *(opposite) he based the portraits of Spanish soldiers, visible under the line of lances, on a group of similar figures painted by El Greco. The canvas commemorates a victory over the Dutch in one of the many wars which Catholic Spain carried on against the Protestants.*

THE GRAND TOUR

"A man who has not been in Italy," Dr. Johnson proclaimed, "is always conscious of an inferiority." English gentlemen agreed. Although Trinity College in Dublin was once praised for keeping young men from being "infected with popery and other ill qualities" while studying abroad, the lure of Italy proved too strong; gentlemen were soon required to complete their education with a Grand Tour which reached its climax in a visit to Rome, the very font of popery. A thriving English guide service welcomed them to the city, ready to lead Gibbon on an eighteen-week tour of antiquities or stroll with Boswell through the Forum, conversing in Latin to sustain the classical ambience. By the nineteenth century, Lord Byron found the city "Pestilent with English—a parcel of staring boobies who go about gaping." But they did not gape alone. Even when Dürer visited Venice to plumb the secrets of Renaissance art, the *Wanderjahr* had been a tradition for German students. They made Rome the focus of their trip, and eventually they were followed there by awed visitors from Scandinavia and America. The Grand Tour was *de rigueur* for gentlemen educated on the Renaissance model, and even more necessary for painters and poets. The dedication with which they inspected Roman remains and Renaissance monuments equaled the fervor shown centuries before by Brunelleschi and Donatello, who first traveled to the city at the dawn of the Renaissance to immerse themselves in the spirit of the past.

Zoffany, an eighteenth-century favorite, painted some of the treasures of Florence's Uffizi Gallery in a souvenir picture for Britain's royal family. Titian's Venus of Urbino *dominates the foreground; at left is a Raphael Madonna surrounded by a swarm of connoisseurs.*

OVERLEAF: *Canaletto, who grew affluent painting views for nostalgic tourists, shows a group of them amid the ruined grandeur of the Forum, studiously inspecting the source from which the Renaissance sprang.*

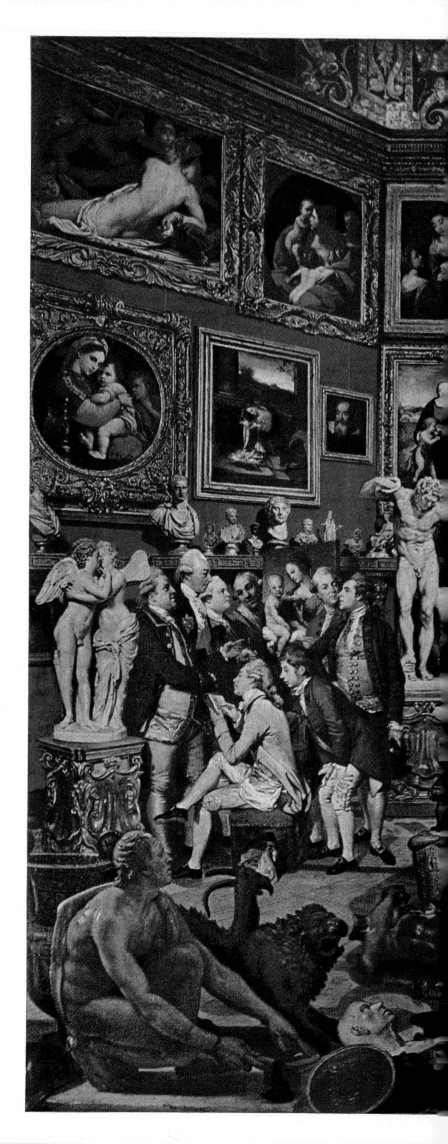

ACKNOWLEDGMENTS AND INDEX

ACKNOWLEDGMENTS

The Editors are especially grateful to the following individuals and institutions for their generous assistance, and for their co-operation in making available pictorial material in their collections:

Archivio di Stato, Siena
    Dr. Sandro de' Colli
Archivio di Stato, Venice
    Prof. Conte Raimondo Morozzo della Rocca
Biblioteca Estense, Modena
    Prof. Pietro Puliatti
Biblioteca Marciana, Venice
    Prof. Tullia Gasparrini Leporace
Biblioteca Mediceo-Laurenziana, Florence
    Prof. Irma Merolle Tondi
Biblioteca Nazionale, Florence
    Dr. Eugenia Levi
Biblioteca Riccardiana, Florence
    Dr. Berta Maracchi Biagiarelli
Biblioteca Trivulziana, Milan
    Prof. Caterina Santoro
Bibliothèque de l'Arsenal, Paris
    Jean-Pierre Seguin
Bibliothèque Nationale, Paris
    Jean Porcher
    Jean Babelon
    Jean Vallery-Radot
Book-of-the-Month Club, New York
    Harry Dale
British Museum, London
    Manuscripts, Prints, and Drawings Departments
Donna Lelia Caetani, Rome
Casa Editrice Aldo Martello, Milan
    Aldo Martello
Centre National de la Recherche Scientifique, Paris
    Miss Jeanne Vielliard
Dr. Enrico Ceramelli-Papiani, Florence
City Art Gallery, Bristol
    H. Schubart
Civici Musei Veneziani d'Arte e di Storia, Venice
    Prof. Giovanni Mariacher
Lord Chamberlain's Office, St. James's Palace, London
    The Comptroller of Paintings
Marcel Destombes, Paris
Prof. H. J. Dow, Sweet Briar College, Virginia
P. Duchartre, Paris
Dr. Colin Eisler, New York
Ente Nazionale Industrie Turistiche, Rome
    Dr. Gian Piero Gallian
Fitzwilliam Museum, Cambridge
    Carl Winter
Frick Art Reference Library, New York
Galleria e Museo Estense, Modena
    Dr. A. Ghidiglia Quintavelle
Prof. Marvin T. Herrick, University of Illinois
Dr. Gilbert Highet, New York
Istituto Geografico de Agostini, Novara
    Dr. M. Nilo
Istituto Italiano d'Arti Grafiche, Bergamo
    Antonio Mancia
Istituto e Museo di Storia della Scienza, Florence
    Prof. Maria Luisa Bonelli
Dr. Hellmut Lehmann-Haupt, New York
Federico Arborio Mella, Milan
Sir Thomas Merton
The Metropolitan Museum of Art, New York
    Marshall B. Davidson
    Stephen Grancsay
    Miss Lillian Green
    Mrs. Edward S. McGill
Mrs. Clarice Milani-Comparetti, Florence
Monumenti, Musei e Gallerie Pontificie, Vatican City
    Prof. Filippo Maggi
    Dr. D. Redig de Campos
Musée de Cluny, Paris
    Francis Salet
Musée Condé, Chantilly
Musée Longchamp, Marseille
    Mrs. Jacques Latour
Musée du Louvre, Paris
Musée Royal des Beaux Arts, Antwerp
    W. Vanbeselaere

Museo Civico, Siena
    Dr. Aldo Cairola
Museo del Prado, Madrid
    Francisco J. Sánchez Canton
Museum of Fine Arts, Boston
    Miss Elizabeth Riegel
Museum of History of Science, Oxford
    H. Josten
    Francis Maddison
National Gallery, London
    Publications Department
National Gallery of Art, Washington
    John Walker
    Huntington Cairns
    Mrs. Elizabeth Ostertag
New York Public Library, New York
    Karl Kup
    Miss Elizabeth Roth
    Wilson G. Duprey
Opera della Metropolitana, Siena
    Conte Ugo del Vescovo Sterbini
Marchesa Iris Origo, Rome
Palazzo Ducale, Venice
    Prof. Egle Trincatanto
The Pierpont Morgan Library, New York
    Frederick B. Adams, Jr.
    John H. Plummer
    Miss Mary M. Kenway
Pinacoteca Ambrosiana, Milan
    Mons. Carlo Castiglioni
Pinacoteca di Brera, Milan
    Dr. F. Russoli
"Réalités-Connaissance des Arts," Paris
    Mrs. Lily LeRoux
Lessing J. Rosenwald, Jenkintown, Pennsylvania
Royal Academy of Arts, London
    Humphrey Brooke
Scala, Florence
    John Clark
Janos Scholz, New York
Soprintendenza alle Gallerie di Firenze, Florence
    Prof. Filippo Rossi
Soprintendenza alle Gallerie per il Lazio, Rome
    Prof. Emilio Lavagnino
Soprintendenza alle Gallerie di Mantova, Mantua
    Prof. Giovanni Paccagnini
Soprintendenza alle Gallerie, Naples
    Dr. Bruno Molajoli
Soprintendenza alle Gallerie di Torino, Turin
    Dr. Noemi Gabrielli
    Col. Vittorio Maglioli
Soprintendenza alle Gallerie, Venice
    Prof. Vittorio Moschini
Time, Inc., New York
    Miss Dorothy L. Smith
Royal Library, Windsor Castle
    Miss A. Scott-Eliott
    Miss Olwen Hedley
Yale University Library, New Haven
    Thomas Marston
Conte Ottavio Zasio, Venice

Grateful acknowledgment is made for permission to quote from the following works:

Michelangelo: A Record of His Life, translated and edited by Robert W. Carden, Constable & Co., London, 1913. *The Notebooks of Leonardo da Vinci,* translated and edited by Edward MacCurdy, Jonathan Cape Ltd., London; Harcourt, Brace & World, Inc., New York (by permission of Mrs. S. W. A. McCurdy). *The Venetian Republic* by William Hazlitt, A. & C. Black, London, 1915. *The Portable Renaissance Reader,* edited by James Bruce Ross and Mary Martin McLaughlin, The Viking Press, Inc., New York, 1958 (from "The Dignity of Man" by Giovanni Pico della Mirandola, translated by M. M. M., and "Self-Portrait of a Universal Man" by Leon Battista Alberti, translated by J. B. R.). *The Book of The Courtier,* by Baldassare Castiglione, copyright ©1959 by Charles S. Singleton and Edgar de N. Mayhew, Doubleday & Company, Inc., New York. *Galateo* by Giovanni della Casa, translated by R. S. Pine-Coffin, Penguin Books, 1958.

PICTURE CREDITS

The following abbreviations are used:

Amb.—Biblioteca or Pinacoteca Ambrosiana, Milan
BAV—Biblioteca Apostolica Vaticana
BEM—Biblioteca Estense, Modena
BLF—Biblioteca Laurenziana, Florence
BM—British Museum
BN—Bibliothèque Nationale, Paris
BNF—Biblioteca Nazionale, Florence
ENIT—Ente Nazionale Industrie Turistiche, Rome
LC—Library of Congress, Washington.
MMA—Metropolitan Museum of Art, New York
MNF—Museo Nazionale, Florence
NGAW, Kress—National Gallery of Art, Washington, Kress Collection
NGAW, Mellon—National Gallery of Art, Washington, Mellon Collection
NGAW, Widener—National Gallery of Art, Washington, Widener Collection
NGL—National Gallery, London
NYPL—New York Public Library
SGF—Soprintendenza alle Gallerie di Firenze

FRONT MATTER—Jacket: "Portrait of a Youth" by Filippino Lippi. NGAW, Mellon. Back jacket: Lodovico Sforza and nephew, Velins 724, BN. Title page: "Triumph of Venus" by Francesco Cossa and others. Detail: Palazzo Schifanoia. Ferrara **4** Angel. Drawing by Filippino Lippi. Collection of Janos Scholz. **8-9** Map by David Greenspan.

THE DAWN OF THE RENAISSANCE

10 Cathedral, Orvieto (John Ross) **12-13** "Effects of Good Government in the City and Country" by Ambrogio Lorenzetti. Palazzo Pubblico, Siena **14-15** Guidoriccio da Fogliano by Simone Martini. Palazzo Pubblico, Siena **16** Genoese banking scene. Add. ms. 27,695, BM—Astrolabe. The Royal Scottish Museum, Edinburgh **17** *Statuti della Società dei Drappieri e Bracciaioli.* Museo Civico, Bologna (Alinari-Giraudon) **18** 14th-century Crusade miniature. Ms. Français 24209, BN **19** Frederick II. Cod. Pal. Lat. 1071, BAV—Castel del Monte (Dr. C. A. Willemsen) **20** "Temptation on the Mountain Top" by Duccio di Buoninsegna. The Frick Collection—Boccaccio Ms. II. II. 38, BNF **21** Sketch by Petrarch. Ms. Latin 6802, BN—Dante. 15th-century copy of lost Taddeo Gaddi fresco. Ms. Palatine 320, BNF **22** Venice. Ms. 264, Bodleian Library, Oxford **23** Miniature by Simone Martini. Amb. **24** Petrarch by Lombardo della Sala. Ms. Latin 6069 F, BN **33** Plaques on Campanile, Florence, by Giotto, Andrea Pisano, and others (All: Alinari) **34-5** "The Crucifix" by Cimabue. S. Domenico, Arezzo (Scala) **36-7** "St. Ambrose, St. Michael, and St. Augustine" by Simone Martini and assistants. Fitzwilliam Museum, Cambridge **38** "The Kiss of Judas" by Giotto. Detail. Scrovegni Chapel, Padua (Anderson) **39** "Pietà" by Giotto. Scrovegni Chapel. Padua (Scala).

THE PRINCE AND THE STATE

40 San Leo, designed by Francesco di Giorgio (ENIT) **42** Guelph emblem (Brogi) **42-3** Orvieto (John Ross) **44** Horrors of tyranny. *De Sphaera.* Ms. A.X. 2.14, BEM (Aldo Martello Editore) **45** "Triumph of Death" attributed to Francesco Traini. Detail. Camposanto, Pisa (Alinari) **46** Presumed portrait of Roberto Malatesta. "Passage of the Red Sea" by Piero di Cosimo. Detail. Sistine Chapel, Vatican (Anderson)—Piccinino by Pisanello. MNF (Alinari) **46-7** *Bastone di comando.* Giovanni Erole, *Erasmo Gattamelata da Narni,* 1877 **47** Gattamelata by Donatello. Piazzo del Santo, Padua (Anderson) **48** "Scene from the Life of San Bernardino" by the Master of Legend of San Bernardino. Pinacoteca Vanucci, Perugia—"Il Bravo" attributed to Titian. Kunsthistorisches Museum, Vienna (Kunst-Verlag Wolfrum) **49** *Biccherna* cover, 1468. Archivio di Stato, Siena (ENIT) **50** Building the Tempio Malatestiano. Ms. 630, Bibliothèque de l'Arsenal—Crab by Agostino di Duccio. Tempio Malatestiano, Rimini (Alinari)—Tempio Malatestiano (Ediz. RIMA) **51** "A Princess of the Este Family" by Pisanello. Louvre (Giraudon) **52-3** "The Return of Lodovico from Exile" by Mantegna. Camera degli Sposi, Castello di Corte, Mantua **53** Federigo da Montefeltro. Urb. Lat. 508, BAV **54** Deposition. Drawing by Raphael. Uffizi (Anderson) **55** Griffin. *L'Histoire et Vite di Braccio Fortebracci et di Nicolo Piccinino,* Perugia, 1623. BAV—"San Bernardino Preaching" by Sano di Pietro. Cathedral, Siena (Anderson) **56** Machiavelli by Santi di Tito. Palazzo Vecchio, Florence **65** Condottiere. Drawing by Leonardo da Vinci. BM **68-9** Battle of Fornovo. A. Vérard. *Mer des Histoires,* Paris, *ca.* 1503 **70-1** Scaling ladder, attack platform, battering ram, and cannon. Valturius, *De Re Militari.* LC, Lessing J. Rosenwald Collection—Mine. Drawing by Francesco di Giorgio Martini, *Trattato di Architettura Civile e Militare,* BLF—Fortress. Drawing by Francesco di Giorgio Martini, *Trattato di Architettura Civile e Militare,* BNF **72** Arabian engine and repeater gun. Valturius, *De Re Militari.* Library of Congress, Lessing J. Rosenwald Collection—Mortar. Drawing by Leonardo da Vinci. *Codice Atlantico,* Amb. **73** Mars. *De Sphaera.* Ms. A.X. 2.14, BEM (Aldo Martello Editore) **74** Presumed portrait of Astorre Manfredi attributed to Romagnol School. Detail of "Beato Bernardino de Feltre." Pinacoteca, Faenza (Alinari)—Letter. Archivio di Stato, Siena—Presumed portrait of Caterina Sforza by Lorenzo di Credi. Pinacoteca, Forlì—Presumed portrait of Duke of Gandia by Pinturicchio. Detail of "Dispute of St. Catherine." Appartamento Borgia, Vatican (Alinari)—Sword. Collection of Donna Lelia Caetani **75** Cesare Borgia, anonymous copy of authentic portrait. Palazzo Venezia, Rome **76** Colleoni hunting, attributed to Girolamo Romanino. Castello di Malpaga, Bergamo **77** Colleoni by Verrocchio. Detail, Campo SS. Giovanni e Paolo, Venice (Anderson) **78-9** "The Rout of San Romano" by Uccello. Uffizi (Aldo Martello Editore) **80** "Battle of the Bonacolsi and Gonzaga" by Domenico Morone. Detail. Castello di Corte, Mantua—"Madonna of Victory" by Mantegna. Louvre **81** "Return of Cardinal Francesco Gonzaga from Rome" by Mantegna. Camera degli Sposi, Castello di Corte, Mantua **82** Gibbet by Pisanello. Detail of "St. George and the Princess of Trebizond." S. Anastasia, Verona **83** Medal of Isotta da Rimini by Matteo de' Pasti. NGAW, Kress—Sigismondo Malatesta by Piero della Francesca. Detail of fresco. Tempio Malatestiano, Rimini (Scala) **84** Document. Detail. Archivio Segreto, Venice **84-5** "King Maurus Dismissing the English Ambassadors" by Carpaccio. Accademia, Venice **86-7** "Fleet of Ferrante I in the Bay of Naples," anonymous. Museo di San Martino, Naples—Four details. M. 801, The Pierpont Morgan Library.

THE ARTS

88 S. Francesco, Arezzo (Gjon Mili) **90-1** "The Tribute Money" by Masaccio. Brancacci Chapel, Sta. Maria del Carmine, Florence (Dmitri Kessel, courtesy *Life*) **92** "David" by Donatello. MNF (Alinari) **92-3** Ideal city attributed to Piero della Francesca. Palazzo Ducale, Urbino (Anderson) **93** Drawing tools. Museum of the History of Science, Oxford **94** Unloading wheat by Fra Angelico. Detail of "Scene from the Life of St. Nicholas of Bari." Pinacoteca Vaticana (Istituto Italiano d'Arti Grafiche, Bergamo) **95** "Madonna and Child" by Piero della Francesca and assistants. Brera, Milan **96** "St. George and the Dragon" by Uccello. NGL **97** Star of Bethlehem and other plants by Leonardo da Vinci. Royal Collection, Windsor Castle. Copyright reserved **98** "St. Jerome in His Study" by Antonello da Messina. NGL **99** "The Castelfranco Madonna" by Giorgione. Cathedral, Castelfranco Veneto (Conzett & Huber) **100** "Hercules and Antaeus" by A. Pollaiuolo, MNF (Alinari) **100-101** Bas-relief of craftsmen by Nanni di Banco. Orsanmichele, Florence (Alinari) **101** Plate from Cafaggiolo, Victoria and Albert Museum. Copyright reserved—Old woman. Tuscan majolica. Fitzwilliam Museum, Cambridge **102** "Apollo and Daphne" by A. and P. Pollaiuolo. NGL **103** "The Feast of the Gods" by Giovanni Bellini and Titian. NGAW, Widener **104** Michelangelo, from his atelier. Louvre **113** Drawings of Hercules by Michelangelo. Royal Collection, Windsor Castle. Copyright reserved **114** Torso of a seated man by Michelangelo. BM—Model of a river god by Michelangelo. Galleria dell' Accademia, Florence **115** Nude athlete by Michelangelo. Detail of ceiling. Sistine Chapel, Vatican (Anderson) **116** "Captive" by Michelangelo. Galleria dell' Accademia, Florence (Evelyn Hofer) **117** "Rondanini Pietà" by Michelangelo. Castello Sforzesco, Milan (Arc. Fot. dei Civici Musei, Milan) **118-19** Ceiling of the Sistine Chapel by Michelangelo. Detail. Vatican (Anderson) **120** Chalice by Uccello. Uffizi (SGF)—Face by Leonardo da Vinci. Palazzo Reale, Turin (Anderson)—Mosaic attributed to Uccello. Atrium, San Marco (Osvaldo Böhm)—Head by Piero della Francesca, *De prospettiva pingendi.* Amb. **120-21** "The Flagellation of Christ" by Piero della Francesca. Palazzo Ducale, Urbino (Scala) **122** Presumed portrait of Cecilia Gallerani. "Lady with an Ermine" by Leonardo da Vinci. Museum Czartoryskich, Cracow (Kindler Verlag, Munich)—Leonello d'Este by Pisanello. NGAW, Kress **123** Giovanni di Pierfrancesco de' Medici by Botticelli. Collection of Sir Thomas Merton **124-25** "Diana and Actaeon" by Titian. Ellesmere Collection, National Gallery, Edinburgh (Larry Burrows, courtesy *Life*) **125** Drawing by Signorelli. Louvre (Giraudon) **126** "The Adoration of the Shepherds" by Giorgione. Detail. NGAW, Kress—"Thebaid" attributed to Starnina. Detail. Uffizi—"St. Jerome" attributed to Lazzaro Bastiani. Museum of Fine Arts, Boston **126-27** "St. Francis in Ecstasy" by Giovanni Bellini. The Frick Collection (courtesy *Time*).

FLORENCE CRADLE OF HUMANISM

128 View from Boboli Gardens (Robert Descharnes) **130** Arms of Arte della Lana attributed to Luca della Robbia. Museo dell' Opera del Duomo (Alinari)—Woodcut of market. *Contrasto di Carnevale e Quaresima*—Woodcut of money changer. Jacopo de Cessolis, *Libro di Giuoccho di Scacchi,* 1493—Silk reeler. Ms. 2580,

THE IMAGES
OF MAN

WOMEN OF
THE RENAISSANCE

THE SPREAD
OF THE RENAISSANCE

COLOR PHOTOGRAPHY: New York, Herbert Loebel, Geoffrey Clements; Washington, D. C., Henry C. Beville; London, Zoltan Wegner; Paris, Giraudon, Claude Michaelsides, Louis Laniepce, Albane, Bibliothèque Nationale (Service Photographique); Bergamo, Foto Wells; Florence, Scala, G. B. Pineider; Milan, Claudio Emmer, Walter Scansani; Modena, Umberto Orlandini; Siena, Foto Grassi; Vatican City, Sansaini; Venice, Foto Fiorentini.

NOTE: *Where page numbers appear in italics, it indicates that the subject is illustrated. Usually the italicized page number refers to the page on which the picture caption appears. Where the creator of a work of art is unknown, the work is listed by title.*